ACADEMIC FREEDOM

ACADEMIC FREEDOM

From Professional Norm to First Amendment Right

DAVID M. RABBAN

HARVARD UNIVERSITY PRESS

Cambridge, Massachusetts,
and London, England

FIRST HARVARD UNIVERSITY PRESS PAPERBACK EDITION, 2024

FIRST PRINTING

Publication of this book has been supported through the generous
provisions of the S. M. Bessie Fund.

Library of Congress Cataloging-in-Publication Data

Names: Rabban, David M., 1949– author.
Title: Academic freedom : from professional norm to first amendment right / David M. Rabban.
Description: Cambridge, Massachusetts : Harvard University Press, 2024. |
Includes bibliographical references and index.
Identifiers: LCCN 2024002744 (print) | LCCN 2024002745 (ebook) |
ISBN 9780674291058 (cloth) | ISBN 9780674295957 (paperback) |
ISBN 9780674297807 (pdf) | ISBN 9780674297814 (epub)
Subjects: LCSH: United States. Constitution. 1st Amendment. |
Academic freedom—United States. | Freedom of speech—United States.
Classification: LCC KF4242 .R33 2024 (print) | LCC KF4242 (ebook) |
DDC 344.73 / 078—dc23 / eng / 20240209
LC record available at https://lccn.loc.gov/2024002744
LC ebook record available at https://lccn.loc.gov/2024002745

CONTENTS

Contents

Conclusion   298

NOTE TO READERS

My web page, https://law.utexas.edu/faculty/david-rabban/academic-freedom, contains charts that provide an overview and comparison of the legal decisions discussed in this book. The charts list the decisions, summarize their facts, and identify the source of the threat to academic freedom, the subject of expression, the competing interests to academic freedom, the legal issues addressed by the judges, and the results.

ACADEMIC
FREEDOM

Introduction

IN THIS BOOK, I provide the first comprehensive synthesis of the extensive case law addressing academic freedom and the First Amendment at American universities. Responding to the judicial decisions, I develop a theory of academic freedom as a distinctive subset of First Amendment law. Beyond rethinking existing case law, the theory helps analyze many current disputes over academic freedom that are likely to generate litigation in the future. In developing the theory, I rely on key justifications for academic freedom as a professional norm, dating from the 1915 Declaration of Principles by the American Association of University Professors (AAUP) and elaborated over the following century within the academic world.

Ever since debates over evolutionary theories in the late nineteenth century, issues of academic freedom and free speech at American universities have received widespread attention from the public as well as within universities themselves. Very few of these issues reached the judiciary before the 1950s, when the Supreme Court began applying the First Amendment to the speech of college professors in cases reflecting general concerns about subversive activities throughout American institutions during the Cold War. Whereas the constitutions of many other countries refer explicitly to academic freedom, the US Constitution does not. The protection of expression in the First Amendment addresses freedom of speech, freedom of the press, freedom of assembly, and freedom to petition. In *Sweezy v. New Hampshire*, decided in 1957, the Supreme Court for the first time identified "academic freedom" as a First Amendment right, differentiating it from "political expression."[1] In *Keyishian v. Board of Regents* ten years later, it called academic freedom "a special concern of the First Amendment."[2] Initially identified as a right of professors, judges subsequently extended the First

Amendment protection of academic freedom to universities as institutions and occasionally indicated that it might cover students as well.

Litigation has raised issues about academic freedom and the First Amendment in an increasing variety of contexts. Many of the cases brought by professors have challenged federal and state laws. Some examples include laws that preclude teaching Darwinian theories of evolution and require teaching "creation science"; laws that limit access to research material, such as sexually explicit material on the internet and the use of abortive fetal tissue to study Alzheimer's disease; and laws that require approval from government funding agencies before publishing research. Professors have challenged surreptitious police surveillance of classes, grand jury questions about classroom discussion of drug policy, and government subpoenas for oral histories from members of the Irish Republican Army gathered by researchers who promised confidentiality to the participants.

In addition to challenging government regulation, professors have brought claims against administrators and trustees. Some have claimed retaliation for expressing controversial ideas in class, such as the value of diversity, the existence of sex-based differences in mental abilities, or the merits of vaginal delivery over cesarean procedures. Cases have asserted that professors had legitimate pedagogical reasons for assigning material that contained offensive and vulgar language, including racist and sexist epithets, and for conducting classroom discussions in which these words were used by students as well as professors. Professors have also denied the university's right to preclude unorthodox teaching methods or to change the grades they have assigned. They have challenged administrative requirements that mandated curricular coverage, teaching upper-level language courses in the foreign language, following a grading curve, distributing a syllabus, conducting student course evaluations, and using gender-neutral pronouns in class.

Beyond the classroom, professors have claimed that universities retaliated against them for speech about university affairs. Professors have condemned the university for not implementing an effective ethnic studies program, opposed the university's efforts to promote diversity and multiculturalism, and bemoaned grade inflation. They have also criticized administrators for poor fundraising, financial mismanagement, and violating university regulations that required participation by professors in making new appointments.

Professors have maintained that retaliation by administrators and trustees extended to speech off campus, such as publications by a philosophy professor asserting that the lower IQ scores of Blacks explain their low percentage in philosophy departments and demonstrate the futility of affirmative action programs. Professors have also claimed that their expression of Marxist or conservative political views, opposition to American involvement in the Vietnam War, support for the civil rights movement, collaboration with the CIA, and criticism of the US Army Corps of Engineers for its response to Hurricane Katrina provoked administrators and trustees to deny appointment.

Universities have asserted their own right of institutional academic freedom, often to justify actions about which professors complained. Institutional academic freedom, they claim, protects against the disclosure of confidential peer review material gathered while considering the appointment and tenure of faculty and limits judicial review of the ultimate decisions, even when professors allege violations of their own First Amendment rights or unlawful employment discrimination. Universities have claimed institutional academic freedom to justify the use of affirmative action in admitting students and the denial of admission to students from a religious high school whose curriculum had not prepared them for college work. They have relied on it to discipline or expel students who had not met academic standards or who had violated campus rules regulating offensive speech. One university asserted its institutional academic freedom to defend the right of students to perform a play that depicted Jesus as a homosexual, opposing a lawsuit brought by citizens who maintained that by permitting this performance the university had endorsed anti-Christian beliefs. Based on general First Amendment doctrines, universities have maintained that they had the right to decide whether student organizations could use campus facilities and to impose a mandatory student activity fee on students that would be distributed to student extracurricular organizations having a wide range of ideological goals.

Universities have relied on institutional academic freedom and general First Amendment doctrines to challenge laws that restricted their discretion in other contexts. One university attacked a licensing law that gave a government agency authority to determine whether a university could grant degrees. Institutional academic freedom and general First Amendment doctrines, other universities maintained, invalidated a law denying federal funds to universities that applied their antidiscrimination policies to limit access of military recruiters to campus during the period when homosexuals could not enlist. Relying on general First Amendment doctrines, universities have resisted attempts by members of the public to express themselves on university property.

In response to many of these cases and numerous others, some Supreme Court decisions and hundreds of lower-court decisions have recognized academic freedom as a First Amendment right. The First Amendment applies only to state action. Judges have largely rejected efforts to expand the concept of state action to the activities of nominally private universities. The First Amendment protection for academic freedom, therefore, applies to legislative and executive actions that affect professors and universities, and to disputes between professors and administrators or trustees at public universities. But it does not apply to disputes within private universities, although some private universities voluntarily agree to follow the requirements of the First Amendment. Unfortunately, judges have not clarified the meaning of academic freedom or explained its relationship to other First Amendment rights. Scholars, and often judges themselves, have accurately observed that these decisions are frustratingly inconsistent and confusing.

Just as courts began incorporating academic freedom within the First Amendment in the 1950s, they have developed since the 1960s a distinctive analysis of the First Amendment rights of public employees, helpfully labeled "employee-speech jurisprudence" by Justice Kennedy.[3] Judges often apply general First Amendment law, employee-speech jurisprudence, and the First Amendment law of academic freedom interchangeably in identical or similar contexts, sometimes even in the same case. They have variously asserted that general First Amendment law and employee-speech jurisprudence apply with greater force in universities, apply in particular ways, or do not apply at all. Other opinions add further layers of complication and confusion. Some refer only to the First Amendment generally or to employee-speech jurisprudence while ignoring issues of academic freedom that are clearly presented. By contrast, an occasional opinion refers to academic freedom when none of its meanings seem relevant and only general First Amendment law or employee-speech jurisprudence seems applicable.

The most fundamental questions remain unresolved, often barely discussed or even raised, either in the decisions themselves or in academic scholarship. Is academic freedom really a distinctive liberty, "a special concern of the First Amendment"? If so, how is it distinctive or special compared to general First Amendment rights? Are some general First Amendment concepts and doctrines—such as "the marketplace of ideas," content and viewpoint neutrality, and the concept of a public forum— inapplicable to, or even inconsistent with, academic freedom in universities? Rather than a public marketplace of ideas committed to content and viewpoint neutrality, doesn't a university appropriately limit speech based on academic standards as determined by academic experts? To what extent does or should the First Amendment law governing public employees cover those public employees who are professors at state universities? Does or should the requirement that the speech of public employees address a matter of "public concern" to qualify for First Amendment protection apply to professors, whose academic speech may make huge contributions to specialized disciplines that are inaccessible or uninteresting to members of the general public? Does the exclusion from First Amendment protection of speech by public employees "pursuant to their official duties" apply to professors, whose most significant official duties are scholarship and teaching? To what decisions does institutional academic freedom apply? Who exercises institutional academic freedom on behalf of universities? Does institutional academic freedom have different meanings for public than for private universities? Do student interests in learning justify a distinctive First Amendment right of academic freedom for them? If so, what is its scope? How does it differ from the academic freedom of professors?

Overview

The organization of this book reflects two major goals. My first goal is to organize and classify the morass of case law about academic freedom and the First Amendment at American universities. No such study currently exists. Though drawn from the cases themselves, the classifications are my own, not ones necessarily identified by the judges in their opinions. Like an initial restatement in any substantive area of the law, this organization of the vast and messy case law should impose some clarity on existing law while also highlighting key areas of confusion. Informed by this analysis of case law, which reveals the inherent difficulties in applying general First Amendment law and employee-speech jurisprudence to universities, my second goal is to develop a theory of academic freedom as a distinctive First Amendment right. The case law provides realistic examples of issues the theory must address and contexts for illustrating how it would operate in practice. The theory would also apply to many current controversies, such as legislative restrictions on teaching "critical race theory," nonrenewal of a professor's appointment for showing a portrait of the Prophet Muhammad in class, university restrictions on the freedom of professors to receive funding from corporate or government sources, and university mandates of "trigger warnings" and "diversity statements."

The policy statements and legal briefs of the AAUP feature prominently both in my analysis of case law and in my development of a theory of academic freedom as a distinctive First Amendment right. Established in 1915, the AAUP has been the principal expositor and defender of academic freedom in the United States. Its founding document, the 1915 Declaration of Principles, was the first major American justification of academic freedom and remains broadly influential throughout the academic world a century later. Though not a legal document, it provides a convincing theoretical justification of academic freedom that is compatible with and can inform analysis of academic freedom as a First Amendment right. Subsequent AAUP policy statements, sometimes formulated jointly with associations of universities and trustees, provide additional guidance in developing a First Amendment theory of academic freedom.

Since the Supreme Court initially recognized academic freedom as a First Amendment right in the 1950s, the AAUP has filed many amicus briefs attempting to translate its policy positions into legal arguments. It has probably participated more than any other organization in cases raising issues of academic freedom. In analyzing AAUP policies and briefs, I draw on my experience as a lawyer in the AAUP's national office from 1976 through 1982 and, after becoming a law professor, as the AAUP's general counsel from 1998 to 2006 and chair of its Committee on Academic Freedom and Tenure from 2006 to 2012. Though I generally agree with AAUP positions, I reject some significant ones, as I indicate throughout this book. In analyzing the meaning of academic freedom, I also draw on important past and contemporary scholarship.

The book begins with two chapters of historical background. In Chapter 1, I analyze the treatment of academic freedom in the AAUP's 1915 Declaration. In Chapter 2, I discuss how the American judiciary had applied other provisions of the Constitution to the university long before it gave academic freedom constitutional meaning by associating it with the First

Amendment. Initially through the impairment of contracts clause in the early nineteenth century, and later through the due process clause of the Fourteenth Amendment ratified after the Civil War, courts addressed issues that since the 1950s have arisen under the different constitutional terminology of the First Amendment. In Chapter 3, I turn to the book's central subject: the meaning of academic freedom as a First Amendment right.

In Chapters 3 through 6, I discuss academic freedom as a First Amendment right of professors. Chapter 3 explores its emergence in Supreme Court decisions during the 1950s and 1960s. Chapter 4 analyzes its development in subsequent Supreme Court and many lower-court decisions. Chapter 5 indicates that this right, while widely recognized, has also been widely ignored in cases applying general First Amendment doctrines and employee-speech jurisprudence to speech by professors. Responding to many issues posed by the case law, I then propose, in Chapter 6, a theory of academic freedom as a distinctive First Amendment right of professors.

Following the discussion of professors and similarly reviewing the case law before proposing a theory, I explore in Chapter 7 the institutional academic freedom of universities. I examine the Supreme Court and lower-court decisions that, most noticeably since the late 1970s, extended the First Amendment right of academic freedom from professors to universities as institutions. In Chapter 8, again responding to case law, I justify a distinctive First Amendment right of academic freedom for universities as well as professors. Chapter 9 asks whether institutional academic freedom can justify limits on free speech, focusing on the regulation of offensive speech on educational grounds and on access to university property. Observing that the academic freedom of professors and universities can conflict, I suggest in Chapter 10 how judges can resolve these cases. In Chapter 11, I consider the possible extension of a First Amendment right of academic freedom to students.

A Theory of Academic Freedom as a Distinctive First Amendment Right

A convincing theory of academic freedom as a distinctive First Amendment right must differentiate academic freedom from general First Amendment rights of free speech while explaining why academic freedom fits within the First Amendment. If academic freedom is the same thing as free speech, there is no need for a separate theory of academic freedom. Yet if academic freedom is different from free speech, its distinctive meaning must be connected to the First Amendment. The societal value of the contribution to knowledge through the expert academic speech of professors, the classic justification for academic freedom in the 1915 Declaration, provides the basis for treating it as a distinctive category of First Amendment analysis. The distinctive meaning of academic freedom is connected to the First Amendment because it fosters two central First Amendment values recognized by courts in a wide range of cases, including in cases arising at universities: the production and dissemination of knowledge, and the contribution of free expression to democratic citizenship.

The 1915 Declaration defined academic freedom as the freedom of professors to perform their essential function of pursuing knowledge and conveying the results of their expert study to students, colleagues, and the broader society. Any indication that professors could be disciplined because people without academic training disagreed with their scholarly views, it stressed, would undermine confidence in the integrity of their work. People would understandably worry that professors had altered their academic judgments to avoid discipline. The 1915 Declaration also took pains to emphasize that academic freedom is not an absolute right of individual professors. It acknowledged that professors should be subject to discipline when their expression violates academic norms. Yet it insisted that only fellow professors have the expertise to determine and apply these norms, adding that involvement by others would raise legitimate suspicions of improper motivations. Peer review thus became a key component of academic freedom.

Without referring specifically to the 1915 Declaration, William Van Alstyne used a similar analysis of academic freedom in his brilliant theoretical essay "The Specific Theory of Academic Freedom and the General Issue of Civil Liberty."[4] Written in 1972 in an attempt to resolve confusion about the status of academic freedom as a First Amendment right, Van Alstyne's convincing distinction between a specific First Amendment right of academic freedom and general First Amendment rights of political expression has gone unheeded by the courts even as the widely lamented lack of clarity among the judicial decisions has persisted and proliferated. In this book, I follow Van Alstyne's distinction, develop the analysis of academic freedom as a distinctive subset of First Amendment law, and apply this analysis to many factual contexts, most of which have arisen in the half century since Van Alstyne's pioneering essay.

Grounding First Amendment academic freedom on the societal contribution of expert academic speech has important implications for its relationship to the general First Amendment right of free speech and to employee-speech jurisprudence. The general First Amendment right of free speech protects the right of all citizens to express themselves about a broad range of subjects. It requires content and viewpoint neutrality in "the marketplace of ideas." The specific First Amendment right of academic freedom primarily protects the right of a limited group of people within universities to pursue and convey their expert knowledge. It does not extend to content or viewpoints that fail to meet academic standards as determined by faculty peers. *Whereas the general First Amendment right of free speech is individualistic and egalitarian, the specific First Amendment right of academic freedom is communitarian and meritocratic.*

Employee-speech jurisprudence limits First Amendment protection to speech about matters of public concern that are not made pursuant to an employee's official duties. The First Amendment right of academic freedom protects the expression of expert speech in scholarship and teaching, the core official duties of professors, even if that speech is not about a matter of public concern.

Academic freedom provides both more and less protection for professors than the general right of free speech provides for citizens or employee-speech jurisprudence provides for public employees. As Van Alstyne stressed in his theoretical essay, academic freedom gives professors more protection for their expert academic speech, but it subjects them to discipline for failing to meet academic standards that do not apply to others.

Just as the 1915 Declaration focused on the academic freedom of professors, a theory of academic freedom as a distinctive First Amendment right applies most easily to them. Beyond protecting scholarship and teaching, this right extends to speech by professors about institutional educational policy. Yet it does not cover the political speech of professors unless it relates to their academic expertise. The assertion by the 1915 Declaration that academic freedom protects all political expression by professors is inconsistent with its own emphasis on the societal value of academic expertise as the justification for academic freedom. With respect to expression outside their expertise, professors should be governed by the First Amendment law of free speech that applies to all citizens and the employee-speech jurisprudence that applies to all public employees.

The centrality of peer review to academic freedom suggests that the First Amendment right of academic freedom should not only protect speech on peer review committees, but also require that universities establish them and provide basic procedural rights for faculty under review. As judges and commentators have often observed in many contexts, substantive First Amendment rights depend on procedural protections. It is also plausible to maintain that the substantive right of professors to speak about the educational policies of universities should require structures of faculty governance in which these policies are discussed, though it would not be a significant mistake to reject this view.

In addition to recognizing academic freedom as a First Amendment right of professors, courts have attributed First Amendment rights of academic freedom to universities as institutions and, much more tentatively, to students. The 1915 Declaration limited academic freedom to professors. It might have been wiser similarly to limit academic freedom as a First Amendment right. Perhaps terms such as "educational autonomy" and "freedom to learn" could have more effectively identified the educational interests of universities and students that merit distinctive First Amendment protection. But it is plausible to analyze these interests under the rubric of institutional and student academic freedom.

The ability of independent universities to protect the academic freedom of professors from external interference, highlighted in both the 1915 Declaration and in judicial decisions, provides the strongest justification for institutional academic freedom. Grounding institutional academic freedom in its instrumental support for the academic freedom of professors connects it to the context in which the concept of academic freedom first arose and most convincingly applies. It also makes sense to include the educational policy decisions of universities within institutional academic freedom because these decisions affect the production and dissemination of knowledge and the training of students for democratic citizenship, the general First Amendment interests that support academic freedom. Because many university decisions are not related to educational policy, institutional academic freedom is not a general right of university autonomy. Determining what constitutes an educational decision by a university, therefore, is as crucial to institutional academic freedom as determining what constitutes expert speech by a professor is to individual academic freedom. And just as general First Amendment doctrines could protect the political speech of professors that is outside their academic expertise, the First Amendment doctrine of freedom of association or the liberty and property clauses of the Fourteenth Amendment could protect the autonomy of universities to make decisions on grounds that are not educational.

The validity of an institutional claim to academic freedom may depend on who makes the decision on behalf of the university. Many educational decisions, especially those related to appointment and tenure, are within the primary responsibility of the faculty, subject to limited administrative and board review. Broader issues of educational policy, by contrast, are within the primary responsibility of the administration and governing board, though faculty should have meaningful input.

In many instances, the extent of institutional academic freedom from state action applies equally to public and private universities. Public as well as private universities should have institutional academic freedom from state regulation of the content of teaching and scholarship. State interests in national security, public health, prevention of fraud, and enforcing laws that protect freedom of expression and prohibit employment discrimination may justify limits on the institutional academic freedom of private as well as public universities. But in some matters, the state should have more authority to regulate public universities than private ones. A state legislature should be able to decide whether to fund a research university, an agricultural college, or a community college. Legislative requirements that a public university serve a broad or elite student body, enroll a certain percentage of state residents, or admit all high school graduates in the top 10 percent of their class seem reasonable. So does legislation compelling public universities to teach courses in state history or the US Constitution, though it would violate the academic freedom of professors if the legislation restricted the materials they could assign or the academic views they could express. But I do not think the legislature should be able to impose any of these decisions on private universities.

The theoretical analysis developed in this book should resolve many disputes about whether a claim raises a First Amendment issue of academic freedom. Some disputes, however, present conflicts between plausible academic freedom claims by professors and universities. In response to a professor's assertion that the university violated academic freedom in denying tenure, the university could claim that it exercised its institutional academic freedom over the selection of faculty while making the decision on valid academic grounds. As judges often concede, they are not competent to evaluate the academic merits. But they are competent to determine whether stated reasons are pretexts. And if a case turns on analysis of the academic merits, judges should defer to the determinations of expert faculty peers, ordering peer review if it has not already occurred and overruling it only when there is compelling evidence that the peer review failed to meet academic standards or resulted in a decision that violated the law.

The extension of academic freedom beyond its core protection of the scholarship and teaching of professors can include student interests in learning as well as institutional interests in educational policy. Students lack the academic expertise that is the foundation of the academic freedom of professors and, particularly as undergraduates, rarely participate in the production of knowledge. But student interests in learning at public universities implicate the First Amendment interests of disseminating knowledge and education for democratic citizenship.

In the classroom, student academic freedom is constrained but not precluded by the academic freedom of professors to make expert judgments about the relevance, quality, and pedagogical value of student speech. If students meet academic standards, they should be able to express views about the subject matter of a class even if they challenge the professor. Students should not be subject to indoctrination, harassment through speech, and other abusive speech that interferes with their ability to learn, even if similar speech off campus would be protected by general First Amendment doctrines. Students are entitled to competent instruction. Student academic freedom plausibly encompasses these student interests in learning. Students, like professors, should have academic freedom for their speech about matters of educational policy. Extracurricular activities, as both educators and judges have observed, constitute "a second curriculum" in which learning occurs. Student academic freedom should protect student journalists and actors. It should also extend to student participation in extracurricular organizations engaged in political and other ideological activity, which contributes to their education for democratic citizenship. Just as academic expertise provides the basis for faculty but not student academic freedom, the educational benefit of extracurricular political activities provides the basis for student academic freedom that is not available for bringing political expression by professors within their academic freedom.

This book should enable readers to reach their own conclusions about how to apply the First Amendment to the educational functions of universities. They can evaluate the variety of judicial approaches in the case law I discuss, and my theoretical justification of academic freedom as a distinctive First Amendment right.

As the case law reveals, to some extent general First Amendment law and employee-speech jurisprudence can be interpreted to recognize interests in academic freedom. For example, in balancing employee interests in speech against employer interests in efficiency, some judges have concluded that university professors have more discretion than other employees to criticize their colleagues and administrators. Beyond selecting from alternative approaches within the existing case law, it is possible to incorporate additional consideration of academic freedom into traditional First Amendment analysis. Points I make while developing a theory of academic freedom as a distinctive First Amendment right, such as the importance of peer review in evaluating academic expression, could inform the application of general First Amendment law and employee-speech jurisprudence to the university.

Yet some doctrines of general First Amendment law and employee-speech jurisprudence are impediments to the educational functions of academic speech in universities. The fundamental First Amendment doctrines of content and viewpoint neutrality, as Justices Stevens and Souter have pointed out, are in tension with the legitimate interests of universities in preferring some ideas over others while making decisions about the merits of candidates for appointment and tenure and of courses to include in the curriculum. Judges have varied in their willingness to treat speech by professors as "matters of public concern" eligible for First Amendment protection, but it is difficult to extend even a broad interpretation of public concern to subjects of esoteric academic interest. The greatest impediment to academic speech comes from the rule that the First Amendment does not protect speech by public employees made "pursuant to their official duties." The official duties of professors most obviously consist of scholarship and teaching. In announcing the "official duties" test, the Supreme Court left open a possible exception for professors. But it has never resolved this issue, and lower courts have differed about whether to recognize an exception.

These difficulties with general First Amendment law and employee-speech jurisprudence highlight the promise of a clarified and developed First Amendment law of academic freedom. Just as employee-speech jurisprudence emerged as a subset of First Amendment law to address the distinctive First Amendment issues that arise in the context of public employment, a First Amendment theory of academic freedom can address the distinctive First Amendment issues that arise in universities. Beyond providing a convincing basis for protecting academic speech left vulnerable by broader areas of First Amendment law, a theory of academic freedom as a distinctive First Amendment right directs attention to the important issues at stake in the regulation of academic speech. For example, even if a judge would reach the same result, it makes more sense to ask whether academic speech by professors meets academic standards than to ask whether it is about a matter of public or private concern. I hope in this book to demonstrate the value of academic freedom as a distinctive subset of First Amendment law by developing its theory and illustrating how it would apply in practice.

1

Defining Academic Freedom in the AAUP's 1915 Declaration

THE "1915 Declaration of Principles on Academic Freedom and Academic Tenure" by the newly formed AAUP remains the most thorough and influential analysis of academic freedom in the United States.[1] It established the meaning of academic freedom as a professional norm within the academic community decades before the Supreme Court identified it as a First Amendment right. Familiarity with academic freedom as a professional norm helps evaluate its subsequent emergence as a First Amendment right. More specifically, the detailed and sophisticated treatment of academic freedom in the 1915 Declaration provides useful guidance for remedying the unelaborated and often confusing judicial application of the First Amendment to academic freedom.

Three key features of the 1915 Declaration are particularly relevant for legal analysis. It justifies academic freedom by tying it to the function of professors in universities. It emphasizes the vital role of peer review in monitoring academic freedom. And it extends the scope of academic freedom to the general political expression of professors.

Legal analysis of the First Amendment right of academic freedom should adopt the justification for academic freedom and the focus on peer review from the 1915 Declaration. But it should reject the extension of academic freedom to general political expression, which was controversial among the framers of the 1915 Declaration and is inconsistent with the Declaration's own justification for academic freedom. Subsequent policy statements by the AAUP have elaborated the application of academic freedom to general political expression without revisiting its initial unconvincing extension in the 1915 Declaration. Pointing out the underlying inconsistency between the justification for academic freedom and its extension to general political expression should help resolve legal confusion about the relationship between free speech and academic freedom in current First Amendment law.

The 1915 Declaration defines academic freedom as the freedom of professors to perform their essential function of pursuing knowledge and conveying the results of their expert study to students, colleagues, and the broader society. Any indication that professors could be disciplined because people without academic training disagree with their scholarly views, it stresses, would interfere with this function by undermining confidence in the integrity of their work. People would understandably worry that professors had altered their academic judgments to avoid punishment. Legal decisions occasionally make this point, but rarely rely on it as the fundamental justification for academic freedom.

The 1915 Declaration also takes pains to emphasize that academic freedom is not an absolute right of individual professors. Speech that fails to meet academic standards, it recognizes, is not the expert academic expression that merits the protection of academic freedom. Yet it insists that only fellow professors have the expertise to determine and apply these standards. Peer review thus became a key component of academic freedom. Judges have occasionally recognized the importance of peer review. But they have not treated it as essential in analyzing the First Amendment right of academic freedom. Interpreting the First Amendment right of academic freedom to require a role for peer review would address the concern of many judges and commentators about the lack of judicial competence to resolve academic disputes. It would encourage judicial deference to expert faculty peers to determine whether faculty speech meets the academic standards that justify the protection of academic freedom.

The justification for academic freedom in the 1915 Declaration—the societal interest in protecting the expression of academic expertise by professors—does not apply to general political expression unrelated to their specialties. Academic freedom should be recognized as a distinctive First Amendment right limited to expert academic speech. This distinctive right should be differentiated from the general First Amendment right of free speech about matters of public concern equally shared by all citizens, including professors when they are speaking on subjects beyond their expertise.

The Historical Background of the 1915 Declaration

The conception of academic freedom formulated in the 1915 Declaration derived from the intellectual ramifications of Darwinian evolutionary thought, the experiences of American professors who had studied in Germany, and the growing interest of American professors, often influenced by philosophical pragmatism and political progressivism, in applying their academic expertise to contemporary social issues.[2] They believed that the search for truth was a continuous process in which apparent errors must be tolerated because truth is never definitively known or even knowable.[3]

Yet they maintained that this search must be pursued by competent experts who followed the procedures of academic disciplines. Stressing that the expert search for truth precludes commitments to competing values, they associated it with ideological neutrality. These views about the search for truth affected pedagogy as well as research. Rather than the traditional transmission of truths from professor to student through recitation, professors engaged students as active learners through class discussions and laboratories. Conflicts with trustees who opposed evolutionary theory prompted professors to establish links with colleagues at other universities and to assert their academic competence in justifying resistance to administrative interference with their work.[4]

The German research university, with its established traditions of academic freedom, was an important model for American professors in the decades before World War I. Many American professors, including many members of the committee that drafted the 1915 Declaration, had studied in Germany. They sought commitments to research and academic freedom in the American universities to which they returned. American professors increasingly viewed academic freedom as the essential attribute of a university, as it was in Germany. Yet the German conception of academic freedom did not adapt easily to the United States. In Germany, academic freedom protected a professor's scholarship and teaching against interference from the state. But Germany lacked a strong commitment to general rights of political expression, and academic freedom did not apply to speech by professors outside the university. The powerful boards of trustees that governed American universities did not exist in Germany, where professors themselves largely operated the university. American professors wanted the protection for scholarship and teaching available in Germany, but they also wanted to prevent universities from restricting their external expression. The strong influence of philosophical pragmatism and progressive political thought in the United States encouraged professors to share their academic expertise with the general public and more specifically to advise public officials.[5] Professors tried to construct a theory of academic freedom that addressed these interests and concerns.

During the last decades of the nineteenth century, wealthy businessmen increasingly dominated the boards of trustees at American universities while professors in the emerging social sciences addressed their academic expertise to the analysis and remediation of social problems.[6] These simultaneous developments triggered many of the disputes over academic freedom that stimulated both the founding of the AAUP and its 1915 Declaration. The disputes arose especially when the academic views of professors challenged the concrete interests, and not just the general ideology, of trustees. Yet some trustees vigorously supported academic freedom, and disputes over academic freedom did not always pit conservative trustees against progressive professors. Some boards of trustees and administrators fired conservative professors and replaced them with populists. Conservative as well as progressive professors supported academic freedom and became activists on its behalf.[7]

The forced resignation in 1900 of Edward Ross, an economist at Stanford University, prompted the first investigation by an organization of professors into conflicts within universities over faculty speech. Stanford had only one trustee, Jane Stanford, the widow of its founder. She put pressure on Stanford's president, David Starr Jordan, to fire Ross. Already displeased with Ross when he supported the presidential campaign of William Jennings Bryan in 1896, Mrs. Stanford demanded his firing when he advocated a ban on immigration of Chinese workers, who had labored on the railroads that formed the basis for the Stanford fortune. Jordan had recruited Ross to the Stanford faculty and tried to convince Mrs. Stanford that he should be retained. But he ultimately acceded to her insistence that he must be dismissed. The American Economic Association decided to investigate the dismissal of Ross. Edwin R. A. Seligman, a professor of economics at Columbia University, chaired the investigating committee and wrote its report, which condemned Mrs. Stanford for using her opposition to Ross's ideas to force his dismissal.[8] The report stated that the allegations against Mrs. Stanford raised issues of freedom of speech, but it did not refer specifically to academic freedom. Jordan, it stressed, had never indicated that Ross "in his utterances on the silver question, on coolie immigration, or on municipal ownership, overstepped the limits of professional propriety."[9]

The next major investigation of a campus controversy by academic disciplinary societies occurred in 1913, when a joint committee of the American Psychological Association and the American Philosophical Association concluded that the president of Lafayette College had forced a professor to resign because his teaching did not conform to the doctrines of the Presbyterian Church.[10] Arthur O. Lovejoy, who had resigned from Stanford in protest against Ross's dismissal,[11] chaired the joint committee. This report, like the Ross report, did not refer to academic freedom.[12]

In December 1913, three associations of social scientists—the American Economic Association, the American Sociological Society, and the American Political Science Association—coordinated to pass identical resolutions establishing committees on academic freedom and tenure that would cooperate with each other. The three separate committees combined into a single joint committee in June 1914.[13] The joint committee decided at its first meeting to write a statement of principles on academic freedom as well as to investigate individual cases.[14] Its preliminary report, published in the March 1915 issue of the *American Economic Review*, raised many issues that the AAUP's 1915 Declaration would soon address.[15] Seligman, the primary author of the preliminary report and of the 1915 Declaration, believed that that the newly founded AAUP, which had its organizational meeting in January 1915, was more suited to sponsoring the document than a joint committee of disciplinary associations.[16]

Following discussions with Seligman and with the approval of other members of the joint committee of the three social science associations, John Dewey, the first president of the AAUP and a professor of philosophy at Columbia, established its first committee, the Committee on Academic Freedom and Academic Tenure. The new AAUP committee, chaired by Seligman, would write a report that built on the joint committee's preliminary one. Dewey appointed fifteen members, seven of the nine members of the joint committee and professors from additional academic disciplines.[17] Seligman drafted the report, as he had the preliminary one, circulated it to the full committee in late November 1915, and after revisions presented it to the AAUP's second annual meeting in January 1916. Following substantial debate, the annual meeting approved the report, which became known as the 1915 Declaration.

Drafting the 1915 Declaration: Should Academic Freedom Extend to Extramural Speech?

Much of the drafting and commentary in 1915 that preceded the final report later known as the 1915 Declaration focused on whether academic freedom should extend beyond the expert expression of professors within the university. The preliminary report of the joint committee addressed this issue, and the founding members of the AAUP had sharply different views. These early discussions were substantially more extensive and revealing than the ultimate treatment of this issue in the 1915 Declaration itself. Although the 1915 Declaration extended academic freedom to external political expression, it did not address many of the arguments made on both sides of this issue, perhaps because a consensus could not be reached. The relationship between academic freedom and political expression has continued to generate division and confusion in the AAUP, the courts, and scholarly commentary.

The preliminary report of the joint committee considered whether the extramural speech of "specialists" and "nonspecialists" should be treated similarly. It gave the specific examples of a biologist giving a public speech on an economic issue and a physicist taking part in a political campaign. Without providing an answer, it wondered if interference with such speech should be considered an "infringement of academic freedom."[18]

In somewhat more detail, the preliminary statement addressed the extramural speech of professors who speak within their expertise. It first assumed that the classroom speech of professors is protected by academic freedom and suggested that it should be privileged against disclosure to the general public. It then presented competing arguments about whether academic freedom should extend to expert expression outside the classroom. As examples of extramural speech, it mentioned informal conversations with students, "scientific" addresses, popular talks, participation in politics, and, more specifically, running for and holding public office. It pointed out that the specialized knowledge of academic experts on political, social, or economic questions could contribute to public discussion of them. On the other hand, it observed that speaking on these issues in public could impair a professor's "reputation for impartiality." Yet it immediately qualified this concern about impartiality by stating that it might "exaggerate the distinction between intramural and extramural utterances." It questioned whether a professor impairs his reputation in reaching his own conclusions in class after presenting "in a scientific way" different views of a topic under discussion, suggesting that a similar process of reaching conclusions in public expression might also not impair reputation.[19]

Although it did not resolve these competing concerns, the preliminary statement clearly concluded that a scholar must make "concessions to public sentiment" in expressing opinions. It offered two examples: public support of social equality between Blacks and whites by a professor in a southern university, and public statements by a sociologist who believes in the desirability of trial marriages. It questioned whether opposition to expressing these views in public could "properly be called an infringement of academic freedom." Conceding that no one is capable of determining "what academic teaching shall be suppressed as contrary to good morals," the statement nevertheless asked: "Can we claim for the academic teacher a consideration which will entirely relieve him from the consequences applicable to all others when they advance opinions for which the popular mind is not prepared and which are at variance with the recognized fundamental standards?" Though posed rhetorically, the clear implication in context was that the answer to these two questions is no.[20]

Somewhat in tension with its concessions to public sentiment in limiting the expression of certain opinions, the preliminary statement suggested in its final set of rhetorical questions about extramural speech that the key issue is the method rather than the content of expression. When commenting on matters about which "public opinion is sharply divided or hostile," the professor should "refrain from extreme or intemperate statement." If the "method of expression" of a professor differs so much from professional norms that his colleagues lose "confidence in his scholarship and poise of judgment," the preliminary report asked: "Can he continue to invoke in his behalf the plea of academic freedom?"[21]

Seligman's subsequent draft of the 1915 Declaration used similar language, stressing the distinction between the statement of opinion and the method of its expression. It added that any restrictions on academic freedom should at least initially be determined by faculty peers rather than the administration or trustees. Yet it did not explain why the academic expertise of faculty peers, which may be necessary to evaluate the substantive content of academic speech, provides special insight into "what academic freedom should be suppressed as contrary to good morals or sound politics or real social interests." In its introductory comments addressing whether academic freedom should extend beyond freedom of teaching to extramural utterances, the preliminary draft of the 1915 Declaration observed the "great difficulty" in drawing a line between internal and extramural expression, referring to them as "two classes of academic freedom." The difficulty, brought to the committee's attention during its investigations of actual disputes in 1915, arose because "extramural utterances or actions have not infrequently reacted upon the intramural conditions" of a university. But the subsequent text of the draft did not elaborate or offer guidance about resolving this difficulty. It did assert that depriving the public of academic expertise would be "unfortunate."[22]

A fascinating exchange between John Wigmore and Arthur Lovejoy just before the drafting committee finished revising the 1915 Declaration reflected vastly different views about the scope of academic freedom.[23] Wigmore, an eminent professor at Northwestern law school who would succeed Dewey as president of the AAUP the next month, responded to the draft by writing an essay entitled "Academic Freedom in the Light of Judicial Immunity." He maintained that there is a striking analogy between academic freedom and judicial immunity from suit in a civil action by a party who claims wrongful treatment by the judge. Judicial immunity, he pointed out, protects corrupt as well as honest judges, "because you cannot protect the one without protecting the other." Similarly, the protection of academic freedom "cannot be limited to the competent thinker." Unless the incompetent are protected as well, the competent will be hampered by having to defend themselves against allegations of incompetence. But just as the protection of the judge does not go beyond his judicial role, the protection of the professor should only extend to his role as a scholar. The protection of academic freedom, Wigmore stressed, is not given for the "personal sake" of the professor, "but for Truth's sake." Truth, he elaborated, "needs the absolutely untrammeled mind of the physicist in the domain of physics; but it does not need his freedom in politics," which presumably does not contribute to truth.[24]

Wigmore acknowledged that in practice it could be hard to differentiate the academic from the political, but he believed that in most circumstances the boundary is clear. He gave two legal examples of extramural expression within a professor's expertise that should be protected by academic freedom. One was an article by a lecturer on corporation law critical of a judicial decision that imposed a large fine in a widely followed case. The other was a lecture by a specialist on international law who criticized President Cleveland's message to Great Britain about its interference in Venezuela.[25]

Wigmore anticipated the response that it would be wrong to give the university professor less general freedom of expression outside his specialty than other citizens possess. He defended this loss of general freedom by emphasizing that the professor "has been given a special privilege over and above the ordinary citizen" through his "university immunity" for expression within his own field. He stressed that by granting this immunity, the university "abdicated" the general right of employers to dismiss employees for expressing unpopular views. In exchange for this extraordinary immunity for academic expression, Wigmore believed, it is reasonable to require professors to "relinquish" their general rights of political expression. In making these observations, Wigmore compared professors to clerics in the Middle Ages, who received immunity from military service and civil taxation in return for confining themselves to their religious obligations.[26]

Wigmore did not address how equal rights of general expression might jeopardize a professor's capacity to perform his academic functions. He seemed to believe more abstractly that special rights must be offset by corresponding restrictions in order to maintain a general sense of societal fairness. Even if the general expression of professors would not compromise their obligations to the pursuit of truth protected by academic freedom, he might have been uncomfortable about giving professors unique rights of expression at work while enjoying the same general rights of expression as all other citizens.

Seligman found Wigmore's essay "exceedingly well written," but he disagreed with its conclusions and doubted whether it should be incorporated into the 1915 Declaration. He circulated it to the other members of the drafting committee, stating that they could discuss it at their meeting the next month.[27] Lovejoy wrote an immediate response vigorously disagreeing with most of Wigmore's analysis, which Seligman also circulated to the full drafting committee.[28]

Lovejoy rejected Wigmore's analogy between academic freedom and judicial immunity from civil actions. He pointed out that judges, though immune from civil liability, do not have absolute immunity because they can be impeached for misconduct. Similarly, professors should not have absolute immunity from dismissal for incompetence or unprofessional conduct. Lovejoy agreed with Wigmore that lay boards of trustees lack competence to review the "methods and opinions of specialists" and that professors, like judges, should be treated as appointees rather than employees. But instead of academic immunity, Lovejoy advocated review by "judicial members of the academic profession" within the university.[29]

Lovejoy also rejected Wigmore's position that expression by professors outside their academic expertise should not be protected. Invoking Wigmore's analogy to judges, Lovejoy maintained that just as a federal judge cannot be punished by the president who appointed him for personal expression unrelated to his judicial duties, a professor should not be punished for personal expression by the appointing authorities at universities. He worried that Wigmore's approach would allow trustees to use the unprotected speech of professors outside their expertise as a pretext for dismissing them for their academic views. To accept Wigmore's approach "is to give up all practical possibility of maintaining academic freedom." Lovejoy concluded that "in order effectually to protect the investigator within his special province, you must protect him outside of it also."[30]

Roscoe Pound, a Harvard law professor who served on the drafting committee, also commented on the distinction between speech within and outside a professor's academic specialty. "I am doubtful," Pound wrote Seligman, "about any proposition that seems to confine the teacher to a sort of water-tight compartment, labeled his particular subject." Probably influenced by his own pioneering scholarship that drew on the insights of the emerging social sciences and pragmatic philosophy in developing what he called "sociological jurisprudence," Pound added: "While we cannot today take all knowledge for our province, we certainly can and ought to bring all knowledge to bear upon our province and throw light from our province upon all knowledge." Pound suggested to Seligman that their own disciplines of economics and law "can cover a pretty broad ground by our claim of jurisdiction." And Pound considered it plausible for a professor of Greek to assert "that he had learned enough from a study of Thucydides and of the political revolutions and counter revolutions which he describes to pass an expert judgment upon modern politics."[31]

The 1915 Declaration

The 1915 Declaration focused at length on the importance of academic freedom in protecting the valuable function of professors in producing and disseminating knowledge. In developing this argument, it stressed the role of peer review in evaluating claims of academic freedom. More summarily and less convincingly, it extended academic freedom to extramural speech beyond a professor's expertise, ignoring or treating superficially much of the sophisticated debate about this controversial topic during the drafting process.

In its opening paragraph, the 1915 Declaration identified three elements of academic freedom: "freedom of inquiry and research; freedom of teaching within the university or college; and freedom of extra-mural utterance and action." Throughout the rest of the text, it tied the defense of academic freedom to its conception of a professor's function: the pursuit and dissemination of knowledge based on expertise gained through lengthy study. It stressed that professors cannot perform this function if there is even the appearance that others could restrict the honest expression of academic views. "To the degree that professional scholars, in the formation and promulgation of their opinions, are, or by the character of their tenure appear to be, subject to any motive other than their own scientific conscience and a desire for the respect of their fellow-experts," the 1915 Declaration reasoned, "to that degree the university teaching profession is corrupted; its proper influence upon public opinion is diminished and vitiated; and society at large fails to get from its scholars, in an unadulterated form, the peculiar and necessary service which it is the office of the professional scholar to furnish."[32]

Asserting that all rights have corresponding duties, the 1915 Declaration devoted substantial attention to identifying the limits of academic freedom. While free to convey their own academic views, professors should fairly convey the conflicting conclusions of other scholars. They should not provide students with "ready-made conclusions," but train them "to think for themselves." In a recommendation that would seem quaint or overly restrictive to many readers a century later, it encouraged professors to express their conclusions "with dignity, courtesy, and temperateness of language."[33]

The 1915 Declaration emphasized that academic freedom does not immunize professors from discipline for expression that violates academic standards. This limitation on academic freedom corresponds to the rationale for protecting it, though the 1915 Declaration did not explicitly assert the analogy. Speech that does not meet academic standards is not the expert academic speech that contributes to the production and dissemination of knowledge. The 1915 Declaration insisted that only other professors are competent to make this determination. While conceding that the governing boards of universities are competent to assess charges that professors have failed to perform assigned duties or have engaged in immoral behavior, it stressed that members of these boards lack the expertise to evaluate academic standards. Indeed, involvement by the board in discipline for expression by professors that allegedly violates academic standards would allow it to substitute its own "opinions or prejudices." Emphasizing the crucial role of faculty in establishing the boundaries of academic freedom, the 1915 Declaration asserted "not the absolute freedom of the individual scholar, but the absolute freedom of thought, of inquiry, of discussion, and of teaching, of the academic profession."[34]

The 1915 Declaration recognized the novelty of its emphasis on peer review. It observed that professors had not previously had the opportunity to determine whether their colleagues had violated academic standards, might find the obligation to do so "unwelcome and burdensome," and might have to exercise more "impersonal judgment" and "judicial severity" than they currently possess. But it warned that if professors fail to exercise this responsibility and, when necessary, fire their colleagues for incompetence or for invoking academic freedom "as a shelter for inefficiency, for superficiality, or for uncritical and intemperate partisanship," people without the necessary qualifications will do so, which would breed suspicion and controversy.[35]

While acknowledging that the board of trustees is the ultimate source of power in a university, it urged trustees to understand this power as a public trust and to respect the academic freedom of professors. It recognized the existence of a small number of "proprietary" universities established to propagate the doctrines of the people who provided the endowment and cited three actual examples: universities established by religious denominations to teach a religious faith, a university funded by a wealthy manufacturer to teach the advantages of a protective tariff, and a university endowed to teach the doctrines of socialism. Differentiating proprietary universities from the typical university, it observed that "their purpose is not to advance knowledge by the unrestricted research and unfettered discussion of impartial investigators." Trustees of proprietary universities, the 1915 Declaration conceded, must obey the terms of the deed of gift and, whatever their own views, require adherence by professors to the doctrines the university was founded to promote. Expressly refusing to comment on the desirability of proprietary universities, the 1915 Declaration emphasized that they should be clear about their ideological commitments and "should not be able to sail under false colors." It also observed that proprietary universities, already few, were becoming rarer, and mentioned that religious universities increasingly did not require the teaching of specific doctrines.[36]

Except for the few remaining proprietary universities, the 1915 Declaration insisted, universities are a public trust and their trustees are trustees for the public. Private as well as public universities are public trusts because they appeal for public support to maintain "a nonpartisan institution of learning" rather than an instrument of propaganda. At the overwhelming majority of universities that are not proprietary, the 1915 Declaration concluded, trustees violate their public trust if they restrict the academic freedom of professors.[37]

Based on this reasoning, the 1915 Declaration criticized universities that treated professors as employees of the trustees, who could exercise their power as employers to impose their own views about teaching and even dismiss professors with whom they disagreed. This "conception of the university as an ordinary business venture, and of academic teaching as a purely private employment," it stressed, manifests "a radical failure to apprehend the nature of the social function discharged by the professional scholar." It asserted that professors are appointees, not employees, of trustees, and are responsible to the public and to the professional judgment of their colleagues, not to trustees who "have neither competency nor moral right to intervene" in their academic work. In this connection, though not in all respects, it compared the relationship between professors and trustees to the one between federal judges and the president, a point about which Wigmore and Lovejoy agreed despite their vigorous dispute about the appropriateness of the analogy between judges and professors. Just as the president who appoints federal judges cannot control their decisions, the trustees who appoint professors cannot control their scholarship and teaching. And just as the president is not responsible for the legal decisions of the appointed judges, trustees are not responsible for the academic conclusions of the appointed professors.[38] In making these points, the 1915 Declaration did not indicate that existing law treated professors as employees and allowed employers to fire employees "at will."

Before turning directly to the controversial subject of extramural expression, the 1915 Declaration elaborated its initial assertion that academic freedom extends to it. Warning that democracies are subject to the "tyranny of public opinion," which produces conformity and regards with suspicion any deviations from conventional standards, the 1915 Declaration asserted that a university should be an "inviolable refuge from such tyranny."

One of the main functions of a university in a democratic society, it added, is to help public opinion become more self-critical and reflective. Restrictions on the academic freedom of professors prevent universities from serving this vital democratic function.[39]

Reflecting the dominant emphasis in contemporary progressive ideology on the need for expertise in government, the 1915 Declaration maintained that professors in the modern university, in addition to scholarship and teaching, provide expert advice to legislators and administrators confronted with the complexities of modern society. It observed that if professors are not free to pursue their research and express their expert views, however unpopular, their advice cannot be trusted, and they cannot perform this vital function in the public interest.[40]

The 1915 Declaration explicitly addressed "extramural utterances" later in the document, making it clear that the protection of academic freedom should extend beyond the expert advice given by professors to legislators and administrators. It made the "obvious" but unelaborated point that professors "are under a peculiar obligation to avoid hasty or unverified or exaggerated statements, and to refrain from intemperate or sensational modes of expression." But it took Lovejoy's position favoring the protection of extramural expression by professors even if it does not relate to their academic expertise, the position rejected by Wigmore and left open by Seligman in earlier versions. Subject to the restraints it identified, which Lovejoy had not included in his own analysis of extramural expression, it declared that "it is not, in this committee's opinion, desirable that scholars should be debarred from giving expression to their judgments upon controversial questions, or that their freedom of speech, outside the university, should be limited to questions falling within their own specialties."[41]

Though the 1915 Declaration based its justification for academic freedom on the benefit to society at large from the production and dissemination of knowledge by trained experts, it nowhere explained how extramural speech by professors on subjects outside their own specialties relates to this justification. It did not use Lovejoy's argument that trustees could punish the expert speech of professors by using their general political expression as a pretext. Nor did it invoke Pound's emphasis on the difficulty in differentiating expert from political expression. By referring in its opening definition of academic freedom to the findings of all five AAUP investigating committees in 1915 that professors had been dismissed at least in part for their extramural political speech as citizens, it indicated that pragmatic rather than theoretical considerations predominated.[42] As Walter Metzger elegantly observed, the 1915 Declaration "stretched the cloth of protection over an area in which academics proved to be most exposed."[43] How appropriate that John Dewey, the famous philosopher of pragmatism, was president of the AAUP when it adopted the 1915 Declaration!

And how interesting that Lovejoy himself, who supported the extension of academic freedom to political expression in his exchange with Wigmore in 1915, subsequently rejected this position in an entry on "academic freedom" in the 1930 edition of the *Encyclopedia of the Social Sciences,* an influential volume edited by Seligman. Lovejoy observed that professors "have been dismissed or otherwise penalized because of their exercise, outside the university, of their ordinary political or personal freedom in a manner or for purposes objectionable to the governing authorities of their institutions." He called such administrative action "contrary in spirit to academic freedom." But without elaborating what he meant by "spirit," he concluded that "it is primarily a special case of the abuse of the economic relation of employer and employee for the denial of ordinary civil liberties."[44] Writing subsequently as a scholar, rather than as a co-author of a statement by an association of university professors, Lovejoy might have been more inclined to state his academic views freed from pragmatic considerations.

Soon after publication of the 1915 Declaration, Harvard president Abbott Lawrence Lowell provided an alternative and more convincing analysis of the relationship between academic freedom and extramural political expression. In his annual report for 1916–1917, Lowell addressed "the right of a professor to express his views without restraint on matters lying outside the sphere of his professorship." According to Lowell: "This is not a question of academic freedom in its true sense, but of the personal liberty of the citizen. It has nothing to do with liberty of research and instruction in the subject for which the professor occupies the chair that makes him a member of the university." To illustrate, he observed that a professor of astronomy has "no special knowledge of, and no particular right to speak upon, the protective tariff." On this issue, the professor is no different from any other citizen, "and the question is simply whether the university or college by employing him as a professor acquires a right to restrict his freedom as a citizen."[45]

Lowell acknowledged that the political expression of professors as citizens could harm the university. But he maintained that trying to restrain it would be a greater harm. He reasoned that a professor should not be forced "to surrender a part of his liberty" as a condition of university employment. Such a requirement would affect the "dignity of the academic career" and would discourage able people from becoming professors. "If a university or college censors what its professors may say, if it restrains them from uttering something it does not approve," Lowell added, "it thereby assumes responsibility for that which it permits them to say." Lowell saw "no middle ground." "Either the university assumes full responsibility for permitting its professors to express certain opinions in public, or it assumes no responsibility whatsoever, and leaves them to be dealt with like other citizens by the public authorities according to the laws of the land." Lowell himself believed that this "is a responsibility which an institution of learning would be very unwise in assuming." Consistent with his theoretical position, Lowell and the Harvard Corporation resisted the threat by an alumnus to withdraw a bequest of $10 million unless Harvard dismissed a professor who made pro-German statements during World War I. The Corporation issued a rare public statement asserting that "the University cannot tolerate any suggestion that it would be willing to accept money to abridge free speech, to remove a professor or to accept his resignation."[46] By following Lowell's compelling logic, universities could protect the extramural political speech of professors without unconvincingly subsuming it within the concept of academic freedom.

While observing in its first sentence that the traditional German definition of academic freedom had applied to both professors and students, the 1915 Declaration immediately added that it would confine its own analysis to professors. Stating that its focus on the academic freedom of professors "need scarcely be pointed out," it did not elaborate why it was so obvious that student academic freedom would be abandoned.[47] The minutes of the drafting committee do not provide any clarification.[48] As Walter Metzger observed, in its first uses in the United States the term "academic freedom" referred primarily to students, particularly their right to take elective courses. After students received this right, attention turned to the academic freedom of faculty, and by the 1890s the term overwhelmingly applied to professors.[49] The exclusion of student academic freedom from the 1915 Declaration reflects this evolution in meaning.

Possibly the framers of the initial document of a new association of university professors thought they should focus on issues involving professors themselves, either self-interestedly or as a matter of appropriate organizational jurisdiction. They might have also thought that students could advance their interests in academic freedom on their own, as members of the AAUP governing council maintained in 1932 while discussing the possible creation of a special committee to consider the academic freedom of students.[50] Though the 1915 Declaration did not recognize student academic freedom, it did provide some safeguards for student interests by asserting that professors are not protected by academic freedom if they attempt to indoctrinate students.

The 1915 Declaration did contain a section entitled "The Function of the Academic Institution," which maintained that the university cannot fulfill its purposes "without accepting and enforcing to the fullest extent the principle of academic freedom."[51] But even in this section, it continued to associate academic freedom with the professor, in contrast to the subsequent judicial extension of the First Amendment right of academic freedom to universities as well as to professors.

Contemporary college presidents criticized the 1915 Declaration for limiting its conception of academic freedom to professors. Charles H. Van Hise, the president of the University of Wisconsin, wrote a letter to Richard T. Ely, a professor of economics at Wisconsin who served on the drafting committee, complaining that the 1915 Declaration "is written wholly from the point of view of the professors." Van Hise protested that it "wholly ignored" the "rights of students and the public interest," which "are paramount to the individual."[52]

Another college president, Alexander Meiklejohn of Amherst College, criticized the 1915 Declaration's emphasis on the academic freedom of professors for failing to recognize that the university as an institution has interests in academic freedom. In an article in the *Atlantic* in 1918, he maintained that the AAUP "in its proposals and discussions has sundered the college in two" by opposing professors against administrators and trustees. "It sometimes seems as if professors said, 'Let presidents and trustees get money as they can; let them make promises to donors or legislators if need be; but we will see that the promises they give are broken; no man can influence us.' Professors free; trustees and presidents slaves, that seems to be the doctrine." Meiklejohn called this doctrine "false and hateful." Echoing Abraham Lincoln's famous "house divided" speech in 1858 opposing actual slavery, Meiklejohn stated portentously that a college cannot "live half-slave and yet half-free." The academic freedom of professors must exist "within the freedom of the college." In dealing with donors and legislators, he maintained, presidents and trustees must be frank that a university requires academic freedom. He believed that in practice "American colleges are free, trustees and presidents as well as teachers," because most donors and legislators "are eager to give to institutions which no man can buy."[53]

The AAUP after the 1915 Declaration

Over the following century, the AAUP has addressed many subjects. But contrary to the hopes and expectations of its founders, who wanted the new organization to focus on general issues of educational policy and governance at universities, the defense of academic freedom has remained its primary and most recognized function.[54] The 1915 Declaration was the foundation for the subsequent "1940 Statement of Principles on Academic Freedom and Tenure," jointly formulated and endorsed by the AAUP and the Association of American Colleges (AAC) and subsequently endorsed by more than 200 societies of academic disciplines and other educational associations.[55] The provisions of the 1940 Statement have been incorporated into the institutional regulations of many American universities and into collective bargaining agreements between universities and faculty unions.[56]

The 1940 Statement of Principles included extramural political utterances within its definition of academic freedom. It asserted that when professors "speak or write as citizens, they should be free from institutional censorship or discipline, but their special position in the community imposes special obligations." Professors "should remember that the public may judge their profession and their institution by their utterances." They, therefore, "should at all times be accurate, should exercise appropriate restraint, should show respect for the opinions of others, and should make every effort to indicate that they are not speaking for the institution."[57] In an interpretation of this language, the AAUP and the AAC agreed that the university administration, in pressing charges against a professor whose extramural utterances it believes "raise grave doubts" about "fitness" for a teaching position, "should remember that teachers are citizens and should be accorded the freedom of citizens."[58]

The AAUP's subsequent 1964 Statement on Extramural Utterances clarified the limitations on invoking them as grounds for university discipline. "The controlling principle," the Statement asserted, "is that a faculty member's expression of opinion as a citizen cannot constitute grounds for dismissal unless it clearly demonstrates the faculty member's unfitness for his position." "Extramural utterances," it immediately added, "rarely bear upon the faculty member's fitness."[59] Yet the 1964 Statement did not attempt to specify or illustrate the rare circumstances in which extramural political expression legitimately raises grave concerns about fitness. Nor have subsequent statements by the AAUP addressed these issues.[60] To my knowledge, the AAUP has never found that expression by a professor as a citizen justifies disciplinary action by a university.

The AAUP thus retains the 1915 Declaration's extension of academic freedom to cover extramural political expression while asserting that most of the restrictions on it advocated by the 1915 Declaration should not apply. If professors make extramural political statements unrelated to their disciplinary expertise that contain "hasty or unverified or exaggerated statements" or "intemperate or sensational modes of expression," language the 1915 Declaration asserted professors should avoid, the AAUP today would not consider them evidence of unfitness. It would maintain that professors as well as other citizens should have the right to make such statements. In the 1915 Declaration, the extension of academic freedom to extramural political speech came at the price of academic standards of care even in expressions unrelated to the professor's expertise. The current AAUP, by contrast, wants to preserve the expansive definition of academic freedom to include extramural political speech while eliminating the "peculiar obligation" of professors to express themselves more carefully than other citizens. Reports of AAUP investigating committees reflect this position.[61] Whereas the 1915 Declaration provided some symmetry by linking academic freedom to similar academic standards in all expression, the 1964 Statement on Extramural Utterances does not apply academic standards to extramural expression unrelated to disciplinary expertise.

Throughout its history, the AAUP has investigated only a small proportion of the alleged violations of academic freedom that professors brought to its attention. Lovejoy wrote in January 1916 that the committee on academic freedom would only investigate cases that seemed especially important.[62] This policy has persisted ever since, as required by limited resources as well as by broader considerations about the appropriate role of the AAUP.[63] In a 1937 response to a book that criticized the AAUP for insufficiently protecting academic freedom, Lovejoy provided a description of its work that remains accurate. He acknowledged that AAUP investigations rarely resulted in the reinstatement of a professor after a finding that a university dismissal violated academic freedom. Yet he stressed the deterrent effect of publishing careful reports by investigating committees based on verification of the facts. After investigations, universities often revise their institutional regulations to provide more protection for academic freedom, which helps to prevent violations in the future. Other universities are deterred from violating academic freedom by the threat of similar shaming. Lovejoy also pointed out that the AAUP often mediates disputes between professors and universities, thwarting violations of academic freedom before they occur.[64]

Litigation under the First Amendment provides substantially greater opportunities for remedying violations of academic freedom than do AAUP procedures designed to implement understandings of academic freedom derived from the 1915 Declaration. Whereas the AAUP can pursue only a fraction of the complaints it receives alleging violations of academic freedom, the courts are open to all. The AAUP has difficulty obtaining back pay and reinstatement for professors dismissed in violation of their academic freedom, but judges can order and enforce these remedies. Despite its limited powers of enforcement, the AAUP has had an enormous influence on the widespread implementation of policies protecting academic freedom in American universities and on securing adherence to them. But judicial enforcement of academic freedom as a First Amendment right is more powerful than any sanction available to the AAUP.

Conclusion

In developing a theory of academic freedom as a First Amendment right, I rely heavily on the justification for academic freedom in the 1915 Declaration. Its argument that professors need academic freedom to fulfill their functions as scholars and teachers powerfully applies to First Amendment analysis. Its emphasis on the role of peer review in the system of academic freedom provides useful guidance for judicial review of First Amendment claims. But its extension of academic freedom to extramural political expression, which is inconsistent with its own logic, is a conception of academic freedom that impedes the differentiation of a distinctive First Amendment theory of academic freedom from general First Amendment rights of free speech.

2

Initial Applications of the Constitution to the University

THE AAUP's 1915 Declaration was the first major analysis of academic freedom in the United States, but judicial treatment of issues arising at universities as matters of constitutional law began soon after the ratification of the US Constitution. From the famous *Dartmouth College* case decided by the Supreme Court in 1819 through the remainder of the nineteenth century, the "impairment of contracts" clause of the Constitution was the major vehicle for constitutional analysis of the relationship between the university and the state. Only in the 1950s did the First Amendment become the primary constitutional approach, focusing on disputes within universities as well as between the university and the state. In some significant respects, analysis under the impairment of contracts clause foreshadowed and provides historical context for understanding the subsequent application of the First Amendment to the university. Most significantly, the legal distinction between public and private universities introduced by *Dartmouth College* also governs modern First Amendment law, which only limits state action.

Beyond this fundamental similarity, modern First Amendment decisions, like previous decisions under the impairment of contracts clause, address the boundaries of permissible state regulation of universities and indicate when differences between private and public universities should affect this determination. More generally, throughout the history of constitutional review of disputes arising at universities, judges have emphasized that universities contribute to the entire society through the advancement of knowledge and by preparing students for democratic citizenship. In these important respects, the cases share the underlying values the 1915 Declaration invoked to justify academic freedom. To fulfill their vital functions, the cases often maintain, universities must have substantial but not unlimited independence from the state.

Impairment of Contracts

For much of the nineteenth century, judges applied the provision of the Constitution that prohibits any state from passing a law "impairing the obligation of contracts" to determine whether legislation impaired the "contract" created when the state granted a charter of incorporation to a university. By emphasizing that the impairment of contracts clause applies only to private property, the Supreme Court created an influential distinction between private and public institutions of higher education. This distinction had not previously been recognized by the institutions themselves, which typically relied on both public and private support and included public officials as well as private figures on their governing boards.[1] Decisions throughout the nineteenth century elaborated the characteristics that define universities as private or public, when state regulation impairs the charter of a private university, and circumstances in which even public universities are protected from the state.

The Supreme Court initially invoked the impairment of contracts clause to analyze a dispute arising at a university in its 1819 decision, *Trustees of Dartmouth College v. Woodward.*[2] This decision has become justifiably famous for its role in the emerging legal treatment of the business corporation.[3] Commentators have given relatively little attention to its importance for judicial review of universities, the context of the decision itself.

Although it originated as an internal dispute at Dartmouth College, by the time it reached the Supreme Court the case had become a major political issue in New Hampshire and reflected a broader national debate about the interplay among government, universities, and religion in the early American republic. Many of the most interesting underlying facts do not appear in the judicial opinions.

Growing tension between the president of Dartmouth College, John Wheelock, and the board of trustees led to the litigation. As the son of the founder and the leading source of financial support, Wheelock had dominated Dartmouth College for decades.[4] During the years before the litigation, he increasingly lost control of the trustees, who rejected his candidates for the board and the faculty.[5] Wheelock accused a faction of the trustees, under the influence of evangelical revivalism, of trying to transform

Dartmouth into a sectarian religious institution. These trustees and their faculty supporters portrayed Wheelock as a religious liberal who threatened the traditional orthodoxy of New England Calvinism.[6]

In 1815 Wheelock asked the New Hampshire legislature to intervene in his controversy with the board. Reluctant to become directly involved, the legislature recommended that the governor appoint a special committee of non-legislators to investigate. The governor agreed and named three members acceptable to Wheelock and the trustees, two religious liberals and an orthodox Presbyterian. Given the frequent tension throughout American history between universities and legislatures over legislative involvement in university affairs, it is striking that the president and the board apparently assumed that the legislature had an appropriate role, and that the legislature kept its distance through the special committee. When the investigators decided not to recommend any action to the legislature, supporters of Wheelock attempted a reconciliation with the trustees. The attempt failed, and the trustees dismissed Wheelock.[7]

The dispute between Wheelock and the trustees became a major issue in the New Hampshire gubernatorial election of 1816. William Plumer, the candidate of the Jeffersonians, expressed views shared by many in his party, including Jefferson himself. He maintained that because Dartmouth College was supported by public funds, it should be subject to state control and should not retain its affiliation with the Congregational Church. Many Federalists, by contrast, approved state support of colleges that, like Dartmouth, were often led by people who combined Federalist politics with Congregationalist religion. Yet Federalists resisted state involvement in the institutions it supported, probably at least in part because Jeffersonians often controlled the state legislatures.[8]

After Plumer won the election, he drew attention to Dartmouth College in his inaugural address to the legislature. Echoing central Jeffersonian themes, he emphasized that "the general diffusion of knowledge" is particularly necessary in a republic and maintained that the state should "patronize and support the cause of literature and the sciences." New Hampshire, he observed, had made substantial contributions to the funds of Dartmouth College, giving citizens of the state legitimate interests in its condition. The original charter from the British king that established the college in 1769, Plumer added, naturally reflected "principles congenial to monarchy." They included the power of the board of trustees to perpetuate itself by electing new trustees to fill vacancies, which "is hostile to the spirit and genius of free government." After pointing out that Dartmouth College "was formed for the public good, not for the benefit and emolument of its trustees," Plumer asserted that all governments have amended acts of incorporation. In New Hampshire itself, the legislature had frequently changed the boundaries of incorporated towns, and legislatures in other states had materially revised their college charters. Just as the laws of the United States and New Hampshire implicitly abolished the requirement in the original charter that all officers of Dartmouth College take an oath of loyalty to the British king, Plumer reasoned, the legislature could now make express changes to the charter in the public interest.[9]

The New Hampshire legislature acted on Plumer's recommendation. In "an act to amend the charter and enlarge and improve the corporation of Dartmouth College," it changed the name of Dartmouth College to Dartmouth University, gave the governor power to appoint new members to an enlarged board of trustees, and established a new board of overseers, appointed in part by the governor, with control over the trustees. The legislation also required the president and faculty to take an oath of loyalty to the United States and New Hampshire and guaranteed "perfect freedom of religious opinion."[10] In exercising his new powers, Plumer appointed Federalists as well as Jeffersonians and adherents of various religious sects.[11]

Although the original trustees had internal divisions about the appropriate role for religion in college life and the wisdom of firing President Wheelock, they united in bringing a lawsuit in New Hampshire state court to challenge the new legislation.[12] The state court rejected their claim that the amendments to the charter constituted an unconstitutional impairment of the contract created by the original charter. The impairment of contracts clause, it maintained, was clearly intended to protect private rights of property, not to limit the power of states over "civil institutions" such as "public corporations." The key question for the court, therefore, was whether Dartmouth College was a private or a public corporation. Private corporations are "created for the immediate benefit and advantage of individuals," who own the corporate property. Public corporations "are created for public purposes" and their property is devoted to these purposes, not to the private interests of the corporators. As examples of private corporations incorporated in New Hampshire, the court listed companies that built canals, roads, and bridges as well as banking, insurance, and manufacturing companies. As example of public corporations, it listed counties and towns.[13]

Based on its reading of the original charter of Dartmouth College from the British king, the court stated that it "was founded for the purpose of 'spreading the knowledge of the great Redeemer' among the savages and of furnishing 'the best means of education' to the province of New-Hampshire." These purposes, the court concluded, are clearly matters of important public concern in which the trustees have no greater interest than any other members of the community. According to the court, the office of trustee of Dartmouth College, like the office of governor or state judge, is a public trust. Any loss to the property of Dartmouth College would be a loss to the public, not a private loss to the trustees. The trustees have no private rights in Dartmouth College other than to their offices as trustees. The court maintained in passing, by contrast, that the faculty and students have private rights in Dartmouth College that are judicially enforceable, noting that no such claims had been made in the litigation and suggesting that none could have been because the legislation did not injure any of these unnamed private rights.[14]

The decision concluded by emphasizing that its legal analysis promoted the public interest in education. After highlighting the need to maintain the "just rights and privileges" of universities, the court expressed concern about the unchecked power of university trustees. Higher education, the court reasoned, "is a matter of too great moment, too intimately connected with the public welfare and prosperity," to be entrusted to the "absolute control of a few individuals, and out of the control of the sovereign power." It warned that independent trustees "will ultimately forget that their office is a public trust—will at length consider these institutions as their own—will overlook the great purpose for which their powers were originally given, and will exercise them only to gratify their own private views and wishes, or to promote the narrow purposes of a sect or a party."[15] It is fascinating that almost a century later the AAUP's 1915 Declaration used very similar language, although there is no evidence of any borrowing from this decision. Asserting that private as well as public universities constitute a "public trust" whose trustees are "trustees for the public," the 1915 Declaration complained about trustees who employed their legal power of dismissal "to gratify their private antipathies or resentments."[16] The New Hampshire court conceded that legislative power, like any power, may be unwisely exercised, but concluded that there was no better alternative. "If those whom the people annually elect to manage their public affairs cannot be trusted," it asked rhetorically, "who can"?[17]

39

The Supreme Court reversed, holding that the New Hampshire legislation violated the impairment of contracts clause. Chief Justice Marshall's majority opinion acknowledged that the framers of the Constitution did not have legislative amendment of a college charter in mind when drafting this clause. But there was no evidence, it also asserted, that they would have created an exception to the clause or would have written a different clause had this possible application been suggested. Indeed, Marshall quoted the constitutional provision giving Congress the power to grant copyrights and patents as evidence that the framers would have wanted the impairment of contracts clause to cover the facts of *Dartmouth College*. He maintained that both constitutional provisions manifested the respect of the framers for science and literature and that each constituted a "different mode" for promoting them. Just as the congressional power to grant copyrights and patents had "withdrawn science, and the useful arts, from the action of state governments," so the impairment of contracts clause protected from state legislative interference "contracts made for the advancement of literature" through a charter to a college.[18]

Chief Justice Marshall agreed with the New Hampshire court that the impairment of contracts clause applies only to private property and not to "civil institutions," but he disagreed with its conclusion that Dartmouth College was a civil institution. He acknowledged that "education is an object of national concern and a proper subject of legislation." A legislature could create a university entirely under its control, which would be a civil institution. But he rejected the claim that all colleges are civil institutions simply because their general purpose is education. This position, he pointed out, would treat education as an exclusive function of government, making all teachers public officers, all donations public property, and the will of the legislature paramount to the will of the donor. He observed that Dartmouth College was funded entirely from private donations at the time of its founding and incorporation, and denied that a charter of incorporation from the state automatically creates a civil institution. He doubted that any private donor would endow a college if the state could control its funds immediately upon incorporation. Having determined that Dartmouth College was a private rather than a civil institution, Marshall concluded that the New Hampshire legislation violated the impairment of contracts clause by transferring control of the college from the self-perpetuating private board of trustees guaranteed by the original charter to "a machine entirely subservient to the will of the government."[19]

Even though his constitutional conclusion differed from the reasoning of the New Hampshire court, Chief Justice Marshall echoed the New Hampshire court by maintaining that his legal analysis promoted the interests of higher education and that those interests require freedom from external interference. The New Hampshire court worried about interference from self-interested trustees, but Marshall referred to the pernicious influence of legislative bodies, "whose fluctuating policies and repeated interferences, produced the most perplexing and injurious embarrassments." In contrast to the New Hampshire court, which recognized the potential abuse of legislative power while concluding that it posed a lesser threat to universities than the trustees, Marshall did not address the potential abuse of power by trustees even as a lesser threat than legislative interference. Justice Story's concurring opinion did respond to this concern by pointing out that a court of equity has jurisdiction to remedy abuses of trust and can even vest the trust in others.[20] The New Hampshire court, by contrast, had denied the efficiency of judicial review, claiming that many abuses by trustees can be corrected "by sovereign power alone."[21]

Story's concurring opinion is particularly helpful in elaborating Marshall's conclusion that the public interest in education does not justify categorizing all universities as civil institutions. He acknowledged that "in a certain sense, every charity which is extensive in its reach, may be called a public charity, in contradistinction to a charity embracing but a few definite objects." In this sense, he observed, a university is a public charity whenever it offers its charitable purpose of promoting learning and piety to a broad community. But he stressed that a public charity is often a private corporation. The assumption that "because a charity is public, the corporation is public," he declared, "manifestly confounds the popular with the strictly legal sense of the terms." In the legal sense, a public corporation means more than that "the whole community may be the proper objects of the bounty, but that the government have the sole right as trustees of the public interests, to regulate, control and direct the corporation, and its funds and its franchises, at its own good will and pleasure." A public corporation, he added, must be "the exclusive property and domain of the government itself."[22]

Under the terms of Dartmouth's original charter, Story maintained, the land and property held and subsequently acquired by the board, including from the states of Vermont and New Hampshire, was for the use of Dartmouth College in promoting piety and learning, not for the more general use of the people of New Hampshire. Story observed that the charter provided no endowment from the crown and did not reserve any power of amendment in the crown. This charter, Story reasoned, created an implied contract between the crown and every benefactor to Dartmouth College "that the crown would not revoke or alter the charter, or change its administration, without the consent of the corporation." The American Revolution, he added, did not alter the validity of the original charter.[23]

Neither Marshall nor Story addressed Governor Plumer's Jeffersonian claim that state support of Dartmouth College should preclude Dartmouth's affiliation with the Congregational Church. But by invalidating the legislative amendments to Dartmouth's charter, these Federalist justices permitted state support but not state control of such colleges, the status quo widely favored by Federalists generally.

Despite the disagreement between the New Hampshire court and the US Supreme Court about the application of the impairment of contracts clause, the *Dartmouth College* litigation revealed two key areas of agreement that would continue to be endorsed by American courts in cases arising at colleges and universities ever since. Both courts stressed that higher education serves the vital social function of diffusing knowledge, which is essential to the effective operation of American society. And both stressed that external interference can jeopardize the ability of universities to perform this central institutional function. Their differing interpretations of the impairment of contracts clause reflected their disagreement over the source of the greatest threats to the necessary independence of universities. Viewing trustees as the greatest threat, the New Hampshire court did not construe the clause as a barrier to legislative checks on their power. Viewing legislators as the greatest threat, the US Supreme Court construed it to limit their ability to intervene in university affairs.

Often citing *Dartmouth College,* subsequent decisions throughout the nineteenth century elaborated its analytical categories. While clarifying the differences between public and private institutions of higher education, they indicated limits on the broad discretion of trustees at private institutions and on the power of state legislatures over public ones. The cases also upheld some general legislation that restricted the autonomy of both private and public universities.

Decisions held that receiving original funding or subsequent support from the state did not make a university public. Nor could subsequent legislation or action by the board of trustees amend the charter of a private university. Applying this reasoning, judges found that legislatures violated the impairment of contracts clause by firing a college president and by initiating a popular election for an entirely new and enlarged board of trustees.[24]

Yet some courts cautioned that trustees could modify the original provisions of a charter as long as they did not deviate from its central purposes. Even while holding that legislation requiring concurrence of an ecclesiastical body in the choice of college trustees violated the impairment of contracts clause, the Missouri Supreme Court asserted that "strict adherence to all the formal requirements of a foundation might defeat its object" and observed that trustees have a right to alter the curriculum of a college based on changes in the conditions of knowledge. It maintained that "if in centuries past the founder of a college had enumerated alchemy and astrology among its studies, the study of chemistry and astronomy might be deemed a truer compliance with the object of the charity."[25]

While many subsequent decisions elaborated the distinction between private and public universities in *Dartmouth College* to create a broad definition of private universities, courts also applied the distinction to identify public universities over which the state had substantial control. The Missouri Supreme Court differentiated Dartmouth College, a "private corporation," from the State University of Missouri. In founding the state university, the legislature established its own institution, "a public corporation for educational purposes," and "provided for its control and government, through its own agents and appointees." The power vested in the board of curators "was made subject to the pleasure of the Legislature." In contrast to the origins of Dartmouth College, the court observed, the legislature did not contract with private parties in creating the university, so there was no contract to impair. Just as some cases held that public funding did not make private universities public, this decision held that private contributions to the university's original building fund did not make a public university private. Finding that the legislature had the power to pass a law firing the entire faculty, the court denied a professor's suit for lost salary.[26] Decisions in other states held that legislatures had the power to remove the boards of trustees of public universities and appoint successors, and to close a public agricultural college.[27]

Occasionally courts indicated constraints on the power of state legislatures even over public universities. Not all universities that are public corporations, the Alabama Supreme Court held, are under absolute state control. While determining whether legislative appropriations for a college required a two-thirds vote, the court found that the charter of the Medical College of Alabama, a public corporation, gave its self-perpetuating board of trustees entire control over its management. The board could change the curriculum or close the college entirely, although the legislature could amend the charter to place the Medical College under its absolute control.[28]

Although courts provided substantial independence from legislative control to private and even to some public universities, decisions also upheld general legislation that both private and public universities challenged as illegal interference in their internal affairs. A Maryland appellate court rejected the claim by the board of trustees of the University of Maryland that legislation establishing a state board of examiners to license physicians violated the charter granting the college of medicine the authority to award diplomas and certificates to practice medicine. The court concluded that the legislation was a "general police regulation" within the "political power" of the state, which was enacted "to shield the community from the pernicious effects of the ignorance of unskillful pretenders." Nothing in the charter of the medical school, the court stressed, indicated that the state gave up and transferred this "inviolable power."[29]

The California Supreme Court interpreted legislation in the state's general "political code" to give females the right to attend the University of California. The legislation provided that "words used in the masculine gender comprehend as well the feminine gender." The court rejected the claim by the board of the university's Hastings College of Law that this interpretation violated its charter, which gave it power to admit students. Acknowledging that the power to admit includes discretion to determine "who, for any sufficient reason, ought not to be admitted," the court denied that the board had unlimited discretion to violate general laws and to reject any student "who does not possess some qualification arbitrarily selected by them."[30]

The conclusion of the US Supreme Court that a state law prohibiting racially integrated classes did not violate the charter granting Berea College authority to educate "all persons" is another example of how judicial enforcement of general legislation limited institutional independence.[31] The college, which taught integrated classes, was convicted for violating this law and fined $1,000. The majority reasoned that the law only separated the students "by time and place of instruction," which did not prevent the college from furnishing an education to all of them.[32]

44

These cases since *Dartmouth College* reiterated and extended its fundamental distinction between private and public universities. Yet they also recognized legitimate exercises and limitations of state power at both.

The Transition to First Amendment Analysis

By the early twentieth century, the provision in the Fourteenth Amendment that a state cannot "deprive any person of life, liberty, or property without due process of law" superseded the impairment of contracts clause as the constitutional vehicle for judicial review of legislation affecting educational institutions. In his dissent in *Berea College* in 1908, Justice Harlan stepped outside the framework that had prevailed since the opinions of Marshall and Story in *Dartmouth College*. Rather than analyze whether the state legislation violated the college's charter and constituted an impairment of contract, Harlan maintained that "the right to impart instruction" was both a property and a liberty interest and that the "right to receive instruction" was a liberty interest. He concluded that the statute precluding integrated classes was an arbitrary invasion of these rights guaranteed against hostile state action by the Fourteenth Amendment. Yet Harlan limited his analysis to state legislation affecting a "private institution of learning." He explicitly left undecided whether "public schools, established at the pleasure of the state and maintained at the public expense," could invoke these rights under the Fourteenth Amendment.[33]

Whereas Harlan applied the Fourteenth Amendment in dissent, four majority decisions by the United States Supreme Court in the 1920s relied on its general protection of liberty and property to invalidate state legislation regulating primary and secondary schools.[34] They struck down laws that prohibited schools from teaching any subject in a language other than English and required all children between eight and sixteen to attend public schools.[35] Subsequent cases did not address whether teachers, parents, or schools had liberty or property rights that posed barriers to state regulation of education. No similar cases arose at universities.

Yet the word "liberty" acquired new meaning in 1925 when the US Supreme Court asserted that freedom of speech and of the press, which the First Amendment guarantees against abridgment by Congress, "are among the personal rights and 'liberties' protected by the due process clause of the Fourteenth Amendment from impairment by the states."[36] Though sometimes referring interchangeably in the following decades to Fourteenth

Amendment "liberty" and First Amendment "freedom of speech," courts eventually used distinctively First Amendment terminology in addressing state regulation of speech, including speech at universities, rarely referring to the general protection of "liberty" in the Fourteenth Amendment.

Although courts now rely on the First Amendment rather than the impairment of contracts clause while applying the Constitution to the university, they still occasionally cite *Dartmouth College*. A few decisions have invoked it while rejecting First Amendment claims by universities. Some cited it for the general proposition that states can regulate universities in certain circumstances and quoted Marshall's statement that "education is an object of national concern, and a proper object of legislation."[37] Resembling the nineteenth-century decisions that relied on it to uphold legislation against university claims to independence, these cases sustained a state law regulating the granting of baccalaureate degrees, the denial of accreditation by a state agency, and the refusal of a state higher education coordinating board to give "certificate authority" to an institution that offered a major in science education from "a Biblical scientific creationist viewpoint."[38] More significantly, in assessing whether universities are engaging in state action to which the First Amendment applies, scholars and judges have referred to the distinction in *Dartmouth College* between public and private universities.

Many scholars and litigants in the 1960s and 1970s advocated a broader conception of "state action" that would encompass the decisions of many nominally private institutions. This conception was often directed at enabling more enforcement of the Fourteenth Amendment's prohibition against race discrimination.[39] But an expanded conception of state action could also protect First Amendment rights in private universities. Despite attracting prominent advocates, the expansion of state action was quite limited, leaving the long-standing legal distinction between private and public universities largely unchanged and allowing the internal operations of private universities to remain free from First Amendment scrutiny.

Henry Friendly, the eminent federal judge, made an influential contribution to the analysis of state action at universities in a lecture he delivered in 1968 at Dartmouth College itself, which was honoring the sesquicentennial of the oral argument of its eminent alumnus, Daniel Webster, in *Dartmouth College*. Friendly asserted that Chief Justice Marshall, in construing the impairment of contracts clause, had "made things too easy for himself, as he was wont to do, by drawing too bright a line between 'a civil institution' and 'a private eleemosynary institution.'" Friendly proposed a more flexible approach to this distinction in determining the existence of state action, rejecting the views of "constitutional absolutists" that all eleemosynary institutions are bound by the guarantees of the Fourteenth Amendment or that none are.[40]

In the context of higher education, Friendly disagreed with the position that the similarity in the educational functions of private and public universities should encourage the application of the same constitutional standards to all of them, particularly in an era when private as well as public universities depend on substantial public support. He praised *Dartmouth College* for promoting the independence of voluntary associations in the United States and suggested that preserving this independence, "subject to corrective legislative action," would be a greater contribution to liberty and the healthy pluralism of American society than imposing "a rigid and uniform constitutional absolutism—even if in some instances what seems a wrong goes unrighted." The distinction between public and private institutions, Friendly maintained, should depend on "the nature and amount of state aid and the particular grievance asserted." He especially favored finding state action in cases alleging discrimination and was less inclined to do so in cases alleging violations of free speech or unfair dismissal procedures. But even in cases alleging discrimination, he maintained that the magnitude of the discrimination and its potential social consequences should be taken into account. He believed, for example, that discrimination in admission to a private hospital is more serious, and therefore more amenable to a determination of state action, than discrimination in admission to a private school.[41]

Advocating a much broader conception of state action, and written in part as a response to Friendly, Professor Robert O'Neil stressed the substantial government financial support and regulation of private higher education, and the public function of private as well as public universities in educating students for productive lives.[42] While claiming that a strict distinction between public and private universities did not reflect the current realities of American higher education, O'Neil helpfully reviewed its history. The differentiation of public and private universities, stimulated partly by *Dartmouth College* and partly by the increasing reluctance to provide state support to colleges with religious affiliations, was reinforced throughout the nineteenth century as states established explicitly public universities. But the gradual secularization of many private universities and the growth of both state and federal support of private universities blurred the distinction between private and public universities, reintroducing the mixture of public and private attributes that characterized the colleges established during the colonial period, including Dartmouth College itself at the time of the famous Supreme Court decision. Increased private support in the twentieth century of the public universities created in the nineteenth century further blurred the distinction.[43]

To illustrate the weaknesses of a rigid distinction between public and private universities in determining the existence of state action, O'Neil discussed an opinion, written by Friendly himself, generated by an incident at Alfred University in New York the day after Friendly's lecture at Dartmouth. Alfred University, like Cornell University and a few other institutions, combined privately and publicly funded colleges within the same university. The dean of students at Alfred suspended seven students for alleged disciplinary infractions during a demonstration. Four of the students were enrolled in the privately funded liberal arts college and three of them were enrolled in the publicly funded Ceramics College. The suspended students sued for reinstatement. Judge Friendly found state action in the suspension of the students enrolled in the Ceramics College, but no state action in the suspension of the students enrolled in the liberal arts college. Suspended by the same dean for their participation in the same demonstration, the students at the same university had different constitutional rights based on the source of funding of the college in which they were enrolled. In considering the impracticability of having different rules for these two groups of students, Friendly remarked, "[T]hat would be Alfred's problem."[44]

O'Neil supported findings of state action in more circumstances than did Friendly, though he agreed with Friendly that the degree of government involvement and the nature of the challenged decision should affect the determination of state action. In O'Neil's opinion, state action should apply to restrictions on unpopular political speakers and student disciplinary procedures at private universities, but not if speech threatened a core institutional value or if the potential sanctions for a disciplinary infraction were relatively minor.[45]

Judicial decisions construing the meaning of "state action" in higher education overwhelmingly followed the strict formal separation of private and public universities to which Friendly as well as O'Neil objected. A 1962 decision addressing the refusal of Tulane University to admit Black students was a rare exception. Judge J. Skelly Wright, who often used innovative legal analysis especially in combatting discrimination, found that Tulane was a public university engaged in state action and, therefore, subject to claims that it violated the equal protection clause. "At the outset," he wrote, "one may question whether any school or college can ever be so 'private' as to escape the reach of the Fourteenth Amendment." Quoting letters from Thomas Jefferson calling education the only "sure foundation of freedom" in a republic, Wright asserted that in the United States "institutions of learning are not things of purely private concern." The great public interest in education does not depend on "whether it is offered by a public or private institution." He maintained that "the administrators of a private college are performing a public function" and are "agents of the state, subject to the constitutional restraints on governmental action." Invoking "reason" as well as "authority," Wright argued that "the Constitution never sanctions racial discrimination in our schools and colleges no matter how 'private' they may claim to be."[46]

Under the facts of the Tulane case, Wright concluded, his holding did not have to extend this far. He cited the origins of Tulane as a public college, continuing state financial support, and the presence of three state officials on its governing board as sufficient evidence of state action.[47] After further judicial proceedings, another judge heard this case, disagreed with Wright's interpretation of the extent of government involvement at Tulane and, discussing *Dartmouth College* at length, concluded that no state action existed.[48] The judge observed that the Tulane board of trustees considered itself bound by state law to remain segregated and asserted that it would integrate if permitted to do so. He held that the state law requiring segregation was itself unconstitutional and that Tulane was free to integrate.[49]

In contrast to Judge Wright, the overwhelming majority of cases rejected claims that nominally private universities engaged in state action. Some of these decisions cited *Dartmouth College* to support this conclusion. Soon after his lecture and his decision in the Alfred University case, Judge Friendly denied that the grant of state property to assist in the construction of a law school converted it from a private to a public institution. He pointed out that *Dartmouth College,* although decided decades before the prohibition against state action in the Fourteenth Amendment, was the first important case to address the distinction between private and public universities. The substantial grants of land to Dartmouth by the states of Vermont and New Hampshire, he emphasized, did not prevent the Court from concluding that Dartmouth was a private university. Without referring again to *Dartmouth College*, Friendly also maintained that the public function of universities in offering education does not constitute state action, reasoning that resembles the conclusion of Justices Marshall and Story that the public interest in higher education does not make universities public institutions.[50] Citing *Dartmouth College*, other decisions denied that public funding for programs and capital expenditures, or the receipt of a charter from the state subjected universities to the requirements of state action.[51] Because courts did not find state action under these circumstances, they did not address the constitutional claims by a professor that he was fired in retaliation for articles he had published, or by students that they were dismissed for their unpopular speech.[52]

In a rare decision concluding that a previously private university had become sufficiently public to come within the scope of state action, Judge Higginbotham found that Temple University had been integrated into the state system of higher education. Based on this finding, he reversed the summary judgment against professors who claimed that the university dismissed them for exercising rights protected by the Fourteenth Amendment. Discussing *Dartmouth College* at length, Higginbotham conceded that a college does not become a public institution simply because the state charters it or conveys real property to it. But he maintained that if Dartmouth had received the amount of funding provided to Temple by the state of Pennsylvania, Marshall would have characterized Dartmouth as a public institution. The extent of state support in this case seemed substantially greater than in those that did not find state action. In a lengthy discussion of the relationship between Temple and the state, Higginbotham cited legislation that designated Temple a state-related institution while permitting it to retain its private corporate identity, reorganized the board of trustees to ensure that one-third would be appointed by elected public officials, authorized the legislature to set tuition, gave Temple access to state funds for capital expenditures, allowed Temple to issue tax-exempt bonds, and required extensive reporting by Temple to the state. Under this legislation, Temple received over half its operating income from the state, and the state was about to become the owner of the majority of Temple's physical plant. Temple itself had even invoked its state-related status to escape the jurisdiction of the National Labor Relations Board over private but not public employers.[53] These exceptional elements of state involvement, which easily distinguish this case from those finding that substantially less state support did not constitute state action, underline the general difficulty in convincing a court to find state action by private universities.

Yet some states have provided free speech rights at private universities through interpretation of state constitutional protection for free speech and through legislation that applies the First Amendment to private universities. The New Jersey Supreme Court concluded that the New Jersey Constitution is "more sweeping in scope than the language of the First Amendment" and protects rights of speech and assembly against private as well as governmental entities. Based on this reasoning, it recognized the right to distribute political literature on the campus of Princeton University.[54] To invalidate a speech code at Stanford University, a judge applied a California law providing that no private university shall subject a student to disciplinary sanctions for speech protected from governmental restriction by the First Amendment.[55] Some private universities, moreover, have voluntarily agreed to follow the requirements that the First Amendment imposes on public universities through the state action provision of the Fourteenth Amendment. In a dismissal proceeding brought by Stanford University against a tenured professor for speeches allegedly inciting to violence, the faculty hearing committee decided that it would review the professor's speech by the Supreme Court's definition of incitement in First Amendment cases.[56]

Conclusion

The history of judicial interpretation of the relationship between the university and the state through the impairment of contracts clause provides helpful historical context for examining the subsequent application of the First Amendment to the university. As the following chapters illustrate, First Amendment analysis, while echoing many of the points made in decisions construing the impairments of contracts clause, encompasses a much broader range of issues. Chapter 3 begins the First Amendment analysis by exploring the emergence of academic freedom as a First Amendment right of professors.

3

The Emergence of Academic
Freedom as a First Amendment
Right of Professors

THE IDENTIFICATION of academic freedom as a First Amendment right emerged through a series of Supreme Court cases in the 1950s and 1960s. These cases examined the application to professors of general laws addressing subversive speech and conduct. Whereas the 1915 Declaration focused on the relationship of professors to trustees, and the earlier application of the Constitution to the university under the impairment of contracts clause focused on the relationship of the state to trustees, these cases focused on the relationship of the state to professors. Like the 1915 Declaration, they emphasized that the societally valuable function of professors in advancing knowledge and preparing students for democratic citizenship requires protection for the expression of their expert academic views. And like the earlier constitutional cases under the impairment of contracts clause, they recognized the dangers of state intrusion into the academic affairs of universities.

These cases about professors in the 1950s and 1960s formed part of a much larger group of cases generated by concerns about subversive activities during the Cold War against Communism.[1] In these years, worries about Communist infiltration and subversion of American institutions prompted Congress and many state legislatures to launch investigations that extended well beyond Communists and former Communists to members of many organizations on the political left. In addition to legislative investigations, prosecutors throughout the country brought charges under laws that required public employees to disclose their organizational affiliations, take mandatory loyalty oaths to the United States and to the state in which they work, and disclaim membership in the Communist Party or other "subversive organizations." These investigations and prosecutions reached professors along with many other Americans in both the public and the private sectors of employment. Congressional investigations of alleged Communist influence in the film industry, for example, attracted substantial public attention.[2]

Many universities, like other organizations, themselves investigated employees and fired them if they were members or former members of the Communist Party or other "subversive organizations," or if they refused to answer questions about their associations.[3] In 1953 the presidents of the thirty-seven member institutions of the Association of American Universities (AAU), the organization of the major American research universities, issued a statement proclaiming that current membership in the Communist Party "extinguishes" a professor's right to a faculty position. The AAU statement also asserted that the invocation of the Fifth Amendment privilege against self-incrimination to refuse to answer questions during congressional investigations "places upon a professor a heavy burden of proof of his fitness to hold a teaching position." Although many of its internal bodies had opposed the legislative investigations and loyalty oaths, the AAUP did not publicly oppose them until 1956, when it published a comprehensive report entitled "Academic Freedom and Tenure in the Quest for National Security." And although this report objected to the AAU's position on the Fifth Amendment, it acknowledged that "indications of past or present Communist associations and activities," including invocation of the Fifth Amendment, justify at least preliminary university inquiries into faculty "unfitness."[4]

The Supreme Court decisions about professors during this period focused on many of the same constitutional issues that affected other employees. They analyzed the privilege against self-incrimination in the Fifth Amendment, procedural rights under the due process clause of the Fourteenth Amendment, and First Amendment rights of political expression. Yet they also addressed the impact of state laws and regulations on professors, often using the terminology of "academic freedom." Like the larger group of cases presenting conflicts between the individual constitutional rights of public employees and state interests in national security, these university cases reached different and often inconsistent results, sometimes favoring the individual right and sometimes favoring the government interest in national security. Whatever the result, many of the opinions stressed the danger that government investigations of professors, loyalty oaths, and disclaimer oaths could inhibit the societally valuable academic discussion of controversial ideas in the classroom.

The emergence of academic freedom as a First Amendment right of professors was fitful and uncertain. Some opinions identified academic freedom as a First Amendment right, including in cases that found no violation. Some discussed the importance of academic freedom without tying it directly to the First Amendment. Some applied general First Amendment principles, though they invoked the same values other opinions associated with academic freedom. Some claimed that earlier opinions had recognized academic freedom as a First Amendment right even though they had not done so explicitly. Even cases that treated academic freedom as a First Amendment right did not elaborate its meaning or rely on it as the doctrinal ground for the decision. These cases often gave conflicting signals about whether the First Amendment right of academic freedom provided distinctive rights to professors or applied general First Amendment principles to them with particular force. Yet by the 1967 decision in *Keyishian v. Board of Regents*, the Supreme Court majority identified academic freedom as "a special concern of the First Amendment."[5] From 1967 to the present, numerous federal and state judges have invoked this phrase while treating academic freedom as a First Amendment right.

The Hook-Meiklejohn Debate

The debate between Sidney Hook and Alexander Meiklejohn in 1949 about the propriety of dismissing professors for membership in the Communist Party provides valuable background for understanding these Supreme Court decisions. The immediate occasion for the debate was action by the board of regents of the University of Washington, dismissing two members of the Communist Party and placing three former members on probation for two years. Hook, who had studied with Dewey as a graduate student in the 1920s, was a professor of philosophy at New York University. Meiklejohn, who while serving as president of Amherst College in 1918 had criticized the 1915 Declaration for focusing exclusively on the academic freedom of professors, was a professor of philosophy at the University of California, Berkeley. He had written extensively about the First Amendment, publishing his major book, *Free Speech and Its Relation to Self-Government,* in 1948. Hook maintained that Communist Party membership justifies dismissal; Meiklejohn disagreed.

At the beginning of his 1949 article "Should Communists Be Permitted to Teach?," Hook highlighted that the dispute at the University of Washington was the first time professors themselves had been accused of violating academic freedom. He called this situation "a startling reversal which reflects the emergence of new problems in culture and education not dreamed of when John Dewey and Arthur T. Lovejoy organized the American Association of University Professors to further the interests of their profession and defend academic freedom." In concluding that membership in the Communist Party itself violates academic freedom, Hook reasserted the major premises of the 1915 Declaration. He maintained that the search for truth requires protection for controversial academic views, that only intellectual peers can judge academic competence, and that academic freedom entails duties correlative with rights. Without academic freedom, he declared, a university loses the independent research and critical teaching that are its institutional reasons for existence.[6]

Hook based his analysis on the distinction between belief in Communism, which he considered protected so long as it was reached through "the honest exercise of academic freedom," and membership in the Communist Party, which he considered an abandonment of academic freedom because it required adherence to the "Party line." Quoting from Communist Party documents, Hook pointed out the Party's directive to professors that "Marxist-Leninist analysis must be injected into every class" in a way that prevents "exposing themselves" as Party members.[7] The requirement to follow the Party line, he emphasized, extends to every subject from art to zoology. He pointed out as well that the Party line had changed with political exigencies, requiring professors to reverse their former academic views. As examples, he asserted that changes in the Party line forced English professors to alter their views about particular novelists and even particular books, and had instructed social scientists to treat President Franklin Roosevelt as a Fascist in 1934, as a progressive in 1936, as a warmonger in 1940, and, after Hitler invaded the Soviet Union in 1941, as a leader of oppressed people throughout the world. Once a professor joins the Communist Party, Hook concluded, "he is not a free mind." And when professors allow their academic opinions to be dictated by others rather than by "free inquiry into the evidence," they violate academic freedom.[8]

While reasoning that membership in the Communist Party constitutes a violation of academic freedom that justifies dismissal, Hook ended his article by cautioning that it might not be prudent to dismiss in all circumstances. He acknowledged that "reactionary elements" may use Communist Party membership "as a pretext to hurl irresponsible charges against professors whose views they disapprove," which could present a legitimate reason not to dismiss. Consistent with the emphasis on peer review in the 1915 Declaration, he concluded that university policy about the treatment of members and former members of the Communist Party should be "*left to university faculties themselves,* and not to administrators and trustees who are harried by pressure groups."[9] Yet Hook did not apply his own conclusion to the facts at the University of Washington itself. The board of regents, on the recommendation of the president, reversed the decision of the faculty committee that had responsibility under the university's code for reviewing academic freedom cases. The committee determined that no grounds existed for dismissing the former or current members of the Communist Party.[10] Though this reversal violated Hook's own position, he did not criticize the president and trustees or even mention these facts.

Meiklejohn agreed with Hook's presentation of the principle of academic freedom but vigorously disagreed with his conclusion that membership in the Communist Party provides grounds for dismissal. Meiklejohn acknowledged that Communist Party membership requires following the Party line, but he maintained that professors join and remain in the Communist Party because they agree with it, not because the Party orders compliance. He pointed out that three of the five professors dismissed at the University of Washington had resigned from the Communist Party, demonstrating that they remained capable of thinking freely. "Slaves," he tersely concluded, "do not resign." Contrasting the use of police and military power in the Soviet Union to compel adherence to Party orders, he observed that in the United States Communist Party membership is voluntary and that the only weapon of the Party is expulsion. As the cases at the University of Washington illustrated, moreover, joining the Communist Party can ruin an academic career, indicating that professors who do so generally "are moved by a passionate determination to follow the truth where it seems to lead, no matter what may be the cost to themselves and their families."[11]

More broadly, Meiklejohn maintained that dismissing professors solely because they are members of the Communist Party makes "a mockery of freedom by using in its service the forces of suppression." He expressed confidence in the "American doctrine" that "whenever in the field of ideas, the advocates of freedom and the advocates of suppression meet in fair and unabridged discussion, freedom will win."[12] But he did not address Hook's claim that the Communist Party policy and practice of anonymous indoctrination precludes fair discussion.

Intriguingly, at the beginning of his article Meiklejohn asserted that the principle of academic freedom "corresponds closely" to the First Amendment. Just as the First Amendment protects freedom of speech from abridgment by Congress, so academic freedom protects the scholarship and teaching of professors from university administrators.[13] Meiklejohn did not assert that this correspondence should prompt the incorporation of academic freedom into First Amendment analysis, and he did not develop the analogy between them any further in his article. Within a few years, the Supreme Court would use this correspondence to identify academic freedom as a First Amendment right of professors.

The Prelude to *Sweezy*

The Supreme Court majority first recognized academic freedom as a First Amendment right in the 1957 case *Sweezy v. New Hampshire*. But the two former law professors on the Court, William O. Douglas and Felix Frankfurter, wrote opinions in 1952 that stressed the importance of independent critical inquiry by professors. Other justices agreed with their views, and often cited them in subsequent cases, including cases that referred explicitly to academic freedom as a First Amendment right.

The dissent by Justice Douglas in *Adler v. Board of Education* in 1952 was the first Supreme Court opinion that referred to academic freedom. The plaintiffs in *Adler* sought a declaratory judgment that a New York law, designed to combat the infiltration of subversive groups into state educational institutions, was unconstitutional. The law provided for the disqualification and dismissal of an employee of these institutions who "deliberately advocates, advises or teaches" that the government of the United States at any level "should be overturned by force, violence or any unlawful means" or who "helps to organize or becomes a member of" any organization that does so.[14] The law also required the state board of regents, after notice and a hearing, to make a list of such organizations and to provide that membership in any listed organization constitutes prima facie evidence of disqualification, subject to challenge by the affected employee in a hearing with rights to cross-examination.[15]

In their brief to the Supreme Court, the plaintiffs referred to academic freedom under the heading of the argument that this law unconstitutionally abridged "freedom of speech and of assembly." To support its claim that "laws such as these create fear and timidity wholly incompatible with the intellectual atmosphere in which teachers should live," the brief cited recent surveys and articles about the status of academic freedom.[16] The amicus brief filed by the State of New York responded that the law did not raise issues of free speech or academic freedom. Emphasizing the great influence of teachers on students, the brief quoted a few sentences from a 1940 decision by a New York appellate court that made this point while referring to the limits of academic freedom in a case construing the state penal code. "Academic freedom," one of those sentences declared, "cannot authorize a teacher to teach that murder or treason are good." The brief added italics to the word "treason," presumably to highlight the connection to the concern about subversion in *Adler*.[17]

The earlier case, which the brief did not discuss beyond the quoted sentences, overturned the visiting appointment of the eminent British philosopher, Bertrand Russell, to New York's City College. While conceding that the New York Board of Higher Education had the exclusive and unreviewable power to appoint faculty, the judge maintained that this power could not be used to "encourage any course of conduct tending to a violation of the Penal Law."[18] The judge concluded that Russell's published opposition to laws regulating adultery and homosexuality, and his support of temporary childless marriages for university students, had this unlawful tendency and required judicial revocation of his appointment. Asserting that he would not interfere with any action of the board regarding "a pure question of 'valid' academic freedom," the judge did "not tolerate academic freedom being used as a cloak to promote the popularization in the minds of adolescents of acts forbidden by the Penal Code." He differentiated academic freedom from "academic license" without indicating what would constitute "valid" academic freedom.[19]

After quoting from this decision, the New York State amicus brief in *Adler* returned to the subject of academic freedom in its concluding paragraphs. Teachers who become "disciplined agents of organizations advocating the overthrow of our government by force and violence," it observed, "are under compulsion not to speak truth, but only that which will lead or mislead into their fold." Academic freedom and free speech, the brief asserted, can flourish only if such teachers are "eliminated" from their positions.[20]

The Supreme Court majority in *Adler* upheld the legislation without referring to academic freedom. Relying on the long tradition of First Amendment analysis differentiating the "right" of citizens to free speech from the "privilege" of public employment, the majority asserted that if teachers are unwilling to work under reasonable terms required by the government, "they are at liberty to retain their beliefs and associations and go elsewhere." Finding the terms of the legislation reasonably related to the fitness of professors, the majority also denied that it violated due process of law.[21]

Justice Douglas's dissent, joined by Justice Black, began by stressing that the Constitution guarantees freedom of thought and expression to all and that "none needs it more than the teacher." The threat of dismissal for disloyalty, Douglas wrote, "is certain to raise havoc with academic freedom." He maintained that the New York law created "a spying project" for evidence of disloyalty, in which "the prejudices of the community" encourage "searches for hidden meanings in a teacher's utterances." As hypothetical examples, he observed that disloyalty could be inferred from references by an art teacher to socialism, hostility of a history teacher to Franco's rule in Spain, overtones of revolution in an English teacher's discussion of *The Grapes of Wrath*, praise by a chemistry teacher of Soviet progress in metallurgy, and skeptical comments about American involvement in Korea. "There can be no real academic freedom in that environment," he concluded. "Where suspicion fills the air and holds scholars in line for fear of their jobs," he added, "there can be no exercise of the free intellect." Rather than promoting "free inquiry," "adventurous thinking," and the "pursuit of knowledge," teachers become "a pipeline for safe and sound information," conveying a "deadening dogma" that is as dangerous a "party line" as the one required by Communists.[22] Douglas did not elaborate how disloyalty could be construed as meeting the statutory requirement of advocating the overthrow of government "by force, violence or any unlawful means." He apparently felt that "the prejudices of the community" during the anxieties of the Cold War would treat unfounded evidence of disloyalty as advocacy prohibited by the law.

The opinion then made its most explicit connection between academic freedom and the First Amendment. The system established by the New York law, it maintained, "cannot go hand in hand with academic freedom. It produces standardized thought, not the pursuit of truth. Yet it was the pursuit of truth which the First Amendment was designed to protect." Douglas conceded that teachers could be dismissed for creating cells of Communist activities in the schools or for turning their classrooms into "forums for propagandizing the Marxist creed." But as long as they met "professional standards" and did not commit overt illegal acts, he concluded, they should not be subject to dismissal for their political views and associations.[23]

Justice Frankfurter also dissented in *Adler,* but on a technical jurisdictional ground.[24] Yet it is interesting that Frankfurter's file on the *Adler* case contains a list of sources he consulted regarding "the effects of loyalty investigations etc. on academic activity and performance." The list contains the statement that none of the material was used because Frankfurter ultimately relied on other grounds.[25] But the list probably reflects Frankfurter's concerns about the substantive issues he decided not to address in his opinion, and it is likely that he did consult the sources on the list in preparing the concurring opinion he wrote later the same year in *Wieman v. Updegraff,* which unanimously invalidated a loyalty oath required by the Oklahoma legislature for all state employees.[26]

Faculty and staff at Oklahoma Agricultural and Mechanical College challenged the Oklahoma law, which required an oath that the employee was not, nor within the past five years had been, affiliated with any group determined by government officials to be a communist front or subversive organization, and that the employee would fight for the United States in time of war or national emergency. Neither the faculty and staff challenging the law nor the Supreme Court majority opinion referred to academic freedom. The majority focused on the fact that this law, unlike the ones in *Adler* and other prior cases, allowed exclusion of individuals from employment based solely on organizational membership, without investigating a person's knowledge of the organization. "Indiscriminate classification of innocent with knowing activity," it concluded, "must fall as an assertion of arbitrary power," which "offends due process."[27]

Frankfurter's concurrence was a lengthy and impassioned testament to the role of teachers at all levels of education "as the priests of our democracy."[28] Douglas wrote "as one professor to another" in a note informing Frankfurter that he would join the concurrence.[29] Just as Douglas began his dissent in *Adler* by stressing that none needs the constitutional protection for rights of free expression more than the teacher, Frankfurter asserted that "the teacher's relation to the effective exercise" of these rights brings the constitutional protection "vividly into operation." Like Douglas in *Adler,* he objected to the "unwarranted inhibition" produced by the law, which unmistakably tends "to chill that free play of the spirit which all teachers ought especially to cultivate and practice."[30] Tying the function of the teacher to the health of American democracy and to the search for "understanding and wisdom," Frankfurter wrote a passage that became frequently cited:

> It is the special task of teachers to foster those habits of open-mindedness and critical inquiry which alone make for responsible citizens, who, in turn, make possible an enlightened and effective public opinion. Teachers must fulfill their function by precept and practice, by the very atmosphere which they generate; they must be exemplars of open-mindedness and free inquiry. They cannot carry out their noble task if the conditions for the practice of a responsible and critical mind are denied to them. They must have the freedom of responsible inquiry, by thought and action, into the meaning of social and economic ideas, into the checkered history of social and economic dogma. They must be free to sift evanescent doctrine, qualified by time and circumstance, from that restless, enduring process of extending the bounds of understanding and wisdom, to assure which the freedom of thought, of speech, of inquiry of worship are guaranteed by the Constitution of the United States against infraction by national or state government.[31]

Whereas Douglas referred explicitly to academic freedom several times in his dissent in *Adler*, Frankfurter never used this term in an opinion that so passionately expressed the values associated with it. Yet "freedom of inquiry" and "critical inquiry," phrases he used throughout his opinion, are closely related to academic freedom. His reference to the role of teachers in fostering "an enlightened and effective public opinion" resembles the statement in the AAUP's 1915 Declaration that the academic freedom of professors serves a democratic society by helping public opinion become more self-critical and reflective. Subsequent Supreme Court opinions, including some by Frankfurter himself, invoked the themes of Frankfurter's concurrence in *Wieman* while discussing academic freedom explicitly.

Sweezy v. New Hampshire

Sweezy v. New Hampshire, decided in 1957, was the first case in which a majority of the Supreme Court indicated that academic freedom is a distinctive right protected by the First Amendment. Chief Justice Warren's plurality opinion, signed by four justices, differentiated "academic freedom" from "political expression" while treating both as rights protected by the Bill of Rights and the Fourteenth Amendment.[32] Justice Frankfurter's concurrence, joined by Justice Harlan, contained a lengthy discussion of the importance of academic freedom in universities. In providing constitutional protection for academic freedom, Frankfurter relied on the judicial responsibility to enforce the "substantive content" of the due process clause of the Fourteenth Amendment.[33] Neither opinion explicitly cited the First Amendment in connection with academic freedom. But the First Amendment's protection of free speech is the provision of the Bill of Rights that relates to academic freedom and political expression and that constitutes part of the "substantive content" of the due process clause cited by Frankfurter. Since the Supreme Court declared in 1925 that First Amendment guarantees are rights and liberties protected by the due process clause against state action, many opinions referred generally to the Bill of Rights and the due process clause when analyzing alleged state infringement of First Amendment rights, sometimes without adding a reference to the First Amendment itself.

The New Hampshire law challenged by Paul Sweezy, a guest lecturer at the University of New Hampshire, authorized the state attorney general to investigate possible violations of an earlier state law that made subversive persons ineligible for employment by the state government and that declared subversive organizations unlawful. The attorney general twice summoned Sweezy, a well-known Marxist economist, to testify. In a long statement he read at the beginning of his first hearing, quoted in full in a footnote to Warren's plurality opinion, Sweezy stated that he had no knowledge of any violations of the law or of subversive persons in New Hampshire. He added that he was willing to answer certain questions about himself and his views about "the use of force and violence to overthrow constitutional forms of government," making it clear that in doing so he was not conceding the right to ask them. But he maintained, "I shall respectfully decline to answer questions concerning ideas, beliefs, and associations which could not possibly be pertinent to the matter here under inquiry and / or which seem to me to invade the freedoms guaranteed by the First Amendment." Sweezy did not refer to academic freedom in his statement, though he did observe that most of the people subpoenaed by the attorney general fell into one or both of two groups: professors at Dartmouth College and the University of New Hampshire "who have gained a reputation for liberal or otherwise unorthodox views," and activists in the Progressive Party. These subpoenas convinced Sweezy that the main purpose of the investigation was not to uncover subversion but to expose the few people in the state who had expressed any political dissent.[34] He seemed more concerned about the general suppression of political dissent than about issues of academic freedom.

Consistent with his opening statement, Sweezy answered many of the questions asked at the hearings, stating that he had never been a member of the Communist Party or participated in any effort to overthrow the government by force or violence. But he refused to answer questions that the Court grouped into two categories: questions about the Progressive Party, and questions about his lecture at the University of New Hampshire. The questions about his lecture asked whether he said that socialism was inevitable in the United States, whether he advocated Marxism, and whether he espoused the theory of dialectical materialism.[35] The New Hampshire courts held Sweezy in contempt and ordered him jailed until he answered the questions.

Thomas Emerson, a professor at Yale Law School and a leading First Amendment scholar, represented Sweezy in the Supreme Court. His brief explicitly connected academic freedom with the First Amendment as part of a broader attack on the law. One of the brief's five major headings stated that the questions about Sweezy's lecture violated the First Amendment. The first sentence under this heading maintained that the effort to force Sweezy to answer these questions "presents the issue of freedom of speech in one of its most significant and sensitive aspects—the area of academic freedom." In effect, Emerson added, these questions brought "the potent sanctions of the state investigatory power to bear in hampering and repressing academic discussion of socialist and Marxist theory." He quoted from a recent book, *Academic Freedom in Our Time,* which asserted that legislative committee investigations had produced an atmosphere of apprehension and intimidation on American campuses. Emerson noted other books that made the same point and reiterated this theme throughout his brief.[36]

Although the AAUP subsequently participated extensively in litigation about academic freedom, it did not file an amicus brief. It had never previously filed one, and only in 1956 had its governing council voted to do so in the future.[37] The AAUP considered filing an amicus brief in *Sweezy,* but ultimately decided not to write one. It doubted that the case would be decided on grounds related to the AAUP's traditional concerns about academic freedom expressed in the 1915 Declaration. A legal challenge to legislative investigations of subversive activities, it concluded, was not the best context in which to ask the judiciary to recognize and protect academic freedom. More generally, it worried about judicial appropriation of a concept the AAUP had largely defined and successfully advocated throughout the academic world. Even a favorable legal definition of academic freedom would be subject to further judicial interpretation. What the Court might give, many within the AAUP feared, it might also take away. Constitutional recognition of academic freedom, moreover, could prompt many within the university community to refrain from any continuing independent effort to define and refine this crucial concept. The constitutional meaning of academic freedom could preempt rather than complement the one set forth in the 1915 Declaration and accepted in the institutional regulations of many universities. Principles of academic freedom not incorporated in the First Amendment could thereby be abandoned entirely.[38] These concerns were plausible, but by not filing an amicus brief the AAUP missed what in retrospect was a crucial opportunity to influence judicial interpretation of the relationship between academic freedom and the First Amendment at its inception.[39]

A fascinating exchange between Chief Justice Warren and Justice Frankfurter preceded their published plurality and concurring opinions. Warren wrote the first draft opinion in *Sweezy*. It contained most of the content of his published plurality opinion, but not the language about academic freedom, which was inserted after Frankfurter challenged much of Warren's analysis. Warren claimed that the New Hampshire law defining subversive organizations, like the Oklahoma law invalidated in *Wieman*, unconstitutionally allowed the punishment of innocent members of an organization even if they did not knowingly engage in any illegal activities. He also quoted from the decision of the New Hampshire Supreme Court, which acknowledged that "the right to lecture and associate" are constitutionally protected individual liberties and that the questions to Sweezy "undoubtedly interfered" with his exercise of these liberties. Yet the New Hampshire court added that these "are not absolute rights" and that the state interest in conducting the investigation outweighed them. Disagreeing with this deference to the state's interest, Warren stressed that the legislation gave the attorney general "such a sweeping and uncertain mandate" that it was impossible to know whether the legislature wanted the attorney general to ask the questions he posed to Sweezy. Without this knowledge,

Warren maintained, the state interest in the answers to the questions cannot be assessed, and without a valid state interest there can be no justification for endangering Sweezy's constitutional rights, which he did not elaborate beyond the quotation from the New Hampshire Supreme Court. Warren concluded that "the use of the contempt power, notwithstanding the interference with constitutional rights, was not in accordance with the due process requirements of the Fourteenth Amendment."[40]

In a letter to Warren responding to this draft, Frankfurter wrote that he found most of it unpersuasive, except for the discussion of the limits on state power in the Bill or Rights and the due process clause. "I suppose I am influenced," he wrote Warren, "by the fact that a quarter-century of my life was lived as a university teacher and throughout my whole life, both before I came to the Harvard Law School and since coming here, the problem of the relation of universities to the state has become a chief concern of mine."[41] The day after writing this letter, Frankfurter circulated a memorandum on the *Sweezy* case, followed the next day by a nearly identical "separate" opinion that eventually became his published concurring opinion.[42] Frankfurter did not mention that when he was a professor at Harvard Law School he served on a committee appointed by the president to investigate the nonrenewal of instructors in the Economics Department, including Sweezy.[43]

The day after Frankfurter circulated his separate opinion Warren circulated a revised draft opinion that added several paragraphs. These new paragraphs, probably written in response to Frankfurter's memo and separate opinion, included Warren's first references to academic freedom and were incorporated into his published opinion.[44] Placed immediately after his original summary of the decision by the New Hampshire Supreme Court, Warren began by agreeing with the court's concession that the investigation abridged Sweezy's constitutional rights to lecture and associate, a conclusion that "could not be seriously debated." After asserting that these rights are safeguarded by the Bill of Rights and the Fourteenth Amendment, Warren more specifically stated: "We believe that there unquestionably was an invasion of petitioner's liberties in the areas of academic freedom and political expression—areas in which government should be extremely reticent to tread."[45] By using the plural "liberties" and "areas," Warren indicated that "academic freedom" and "political expression" are distinctive liberties protected by the Bill of Rights. The protection of "the freedom of speech" in the First Amendment is clearly the provision in the

Bill of Rights that encompasses them. Surely the facts of the *Sweezy* case contributed substantially to this separate identification of academic freedom and political expression as First Amendment rights. The questions about Sweezy's lecture raised issues of academic freedom, and the questions about the Progressive Party raised issues of political expression.

The next two new paragraphs reinforced the identification of academic freedom and political expression as distinctive First Amendment rights by apparently devoting a paragraph to each. The first paragraph discussed the importance of intellectual freedom in the university, elaborating the earlier reference to academic freedom without repeating the term or citing the First Amendment. "Equally manifest as a fundamental principle of a democratic society," the next paragraph began, "is political freedom of the individual," language indicating that academic freedom and political expression are distinctive rights. In contrast to the lack of additional references to academic freedom or the First Amendment in the prior paragraph, this paragraph stated that "political expression" is a "right" that was "enshrined in the First Amendment of the Bill of Rights."[46] This lack of symmetry raises questions about why Warren did not similarly state in the prior paragraph that academic freedom is a First Amendment right. I do not think that the more explicit connection of political expression as a First Amendment right undermines the conclusion that Warren also intended the prior paragraph to elaborate the meaning of academic freedom as the other of the two First Amendment "liberties" he had already identified. Reinforcing this conclusion, at the beginning of the paragraph following the discussion of political expression, Warren again used the plural "areas" in referring to Sweezy's "rights under the Constitution."[47]

I think the lack of symmetry was inadvertent. Warren had written the paragraph on political expression in his original draft. He added the previous paragraph about intellectual freedom in the university after receiving Frankfurter's memo and revised the beginning of the existing paragraph on political expression by inserting the phrase "equally manifest." The purpose of the new paragraph was to elaborate his other new language referring to academic freedom, and he probably did not consider how much it should parallel the existing paragraph on political expression. Yet this lack of symmetry could also indicate that Frankfurter had not developed his views about the relationship between academic freedom and the First Amendment.

In a case two years later involving the same statutory scheme, the Court reinforced the identification of academic freedom and political expression as separate First Amendment rights. Upholding the conviction of the executive director of an organization that sponsored lectures at a summer camp, the majority observed that "the academic and political freedoms discussed in *Sweezy*" did not easily apply because the organization was "neither a university nor a political party."[48] The lawyer for the executive director complained decades later that the "brave words about academic freedom in *Sweezy*" turned out to be "an example of narrow elitism." He maintained that the guest lectures at the summer camp "were certainly as educational as those given at the University of New Hampshire or any other formal educational institution." Reflecting the connection between the emerging First Amendment right of academic freedom and the distinctive functions of university professors, he complained that the justices "had a respect for university teaching, scholarship, and scholars, which limited their vision of academic freedom."[49]

To understand the Court's initial conception of academic freedom, Warren's new paragraph elaborating its meaning merits quotation in full.

> The essentiality of freedom in the community of American universi-
> ties is almost self-evident. No one should underestimate the vital role
> in a democracy that is played by those who guide and train our youth.
> To impose any straight jacket upon the intellectual leaders in our col-
> leges and universities would imperil the future of our Nation. No field
> of education is so thoroughly comprehended by man that new dis-
> coveries cannot yet be made. Particularly is that true in the social
> sciences, where few, if any, principles are accepted as absolutes. Schol-
> arship cannot flourish in an atmosphere of suspicion and distrust.
> Teachers and students must always remain free to inquire, to study
> and to evaluate, to gain new maturity and understanding; otherwise
> our civilization will stagnate and die.[50]

This paragraph reiterates themes expressed in Douglas's dissent in *Adler* and Frankfurter's concurrence in *Wieman*. The "vital role" in a democracy of the "intellectual leaders in American colleges and universities" echoes Frankfurter's description of teachers as "the priests of our democracy." But in contrast to Frankfurter, who explained that teachers fulfill this role by teaching habits of critical inquiry that are required for responsible citizens and effective public opinion, Warren did not specify how professors contribute to democracy. He turned to the societal value of the pursuit of knowledge through scholarship and teaching at universities, and, like Douglas and Frankfurter before him, maintained that it is inhibited in an atmosphere of suspicion. Yet Douglas, joined only by Black, wrote in dissent in *Adler*, and Frankfurter, joined only by Douglas, wrote in concurrence in *Wieman*. Warren made these points in a plurality opinion signed by four justices, and the concurrence by Frankfurter, joined by Harlan, endorsed and expanded Warren's discussion of them. For the first time, in *Sweezy*, a majority of Supreme Court justices indicated that academic freedom is a distinctive First Amendment right.

The paragraphs Warren added to his initial draft in *Sweezy* did not persuade Frankfurter to abandon his separate opinion. It became a concurrence, joined only by Justice Harlan. Frankfurter began his opinion by vigorously disagreeing with the plurality's primary reliance on the lack of clarity in the scope of the legislature's mandate to the attorney general. He maintained that this issue was a matter of state law beyond the powers of the Supreme Court to review.[51] He objected instead that the state's asserted interest in preventing subversion did not justify the infringement of Sweezy's "constitutionally guaranteed right to lecture" recognized by the New Hampshire Supreme Court. Frankfurter stressed "the grave harm resulting from governmental intrusion into the intellectual life of a university" through the questions the attorney general asked Sweezy about his lecture. The fact that Sweezy swore that he had never advocated overthrowing the government by force or violence underlined Frankfurter's position that the state's justification for compelling him to discuss the contents of his lecture "appears grossly inadequate."[52] He elaborated in a paragraph that emphasized the societal value of free inquiry in universities, as he had in his concurrence in *Wieman*, while adding more discussion about the danger of state intervention. An initial draft preceded this discussion with the heading *"ACADEMIC FREEDOM,"* which he crossed out and which did not appear in the published opinion.[53]

> Progress in the natural sciences is not remotely confined to findings made in the laboratory. Insights into the mysteries of nature are born of hypothesis and speculation. The more so is this true in the pursuit of understanding in the groping endeavors of what are called the

social sciences, the concern of which is man and society. The problems that are the respective preoccupations of anthropology, economics, law, psychology, sociology and related areas of scholarship are merely departmentalized dealing, by way of manageable division of analysis, with interpenetrating aspects of holistic perplexities. For society's good—if understanding be an essential need of society—inquiries into these problems, speculations about them, stimulation in others of reflection upon them, must be left as unfettered as possible. Political power must abstain from intrusion into this activity of freedom, pursued in the interest of wise government and the people's well-being, except for reasons that are exigent and obviously compelling.[54]

Frankfurter then asserted "the dependence of a free society on free universities," which, repeating his major theme, "means the exclusion of governmental intervention in the intellectual life of a university." Government intervention can occur "avowedly," but also, as he and Douglas had stressed in their prior opinions, "through action that tends to check the ardor and fearlessness of scholars, qualities at once so fragile and so indispensable for fruitful academic labor." He cited a few sources from a "vast body of literature" to support his own language, though none from the AAUP, and decided to quote several paragraphs from one of them, a publication recently issued by a conference of senior scholars in South Africa titled *The Open Universities in South Africa*. Calling the search for knowledge in a university its own end, not just a means to an end, the statement maintained that a university must foster free inquiry and remain independent from the government or other external influences. It then described "the four essential freedoms of a university—to determine for itself on academic grounds who may teach, what may be taught, how it shall be taught, and who may be admitted to study."[55] Neither the statement itself nor Frankfurter asserted that these freedoms constitute "academic freedom." But scores of subsequent decisions have quoted this language, generally ascribing it to Frankfurter himself rather than to the original South African statement, as elements of the academic freedom protected by the First Amendment.

Although the excerpt quoted by Frankfurter did not explicitly refer to "the four essential freedoms of a university" as academic freedom, the publication in which this sentence appeared emphasized that the introduction of apartheid in South Africa violated academic freedom. The "open universities in South Africa" were the two universities in the country that were not segregated. The publication protested the government's proposed legislation to prohibit them from admitting nonwhite students. In presenting "the essence of the case" against the legislation, the first chapter declared that "legislative enforcement of academic segregation on racial grounds is an unwarranted interference with university autonomy and academic freedom."[56] The next chapter, "The Idea of a University," contained the paragraphs quoted by Frankfurter.[57] A South African judge who had studied with Frankfurter at Harvard Law School wrote him a letter in May 1957, weeks before Frankfurter drafted his opinion in *Sweezy*, alerting him to this publication and enclosing several articles and editorials opposing apartheid as an attack on academic freedom.[58] One of these articles did explicitly tie "the four essential freedoms" to academic freedom. Entitled "Sacred Principle of Academic Freedom," it was written by Albert Centlivres, the chancellor of the University of Cape Town, who had recently retired as Chief Justice of South Africa and who signed *The Open Universities in South Africa*. In his article, Centlivres referred to a definition of academic freedom "to be the freedom to decide what to teach, whom to teach, how to teach and who should teach."[59] These are the "four essential freedoms of a university" listed in different order and somewhat different language in the publication quoted by Frankfurter in his concurrence. Frankfurter sent a copy of his opinion to Centlivres, who thanked him in a letter stating, "[W]hat you said is a great encouragement to those of us who are endeavoring, against great odds, to support the principles of university autonomy & academic freedom."[60]

Frankfurter wrote in his concurrence that he would quote from the South African statement because it was the latest in the vast body of literature he mentioned. He also described the statement as "perhaps the most poignant because its plea on behalf of continuing the free spirit of the open universities of South Africa has gone unheeded." After the lengthy quotation, he wrote that he did not consider the New Hampshire legislation challenged by *Sweezy* comparable "to the policy against which this South African remonstrance was directed," but that the situation in South Africa demonstrated the need to resist government intrusions "at their incipiency."[61] Frankfurter never specified that the policy was apartheid, which some readers of his opinion might not have realized at the time and which subsequent readers were even less likely to know. Perhaps Frankfurter quoted a foreign rather than an American source from the vast literature he described not only because it was the most recent and, for those who understood the reference to South Africa, the most poignant, but to highlight the universality of his analysis and to extract it from the especially controversial context of the concern about subversion in the United States during the Cold War.

Thomas Emerson, Sweezy's lawyer, was surprised by the Supreme Court's decision.[62] Soon after the oral argument, he expressed doubt that it would decide the case on First Amendment grounds. He was, therefore, delighted that it addressed First Amendment issues. He found Warren's opinion "somewhat baffling" and hard "to figure out." But he maintained that "the language and the spirit" of the Warren and Frankfurter opinions are much broader than the "complicated technical point" on which Warren focused. He asserted that the Supreme Court, "for the first time in its history," declared that "full freedom in the academic world is fully protected by the First Amendment."[63]

From *Sweezy* to *Keyishian*

Keyishian v. Board of Regents, decided ten years after *Sweezy*, was the next important Supreme Court decision that recognized academic freedom as a First Amendment right. *Keyishian* quoted from *Sweezy* while making a more explicit connection between academic freedom and the First Amendment. Between *Sweezy* and *Keyishian*, three other cases provide valuable insights into the winding path through which academic freedom emerged as a First Amendment right of professors. Of particular interest, Justices Frankfurter and Harlan voted against the claims of professors even as they adhered to their concurrence in *Sweezy*.

Only two years after *Sweezy*, the Supreme Court decided *Barenblatt v. United States*, another case in which a professor relied on the First Amendment while refusing to answer questions in connection with a government investigation into subversive activities. The Subcommittee of the United States House of Representatives on Un-American Activities interrogated Lloyd Barenblatt about his current or past membership in the Communist Party. Barenblatt was a nontenured instructor at Vassar College whose four-year contract expired between his initial summons to appear before the Subcommittee and his hearing. Because the Supreme Court had addressed academic freedom in *Sweezy* and was likely to do so again in *Barenblatt*, the AAUP decided to file its first amicus brief.[64]

The AAUP brief identified two aspects of faculty academic freedom while differentiating both from general First Amendment rights. Disclaiming any reliance on the individual First Amendment rights professors share with others, it maintained instead that a distinctive right of academic freedom should be protected by the First Amendment.[65] The traditional definition of academic freedom, the brief observed, focused on the right of the individual professor to engage in teaching and scholarship free from both institutional and external constraints. Yet even as it encouraged the Court to protect this right from infringement by the government, the AAUP stressed that it based its argument on "a second ground, namely that academic freedom also belongs to a teacher in his representative capacity as a member of the academic community." The brief tied this second ground to the "workable autonomy that academic institutions require in order to carry out their educational and research responsibilities," quoting the reference to the university in the 1915 Declaration as an "intellectual experiment station."[66] Although Barenblatt and the United States were the nominal parties in the case, the brief stressed that the "real antagonists were the Government and the university." Control by the university over the employment and dismissal of faculty, the brief maintained, is an "essential precondition" to academic freedom in teaching and research. If any external body, governmental or private, wrests this control from the university, "academic freedom disappears." The congressional interrogation of the professor infringed his freedom "as an agent of the community and thereby injured that community."[67]

As if to stress the danger of government interference in the university, the brief minimized threats to academic freedom within universities themselves, the concern that had led to the founding of the AAUP and that had dominated its work ever since. Indeed, throughout the more than four decades of its existence the AAUP had devoted much of its organizational work to the mediation and investigation of claims by professors that trustees and administrators had violated their academic freedom. Regarding recent decisions by universities to dismiss faculty members in connection with concerns about Communist influence, the brief reported that the AAUP's own investigations had disclosed "some instances" in which both faculty members and administrators "were not without fault." But the brief stressed what it considered to be the unique threat that exists when "vulnerable institutions of higher learning face the monopolistic power of the state." Asserting that the academic community, under the AAUP's broadly accepted standards of academic freedom, could regulate abuses within universities, it concluded that these established standards, not the "steam roller" of the congressional investigating committee, were "the proper tool for weeding out the unfit." No evidence, it maintained, indicated that the academic community was incapable of exercising its autonomy to correct possible abuses of academic freedom by professors who may have misused their positions to indoctrinate in the classroom or distort their research.[68] Perhaps the same concern about judicial preemption of the definition of academic freedom, which prompted the AAUP not to file a brief in *Sweezy*, led the AAUP in *Barenblatt* to focus on the threat to academic freedom from the state and to divert the Court from disputes about academic freedom within universities.

The AAUP brief conceded that "claims of academic freedom cannot be asserted unqualifiedly." It recognized that national self-preservation and well-informed lawmaking as well as academic freedom are societal interests and that when these interests "collide" none "can claim a priori supremacy." Relying on *Sweezy*, the brief maintained that in *Barenblatt* the interest in academic freedom should prevail because the legislative policy authorizing the investigation lacked statutory authority and had been "obscurely expressed."[69]

In contrast to its reversal of Sweezy's contempt conviction, the Supreme Court upheld Barenblatt's conviction under a federal statute that made the refusal to answer questions from a congressional committee a misdemeanor subject to fine and imprisonment. Writing for the majority, which included Justice Frankfurter, Justice Harlan acknowledged that in general Congress cannot inquire into the teaching at American universities. "When academic teaching-freedom and its corollary learning-freedom, so essential to the well-being of the Nation, are claimed," he declared, "this Court will always be on the alert against intrusion by Congress into this constitutionally protected domain." Yet he also insisted that a university "is not a constitutional sanctuary" from congressional inquiries and that Congress is not precluded from asking questions within its "constitutional legislative domain" when the witness is a teacher.[70]

Harlan maintained that upholding Barenblatt's conviction was entirely consistent with the result in *Sweezy*. Asking Sweezy about his lecture and the Progressive Party, he asserted, was very different from asking about the extent of Communist Party infiltration into American universities with the purpose of overthrowing the government. Finding that Congress had made clear its interest in investigating Communist infiltration in education, which threatened the ultimate societal value of self-preservation, Harlan deemed membership in the Communist Party clearly pertinent to that inquiry.[71]

Barenblatt himself, Harlan observed, had not suggested that Congress could never inquire into Communist activities in universities. He then quoted in a footnote the full paragraph in the AAUP amicus brief conceding that academic freedom can collide with the societal interest in national self-preservation, the only reference to the AAUP brief in either the majority or dissenting opinions. Harlan understood Barenblatt to claim that the investigation of him was aimed at "the theoretical classroom discussion of communism," not at subversion. Harlan disagreed, finding that the record did not reveal that it "was directed at controlling what is being taught at our universities."[72]

Justice Black's dissent for four justices objected that the "obloquy" produced by government investigations into Communist affiliations would "prevent all but the most courageous from hazarding any views which might at some later time become disfavored." This undesirable result, he maintained, "is doubly crucial when it affects the universities, on which we must largely rely for the experimentation and development of new ideas essential to our country's welfare."[73] Black did not associate "the experimentation and development of new ideas" with academic freedom, although earlier Supreme Court opinions had made this connection.

The next year another 5–4 decision, *Shelton v. Tucker*, held unconstitutional an Arkansas law that required all teachers in public institutions to list all organizations to which they belonged or contributed during the prior five years. The majority concluded that the statute unconstitutionally impaired "a teacher's right of free association, a right closely allied to freedom of speech."[74] "The vigilant protection of constitutional rights," it asserted, "is nowhere more important than in the community of American schools." To support this assertion, it quoted passages in Frankfurter's concurrence in *Wieman* and Warren's plurality opinion in *Sweezy* that stressed the importance of freedom of inquiry for teachers.[75]

The majority did not refer to academic freedom, which in *Sweezy* had been "closely allied to freedom of speech," but Frankfurter did in his dissent. He cited his concurring opinions in *Wieman* and *Sweezy*, which did not themselves refer explicitly to academic freedom, as evidence that the reason for his dissent was "not that I put a low value on academic freedom." Indeed, he added, he dissented because he believed that academic freedom depends on the careful selection of teachers based on comprehensive information. Although he indicated his personal reservations about the value of the information sought by the Arkansas law, he did not think that the law exceeded the limits on state action imposed by the Fourteenth Amendment. This conclusion reflected Frankfurter's general belief in limited judicial review of state action, which he expressed to Warren while identifying *Sweezy* as a rare exception. Frankfurter added that if Arkansas used the law to terminate the appointment of teachers merely because they belonged to unpopular organizations, it would then be appropriate for the Court to hold this application unconstitutional.[76] Justice Harlan's separate dissent, joined by Frankfurter and two other justices, made similar points without any reference to academic freedom or to the previous opinions that discussed it.

Baggett v. Bullitt, the third instructive case between *Sweezy* and *Keyishian*, was decided in 1964, after Frankfurter's retirement and death. It was another challenge to a law that required state employees, as a condition of employment, to take loyalty oaths to the federal and state constitutions and to disclaim membership in the Communist Party or other subversive organizations. The district court upheld the law, observing that the fitness and competency of professors extends to their loyalty. It rejected claims by professors that the oath violated their First Amendment right of academic freedom by interfering with their ability to discover and transmit knowledge. "Education, not indoctrination," the district court responded, "is the function of a university teacher." Using the same reasoning as Sidney Hook in his debate with Alexander Meiklejohn, it maintained that members of subversive organizations are incapable of exercising academic freedom because they are "bound by a rigid adherence to an ideology governed by the political expediencies of its revolutionary purpose rather than by dedication to the verities wherever they may be discovered."[77]

The brief to the Supreme Court on behalf of faculty, staff, and students at the University of Washington asserted that the law violated numerous First Amendment rights protected against state action by the Fourteenth Amendment, "particularly academic freedom." The brief contained a separate section recounting "recent abridgments of academic freedom," which included quotations from the opinions by Warren and Frankfurter in *Sweezy*.[78] The Court majority held that the law violated the due process clause because it was too "vague, uncertain and broad." Without referring to academic freedom, the opinion maintained that the statutory language defining subversive activity could be construed to cover academic interchanges with known Communists in teaching, editing, and attending scholarly conferences. The only mention of academic freedom was in a footnote stating that it would not address the standing of students to participate in this case because their interests in academic freedom were fully protected by the judgment in favor of the faculty. The dissent by Justice Clark, joined by Harlan, called "absurd" and "ridiculous" the majority's interpretation of the statute as possibly extending to teaching classes whose students included members of the Communist Party, perhaps indicating that they might not have dissented if they thought the statute did extend this far.[79]

Keyishian v. Board of Regents

The Supreme Court's 1967 decision in *Keyishian v. Board of Regents* culminated the series of cases that began with *Adler* in 1952. Justice Brennan's majority opinion identified academic freedom as a First Amendment right more clearly than had any previous opinion, as commentators recognized at the time. The plaintiffs in *Keyishian* challenged the same statutory scheme that the Court had upheld in *Adler*. The majority overruled *Adler*, provoking an unusually angry dissent from Justice Clark, joined by three other justices. As in the other cases beginning with *Adler*, most of the analysis and debate by the justices did not focus on academic freedom and the holding did not depend on it. Even the AAUP amicus brief in *Keyishian*, which was very similar to the eventual majority opinion, dealt mostly with other issues.

The majority opinion stressed the reasons it overruled *Adler*. Concluding that the statutory scheme was unconstitutionally vague, a frequent ground used by the Warren Court to invalidate legislation as unconstitutional, the majority asserted that the Court in *Adler* had refused to consider complaints about vagueness because they had not been made in the pleadings or in the lower courts. It cited well-known language from previous First Amendment cases that did not arise at universities to maintain that vagueness has a "chilling effect" on First Amendment freedoms, does not give them the necessary "breathing space to survive," and induces potential speakers to "steer far wider of the unlawful zone" than constitutionally required.[80]

In addition to its emphasis on vagueness, the majority in *Keyishian* maintained that pertinent constitutional doctrine had changed in several important respects since *Adler*. The premise in *Adler* that "public employment, including academic employment, may be conditioned upon the surrender of constitutional rights which could not be abridged by direct government action," the majority stressed, had been rejected by many subsequent Supreme Court decisions. The development of constitutional law, moreover, required proof of specific intent to further the unlawful aims of an organization, not just the mere knowing membership found sufficient in *Adler,* to justify exclusion from public employment. The New York statutory scheme, the majority concluded, was unconstitutionally overbroad because it extended beyond the legitimate punishment for specific intent to the impermissible proscription of mere knowing membership. The majority emphasized "the stifling effect on the academic mind by curtailing freedom of association," noting various books and articles for support. Some of these books and articles included the term "academic freedom" in their titles.[81]

Clark's dissent angrily disagreed with all the majority's "blunderbuss" attempts to differentiate *Adler.* It maintained that *Adler* was correctly decided and had been frequently followed by other decisions over the intervening fifteen years. Contrary to the majority, it asserted that the issue of vagueness had been raised and rejected in *Adler.* "No court," it concluded, "has ever reached out so far to destroy so much with so little."[82]

Despite their primary focus on other issues, both the AAUP amicus brief and the majority opinion contained substantial discussion of academic freedom. The AAUP brief claimed that Supreme Court decisions since *Adler* "have steadily enhanced the weight and dignity of academic freedom in the constitutional balance," characterizing Frankfurter's concurrences in *Wieman* and *Sweezy* and Warren's plurality opinion in *Sweezy* as giving "official recognition to the constitutional stature of academic freedom" while quoting from them at length. Citing cases between *Sweezy* and *Keyishian,* including *Shelton v. Tucker* and *Baggett v. Bullitt,* it maintained that they "have given even greater recognition and prominence to the constitutional interest in academic freedom."[83]

These assertions about the prior recognition of academic freedom as a constitutional right seem much more sweeping than justified by the opinions themselves, which often did not even refer explicitly to academic freedom. The brief recognized that the cases it cited since *Sweezy* "may well protect the rights of all public employees, and not only of academic personnel," but it asserted that "the most important constitutional principles have been developed in the academic setting," where "the constitutional protections are most needed." Making this point more strongly, the brief asserted that "the particular academic freedom interests of *college and university professors* . . . are of an even higher constitutional order than the claims which can be made for other public employees."[84] Thus, in contrast to its brief in *Barenblatt,* which disclaimed reliance on individual First Amendment rights professors share with others while advocating a distinctive First Amendment right of academic freedom, the AAUP argued in *Keyishian* that constitutional rights shared by all public employees are particularly important for professors. Nor did the AAUP's brief in *Keyishian* reiterate the emphasis in its *Barenblatt* brief on academic freedom as a right of professors in their capacity as representatives of the academic community seeking "workable autonomy" from the state.

The majority opinion addressed academic freedom immediately after its analysis of the unconstitutional vagueness of the statutory scheme. While discussing vagueness, the opinion gave examples of academic speech the New York law could be construed to cover, including teaching or advocacy by a professor of the forceful overthrow of government without any attempt to indoctrinate others; assignments of histories about the evolution of Marxist doctrine or the background of the French, American, and Russian Revolutions; and even carrying a copy of the *Communist Manifesto* on a public street. The dissent denied that the law could conceivably be applied to some of "the strained and unbelievable suppositions that the majority poses," though it added that the possibility of some borderline cases should not invalidate the law. The majority closed its discussion of vagueness by asserting that the legitimate state interest in preventing subversion in the educational system could be achieved by more narrow means that do not violate fundamental First Amendment rights.[85] It then added a paragraph about academic freedom, followed by the quotation of the paragraph from Warren's plurality opinion in *Sweezy* that elaborated his identification of academic freedom as a liberty protected by the Bill of Rights.

Our Nation is deeply committed to safeguarding academic freedom, which is of transcendent value to all of us and not merely to the teachers concerned. That freedom is therefore a special concern of the First Amendment, which does not tolerate laws that cast a pall of orthodoxy over the classroom. "The vigilant protection of constitutional freedoms is nowhere more vital than in the community of American schools" [citing *Shelton v. Tucker*]. The classroom is peculiarly the "marketplace of ideas." The Nation's future depends upon leaders trained through wide exposure to that robust exchange of ideas which discovers truth "out of a multitude of tongues, (rather) than through any kind of authoritative selection" [citing *United States v. Associated Press*].[86]

The reference to academic freedom as "a special concern of the First Amendment" identified academic freedom as a First Amendment right more clearly than any previous Supreme Court opinion. Yet this brief paragraph gave very little guidance about the meaning of academic freedom and gave contradictory signals about its relationship to the First Amendment generally. The words "special" and "peculiarly" connote distinctiveness. They suggest that academic freedom is different from other First Amendment rights, such as speech and association, and that its constitutional interpretation should be informed by legal doctrines sensitive to its distinctiveness, including the need to prevent "a pall of orthodoxy over the classroom." By contrast, the quotation from *Shelton* emphasizes that First Amendment rights shared by everybody must especially be protected in the educational community. The reference to the "marketplace of ideas" and the quotation from the Associated Press case similarly point away from the distinctiveness of academic freedom as a First Amendment right. Justice Holmes, the first justice to use the "marketplace of ideas" metaphor in a First Amendment case, invoked it in his famous dissent in *Abrams v. United States,* a prosecution under the Espionage Act of 1917, as part of his argument for protecting the right of political dissent.[87] The Associated Press case addressed antitrust claims far removed from the educational context.

Although the single paragraph about academic freedom in *Keyishian* left many questions about its meaning unanswered, it was a major step in incorporating academic freedom within the First Amendment. The *New York Times* article reporting the decision began: "Academic freedom, a Johnny-come-lately to constitutional law, won an impressive and perhaps decisive victory this week over its traditional opposing concept, loyalty-security legislation. For a concept that was not even recognized as a constitutional right until a decade ago, academic freedom received a surprisingly strong endorsement from the Supreme Court." The article referred to *Sweezy* as the first time "a majority of the justices declared that a constitutional right of academic freedom did exist, although they left it undefined."[88] The *Keyishian* majority also left academic freedom undefined. Indeed, Frankfurter's concurrence in *Sweezy* discussed issues related to academic freedom in much more detail. But even if *Keyishian* did not define academic freedom more than *Sweezy*, the article was accurate in reporting that *Keyishian* moved substantially beyond *Sweezy* in asserting clearly that academic freedom is a First Amendment right.

Conclusion

Sweezy and *Keyishian* soon became the starting point for judicial analysis of academic freedom as a First Amendment right. The angry dissent in *Keyishian* was the last gasp of a dying tradition that had intermittently persisted in the fifteen years since *Adler*. While frequently bemoaning the lack of clarity about its meaning, judges have invoked it in many contexts beyond the cases about national security in which it emerged. Chapter 4 analyzes decisions since *Keyishian* that illustrate the judicial interpretation of academic freedom as a First Amendment right of professors.

4

The Development of Academic
Freedom as a First Amendment
Right of Professors

CASES SINCE *Keyishian* in the Supreme Court and many more in the lower federal and state courts have substantially expanded the number and variety of judicial encounters with issues of academic freedom. Like the cases that initially recognized academic freedom as a First Amendment right in the 1950s and 1960s, many of these cases attached this right to professors. Beginning in the late 1970s the Supreme Court also attached it to universities. Yet many other cases since *Keyishian* have relied on general First Amendment law when clear issues of academic freedom were raised. In this chapter, I focus on the development of academic freedom as a First Amendment right of professors, saving for subsequent chapters its expansion to universities and the lack of attention to it in cases applying general First Amendment law.

The Supreme Court has continued to identify academic freedom as a First Amendment right while deciding cases on other grounds. Many lower-court cases, by contrast, have explicitly relied on it as the doctrinal basis for the decision, whether upholding or denying the professor's academic freedom claim. These cases have reached inconsistent results and have not provided much analysis. They demonstrate the need for a comprehensive theory that justifies treating academic freedom as a distinctive First Amendment right. They also highlight realistic issues a theory must address. Most importantly, these cases raise questions about the scope of this distinctive right. Does academic freedom in scholarship and teaching extend beyond the content of expert academic expression? Does it protect access to research material, pedagogical decisions in the classroom, and confidentiality for unpublished research and classroom discussions? Are some interests in scholarship and teaching not covered by academic freedom? Does academic freedom extend beyond scholarship and teaching to encompass speech within the university about educational matters and speech outside the university unrelated to the professor's expertise? I return to these questions in Chapter 6, where I propose a theory of academic freedom as a distinctive First Amendment right of professors.

Supreme Court Decisions

After initially identifying academic freedom as a First Amendment right of professors in cases about national security during the Cold War, the Supreme Court decided cases in a broader range of contexts. Cases about national security continued to raise issues of academic freedom. But so did cases construing the clause of the First Amendment that prohibits laws "respecting an establishment of religion," and cases applying federal and state labor law to collective bargaining by professors. Ironically, two cases in which neither professors nor universities were litigants contain perhaps the most revealing and protective language about the distinctiveness of academic speech. Emphasizing that the tradition of free expression within universities is fundamental for the very functioning of American society, one case exempted them from the general First Amendment principle that that the government can control speech in the institutions it funds.[1] The other case indicated that the First Amendment right of academic freedom may require more protection for the scholarship and teaching of professors than the First Amendment provides to expression by other public employees.[2]

Majority decisions have treated academic freedom as a First Amendment right, have cited *Sweezy* and *Keyishian* approvingly, and have endorsed themes associated with academic freedom even when not referring to it. They have relied on AAUP policy statements as defining norms of academic freedom relevant to legal analysis and have responded to arguments in AAUP amicus briefs. The approving references by majority opinions to *Sweezy* and *Keyishian* did not quote their identification of academic freedom as a First Amendment right, but several dissenting opinions did quote this language and no majority opinion questioned this identification. A few dissenting opinions suggested that the academic freedom of professors protected by the First Amendment includes expression about institutional educational policy, participation in institutional governance, and extramural political expression.

Like opinions before *Keyishian,* these subsequent opinions sometimes referred to the First Amendment without mentioning academic freedom, sometimes referred to academic freedom without mentioning the First Amendment, and sometimes ignored issues of academic freedom raised in the briefs or in the courts below. Different justices relied on academic freedom in different cases. Individual justices who relied on academic freedom in some cases did not in others when their colleagues did. Ambiguity persisted about whether academic freedom connotes that the protection of general First Amendment rights is particularly important in the university, or whether it is a "special" First Amendment right—and if so, how.

Addressing Academic Freedom as a First Amendment Right of Professors

The Supreme Court's most significant comments since *Keyishian* about the status of academic freedom as a First Amendment right of professors arose in 2006 as a byproduct of a case brought by a deputy district attorney. In *Garcetti v. Ceballos,* the Court adjudicated the attorney's claim that he had been disciplined in retaliation for challenging the accuracy of an affidavit used to obtain a search warrant. The major legal issue was whether the First Amendment protects speech by public employees made "pursuant to their official duties."[3] Like many other amici, the AAUP filed a brief arguing that it does. The brief then uniquely added its special concern about the potentially devastating impact of a blanket rule denying such protection on the Court's prior decisions recognizing "academic freedom for university professors as a core First Amendment value." These decisions, the AAUP stressed, had never even hinted that academic freedom is limited to expression outside a professor's expertise in performing official duties. To the contrary, they indicated that the more a professor's speech reflects expertise, the greater the First Amendment protection for academic freedom.[4]

The Court majority held that statements by public employees made pursuant to their official duties are not protected by the First Amendment.[5] In a single paragraph of his lengthy dissent, Justice Souter addressed the implications of the decision for academic freedom. Not citing the AAUP brief but echoing its concerns, he worried that the majority's reasoning was "spacious enough to include even the teaching of a public university professor, and I have to hope that today's majority does not mean to imperil First

Amendment protection of academic freedom in public colleges and universities, whose teachers necessarily speak and write 'pursuant to . . . official duties.'" Souter followed this sentence with quotations from *Sweezy* and *Keyishian* that recognized academic freedom as a First Amendment right.[6]

In his majority opinion, Justice Kennedy responded to Justice Souter by acknowledging "some argument that expression related to academic scholarship or classroom instruction implicates additional constitutional interests that are not fully accounted for by this Court's customary employee-speech jurisprudence." He thereby indicated the possibility that the First Amendment right of academic freedom provides more protection to professors than employee-speech jurisprudence provides public employees generally. But Kennedy did not give any hint of his own views. Because the case did not involve a professor, he stated, there was no need to resolve this issue.[7]

Several dissenting opinions in other cases since *Keyishian* also treated academic freedom as a First Amendment right of professors. Dissenting in the 1972 decision in *Board of Regents v. Roth* from a majority opinion denying procedural protections to nontenured faculty, Justice Douglas maintained that a statement of reasons for a nonrenewal and an opportunity to rebut them in a hearing are necessary to protect substantive First Amendment rights, including academic freedom. "No more direct assault on academic freedom can be imagined," Douglas wrote, "than for the school authorities to be allowed to discharge a teacher because of his or her philosophical, political, or ideological beliefs." He quoted passages from Frankfurter's concurrence in *Sweezy* and the language in *Keyishian* referring to academic freedom as "a special concern of the First Amendment."[8] But those quotations addressed the role of academic freedom in teaching and scholarship rather than its relation to "philosophical, political, or ideological beliefs" generally. Indeed, Chief Justice Warren's plurality opinion in *Sweezy* differentiated academic freedom and political expression as distinctive First Amendment liberties. Douglas did not elaborate his own statement about academic freedom, and the majority did not respond to it. Nor have subsequent Supreme Court decisions applied the First Amendment right of academic freedom to political expression. Yet this statement provided the basis for some lower-court judges to extend academic freedom to political expression, the position of the AAUP's 1915 Declaration.

In the very different context of a state labor law governing collective bargaining in higher education, Justice Brennan relied on the First Amendment right of academic freedom while dissenting in *Minnesota State Board of Community Colleges v. Knight,* decided in 1984. The majority, in an opinion by Justice O'Connor, denied the First Amendment claims of professors who challenged their exclusion as nonunion members from "meet and confer" committees established by the collective bargaining agreement to discuss issues of educational policy outside the scope of mandatory bargaining. Even if First Amendment rights of free speech "take on special meaning in an academic setting," she asserted, they do not require the government to include teachers in institutional policymaking. Citing the AAUP brief, she recognized that policy arguments support the strong tradition of faculty participation in academic governance. But she maintained that the Supreme Court had never recognized this participation as a constitutional right. She pointed out as well that the state had not in any way restricted the right of faculty to express their views on any educational issues and had not suppressed any ideas.[9]

In his dissent, Justice Brennan asserted that prior Supreme Court decisions had acknowledged "unequivocally" the statement in *Keyishian* that academic freedom is "a special concern of the First Amendment," though the cases he cited did not quote this statement. He maintained that the freedom to discuss controversial ideas in the classroom may be jeopardized as much by restrictions on the ability to communicate with administrators about issues of academic policy as by the more direct restrictions on classroom speech struck down in previous decisions. Specifying curricular proposals, academic standards, and budgetary issues as matters of academic policy that typically arose in the "meet and confer" sessions, he concluded that excluding professors from these sessions "would plainly violate the principles of academic freedom enshrined in the First Amendment."[10]

Addressing Themes Associated with Academic Freedom

Without referring explicitly to the First Amendment right of academic freedom, some decisions since *Keyishian* expressed themes that other opinions associated with it. *Epperson v. Arkansas,* decided in 1968, reviewed an Arkansas statute enacted in 1928, the year after the famous Scopes trial in Tennessee. Modeled on the Tennessee law under which Scopes was convicted for teaching evolution, the statute forbade teachers in public schools and universities "to teach the theory or doctrine that mankind ascended or descended from a lower order of animals." The Arkansas court that first heard the *Epperson* case held that the statute violated the First Amendment because it "tends to hinder the quest for knowledge, restrict the freedom to learn, and restrain the freedom to teach."[11] In a two-sentence opinion, the Arkansas Supreme Court reversed, holding that the statute was a valid exercise of the legislative power to establish the curriculum in public schools.[12]

In oral argument before the Supreme Court, the lawyer for the state stressed this power as the main defense of the statute while also maintaining its religious neutrality. Questions from the justices pushed how far the state was willing to assert the right to establish the curriculum. Asked if the state would defend statutes that prohibited teaching theories of racial inferiority, the lawyer answered that to be consistent with his argument he would have to answer yes. But when asked if the state would defend statutes making it illegal to teach geometry or theories that the earth is round, the attorney retreated. Acknowledging that a line must be drawn somewhere, he indicated that these restrictions would be unreasonable and, therefore, unlawful. In general, he maintained, the courts should restrain from encroaching on state curricular decisions as much as possible.[13]

Even though the lawyer for the state relied primarily on the right of the state to establish its curriculum, the majority of the Supreme Court, in an opinion by Justice Fortas, focused instead on the establishment clause of the First Amendment. The opinion declared the statute unconstitutional based on the overriding fact that it precluded teaching a segment of knowledge because a theory conflicted "with a particular interpretation of the Book of Genesis by a particular religious group." Yet Justice Fortas mentioned, in passing, issues related to academic freedom. He quoted approvingly the passage in *Shelton* about the importance of protecting constitutional freedoms in the public schools and the passage in *Keyishian* asserting that the First Amendment "does not tolerate laws that cast a pall of orthodoxy over the classroom." He also recognized that the *Meyer* decision in 1923 condemned under the liberty clause of the Fourteenth Amendment "'arbitrary' restrictions upon the freedom of teachers to teach and students to learn."[14] Indeed, a pre-argument note in Fortas's files stated that the case is governed by *Meyer*. The pre-argument note also listed prior Supreme Court decisions that addressed the First Amendment rights of teachers and professors.[15] Fortas stressed in his written opinion, by contrast, that his reliance on the establishment clause to resolve the case precluded the need to revisit these decisions.[16]

Justice Black's concurrence treated the majority opinion, which did not refer to academic freedom, as implicitly recognizing it. He questioned "whether it is absolutely certain, as the Court's opinion indicates, that 'academic freedom' permits a teacher to breach his contractual agreement to teach only the subjects designated by the school authorities who hired him." Stressing that scientists as well as religious figures had criticized Darwin's theory, Black closed his opinion by urging the Court to refrain from reviewing the merits of curricular decisions. In a dyspeptic rebuke to his colleagues, he doubted that they were "so nearly infallible" that they could "successfully supervise and censor the curriculum of every public school in every hamlet and city in the United States." Yet the majority made no conclusion about the merits of Darwin's theory while holding that the law violated the establishment clause by attempting "to blot out a particular theory because of its supposed conflict with the Biblical account, literally read."[17]

While reviewing the exclusion of a foreign professor from the United States, the Supreme Court also addressed issues associated in other opinions with the First Amendment right of academic freedom. Its 1972 decision in *Kleindienst v. Mandel* construed a federal statute excluding from admission to the United States aliens who advocate "the economic, international, and governmental doctrines of world communism or the establishment in the United States of a totalitarian dictatorship." The law gave the attorney general discretion to grant visas for temporary visits to otherwise ineligible aliens. Professors at several universities challenged the exclusion of Ernest Mandel, a prominent Belgian Marxist, under this law. These professors had invited Mandel to speak at their universities and at other forums or had expected to participate in academic exchanges with him.[18]

In holding that the exclusion of Mandel violated the First Amendment, the federal district court judge referred to *Keyishian* as identifying "the national commitment to academic freedom" and quoted its language calling academic freedom "a special concern of the First Amendment."[19] The Supreme Court reversed, emphasizing the long-standing judicial deference to executive power over the exclusion of aliens. But the Court acknowledged that the exclusion of Mandel implicated the First Amendment rights of professors. Recognizing the value of sustained personal communication, Justice Blackmun's majority opinion rejected the government's claim that the

First Amendment rights of professors were sufficiently vindicated by their access to Mandel's ideas though his publications and through technological developments such as tapes and telephone connections. Quoting *Shelton,* the opinion maintained that the general First Amendment right to hear "is nowhere more vital" than in schools and universities. It cited the portions of Warren's plurality opinion in *Sweezy* and the majority opinion in *Keyishian* that discussed academic freedom as a First Amendment right.[20] But it did not quote from them or use the phrase "academic freedom."

Although he did not refer explicitly to the First Amendment right of academic freedom, Chief Justice Rehnquist's majority opinion in *Rust v. Sullivan,* decided in 1991, cited *Keyishian* while asserting that the government's general power to control the speech it funds does not extend to universities. Rust upheld government regulations prohibiting doctors from discussing abortion with patients in federally financed family planning clinics. Doctors who worked in the clinics claimed that this prohibition constituted viewpoint discrimination prohibited by the First Amendment because the regulations also compelled them to provide information about continuing a pregnancy to term.[21] Writing for the Court majority, Rehnquist disagreed. Rather than discriminating against viewpoint, he concluded, the government had simply chosen to fund one activity rather than another. He observed that when Congress created the National Endowment for Democracy to promote democratic principles in other countries, the Constitution did not require it to fund an additional program encouraging communism or fascism to avoid viewpoint discrimination.[22]

Yet language proposed by Justice Souter that Rehnquist incorporated into his opinion took pains to emphasize that his analysis of this controversy should not suggest that the government can always control the content of the speech it funds.[23] He gave two examples of government funding that did not justify restrictions on speech. The first was property owned and maintained by the government that traditionally had been open for public expression. "Similarly," he added, "we have recognized that the university is a traditional sphere of free expression so fundamental to the functioning of our society that the Government's ability to control speech within that sphere by means of conditions attached to the expenditure of Government funds is restricted by the vagueness and overbreadth doctrines of the First Amendment." He cited *Keyishian* immediately after this sentence, listing the page that contained the identification of academic freedom as "a special concern of the First Amendment" and the pages about the rejection of the premise in prior cases that public employment could be conditioned on the surrender of constitutional rights.[24]

This brief passage is simultaneously extremely suggestive and extremely frustrating. It is extremely suggestive because it identifies the societal function of the university as requiring exceptional protection for expression. It indicates that government funding cannot justify government control over the content of faculty expression. It is extremely frustrating because the text refers only to the vagueness and overbreadth doctrines of the First Amendment as the doctrinal basis for this exceptional protection. But vagueness and overbreadth are general First Amendment doctrines that the Court used to invalidate many laws affecting speech, mostly in settings outside the university but also, as in *Keyishian,* within it. These doctrines do not provide a rationale for the exceptional protection of speech within universities that Rehnquist recognized in *Rust.* The language in *Keyishian* identifying academic freedom as "a special concern of the First Amendment" does provide this rationale. The "free expression" in a university that Rehnquist observed is "so fundamental to the functioning of our society," as *Keyishian* and other previous Supreme Court decisions recognized, consists largely of the teaching and scholarship of professors that academic freedom protects. The majority in *Keyishian* highlighted how the vagueness and overbreadth of the New York law inhibited the academic freedom of professors to discuss controversial ideas in the classroom, but Rehnquist did not connect vagueness and overbreadth with academic freedom.

Rehnquist referred to the exceptional tradition of freedom of expression in universities only to limit the scope of the Court's holding in a case addressing the First Amendment rights of doctors in a federally funded family planning clinic to discuss abortion with their patients. There was no reason for him to address the academic context at length, just as there was no reason for him to address at length the law governing speech in public forums, his other example of an exception to the general holding in *Rust.* More than most of the prior decisions arising at universities, his short discussion highlights that the functions of universities require additional and distinctive protection for expression within them. Though not referring directly to academic freedom, this discussion provides resources for treating it as a distinctive First Amendment right. Yet in private correspondence with

Souter, Rehnquist maintained that *Keyishian* was based only on considerations of vagueness and overbreadth, and did not address the substantive limits imposed by the First Amendment.[25]

References to Academic Freedom without the First Amendment

Other Supreme Court decisions referred to academic freedom without connecting it to the First Amendment. In its 1986 decision in *Edwards v. Aguillard,* the Court reviewed a Louisiana law that required "balanced treatment" for "creation-science and evolution-science."[26] In response to the charge that this law, like the Arkansas law invalidated in *Epperson,* violates the establishment clause, the state asserted that its balanced approach advanced the legitimate secular purpose of promoting the academic freedom of students in learning different scientific views about the beginnings of life.[27]

Relying heavily on legislative history, Justice Brennan's majority opinion disagreed and found an unconstitutional religious purpose, as in the previous *Epperson* case. But he briefly addressed the meaning of academic freedom while rejecting the state's defense. He observed that academic freedom normally refers to the freedom of teachers to make their own decisions about what to teach. Agreeing with the AAUP amicus brief, he concluded that the act "actually serves to diminish academic freedom by removing the flexibility to teach evolution without also teaching creation science, even if teachers determine that such curriculum results in less effective and comprehensive science instruction." Yet unlike the AAUP, which emphasized that a legislature should not interfere in the merits of academic judgments, the majority opinion took pains to avoid the implication that "a legislature could never require that scientific critiques of prevailing scientific theories be taught."[28] If the legislature imposes this requirement for secular educational purposes rather than for religious ones, the majority indicated, it does not violate academic freedom. And unlike the AAUP, the majority opinion did not tie academic freedom to the collective role of the faculty in determining whether a theory has academic merit.

In other decisions in the 1970s, the Supreme Court relied on the adoption by religiously affiliated universities of the AAUP's 1940 Statement of Principles of Academic Freedom and Tenure to reject claims that government financial support to them was an unconstitutional establishment of religion.[29] Adherence to the 1940 Statement, one decision observed, demonstrated that universities "were characterized by an atmosphere of academic freedom rather than religious indoctrination."[30]

Dissents by Justices Brennan and Stevens in cases applying labor law to collective bargaining by professors produced additional commentary on academic freedom without treating it as a First Amendment right. In *National Labor Relations Board v. Yeshiva University*, decided in 1980, the Supreme Court majority held that its previous exclusion of managerial employees from the coverage of the National Labor Relations Act applied to the full-time faculty of Yeshiva University. The managerial exclusion, the Court pointed out, is based on the assumption that employers are entitled to the undivided loyalty of their managers, which would be jeopardized if the managers engaged in collective bargaining with the very employers whose interests they were hired to promote.[31]

The "notion that a faculty member's professional competence could depend on his undivided loyalty to management," Justice Brennan maintained among his many reasons for dissenting, "is antithetical to the whole concept of academic freedom." The evaluation of faculty, he added, depends on their teaching and scholarship, "not on the compatibility of their advice with administration policy." He observed that academic freedom extends to criticism of administrative policies, which cannot be punished as a breach of loyalty.[32] Despite this understandable focus on the relative power of faculty and administration in interpreting the managerial exclusion as an issue in labor law, Brennan's references to academic freedom had important implications for its meaning as a First Amendment right. He indicated that it could be construed to protect faculty criticism of institutional policies as well as teaching and scholarship, as his later analysis of the Minnesota law establishing "meet and confer" sessions directly asserted.

Another labor law case provoked Justice Stevens to write about academic freedom in dissent. In *Central State University v. American Association of University Professors, Central State University Chapter*, decided in 1999, a local AAUP collective bargaining chapter challenged an Ohio law that exempted instructional workloads for professors from the scope of collective bargaining in the public sector. Upholding the law, the Supreme Court maintained that it was rational for the state legislature to believe that collective bargaining over faculty workload could undermine the legitimate state purpose of increasing faculty attention to teaching.[33]

Underlying the legal issues in the case, Justice Stevens maintained in dissent, "lies a debate about academic freedom." Without referring to the

First Amendment, Stevens asserted that the interest in protecting the academic freedom of professors could be a rational basis for giving them more rights than other public employees to bargain over workload. Even if not, he maintained that the state had provided no rational basis for providing fewer bargaining rights to faculty.[34] Stevens never specified the academic freedom issues he perceived in debates about faculty workload. But his opinion indicated that he, like some of his colleagues, conceived the academic freedom of professors to extend beyond the content of teaching and scholarship to issues of educational policy.

The Supreme Court cases since *Keyishian* have reinforced the identification of academic freedom as a First Amendment right. More cases involving more contexts have addressed issues of academic freedom. Some opinions maintained that academic freedom extends to speech about educational issues on campus and to general political expression off campus as well as to the scholarship and teaching identified in earlier cases. Most importantly, cases in which professors were not litigants indicated that speech in universities requires greater First Amendment protection than speech in other institutions. One case left open the possibility that the First Amendment right of academic freedom exempts the scholarship and teaching of professors from the general doctrine that the First Amendment does not apply to speech by public employees made pursuant to their official duties. These cases provide the basis for treating academic freedom as a distinctive First Amendment right. But they do not elaborate its meaning or how it relates to the First Amendment generally. As in the cases through *Keyishian*, justices often ignore clear issues of academic freedom. Even when identifying academic freedom as a First Amendment right, they continue not to invoke it as the basis for their decisions. While more firmly established by the Supreme Court, the First Amendment right of academic freedom has not been extensively applied or clarified.

Lower-Court Decisions

The many more decisions in the lower courts than in the Supreme Court present a much fuller picture of the status of academic freedom as a First Amendment right of professors. Unsurprisingly given this much larger sample, academic freedom claims by professors in the lower courts have arisen in many more factual contexts, prompting judges to elaborate its meaning beyond the relatively sparse pronouncements of the Supreme Court. I have covered virtually all the Supreme Court cases that touched on the meaning of academic freedom as a First Amendment right of professors. In this section, I select only the most informative of the many more lower-court decisions.

These lower-court decisions reinforce and extend the indications by the Supreme Court that academic freedom is a distinctive First Amendment right of professors. Even when referring to this right while reaching a favorable result for a professor, the Supreme Court never relied on it as the doctrinal basis for the decision. Many lower courts, by contrast, have based their decisions on the First Amendment right of academic freedom, often citing Supreme Court decisions that endorsed it. Even lower-court decisions that have rejected claims of academic freedom by professors have affirmed the existence of the right itself, frequently indicating how the facts differed from cases that upheld it. Yet an elaborate decision by a divided fourth circuit denied that the First Amendment encompasses any distinctive right of professors to academic freedom.

While overwhelmingly concluding that the First Amendment protects the academic freedom of professors, lower-court judges have disagreed about its meaning. Some decisions have limited it to the content of expert expression in scholarship and teaching. Others have applied it more broadly to protect decisions by professors about pedagogy and course coverage, to invalidate laws that could inhibit academic discussion in the classroom, and to exempt unpublished scholarship and confidential research sources from disclosure in litigation. Beyond scholarship and teaching, some cases have extended it to cover expression about university affairs and about general political and ideological issues.

I organize my analysis of the lower-court decisions around the subject of the academic freedom dispute. Because the production and dissemination of knowledge are the core traditional concerns of academic freedom, I first discuss cases dealing with scholarship and teaching. I start by devoting substantial attention to the exceptional case of *Urofsky v. Gilmore,* decided by the entire fourth circuit in 2000. *Urofsky* is a rare decision at any level of the American judiciary denying that professors have a First Amendment right of academic freedom.[35] It also contains far more thorough discussion and debate about the relationship between academic freedom and the First Amendment than any decision by the Supreme Court or by other lower courts. After discussing cases about scholarship and teaching, I turn to the many fewer cases addressing other speech within universities and extramural political speech. I generally do not refer by name to the judges who decided these cases, except in the interesting context when the judge is a former law professor or, more rarely, when the judge is especially well known or when I discuss different opinions in the same case in detail.

Urofsky v. Gilmore

Urofsky arose as a challenge to a Virginia statute that restricted state employees from using computers owned or leased by the state to access defined categories of "sexually explicit content." Professors asserted that the statute violated the First Amendment rights of all state employees while maintaining that it also violated their distinctive First Amendment right of academic freedom.[36] They urged the court to conclude that the statute abridged their academic freedom even if it rejected the broader First Amendment claims.

The professors gave examples of how the statute interfered with their academic freedom in teaching and research. One maintained that he had not assigned an online project on indecency law because he feared that he could not assess his students' work without violating the statute. Another asserted that the statute restricted his access to sexually explicit poems as part of his study of Victorian poets. Professors investigating human sexuality expressed hesitancy about continuing to use the internet as part of their research.[37]

By a vote of 7 to 4, the judges differed over whether the statute violated the First Amendment rights of all state employees. The majority concluded that it did not. The dissent did not address the separate claim that the law violated the First Amendment rights of professors to academic freedom, but the majority opinion and two conflicting concurring opinions did, all at considerable and revealing length.

Without citing any prior cases, Judge Wilkins concluded in his majority opinion "that to the extent the Constitution recognizes any right of academic freedom above and beyond the First Amendment rights to which every citizen is entitled, the right inheres in the University and not in individual professors." By using the phrase "to the extent," he seemed to leave open whether the First Amendment right of academic freedom exists at all. Citing two law review articles, he added that federal courts had "often used, but little explained" the term "academic freedom," producing decisions that lacked consistency and that often referred to academic freedom in situations to which it does not apply. He briefly reviewed the history of the concept of academic freedom in the United States, observing that the AAUP's 1915 Declaration focused on obtaining professional autonomy for professors from lay administrators and trustees rather than on threats from the federal or state governments. He stressed that the 1915 Declaration treated academic freedom as a professional norm rather than a First Amendment right and pointed out the broad acceptance of this norm within American higher education.[38]

Based on this history, he noted that "as a matter of professional practice" university professors already have the academic freedom they are now asserting as a First Amendment right. Acknowledging that academic freedom promotes advances in learning that benefit society at large, he criticized the professors for failing to realize that a wise policy may not have constitutional status. He also noted that the "audacity" of their academic freedom claim "raises the specter of a constitutional right enjoyed by only a limited class of citizens." Allowing professors at state universities to use sexually explicit material on the internet for research purposes while denying access to the same material by psychologists who are state employees but not professors, he maintained, "is manifestly at odds with a constitutional system premised on equality."[39]

While rejecting the claim that the Supreme Court had identified academic freedom as a First Amendment right of professors, the majority opinion conceded that "homage has been paid to the ideal of academic freedom in a number of Supreme Court opinions, often with reference to the First Amendment." But it stressed that despite these numerous "accolades," the Supreme Court had never relied on a First Amendment right to academic freedom to invalidate a state regulation. The "paean" to academic freedom in Chief Justice Warren's plurality opinion in *Sweezy*, it observed, did not determine the outcome of the case. The Supreme Court vacated Sweezy's contempt conviction because it concluded that the state attorney general lacked the authority to investigate, not because the conviction violated the First Amendment. Justice Frankfurter's concurrence recognized an institutional rather than an individual right of academic freedom. "At best," six justices in *Sweezy* "agreed that the First Amendment protects values of academic freedom," although they disagreed "as to the nature of this right."[40]

As strong further evidence that the Supreme Court had not recognized a First Amendment right of academic freedom for professors, the majority observed that in declaring unconstitutional state laws that limited the teaching of evolution, a context in which this right would apply if it existed, the justices relied instead on the establishment clause. Based on its review of the Supreme Court cases, the majority concluded that the claim of First Amendment protection for the academic freedom of individual professors can mean no more than that teachers were the first to receive the protection all public employees now have against dismissal for exercising their First Amendment rights. And because it concluded that the Virginia statute did not violate the First Amendment rights of public employees, it also concluded that it did not violate the First Amendment rights of professors. The majority did note, however, that an actual refusal by a university to approve a particular research project by a professor, a situation not presented in this case, could raise constitutional issues about the extent of its authority "to control the work of its faculty."[41] Given the majority's rejection of a distinctive First Amendment right of academic freedom for professors, it presumably assumed that these constitutional issues would arise under the general First Amendment protection of the rights of public employees.

While much of the majority's analysis of prior Supreme Court decisions was accurate or plausible, it mischaracterized Frankfurter's concurrence in *Sweezy* as asserting that academic freedom is only an institutional right. Frankfurter discussed the academic freedom of a university while protecting Sweezy's individual First Amendment right to refuse disclosing the contents of his lecture at the University of New Hampshire. The University was not a party to the litigation, and Frankfurter never referred to it.

Judge Wilkinson, who had been a law professor at the University of Virginia before joining the court, vigorously disagreed with the majority's rejection of academic freedom as a distinctive First Amendment right of professors. Though he cited *Sweezy* and *Keyishian* to support this right, he did not discuss them in any detail or attempt to refute the majority's interpretation of *Sweezy*. Highlighting the unique context of academic speech, he pointed out that professors are employed to advance knowledge through independent inquiry. They are not "state mouthpieces," but "speak mainly for themselves." This right of academic inquiry, he maintained, requires access to the internet.[42]

Even though he stressed the importance of academic freedom as a First Amendment right of professors and believed that access to the internet is an increasingly important source for scholarly research, Wilkinson agreed with the majority that the Virginia statute did not violate the First Amendment. He reasoned that that a waiver provision in the statute, which allowed state employees to request approval from agency heads to access sexually explicit content, preserved its constitutionality. Pointing out that the record of the case contained evidence of professors receiving waivers and no examples of denials of requested waivers, he expressed general confidence that the academic administrators who are agency heads would protect the academic freedom of professors. He concluded that the statute had only a minimal impact on academic inquiry while addressing the significant state interest in barring employee access to lascivious material.[43]

Without discussing issues of academic freedom, Judge Murnaghan's dissent disagreed that the prior approval process satisfied the requirements of the First Amendment. Even if agency heads would not withhold approval arbitrarily, he worried that their unfettered discretion to impose prior restraints on expression would intimidate state employees into self-censorship, which would harm the public interest.[44]

Provoked by Wilkinson's opinion, Judge Luttig wrote a lengthy, scathing response. He summarized Wilkinson's opinion as reaching the "analytically indefensible" conclusion "that there is a First Amendment right of 'academic freedom' and that other public employees do not possess an analogous First Amendment right to pursue matters that they believe are important to performance of their public responsibilities." Not referring to any of the Supreme Court decisions that the majority accurately described as discussing academic freedom "with reference to the First Amendment," Luttig maintained that this "new-found right," which "is reserved for professors alone," was Wilkinson's "own unabashed creation . . . out of whole cloth."[45]

After criticizing Wilkinson for identifying a distinctive First Amendment right of academic freedom for professors and for not explaining its meaning and scope, Luttig maintained that by concurring in the majority decision Wilkinson failed to have the courage of his own intellectual convictions. In developing this accusation, Luttig provided a stronger defense of academic freedom as a First Amendment right of professors, which he rejected, than Wilkinson himself. In an italicized portion of his opinion, Luttig asserted that the only principled conclusion from recognizing this right would be to declare that the government's interest in restricting access of professors to the internet pales by comparison.[46]

Wilkinson's reliance on the waiver provision of the statute to uphold its constitutionality did not convince Luttig. Pointing out that the AAUP's "seminal" 1915 Declaration defined academic freedom to protect professors from university trustees, Luttig maintained that "no professor would believe that his right of academic freedom is safeguarded merely because it can be denied only by his politically-accountable university administrators." To illustrate this point, he observed that the waiver provision had not reassured the professors who brought this lawsuit to challenge the Virginia statute as a violation of their academic freedom.[47]

Yet Luttig agreed with the majority's rejection of a distinctive First Amendment right of academic freedom for professors. Like the majority, he stressed that the First Amendment applies equally to all public employees without any special protection for professors in the name of academic freedom. A professor, he maintained, should have the same First Amendment rights as a custodian. Luttig also rejected Wilkinson's position that in their research and writing professors speak for themselves rather than for the state that employs them.[48]

This equal application of the First Amendment, Luttig added, should not be understood to denigrate the societal value of academic inquiry. Like the majority, Luttig stressed that not everything of value is protected by the Constitution. In tension with his assertion that the discretion of university administrators to issue waivers should not assuage concerns that they might violate the academic freedom of professors, he was confident that universities would not attempt to suppress true academic freedom even if they were unconstrained by the First Amendment. If a university violated academic freedom, he maintained, it would lose its faculty and the public support needed to survive.[49] Luttig provided no support for these broad assertions, which are refuted by over a century of AAUP reports of violations of faculty academic freedom by administrators and by similar evidence revealed in many judicial decisions.

Subsequent cases overwhelmingly have not followed the *Urofsky* majority in denying the existence of a First Amendment right of academic freedom for professors. It is a rare exception to the broad judicial recognition and application of this right in the lower courts. But I think many judges share the concern expressed by both Wilkins and Luttig that this right could undermine the fundamental commitment to equality at the core of the First Amendment by giving professors more protection than other employees.

This concern about equality of First Amendment rights may explain why many judges apply general First Amendment law without referring to issues of academic freedom in cases where they are clearly presented. It may also explain why even judges who recognize academic freedom as a First Amendment right often do not differentiate it from general First Amendment rights of free speech. Differentiation would require confronting the argument that a distinctive First Amendment right of academic freedom protects professors more than general First Amendment rights protect everybody else and more than employee-speech jurisprudence protects other public employees. Concern about equality may even help explain why defenders of this distinctive right often point out that it comes with corresponding duties to maintain academic standards that do not apply to others. While this point makes analytical sense, it also mitigates the appearance of inequality. If academic freedom carries additional burdens as well as additional benefits, it is easier to argue that it provides different rather than superior protection for professors.

Scholarship and Teaching

The *Urofsky* decision by the divided fourth circuit stands out as an exception to the numerous lower-court cases that have understood Supreme Court decisions as establishing a First Amendment right of academic freedom for professors. Judicial interpretation of this right has determined the result in many lower-court cases, whether judges upheld or denied claims by professors. Disputes about scholarship and teaching, the core functions of professors, have generated many of these cases.

Cases frequently defined the First Amendment right of academic freedom as protecting the content of expert academic expression by professors, the central concern of the AAUP's 1915 Declaration. Some decisions applied this definition to protect professors. While agreeing with this definition, other decisions refused to extend the First Amendment right of academic freedom to additional issues. They rejected claims that it applied to travel abroad for academic reasons, access to research material, court rules that limited the discretion of clinical law professors to select cases, and the impact of concealed handguns in class on classroom discussion. Yet many judges applied the First Amendment right of academic freedom more broadly to include pedagogical judgments by professors and their interests in maintaining confidentiality while teaching and conducting research. Decisions also indicated the limits of this right by concluding that it did not include expression within a professor's expertise that fails to meet academic standards, claims of financial support for research, deviations from legitimate university regulations and expectations, the assignment and dis-cussion of material irrelevant to the subject matter of a course, or speech that is threatening, harassing, or gratuitously insulting.

Underlining the focus of the First Amendment right of academic freedom on protecting the scholarship and teaching of professors, a few decisions denied academic freedom claims by administrators and other professional employees in universities. In rejecting claims by academic administrators that they were fired for exercising their First Amendment rights, two courts concluded that an academic administrator "does not have the same broad academic freedom as a professor." The primary duties of an administrator, the courts observed, "are to coordinate, delegate, and regulate, not to edu-cate."[50] Similarly linking academic freedom to the distinctive work of professors in a case that did not raise First Amendment issues, Judge Posner refused to apply a state tenure statute to a psychologist employed in an ad-ministrative capacity by a university. He maintained that the "purpose of tenure is to protect academic freedom—the freedom to teach and write without fear of retribution for expressing heterodox ideas—and it is the faculty who engage in teaching and writing."[51] Yet courts have applied academic freedom broadly to college teachers, whether or not they are tenured or on the tenure track. Sweezy himself was a guest lecturer, and other cases have protected the academic freedom of adjunct and part-time professors.

Content

In applying the First Amendment right of academic freedom, judges often focused on the content of the professor's expression. The claim by an as-sistant professor of obstetrics that his department chair had retaliated against him for advocating vaginal delivery instead of unnecessary cesarean proce-dures, a judge reasoned, should be protected by the First Amendment right of academic freedom, at least where the views expressed by the professor "are well within the range of accepted medical opinion." Noting that this range must be carefully defined, the judge observed that the use of leeches by doctors to "bleed" patients, treated as "the height of medieval supersti-tion" when he was an undergraduate, had reemerged as an accepted medical technique when microsurgery was developed in the 1980s. "The disastrous impact on Soviet agriculture from Stalin's enforcement of Lysenko biology orthodoxy," he added, should serve as "a strong counter example to those who would discipline university professors for not following the 'party line.'"[52]

A second circuit decision protected the content of expert academic expression in a very different context. It rejected the claim of a pharmaceutical company that a peer-reviewed article in a medical journal, by drawing incorrect inferences from uncontested data, contained false advertising prohibited under a federal statute and defamatory statements prohibited under state common law. Judges Lynch, Winter, and Calabresi, the three members of the panel, were all former law professors. Lynch, who wrote the opinion, taught at Columbia. Winter and Calabresi taught at Yale. The judges observed that propositions of "fact" in the scientific literature, particularly in novel areas of research, are often controversial. Quoting from the statement in *Keyishian* that academic freedom is "a special concern of the First Amendment," they stressed that these controversies should be addressed by qualified experts in the same discipline or field rather than by federal judges. To the extent that conclusions on subjects of "legitimate ongoing scientific disagreement" are not drawn from fraudulent data, the court reasoned, false advertising or defamation cannot be proved.[53]

While limiting its broader application, other decisions agreed that the First Amendment right of academic freedom protects the content of expert academic expression. A panel of the seventh circuit differentiated the content of scholarship from the conduct of research while denying a challenge to a state law that made the use of aborted fetal tissue in academic research a felony. Professors at Indiana University, supported by the university trustees, maintained that this law violated their First Amendment right of academic freedom. One of the professors, for example, used mixed cell cultures derived from aborted fetal tissue to study Alzheimer's disease through grants funded by the National Institutes of Health.[54] Writing for the court, Judge Easterbrook, formerly a law professor at the University of Chicago, called this argument "a non-starter." He maintained that the statute regulated conduct rather than speech. Acknowledging that the use of fetal tissue in research "could lead to speech" in research papers or in the classroom, he emphasized that "a desire to obtain an input into speech does not convert regulation of conduct into regulation of speech." Rejecting the professors' assertion that the statute cast "a pall of orthodoxy over the classroom," the phrase used in *Keyishian* while defining academic freedom as "a special concern of the First Amendment," Easterbrook observed that the law did not prevent them from saying, writing, or teaching anything, including references to results obtained from research using aborted fetal tissue in states and nations that allowed it.[55]

Similarly limiting the First Amendment protection of academic freedom to the content of teaching and scholarship, courts upheld laws that prohibited travel to designated foreign countries and allowed licensed students to carry concealed loaded weapons in class.[56] Neither restrictions on the ability to teach and conduct research abroad nor concern that the gun law would inhibit the robust exchange of ideas in class, judges observed, prevented professors from expressing their academic positions in the classroom or in scholarship.[57] Another court rejected the claim that a rule of the Louisiana Supreme Court regulating student participation in trials infringed the academic freedom of clinical law professors to select cases based on their potential value to students. The court emphasized that the First Amendment right of academic freedom prohibits state regulation of classroom content and pointed out that the rule regulated the role of students in courts, not the expression of professors in class.[58]

Pedagogical Relevance

Many lower courts have agreed that the First Amendment right of academic freedom extends to pedagogical decisions by professors, protecting only those they found justified on academic grounds. Judges often reached different conclusions about pedagogical value in similar cases. They also maintained that universities could adopt general policies applicable to all faculty that could legitimately constrain the pedagogical choices of individual professors.

One revealing case arose when an adjunct professor at a community college, as part of a class on "language and social constructivism" in a course entitled "Introduction to Interpersonal Communication," asked students to suggest words used in the interests of the dominant culture to marginalize minorities and other oppressed social groups. Student suggestions included the words "girl," "lady," "faggot," "nigger," and "bitch." The court reported that the professor and many students found the class discussion "academically and philosophically challenging," but that one of the nine African American students in a class of twenty-two complained to the professor, to campus administrators, and to a local civil rights activist about the use of the words "nigger" and "bitch" in class. The activist urged the college president to take "corrective action" and stated that he would not allow African American students to attend a college in which they would be "berated" with these words. An acting dean then met with the professor, telling him that a prominent member of the local minority community had threatened to reduce the college's already declining enrollment. The professor defended the educational value of the exercise and maintained that the offending words had not been used abusively. At the end of the semester, the dean informed the professor that the matter had been resolved to the satisfaction of the complaining student. A few weeks later, the dean left him a message that there were no classes for him to teach, and he never heard from the college again.[59]

The professor sued, claiming that administrators had retaliated against him for his constitutionally protected classroom speech. Arguing that the right to free speech in the classroom had not been clearly established as a matter of constitutional law, the college moved to dismiss the suit. Rejecting this argument as "totally unpersuasive," the judge quoted from *Sweezy* and *Keyishian* and stressed the "robust tradition of academic freedom" in American universities. To support his conclusion that the First Amendment right of academic freedom protected the professor, the judge emphasized that the words elicited were "germane to the subject matter" of the class and were not used in a gratuitously abusive manner.[60]

Another decision agreed with theater professors who relied on the First Amendment right of academic freedom to justify their pedagogical decision requiring a student, in violation of her religious principles, to perform a role that included the words "goddam" and "fucking." The professors maintained that theater students need to learn how to play uncomfortable roles, and the judges observed the similarity to other pedagogically defensible requirements that law students or history students argue positions with which they disagree.[61] Similarly relying on the First Amendment right of academic freedom while quoting *Sweezy* and *Keyishian,* decisions protected a professor's frequent analogies to sex in a course on technical writing and references to a union organizing on campus in a political science course.[62]

While often acknowledging that the First Amendment right of academic freedom protects legitimate pedagogical expression, other cases concluded that the classroom speech at issue did not serve any legitimate pedagogical purpose and, therefore, rejected claims by professors. In a divided opinion, the second circuit concluded that a professor acted unprofessionally by allowing a classroom exercise "initiated for legitimate pedagogical purposes" to degenerate into the inappropriate use of vulgarities. During a summer school course in composition designed for pre-freshmen who needed re-medial work prior to matriculation, the professor initiated a "clustering" exercise in which students called out words on a topic as a technique to help them avoid the use of repetitive words in essays. The professor allowed the students to choose the topic for the exercise. The students chose "sex." After initially selecting what the instructor called "very safe words," such as "marriage," "children," and "wedding ring," toward the end of the exer-cise students were yelling phrases including "cluster fuck," "slamhole," and "eating girls out," many of which the professor wrote on the blackboard. Concluding that these "vulgarities" were unnecessary to the clustering exercise, the court found that disciplining the professor for failing to ter-minate the exercise did not violate his First Amendment right of academic freedom. Judge Cabranes, the former general counsel of Yale University, dis-sented. He claimed that the decision would weaken the First Amendment protection of academic freedom for professors who do not conform to aca-demic orthodoxy. Legitimate classroom discussion, he maintained, cannot become illegitimate when its content begins to offend administrators.[63]

Another circuit court found that the First Amendment right of academic freedom did not protect an English professor's classroom use of words such as "pussy," "cunt," and "fuck." The professor maintained that he used these words to "point out the chauvinistic degrading attitudes in society that de-pict women as sexual objects" and that he did not direct them to a partic-ular student. An administrator responded that these words are protected only if they appear in assigned texts and are relevant in discussing them. The court agreed with the administration that the professor's words were not germane to the subject matter of the course and pointed out that the First Amendment rights of academic freedom and free speech "are not ab-solute to the point of compromising a student's right to learn in a hostile-free environment."[64]

Lack of pedagogical relevance has placed religious as well as sexual speech outside the First Amendment protection of academic freedom. During a clinical portion of a course in cosmetology, an instructor gave a student re-ligious pamphlets on the sinfulness of homosexuality. Making the obvious point that these pamphlets were not related to styling hair, Judge Wood, formerly a law professor at the University of Chicago, stressed that a pro-fessor's First Amendment right of academic freedom protects her right to express views on the courses to which she is assigned, but does not give her unconstrained rights in the classroom. Judge Wood illustrated the significance of pedagogical relevance through examples from more traditional academic subjects. "No college or university," she observed, "is required to allow a chemistry professor to devote extensive time to the teaching of James Joyce's demanding novel *Ulysses,* nor must it permit an instructor of mathematics to fill her class hours on the law of torts."[65] The instructor remained free to express her views about homosexuality, but she could not do so while teaching a class in cosmetology, to which religious views on the sinfulness of homosexuality had no relevance.

Some decisions recognized legitimate university interests that could restrict pedagogical decisions without violating the First Amendment academic freedom of individual professors. Relying on a decision that allowed a university to limit the extent to which a professor could give students responsibility over the organization of the class and the selection of assignments, a subsequent case held that a department can require professors to teach upper-level language courses in the foreign language.[66] More broadly, before he became a Supreme Court justice Judge Alito denied that a professor's academic freedom protected by the First Amendment creates "a constitutional right to choose curriculum material in contravention to the university's dictates."[67] Cases have also held that grading, which is arguably related to pedagogy, is not part of a professor's First Amendment right of academic freedom and have allowed administrators to assign or change grades.[68]

Additional Claims

Although most academic freedom claims in the lower courts related to scholarship and teaching have dealt with the content and pedagogical relevance of academic expression, some decisions have addressed a range of other issues as well. They have extended the First Amendment right of academic freedom to limit state intrusion in the classroom. Relying on the Supreme Court's decision in *Sweezy,* which invalidated inquiries by the state attorney general into the contents of a lecturer's classroom statements, the California Supreme Court agreed with a professor who asserted that covert police surveillance of classrooms violated this right. "If the after-the-fact inquiry conducted in *Sweezy* threatened to cast a pall of orthodoxy over classroom debates," the court reasoned, "the covert presence of governmental agents within the classroom itself must cast a deeper shadow." The court worried that the expression of tentative ideas challenging orthodoxy would be stifled by the fear that covert surveillance could lead to possible prosecution, influenced by reports of police informers who may have "incorrectly misstated" or even "maliciously distended" the classroom expression of professors and students.[69] The highest state court in New York held that a subpoena to a professor from a grand jury investigating possible drug abuses on campus did not violate the First Amendment right of academic freedom as long as the questions posed by the Grand Jury are relevant to an investigation of criminal misconduct. Yet a concurring opinion, citing *Sweezy* and *Keyishian,* emphasized that questions about the content of a professor's conversations with students or classroom lectures would violate his First Amendment right of academic freedom except in those rare circumstances when they might be relevant to the commission of a crime.[70]

Decisions have also relied on the First Amendment right of academic freedom to preserve the confidentiality of professors' research material. They have pointed out that people might not agree to participate in research projects without promises of confidentiality,[71] that forced disclosure of incomplete data or preliminary drafts of scholarly papers and of communications about them with colleagues could inhibit the development and testing of ideas,[72] and that providing detailed information about ongoing research can take substantial time away from the research itself.[73] One judge cited statements by professors and professional associations of anthropologists, sociologists, and political scientists about the importance of confidentiality in conducting effective field work in social science. The statements observed that much research by social scientists had uncovered information that benefited the public interest in developing policy about crime, health care, immigration, drug use, and many other subjects, information that researchers could not have obtained without assurances of confidentiality.[74] Decisions have limited attempts by litigants to discover the identity of members of the Irish Republican Army who feared violent retribution if their participation in an oral history project were disclosed,[75] of participants in a medical study concerned about the privacy of their patient records,[76] and of employees who provided information for research on "the sociology of the American restaurant."[77] Other decisions have refused to enforce broad subpoenas from companies seeking documents related to academic research on animal toxicity and on the risks of combining smoking with occupational exposure to asbestos.[78] Yet these decisions allowed limited discovery for corporations seeking to defend themselves in litigation and for the United States government in seeking to comply with its treaty obligations.

Courts have rejected claims of academic freedom by professors in various contexts related to scholarship and teaching. They have denied that it includes access to research funding from the university or the right to participate in grant proposals.[79] Another court rejected the claim that a university violates academic freedom if it denies tenure to a candidate because his research interests overlapped with those of a tenured professor.[80]

In cases raising particularly frivolous assertions of academic freedom, courts have observed that universities denied tenure based on deficiencies in the professor's scholarly record, not on objections to its contents. As one judge crisply observed in finding no violation of academic freedom, the denial of tenure "was based not on what appellant did publish, but on what he failed to publish."[81] A court held that the First Amendment protection of academic freedom does not extend to a professor of philosophy who violated the course catalogue by combining courses with a colleague without receiving the required approval.[82] Nor was a court convinced by a professor's claim that the university violated his academic freedom by firing him for missing classes while lecturing abroad without permission.[83] Other decisions found that professors were not protected by academic freedom when they refused to implement a computer software program designed to write course syllabi and evaluate student achievement, gave every student a grade of 100 percent instead of administering a scheduled exam, objected to giving a teaching demonstration while applying for a position, or when universities relied on student surveys or evaluations.[84]

Intramural Speech

Beyond the core concerns of scholarship and teaching, courts have also addressed claims that the First Amendment right of academic freedom extends to speech by professors about university affairs. While scholarship and teaching are traditional categories, judges have not developed an analogous category to classify these cases. Nor did the AAUP address such expression in the 1915 Declaration, though some of its more recent policies connect academic freedom with rights to participate in university governance. I believe that the term "intramural speech" provides an analytically useful classification. As with scholarship and teaching, courts have recognized some claims to academic freedom in intramural speech and rejected others.

Whereas dissents by Justices Brennan and Stevens were the only Supreme Court opinions that interpreted academic freedom to include speech by professors about educational policy and academic governance, decisions by two lower-court judges who had been law professors explicitly recognized and relied on the First Amendment right of academic freedom to protect intramural speech by professors. Judge Robert Keeton, who previously taught at Harvard Law School, held that it protected a professor who opposed a proposed university exchange program with the Soviet Union, and Judge William Fletcher, who previously taught at the University of California, Berkeley, held that it protected professors who urged curricular reform.[85]

Judge Alex Kozinsky, writing for a panel that included former Supreme Court Justice O'Connor, held that it protected e-mails by a professor of mathematics on a distribution list maintained by the college. The e-mails protested the college's celebration of "Dia de la Raza" (Day of the Race) as a racist event and proclaimed the superiority of Western civilization.[86] Though these comments did not refer to matters within the professor's academic expertise or to educational policy more generally, the opinion characterized them as "academic speech."[87]

Decisions that did not protect intramural speech pointed out that academic freedom, like the general right of free speech under the First Amendment, is not absolute. A seventh circuit panel, which included Professor Stevens before he became a Supreme Court justice, decided that the First Amendment right of academic freedom does not protect a professor who, in front of students, condemned administrators and faculty members for criticizing his course coverage and his extensive personal counseling of students. The court recognized that "it is now clear that academic freedom," although "not one of the enumerated rights of the First Amendment," is "safeguarded" by it. Yet without giving additional details of the professor's criticisms, the court stressed that academic freedom is not a "license for uncontrolled expression at variance with established curricular standards and internally destructive of the proper functioning of the institution."[88]

Quoting approvingly from this decision, a New Mexico state court denied protection to the statement by a professor before the board of regents that criticized the administration for its failure to implement an effective ethnic studies program. The statement asserted that the "lack-luster administration has distinguished itself by its incredible mediocrity," had stifled dissent in ways "that would evoke envy in the Kremlin," and "is morally and ethically bankrupt." The "conglomerate" that ran the university was composed of "pseudo-intellectuals (actually hack politicians), and supposed bleeding-heart WASPS who in reality are street walkers who have prostituted themselves and whatever scrupples (*sic*) they might have had to play token Anglo."[89] Nor did a court protect a professor whose disputes with colleagues and administrators, often about alleged interference with his research, escalated into harassing phone calls and threats.[90] Another court asserted that the First Amendment right of academic freedom did not "immunize" a professor from liability for slander after falsely accusing a colleague of having a sexual relationship with the department chair. If the accusation had been true, the judge observed, academic freedom might have protected it.[91]

These decisions, whatever their results, indicate that the lower courts have included intramural speech within the scope of a professor's First Amendment right of academic freedom. In cases about intramural speech, as in cases about scholarship and teaching, courts recognized the underlying right to academic freedom even when denying specific claims.

Extramural Political Speech

Some decisions have maintained that the First Amendment right of academic freedom extends beyond both the campus and a professor's expertise to protect general political expression by a professor in the public sphere. Decisions reaching this conclusion occasionally relied on the single sentence in Justice Douglas's dissent in *Roth* asserting that the discharge of a professor for philosophical, political, or ideological speech is a "direct assault" on this right.[92] In two cases involving denials of appointments to Marxist professors, judges have cited this sentence approvingly while maintaining that a state university cannot use "the subtle and indirect coercion of refusal to hire" against speech it finds offensive or abhorrent.[93] Yet in neither case did the court grant relief. One judge found that the president had not relied on the expression of Marxist beliefs but had made a good-faith assessment of a candidate's qualifications to be appointed department chair.[94] The other judge found that the regents had taken Marxist political and philosophical views into account but that these constitutionally impermissible considerations were not the primary reason for the denial of appointment. Rather, the regents relied on legitimate concerns about the professor's disruptive behavior at another university. Because the judge determined that the regents would have made the same decision if they had not considered the professor's Marxist views, he upheld it.[95]

More recently, a federal circuit court relied on the same passage from Justice Douglas's dissent and on the passage in *Keyishian* identifying academic freedom as "a special concern of the First Amendment" while reversing a district court's summary judgment against a woman who claimed that she was not offered a position as a legal writing instructor because she had conservative political views. Citing evidence that only one of the fifty faculty members at the law school was a registered Republican, that an associate dean warned the applicant against revealing that she had a tenure-track offer from a conservative law school, that a faculty member had alluded to her conservative views at the faculty meeting held to discuss her potential appointment, and that the two people hired had less prior teaching experience and low teaching evaluations, the judge found that there was sufficient evidence of a violation of her First Amendment academic freedom for the case to proceed.[96] A jury ultimately found no First Amendment violation.[97]

In the case in which he held that opposition to a university exchange program with the Soviet Union is protected by academic freedom, Judge Keeton concluded that it also protects the more general expression of conservative political views. He did not quote Justice Douglas, but he did quote the language in *Keyishian* asserting that the First Amendment right of academic freedom "does not tolerate laws that cast a pall of orthodoxy over the classroom." Without explanation and in apparent contradiction to the focus in *Keyishian* on classroom speech, he added that viewpoint discrimination, "based not what is said in the classroom, but what is expressed in outside writings and public statements . . . is especially inimical" to the concerns articulated in *Keyishian*.[98]

In striking contrast to the extensive debate within the AAUP about whether academic freedom extends to extramural political expression, relatively few legal decisions even addressed this issue. Those few maintained that academic freedom encompasses political expression. To my knowledge, no decision rejected such a claim. The core First Amendment right of political expression may account for the relatively few cases dealing with its protection under the more specific First Amendment right of academic freedom. The availability of the general First Amendment right makes it unnecessary to invoke academic freedom as well.

Conclusion

Decisions since *Keyishian* have reinforced the judicial recognition of academic freedom as a First Amendment right of professors. They identified it in a much broader range of contexts than the concerns about national security that dominated the cases in which this right initially emerged. They addressed threats to the academic freedom of professors from corporations and universities as well as from the state. They treated prior opinions that did not themselves refer to academic freedom as having recognized it. They occasionally referred to AAUP policy as defining norms of academic freedom relevant to legal analysis, though they have also differentiated the policy recommendations of the AAUP from the requirements of the First Amendment. Some recognized a broader scope for academic freedom beyond the focus on scholarship and teaching highlighted in the cases through *Keyishian,* extending it to discussion of educational issues within universities and occasionally to general political expression.

As in the cases through *Keyishian,* the Supreme Court continued to base its decisions on other doctrines even when it recognized and extolled the First Amendment right of academic freedom. But many lower-court decisions relied on this right as the doctrinal vehicle for analyzing and resolving concrete disputes. Cases that rejected assertions of this right reinforced its existence by making clear that it would prevail under different facts. These lower-court decisions provided more specificity about its extent and limitations. They generally agreed that the First Amendment right of academic freedom protects the academic content of scholarship and teaching. They also generally agreed that this right protects pedagogically relevant classroom speech even as they disagreed about the pedagogical value of contested speech in specific cases. While lacking consensus, the lower-court cases have addressed additional issues that relate to academic freedom, including state intrusion into the classroom, the confidentiality of research material, intramural speech within the university, and extramural political speech.

Yet the meaning of academic freedom as a First Amendment right remains unclear. Judges have disagreed about its scope and have reached inconsistent results in many factually similar cases. Even while relying on this right, judges have rarely defined it, which has obscured the relationship of academic freedom to the First Amendment generally. They have continued to give conflicting signals about whether the identification of academic freedom as "a special concern of the First Amendment" in *Keyishian* makes it a distinctive First Amendment right or is a way to signify that general First Amendment rights apply with greater force to the academic expression of professors.

Beyond the overwhelming but not unanimous consensus that there is a First Amendment right of academic freedom, no clear doctrines have emerged from this substantial litigation. As in *Sweezy* and *Keyishian,* some subsequent cases have asserted in very general terms that academic freedom promotes societal interests in advancing knowledge and preparing students for democratic citizenship and leadership. They have expressed concern about laws that inhibit scholarship and teaching, especially when they punish or threaten the expression of unpopular academic views. But in contrast to the justification of academic freedom as a professional norm in the AAUP's 1915 Declaration, the legal decisions have not developed these general themes into a comprehensive analysis of academic freedom as a First Amendment right. The uncertainty about the First Amendment meaning of academic freedom has been exacerbated by the many decisions that rely on general First Amendment principles and employee-speech jurisprudence to resolve disputes about expression by professors that clearly come within the scope of academic freedom. Sometimes the application of general First Amendment principles and employee-speech jurisprudence has undermined the protection of academic freedom. Chapter 5 examines those decisions, which reinforce the need for the theory of academic freedom as a distinctive First Amendment right of professors that I then develop.

5

The Limited Application of Academic Freedom as a First Amendment Right of Professors

DESPITE THE EMERGENCE and development of academic freedom as a First Amendment right of professors, many judges have ignored clear issues of academic freedom while applying general First Amendment principles and the more specific First Amendment law of employee-speech jurisprudence. Beyond revealing the limited influence of the developing First Amendment law of academic freedom, the application of these different First Amendment approaches to academic speech has confused legal analysis. Even when they have yielded similar results, they have focused on very different issues. In cases applying general First Amendment principles, judges have determined whether a government regulation is overbroad or vague, or whether the government has violated First Amendment rights to hear or to associate. In cases applying employee-speech jurisprudence, which protects speech by public employees only if it is about a matter of public concern and is not made pursuant to official duties, judges have evaluated whether speech fits within these categories. In cases applying the First Amendment law of academic freedom, by contrast, judges have evaluated whether the government has punished the content of expert academic expression, interfered with the process of academic research, or imposed unjustifiable restrictions on pedagogical decisions by professors.

General First Amendment principles and employee-speech jurisprudence sometimes protect academic expression. But they generally do so by accident, as a byproduct of legal doctrines directed to other concerns. Particularly in applying employee-speech jurisprudence, moreover, judges have allowed punishment of speech that unquestionably would be protected by the First Amendment right of academic freedom. They have concluded that scholarship, teaching, and comments about educational issues at universities do not qualify for First Amendment protection because they are not about matters of public concern and are made pursuant to official duties. Further complicating analysis, other decisions, often confronting very similar facts, have concluded that speech about these subjects did raise matters of public concern or, confronting the issue left open in *Garcetti,* that the official duties test does not apply to it.

Although the cases discussed in this chapter reveal the lack of clarity and inconsistency of existing law, they can help develop a more convincing analysis of academic freedom as a First Amendment right of professors. The facts in these cases, like the facts in cases that explicitly refer to and rely on academic freedom, provide examples of issues that should be addressed and illustrate how the analysis would operate in practice. The similar issues that arise in both sets of cases cover scholarship, teaching, intramural expression, and extramural political speech.

General First Amendment Principles

The continued application of general First Amendment principles to academic speech without considering issues of academic freedom exacerbates the uncertain relationship between the First Amendment and academic freedom that accompanied the Supreme Court's initial identification of academic freedom as a First Amendment right. Can a professor teach controversial views about mental differences between males and females? Can the government require a professor to receive its approval to publish as a condition of receiving a research grant? Can professors invite controversial foreign scholars to conferences in the United States? Are academic norms violated when a professor collaborates with the Central Intelligence Agency (CIA)? Many lower courts applied the First Amendment right of academic freedom to address similar issues. But judges did not refer to it in cases posing these questions, relying instead on general First Amendment principles.

The influential judicial invalidation in 1989 of a campus "Policy on Discrimination and Discriminatory Harassment" at the University of Michigan, Ann Arbor, provides an excellent example of judicial reliance on general First Amendment principles rather than academic freedom. The policy imposed penalties for "stigmatizing or victimizing" speech directed at various characteristics, including race, ethnicity, religion, sex, and sexual orientation.[1] The teaching assistant who brought the lawsuit asserted that his field, biopsychology, included controversial theories that posited biological differences based on sex and race. He worried that discussing these theories in his class on comparative animal behavior could be considered stigmatizing or victimizing under the policy. He particularly worried about the theory that biological differences account for male superiority over females in some spatially related mental tasks, which may help explain why more men than women become engineers. Asserting his right to teach these theories and claiming that he had a reasonable fear that he could be sanctioned under the policy for doing so, he urged the court to declare the policy unconstitutional on grounds of vagueness and overbreadth and to enjoin its enforcement.[2]

Before addressing the vagueness and overbreadth claims, the judge provided an overview of general First Amendment principles, citing cases that did not arise at universities.[3] He then maintained that these "principles acquire a special significance in the university setting, where the free and unfettered interplay of competing views is essential to the institution's educational mission." He followed this sentence with citations to the pages in the classic *Sweezy* and *Keyishian* cases that identified academic freedom as a distinctive First Amendment right.[4] But he did not quote this language or himself refer to academic freedom, even though the right to teach a controversial academic theory is a core concern of the First Amendment right of academic freedom. Instead, he agreed with the teaching assistant that the policy violated the general First Amendment principles of overbreadth and vagueness.

In concluding that the policy was overbroad, the judge emphasized that the university had interpreted it as extending to "serious comments made in the context of classroom discussion," which the judge without further explanation treated as clearly protected by general First Amendment law. He also stressed the vagueness of its key terms. The judge underlined this point very effectively by quoting the university lawyer, who when asked at oral argument how to distinguish between merely offensive speech, which he conceded is protected, and the stigmatizing or victimizing speech prohibited by the policy, answered, "very carefully."[5]

Another court applied the general First Amendment principles of overbreadth and vagueness without addressing issues of academic freedom while invalidating the confidentiality clause required by the National Institutes of Health (NIH) as a condition of receiving research grants. The confidentiality clause forced grant recipients to provide advance notice to the NIH before publishing their preliminary findings and allowed the NIH contracting officer, who might not be a medical doctor or scientist, to block publication.[6] A professor at Stanford Medical School had submitted a successful proposal for funding research on an artificial heart device. But when Stanford objected to the confidentiality clause, the NIH withdrew the research contract and awarded it to another university.[7]

Explaining why the professor's research was covered by the First Amendment, the court emphasized that it "fits snugly in the 'free expression at a university' category" that *Rust v. Sullivan* "carved out" as an "explicit exception" to the general First Amendment principle that the government can control the speech it funds. After quoting Rehnquist's statement in *Rust* that the vagueness and overbreadth doctrines of the First Amendment restrict government regulation of speech in the university context, the court noted that Rehnquist cited *Keyishian* to support this proposition.[8] But the court, like Rehnquist himself in *Rust,* did not refer to *Keyishian*'s identification of academic freedom as "a special concern of the First Amendment," even though the right to conduct and publish research without government interference, like the right to teach controversial theories, "fits snugly" within the protection of the First Amendment right of academic freedom.

Analyzing the confidentiality clause, the court quoted its language allowing the contracting officer to refuse permission to publish "preliminary unvalidated findings" that "could create erroneous conclusions which might threaten public health or safety if acted upon." These standards, the court concluded, are both vague and overbroad. It observed that grant recipients could only be certain of complying with them by refraining from publishing anything not approved by the contracting officer, even if the reasons for the refusal seem wholly invalid. As a result, they are compelled to surrender their free speech rights to the contracting officer, a result prohibited by the First Amendment. The court also agreed with Stanford's claim that the confidentiality clause violated the general First Amendment principle that prior restraints on publications are permitted only in exceptional cases and bear a heavy presumption against their validity.[9]

In cases raising issues of national security, the context in which the Supreme Court first identified academic freedom as a First Amendment right of professors, other courts relied on the general First Amendment rights of "freedom to hear" and "freedom of association" without discussing academic freedom. The 2007 decision in a highly publicized case brought by the American Academy of Religion, a scholarly society devoted to the study of religion, by the AAUP, and by PEN, an organization of authors, editors, and translators, recognized the First Amendment interests of members of these organizations in meeting with Tariq Ramadan, a foreign scholar of Arab descent who had been excluded from the United States. Ramadan, whose scholarship focused on Muslim identity and the practice of Islam in Europe, had accepted a position as a tenured professor at the University of Notre Dame, which submitted a visa petition on his behalf. After the government initially approved and then revoked a temporary visa, the university submitted a new petition for a visa, which had not been processed within the normal time. Due to this delay, Ramadan resigned from the university and had to cancel or decline numerous speaking engagements in the United States, including from the three organizations that filed the lawsuit.[10] The government gave no explanation for the revocation of the temporary visa or the delay in processing the application for a new one. But it did dissociate itself from an earlier statement by a spokesperson for the Department of Homeland Security, who had declared that the temporary visa was revoked based on the provision of the Patriot Act allowing the exclusion of aliens who "endorse or espouse terrorist activity." The government claimed in litigation that this statement was erroneous. but it did not provide an alternative explanation.[11]

Limitations on the ability of scholars to interact with colleagues clearly raise issues about academic freedom in research, but the judge instead focused on the "well-settled principle" that "the First Amendment includes not only a right to speak, but also a right to receive information and ideas." He concluded that government exclusion of an alien from the United States based on his political views implicates this First Amendment right of citizens even if the alien himself has no constitutional or statutory right to enter the United States to speak.[12] In determining whether the government nevertheless had legitimate grounds to exclude Ramadan, the judge relied on the Supreme Court's prior decision in *Mandel.* Although recognizing the First Amendment right to hear, the Court in *Mandel* upheld the exclusion of a Belgian Marxist invited by American professors, concluding that the executive branch of government can exclude an alien based on any "facially legitimate and bona fide reason."[13] Noting that the Supreme Court had not expressly defined this phrase, the judge construed the Court's reasoning as requiring that a reason must be constitutionally permissible to meet this standard. He observed, for example, that excluding Ramadan because he criticized American foreign policy toward the Middle East or opposed the

Iraq War would not meet this standard. The government cannot exclude an alien, he stressed, solely because it disagrees with the content of his speech and wants to prevent a willing American audience from hearing it. Refusing to conclude that the government had relied on the "endorses or espouses terrorist activity" rationale cited by the spokesperson for the Department of Homeland Security, the judge ordered a formal decision on Ramadan's pending visa within ninety days.[14] When the government subsequently denied the visa, asserting that Ramadan had violated the Immigration and Nationality Act by providing material support to a terrorist organization, the judge found this explanation "facially legitimate and bona fide" and dismissed the case.[15]

In the 1950s and 1960s the Supreme Court recognized freedom of association as well as academic freedom as First Amendment rights, sometimes in conjunction with each other.[16] The cases about whether professors could be forced to disclose and possibly be dismissed for membership in the Communist Party or other subversive organizations raised issues regarding both of these emerging First Amendment rights and their relationship to the First Amendment generally. *Keyishian* came closest to linking them by emphasizing "the stifling effect on the academic mind by curtailing freedom of association."[17] A second circuit decision in 1980 addressed the freedom of association of a professor with a very different organization, the CIA.

The professor who brought this case asserted that he was denied tenure because his colleagues objected to his association with the CIA. A political scientist who specialized in "psychopolitics," he had been enthusiastically recommended for promotion from assistant to associate professor by peer review committees. In pursuing his research about the psychology of Nazi leaders, he had contacted the CIA to gain access to data it possessed and agreed to debrief the CIA about his research trip to Europe after he returned. This debriefing occurred in a short telephone conversation with a CIA officer the summer after the recommended promotion. The following fall, one peer review committee reversed its previous recommendation and another voted against granting the professor tenure.[18] A jury found that the peer review committees voted against him because he had associated with the CIA, and the jury awarded substantial damages. The court majority reversed the jury's verdict and remanded the case based on a flaw in the trial judge's instructions to the jury. But a dissenting judge disagreed with the majority's assumption that the First Amendment protected the professor's association with the CIA and asserted that the case should have been dismissed rather than remanded.[19]

By associating with the CIA, the dissenting judge maintained, the professor raised doubts about his scholarly integrity. The judge reasoned that respect for confidences among scholars is essential to the unrestrained exchange of ideas upon which the advance of knowledge depends. Evidence that a professor had disclosed scholarly conversations to the CIA, moreover, would inhibit further scholarly interactions.[20] These concerns relate to the goals and limits of academic freedom, which other decisions considered while analyzing its meaning as a First Amendment right. Yet the dissenting judge did not refer to it.

Employee-Speech Jurisprudence

Decisions addressing the academic speech of professors through employee-speech jurisprudence, even more than decisions addressing it through general First Amendment principles, indicate the limited development of academic freedom as a First Amendment right of professors. In addition to diverting attention from issues of academic freedom, the employee-speech cases demonstrate that the First Amendment right of academic freedom has been extensively ignored as well as extensively recognized. They often reached results that denied academic freedom by concluding that academic speech is not about a matter of public concern or that it derives from the performance of a professor's official duties.

The Supreme Court's Development of Employee-Speech Jurisprudence

Just as the Supreme Court began in the 1950s to recognize academic freedom as a First Amendment right of professors, especially since the late 1960s it has developed what Justice Kennedy has usefully called "employee-speech jurisprudence."[21] Employee-speech jurisprudence is both more specific than general First Amendment law, which covers all citizens, and less specific than the First Amendment right of academic freedom, which covers the small proportion of employees who teach at universities. The Supreme Court itself has not developed its employee-speech jurisprudence in cases arising at state universities. But many lower courts have applied it to the speech of professors, often in circumstances when other courts relied on the First Amendment right of academic freedom. Some lower courts, moreover, have applied employee-speech jurisprudence and academic freedom in the same case.

Pickering v. Board of Education, decided in 1968, was the first Supreme Court decision that clearly differentiated the government as employer in regulating the speech of its employees from government regulation of speech by citizens. Relying on its prior decisions, including *Keyishian* the year before, the Court rejected the once-prevailing view that the government can condition public employment on the waiver of the First Amendment right of citizens "to comment on matters of public interest" related to their work. Yet the Court also conceded "that the State has interests as an employer in regulating the speech of its employees that differ significantly from those it possesses in connection with regulation of the speech of the citizenry in general." It concluded that judges must balance the employee's First Amendment interests, "as a citizen in commenting upon matters of public concern and the interest of the State, as an employer in promoting the efficiency of the public services it performs through its employees."[22]

In *Connick v. Meyers,* a 5–4 decision in 1983, the Supreme Court narrowed the concept of public concern. Worried that every criticism by a public employee related to the operation of the workplace "would plant the seed of a constitutional case,"[23] the majority emphasized that "government officials should enjoy wide latitude in managing their offices, without intrusive oversight by the judiciary in the name of the First Amendment." As a general principle, the Court reasoned that "the content, form, and context" of employee speech must be considered in determining whether it qualifies as a matter of public concern protected by the First Amendment. The circulation of a questionnaire by an assistant district attorney to her staff colleagues about various office policies and relations with superiors, the court concluded in applying this principle, did not address matters of public concern because the questions overwhelmingly were "mere extensions" of her personal dispute with her supervisors over her transfer within the office.[24]

Stressing that the questionnaire raised issues about office morale and the job performance of elected government officials, the dissent maintained that these topics are matters of public concern. It recognized the validity of the majority's worries, but it asserted that the proper response is not to impose artificial restrictions on the concept of public concern, but to give adequate weight to the public employer's interest in the balancing required by

Pickering. In response, the majority conceded that these topics are related to the efficient performance of a government agency. But it stressed that the focus of the questions was "not to evaluate the performance of the office but rather to gather ammunition for another round of controversy with her superiors."[25]

The *Garcetti* case in 2006, another 5–4 decision by the Supreme Court, further narrowed First Amendment protection for public employees by holding that it does not extend to any speech made "pursuant to their official duties." The majority stressed that public employees retain their First Amendment right to speak about matters of public concern related to their workplace that do not fall within their official duties. In his dissent, Justice Souter objected to the official duties test as "an odd place" to distinguish between protected and unprotected speech. The need for the *Pickering* balancing process, Souter maintained, does not disappear when an employee speaks pursuant to his official duties. Indeed, the value of the speech may be greater when an employee is particularly knowledgeable about a subject precisely because it is within his official duties. Souter, therefore, objected to the "categorical" exclusion of all speech pursuant to official duties from First Amendment protection.[26] In response to concerns raised by Justice Souter in his dissent, the majority left open a possible exception to the official duties test for the scholarship and teaching of professors.[27]

Matters of Public Concern

Lower-court decisions involving academic speech by professors, like lower-court decisions involving speech by public employees generally, have reached different conclusions on similar facts in determining whether it was about a matter of public concern. Some decisions have maintained that all speech related to employment, including the basic functions of scholarship and teaching, cannot raise matters of public concern. Other decisions have reached conflicting conclusions about whether scholarship, teaching, and intramural speech outside the classroom addressed matters of public concern. Some have limited matters of public concern to "socially useful subjects" as opposed to "abstract theorizing."[28] Decisions have also differed about the extent to which the personal interest of a speaker in the outcome of a dispute, the extent to which a speaker has tried to arouse public interest, and the extent of actual public interest should affect the determination of whether the speech is about a matter of public concern. In concluding that academic speech was not about a matter of public concern, many decisions denied protection that was afforded by judges who applied the First Amendment law of academic freedom.

Conflicting Conclusions in the Same Case

Some of these disagreements have occurred in the same case. The extensive opinions in *Urofsky* about the status of academic freedom as a First Amendment right, discussed in detail in Chapter 4, also revealed the broad range of judicial views about what constitutes a matter of public concern. The majority opinion by Judge Wilkins concluded that expression by public employees in the course of performing their jobs, including the scholarship and teaching of professors, can never be about a matter of public concern. Wilkins conceded that much of this expression deals with "matters of vital concern to the public." But he refused to equate it with speech about "matters of public concern" protected by the First Amendment because he felt that doing so would give public employees the "right to dictate to the state how they will do their jobs." Writing for the dissenters in *Urofsky*, Judge Murnaghan asserted that restrictions on the ability of professors to access sexually explicit content on the internet would inhibit research about many matters of public concern, such as sexual themes in the humanities and law, sexually related diseases, and child abuse. While focusing mostly on the First Amendment right of academic freedom, which Judge Murnaghan ignored, Judge Wilkinson's concurrence agreed that academic research encompasses many matters of public concern. But as Judge Luttig accurately observed in his own concurrence, Wilkinson made confusing and sometimes contradictory statements about whether all academic research, or only research on "socially useful subjects," constitutes matters of public concern.[29]

More recently, a circuit court reversed a magistrate judge and held that a professor raised an issue of public concern when he resisted his university's revised policy that subjected faculty to discipline if they "refused to use a pronoun that reflects a student's self-asserted gender identity."[30] The magistrate judge acknowledged that gender identity is a controversial subject of profound concern to the public, but she observed that the professor simply refused to use feminine pronouns in addressing a student who was male at birth. The judge indicated that a broader discussion of gender identity in the classroom could involve matters of public concern.[31] The circuit court, by contrast, stressed that the use of gender-specific titles and pronouns had become a passionate topic of public concern. To support this conclusion, it cited the feminist critique of the generic use of masculine pronouns to perpetuate the invisibility of women.[32] By refusing to use feminine pronouns, the court stressed, the professor was conveying his disagreement with the university's position that people can have a different gender identity than their sex at birth.[33]

Teaching and Scholarship

Other decisions found that classroom expression or scholarly publications addressed matters of public concern. While holding that a professor's comments and assignments advocating diversity related to a core issue of public concern, a judge stressed that this determination should not depend on whether the speech was uttered outside the university or in the classroom. He strongly disagreed with the university's position that classroom speech never implicates the First Amendment.[34] Another judge maintained that a professor was speaking "quintessentially" about matters of public concern when, in a book review and a letter to a scholarly journal, he cited IQ scores to assert that Blacks as a group are less intelligent than whites as a group and that affirmative action programs are, therefore, misguided.[35] In a very different factual context, a judge concluded that speech by a law professor in class and in campus publications advocating the legalization of marijuana and criticizing national policy on drug control clearly raises matters of public concern. To reinforce his conclusion, the judge observed that his own docket indicated the extent to which drug abuse and trafficking are major social problems. Recognizing the distinction between protected speech on matters of public concern and unprotected speech on matters of personal interest, the judge made it clear that he would not have reached this conclusion if a professor faced with termination for personal use of marijuana tried to discredit a drug-testing program.[36]

Some cases that relied on the First Amendment right of academic freedom to protect classroom speech asserted as an independent basis for the decision that the speech was about a matter of public concern. The professor who asked his students to suggest words that marginalized oppressed social groups, the court briefly concluded, addressed conflicts over race, gender, and power, which are matters of overwhelming public concern in our society.[37] Referring to this decision, a judge concluded that a professor's classroom and clinical advocacy of vaginal instead of cesarean delivery addressed a matter of public concern, even if a less overwhelming one.[38]

Other decisions concluded that various disputes related to teaching did not involve matters of public concern, including course coverage and assignments, the removal of a student from class, grading, and performance evaluation.[39] One court acknowledged that class size and the integrity of testing procedures are "inherently" matters of public concern, but it denied protection to a professor who only addressed the impact of these topics on her status as an employee.[40] In a case dealing with scholarship, a court concluded that complex statistical modeling using Keynesian economics and intended for a relatively narrow academic audience did not raise issues of public concern.[41]

Intramural Speech

In assessing whether intramural speech addresses public concerns, as in cases about scholarship and teaching, courts have reached conflicting results. Holding that a professor's own reappointment and tenure is a matter of personal interest rather than public concern, courts have denied First Amendment protection to assertions by unsuccessful candidates that the university's decision was unfair or discriminatory. Cases emphasized that the primary motivation of professors was to achieve reappointment or tenure, not to inform the public.[42] The same reasoning would apply to claims by professors that universities denied them reappointment or tenure in retaliation for their exercise of academic freedom. Though convinced that claims of personal bias were accurate and would upset the public, one court concluded that an issue does not become a matter of public concern just because a community finds it interesting.[43]

Courts have concluded that intramural expression about broader issues did not address matters of public concern. A professor's criticism of his department's leadership and lack of harmony, a judge asserted, was a self-interested personal grievance about work.[44] Another judge reached the same conclusion about a professor's criticism of the dean for not allowing sufficient faculty governance and for unethical decisions. In a revealing passage that illustrated the difference between employee-speech jurisprudence and analysis of academic freedom, the judge observed that the purpose of the professor's speech "was to make the University's medical school better—and not to disclose misconduct or official impropriety."[45] Other judges reasoned that a professor's statements about the internal operations of his department could not qualify as matters of public concern unless they addressed "malfeasance, corruption or fraud." A professor's protest that too many courses were taught by lecturers rather than tenured faculty members, one judge concluded, did not meet this standard.[46] Even Judge Wilkinson, who would have protected at least some academic expression as addressing matters of public concern, maintained that a professor's speech about the curriculum would be a private concern due to its "distinctly institutional character."[47] Judges who applied the First Amendment right of academic freedom to intramural speech about curricular reform and university exchange programs would have reached different results.[48]

Yet many decisions found that intramural expression was about matters of public concern. In contrast to the decisions holding that a professor's own reappointment and tenure were personal concerns, courts treated expression about the hiring or firing of other professors as raising matters of public concern. In one case, a professor referred at a faculty meeting to widespread rumors that a candidate for appointment had participated in inappropriate sexual activities with students and had been too hung over to teach effectively.[49] In another, a professor spoke with colleagues while seeking to revoke the tenure of a professor accused of plagiarism and copyright violations, emotional abuse of students, and receipt of kickbacks from a publisher in return for adopting its textbooks.[50]

Judge Fletcher maintained that many internal departmental disputes over budget, curriculum, departmental structure, and faculty hiring may involve matters of public concern.[51] Fletcher made these comments in a case about departmental reorganization, but he also made it clear that the dispute would not have addressed a matter of public concern if it had involved internal controversies over control of the department or disagreement with the board of trustees regarding the procedures for the reorganization or for choosing a new president.[52] This opinion replaced an earlier one that the court withdrew without explanation.[53] In the withdrawn opinion, Judge Fletcher made some additional interesting comments about the relationship between academic disputes and matters of public concern. Pointing out that it is difficult for judges to assess the public interest in these disputes, he urged them to "hesitate before concluding that academic disagreements about what may appear to be esoteric topics are mere squabbles over jobs, turf, or ego." Though debates in English departments over the literary canon may seem trivial to some, he observed, they address important cultural issues. Academic debates in numerous other disciplines, he added, similarly raise broad issues of public concern.[54]

Judges held professors addressed public concerns in speech at faculty meetings opposing multicultural education and urging that the business school devote more attention in classes to the experiences of minorities and women in the work force and to the social responsibilities of businesses.[55] Yet in declaring opposition to multicultural education a matter of public concern, the judge stressed that it was part of a broader "call to action" against cultural practices that harmed women in India, Africa, and Islamic countries. He acknowledged that "abstract theorizing" unrelated to significant social issues might not raise issues of public concern.[56] Another judge held that a librarian on a committee formed to select a book for assignment to all incoming freshman raised issues of public concern when he suggested a book treating homosexuality as "aberrant behavior" that had become accepted as a result of "political correctness." The librarian suggested this book and three others that would challenge "academic orthodoxy" after other members of the committee had suggested books that he considered to have liberal points of view.[57]

In cases dealing with broader issues of social policy, a court identified "educational standards" and "academic policy" as matters of public concern while protecting a professor at Lincoln University, a historically Black university, who asserted that "grade inflation is a crime" not only against the University and its students but against Black people generally.[58] Another court maintained that a professor's proposal to abolish the tenure system, published in various national journals and newspapers, addressed general public concerns about its value.[59] In cases plausibly but less obviously related to educational issues, courts held that disputes about the relocation of the health science center and the cost of constructing a new arts center involved matters of public concern.[60]

Some decisions stressed the widespread distribution of information about a university dispute and public reactions to it as evidence that it related to a matter of public concern,[61] and the absence of these factors as evidence that it was only a matter of private concern.[62] Other cases maintained that speech in a classroom or in an academic department can be about a matter of public concern even if it does not reach a broader audience.[63]

These cases reveal the inconsistency and confusion among decisions applying the doctrine of public concern to the academic context. Even more striking, whereas courts have overwhelmingly interpreted the First Amendment right of academic freedom as minimally protecting the academic content of a professor's expression, many of these cases have denied protection to academic content by concluding that it does not address a matter of public concern.

Balancing

When applying the *Pickering* test, which balances the public employee's interests in commenting as a citizen on matters of public concern against the government employer's interests in efficiency, some judges have taken the academic context into account. Without referring specifically to academic freedom, a court recognized "that there must be more room for divergent views in a university situation than in a prosecutor's office," the context of the Supreme Court's decision in *Connick*. It also observed that the working relationship between professors and administrators is not generally as close as the one between assistant prosecutors and their supervisors and is, therefore, less likely to be disrupted by speech between them.[64] Another court contrasted the university context from the requirements of discipline and duty in the military.[65] And courts have indirectly protected academic freedom by concluding that loss of legislative or alumni financial support caused by a professor's controversial views cannot be balanced by the university against the professor's First Amendment right to free expression.[66]

Some cases have referred specifically to academic freedom as a factor in the balancing process. The decision that protected the professor who solicited words that marginalized oppressed groups stated that in balancing the competing interests of the professor and the college, "we must take into account the robust tradition of academic freedom in our nation's postsecondary schools."[67] In applying the balancing test the court stressed that the use of offensive words was limited to a single class, that only one of the ten minority students in the class complained, that all the other students provided positive feedback on the course, and that no additional conflicts occurred during the remainder of the semester. The court also stressed the lack of evidence that this one incident had undermined the professor's working relationship with his colleagues, interfered with his duties, or otherwise impaired discipline, factors the Supreme Court had identified as legitimate interests of employers in promoting efficiency.[68] In the case of the professor who resisted the university's policy of using pronouns that "reflect a student's self-asserted gender identity," the circuit court found the professor's "powerful" First Amendment interests in academic freedom among the factors that outweighed the university's "comparatively weak" asserted interest in "stopping discrimination against transgender students." The court stressed that the university rejected the professor's proposed compromise of using the student's last name rather than any pronoun and concluded that the record did not present any evidence that the professor's refusal to use feminine pronouns inhibited the student's education.[69]

The academic context of a professor's speech, courts have observed, does not always support the professor. In balancing in favor of a university, a court observed that a professor has a much closer relationship to a department chair than the schoolteacher in *Pickering* had to the superintendent of schools.[70] While asserting that the balancing test is the same whether the professor speaks off campus about politics or on campus as a professor, a court pointed out that when speaking within his own expertise and in personal relationships with students, a professor may be subject to professional standards that do not apply to citizens generally.[71] This decision ultimately balanced in favor of the professor, finding no violations of professional standards. But another court concluded that a university's interest in disciplining unprofessional comments by a professor at a faculty meeting significantly outweighed the professor's interest in criticizing the dean's management decisions.[72]

Official Duties

Lower courts have responded in different ways to Justice Kennedy's concession to Justice Souter in *Garcetti* that the denial of First Amendment protection for speech by public employees made "pursuant to" their "official duties" might not apply to the scholarship and teaching of professors. Without addressing Kennedy's concession, some have assumed that the official duties test does apply to scholarship and teaching. Others have recognized an exception, sometimes limiting it to scholarship and teaching while applying the test to other speech by professors. And some have found that speech by professors was outside the scope of their official duties and, therefore, not subject to the *Garcetti* analysis.

In a decision the year after *Garcetti,* a federal district court applied the official duties test to speech by a professor without any modification or reference to the First Amendment protection of academic freedom. The professor had questioned the professional ethics of colleagues during the process of peer review, criticized his department for having lecturers rather than tenured faculty teach most courses, and accused the department chair of violating faculty self-governance by appointing an assistant professor prior to faculty approval. Concluding that all this speech was pursuant to the professor's official duties and, therefore, excluded from First Amendment coverage by *Garcetti,* the judge emphasized that "a faculty member's official duties are not limited to classroom instruction and professional research."[73] Courts have held that speech by professors alleging financial misconduct or mismanagement within the university is part of their official duties and, therefore, unprotected.[74]

Other decisions, by contrast, have addressed the issue Justice Kennedy left unresolved in *Garcetti* and have asserted that the official duties test does not apply to scholarship and teaching. In holding that the First Amendment right of academic freedom protects a professor's classroom advocacy of vaginal delivery rather than cesarean procedures, the judge endorsed "an academic freedom exception to *Garcetti.*"[75] A panel of the fourth circuit, as urged by the AAUP in an amicus brief, reversed a district court that applied the official duties test to the books, columns, and public speeches of a professor. The professor claimed that the university had denied his application for tenure because he had expressed conservative religious and political views. The panel agreed with the university and the district court that the professor produced this material as part of his job responsibilities as a professor, and that they related to his work as a scholar and teacher.[76] But it maintained that this is precisely the context in which the exception to the official duties test, contemplated in *Garcetti* itself, should be recognized. Although this fourth circuit panel quoted the statement in the earlier en banc decision by the entire fourth circuit in *Urofsky* that the Supreme Court had not established a First Amendment right of academic freedom for professors, its analysis of *Garcetti* did not follow the *Urofsky* precedent. It even quoted approvingly Souter's concern in *Garcetti* that applying the official duties test to scholarship and teaching would imperil the First Amendment protection of academic freedom.[77]

Citing this decision as support, Judge Fletcher more explicitly expanded the academic speech exempted from the *Garcetti* official duties test. Like the fourth circuit panel, and as urged by an AAUP amicus brief, Fletcher's opinion criticized the district court for not recognizing that *Garcetti* left open a possible exception for professors from the official duties test. Discussing

Keyishian and subsequent decisions about the constitutional meaning of academic freedom, he concluded that *Garcetti* would directly conflict with them if applied to professors.[78]

Fletcher observed that the professor developed his plan to reorganize the department in an effort to restore the critical connection to the professional needs of practitioners in the field of mass communications. The professor believed that this connection had been lost by requiring students to take more courses in theory than in practical skills. Fletcher acknowledged that the boundaries of the academic freedom exception might be imprecise. But he felt strongly that the professor's plan was not a close case. In contrast to a proposal to allocate more teaching credits for a large class than for a seminar, to impose a dress code for professors, or to change the menu at the student cafeteria, which he indicated might not be related to scholarship or teaching, the plan for the school of communications, if implemented, would have substantially changed both the curriculum and the composition of the faculty. Those consequences, Fletcher believed, obviously brought the plan within the *Garcetti* exception. Yet the plan was not itself "academic scholarship or classroom discussion," the phrase used in *Garcetti* to describe the possible exception based on concerns about academic freedom. Perhaps recognizing this somewhat awkward fit, Fletcher referred to the *Garcetti* exception as covering "teaching and academic writing."[79] Substituting the phrase "academic writing" for *Garcetti*'s own reference to "academic scholarship" expanded the scope of the exception to include a broader range of academic speech.

Other decisions have recognized the academic freedom exception to the *Garcetti* official duties test while denying its applicability to speech by professors that was not "academic scholarship or classroom discussion." Judges determined that the exception did not apply to speech made as a member of a faculty committee, such as comments objecting to the imposition of academic orthodoxy by the librarian who served on the faculty-staff committee to select a book for assignment to incoming freshmen, and allegations by the chair of a faculty search committee about gender discrimination in the hiring process.[80] Speech at a faculty meeting asserting that evaluations of faculty were arbitrary and that the college's fundraising was insufficient did not qualify for the academic freedom exception.[81] Nor did expression by professors to administrators reporting a colleague's claim of sexual harassment and a student's violation of a federal law designed to protect patient privacy.[82] Another court refused to apply the exception to advice by a professor to a student accused of violating campus policy prohibiting the possession of weapons.[83] All of these cases applied the *Garcetti* official duties test to reject the First Amendment claim.

In one very interesting case, a professor claimed that he had been terminated for criticizing actions by the US Army Corps of Engineers in the aftermath of Hurricane Katrina. The university moved for summary judgment, asserting that the professor's speech was made pursuant to his official duties. The court denied the motion, finding that the professor's job duties did not include speaking to the media, the context in which he made his criticisms. Although the professor had not argued for an academic freedom exception, the court nevertheless indicated sympathy for recognizing one in an appropriate case. It observed that applying the official duties test to professors could allow administrators to discipline them for expressing unpopular or unorthodox opinions.[84]

The fact that lower courts have differed in their interpretations of the possible academic freedom exception to the official duties test of *Garcetti* obviously has enormous implications for the future of academic freedom as a First Amendment right. Scholarship and teaching are the core official duties of a professor. *Garcetti* excludes speech by public employees pursuant to their official duties from the protection of the First Amendment. If there is no academic freedom exception from the official duties test, academic freedom as a First Amendment right of professors is imperiled, as Souter warned in his *Garcetti* dissent. If there is an academic freedom exception, its impact on the First Amendment right of academic freedom depends on its reach. As the lower-court decisions illustrate, some judges have limited it to scholarship and teaching, the areas specifically identified by Kennedy and Souter, while others have extended it to intramural and extramural speech.[85]

Is Academic Freedom a Distinctive First Amendment Right?

Adding to the confusion produced by the continued application of general First Amendment principles and employee-speech jurisprudence to academic speech, decisions have reached different conclusions about whether academic freedom can be differentiated from other First Amendment rights. Some cases have explicitly referred to the "long recognized . . . significance" and "invaluable role" of academic freedom, acclaimed in "abundant cases," while claiming that it is not an "independent" or "separate right apart from the operation of the First Amendment within the university setting."[86] Yet these cases, frustratingly, do not go further in explaining how the "university setting" affects "the operation of the First Amendment."

Other courts, by contrast, have stressed the distinctiveness of the First Amendment right of academic freedom. One influential decision maintained that this right provided an additional reason not to enforce a company's subpoena of the research notes and data of professors, rejecting the company's claim that professors have no greater First Amendment interests in nondisclosure than anybody else.[87] In a case involving the technical doctrine of collateral estoppel, a judge concluded that academic freedom and speech about matters of public concern are distinct doctrines. He, therefore, rejected a university's argument that a professor's academic freedom claim should be dismissed because he had an opportunity in a previous case to litigate about whether he spoke on a matter of public concern.[88] Judge Wood pointed out that speech about matters of public concern, which would be protected by the First Amendment in many contexts, would not be protected by academic freedom if uttered in class without any pedagogical purpose.[89]

Conclusion

The many cases applying general First Amendment principles and employee-speech jurisprudence to academic speech by professors demonstrate that the judicial recognition of academic freedom as a First Amendment right of professors, though often the doctrinal basis for decisions, has not become the standard method of judicial analysis. Judges also rely on general First Amendment principles and employee-speech jurisprudence in cases that raise issues of academic freedom.

In addition to contributing to the conceptual confusion produced by the judicial application of these three different approaches, employee-speech jurisprudence has often allowed the punishment of speech that would have been protected by the First Amendment right of academic freedom. Most strikingly, judges have sometimes concluded that scholarship and teaching never raise issues of public concern and are official duties of professors, thereby precluding First Amendment protection and undermining the most fundamental protection of academic freedom. Without denying protection to all scholarship and teaching, other judges have found that speech about many subjects that could be protected by academic freedom are not about matters of public concern. Examples include comments about course coverage, curriculum, unfairness and discrimination in tenure decisions, declining academic standards, departmental reorganization, and, most dramatically, "abstract theorizing" and speech "to make the university better."

Sometimes general First Amendment principles and employee-speech jurisprudence yield similar results as the First Amendment analysis of academic freedom, but they do so through conceptual categories that do not examine the First Amendment value of distinctively academic expression. General First Amendment principles of overbreadth and vagueness have protected classroom discussion of controversial scholarly theories, and employee-speech jurisprudence has protected it as relating to matters of public concern. But these decisions have not addressed whether the controversial theories were relevant to the subject matter of the course or met scholarly standards, key issues for determining the protection of academic freedom. Classroom discussion of controversial scholarly theories about the relative mental abilities of males and females should be protected to the extent that they meet these standards, even if university regulations are not overbroad or vague. The protection of a professor who advocates vaginal instead of cesarean delivery should depend on whether this view is "within the range of accepted medical opinion" and is relevant to a course in obstetrics, not on whether this subject is sufficiently about a matter of public concern.

Some judges have recognized the lack of fit between employee-speech jurisprudence and the First Amendment protection for the academic freedom of professors. In a particularly thoughtful opinion, a judge worried that employee-speech jurisprudence "does not explicitly account for the robust tradition of academic freedom" that the Supreme Court had repeatedly recognized as "a special concern of the First Amendment." But he concluded that academic freedom could receive appropriate consideration in the process of determining the extent of a professor's right to speak about matters of public concern.[90] Judges occasionally have indicated that the current lack of clarity about the meaning of academic freedom as a First Amendment right of professors prompted them to avoid relying on it as the basis for their decisions. After a lengthy review of previous case law, a district court judge concluded in 1995 that "their rhetoric is broader than their holdings" and that "the parameters of academic freedom are not distinct."[91] He, therefore, did not consider a professor's academic freedom claims and used employee-speech jurisprudence instead to analyze whether the First Amendment protected classroom expression. In the case challenging bans on academic travel to Cuba, Judge Harry Edwards, a former professor at the University of Michigan, wrote a lengthy concurring opinion criticizing his colleagues for even addressing the "difficult" and "complicated" issues about the meaning of academic freedom as a First Amendment right. The concept of academic freedom, he stressed, is hard to grasp and its breadth is unclear. According to Edwards, the case could have been easily resolved through the "relatively straightforward and uncomplicated" application of the general First Amendment principle of content neutrality.[92] Perhaps similar but unstated reasoning accounts at least in part for the widespread lack of judicial attention to issues of academic freedom in cases that clearly present them.

To some extent, as the judge indicated in urging attention to considerations of academic freedom in construing matters of public concern, it is possible to apply general First Amendment principles and employee-speech jurisprudence with more sensitivity to academic speech than currently prevails. Interests in protecting scholarly communications could inform interpretation of the general First Amendment rights to hear and to associate. The definition of a matter of public concern could cover more academic speech, perhaps even the general pursuit of knowledge through abstract theorizing about esoteric subjects unrelated to current societal problems. As some judges have asserted, consideration of academic freedom, including its limitation to expression that meets professional standards, could be explicitly considered in applying the *Pickering* balance to disputes between professors and universities.

For the situations in which even distinctive applications of general First Amendment principles and employee-speech jurisprudence cannot sufficiently protect academic freedom, courts could develop explicit exceptions. Examples already exist. The general principle that the First Amendment allows the government to control speech through conditions on funding, Chief Justice Rehnquist concluded in his majority opinion in *Rust*, does not apply to the university because it is "a traditional sphere of free expression so fundamental to the functioning of our society."[93] In a subsequent case declaring that conditions on a federal grant to a university professor violated the First Amendment, a district court judge referred to this language as an "explicit exception" to the general principle.[94] Justice Kennedy's acknowledgment that the "official duties" test of "customary employee-speech jurisprudence" might not apply to "speech related to scholarship or teaching" indicates the possibility of another exception, which some lower courts have recognized.[95]

Yet the need for numerous modifications and exceptions casts doubt on the explanatory power of general First Amendment principles and employee-speech jurisprudence to address the academic speech of professors. Even with significant modifications and exceptions, moreover, their conceptual categories would remain focused on other issues. For example, they would examine whether a regulation is vague or overbroad, or whether speech is about a matter of public concern or expressed pursuant to official duties, rather than on whether speech is within a professor's academic expertise. An improved analysis of academic freedom as a distinctive First Amendment right of professors is a better way to address the confusion and inconsistency in current legal analysis. It could clarify the meaning of this right itself as well as its relationship to other areas of First Amendment law. It could provide more convincing justifications for decisions even in situations where general First Amendment principles or employee-speech jurisprudence could plausibly be invoked. This theory would identify when cases raise issues of academic freedom. If they do, the distinctive theory First Amendment law of academic freedom, rather than general principles of First Amendment law or employee-speech jurisprudence, would apply.

I turn in Chapter 6 to developing this theory. I build on the justification of academic freedom in the AAUP's 1915 Declaration, adapting it to First Amendment analysis, and on the issues raised by the case law discussed thus far. I also use the facts of the case law to illustrate how the theory would operate in practice, often in ways that use different reasoning and reach different results than in the cases themselves.

6

A Theory of Academic Freedom as a Distinctive First Amendment Right of Professors

IN THIS CHAPTER I propose and illustrate a theory of academic freedom as a distinctive First Amendment right of professors. With this theory I seek to remedy the confusion, inconsistency, and frequently unsatisfactory results reflected in the judicial decisions. Beyond providing needed protection in areas left vulnerable by current First Amendment law, the theory directs attention to the educational issues at stake and offers better justifications for decisions even when current law would yield the same result. Just as judges have developed employee-speech jurisprudence as a distinctive subset of First Amendment law to differentiate the more specific context of government employment from the general role of government as sovereign, the expressive functions of university professors justify a distinctive theory of academic freedom as a still more specific subset of First Amendment law. The judicial recognition since the 1970s of "commercial speech" as another distinctive subset of First Amendment law provides additional support for a distinctive theory of academic freedom.

A convincing theory must differentiate academic freedom from general First Amendment rights of free speech while explaining why it fits within the First Amendment. If academic freedom is the same thing as free speech, there is no need for a separate theory. If academic freedom is different from free speech, its distinctive meaning must be connected to the First Amendment. The societal value of the contribution to knowledge through the expert academic speech of professors provides the most convincing justification for treating it as a distinctive category of First Amendment analysis differentiated from the general free speech rights of all citizens, including professors when they are speaking as citizens rather than as academic experts.

In elaborating this theory, I draw on the analysis of academic freedom in the AAUP's 1915 Declaration of Principles. Broadly accepted within the academic world before the Supreme Court began to recognize academic freedom as a First Amendment right in the 1950s and 1960s, it remains enormously influential today. Most importantly, the 1915 Declaration emphasizes the function of professors in the production and dissemination of knowledge, the same societal goal that the Supreme Court in many contexts has repeatedly highlighted as a fundamental First Amendment interest. Yet the 1915 Declaration specifies the relationship between academic freedom and the production and dissemination of knowledge much more clearly than the generally terse and conclusory language in scattered judicial decisions. Though not a legal document, the 1915 Declaration provides a convincing theoretical justification of academic freedom that is compatible with and can inform analysis of its meaning as a First Amendment right.

I rely especially on two central arguments of the 1915 Declaration. First, professors cannot perform their distinctive societal function in producing and disseminating expert knowledge unless they are protected from discipline for the honest expression of their academic views. Any indication that professors could be disciplined based on disagreement with their scholarly views would undermine confidence in the integrity of their work. Second, peer review by other professors is essential to determining whether speech by a professor meets the academic standards that justify the protection of academic freedom.

The 1915 Declaration took pains to emphasize that academic freedom does not protect speech by professors that violates academic norms. This limitation on academic freedom corresponds to the rationale for protecting it, though the 1915 Declaration itself does not explicitly assert the analogy. Speech that does not meet academic norms is not the expert academic speech that contributes to the production and dissemination of knowledge. And the 1915 Declaration convincingly insisted that only fellow professors have the expertise to determine and apply these norms, adding that involvement by others, including university administrators and trustees, would raise legitimate suspicions of improper motivations. Peer review thus became a key component of academic freedom.

The facts of the litigated cases illustrate the appropriate scope of the distinctive First Amendment right of academic freedom, whether or not these cases themselves relied on it or reached conclusions consistent with my own. Academic freedom in scholarship and teaching should protect the content of expert academic expression, access to research material and to other scholars, the pedagogical decisions of professors, and confidentiality in research and teaching. It should not protect scholarship and teaching that fails to meet academic standards as determined by peer review, classroom expression unrelated to the subject matter of a course, or failure to meet reasonable university policies about topics such as the distribution of a syllabus and course evaluations in class, grading curves, and teaching upper-level language courses in the foreign language. As the cases reveal, facts often present close questions about whether the speech fits within a protected or unprotected category.

The protection of the distinctive First Amendment right of academic freedom should extend beyond the core functions of professors in scholarship and teaching. Because academic freedom applies only to expression that meets academic standards, it should cover speech by faculty peers in making this determination. In addition to specialized knowledge within their academic disciplines, professors have general expertise in matters of educational policy. Because educational policy influences the production and dissemination of knowledge, academic freedom should extend to expression of this general expertise. It should protect speech about academic standards, curricular reform, and university governance. But it should not protect comments about whether a university should celebrate an ethnic holiday on campus, university fundraising efforts, athletic policy, and land acquisition. Faculty have no special expertise about these subjects, whose relation to the production and dissemination of knowledge is often tenuous at best. Nor should it protect language that is unprofessional, false, threatening, or harassing. As in cases about scholarship and teaching, close questions can arise about whether speech fits within a protected or unprotected category.

It is also plausible, though more of a stretch, to extend the reach of the First Amendment right of academic freedom beyond academic expression itself to procedural and structural protections for it, just as current First Amendment law requires procedural and structural protections before the government can limit public meetings or seize allegedly obscene material. Yet the justification for academic freedom does not extend to speech by professors about political issues that are unrelated to their expertise, whether on or off campus. The controversial inclusion of such expression within the conception of academic freedom in the 1915 Declaration is inconsistent with its own emphasis on the societal value of academic expertise, as some of its framers complained at the time. With respect to expression outside their expertise, professors should be governed by the First Amendment law of free speech that applies to all citizens and the employee-speech jurisprudence that applies to all public employees.

In developing a theory of academic freedom as a distinctive First Amendment right of professors, I differentiate academic freedom from free speech and connect it to general First Amendment values. I then discuss how this distinctive right applies to scholarship and teaching, to other speech within the university, and to political speech outside the university. I close by examining whether the First Amendment right of academic freedom should include procedural and structural protections.

Differentiating Academic Freedom from Free Speech

The distinctive function of academic freedom in protecting the societal interest in the expert expression of professors differentiates it in several respects from the general right of free speech. The general right of free speech is egalitarian and individualistic. It is egalitarian because all citizens have equal rights to free speech on a broad range of subjects. It is individualistic because its exercise does not depend on others. Academic freedom, by contrast, is meritocratic and communitarian. It is meritocratic because expression is protected only if it meets academic standards. It is communitarian because the community of faculty peers makes the determination of merit.

In further contrast to the general right of free speech as well as to employee-speech jurisprudence, academic freedom entails both more and less protection for expression by professors within their areas of expertise, as William Van Alstyne highlighted in a classic article published in 1972. Professors who meet academic standards have more protection than other employees because the university employer cannot direct the topics they investigate or the conclusions they reach, even if those conclusions lead to public hostility and financial hardship for the university.[1] Professors also have more protection than citizens generally from laws that jeopardize their expert academic speech. Van Alstyne convincingly asserted, for example, that a professor who uses hard-core pornography as part of a study that meets academic standards should be protected even if it otherwise violates state criminal law and constitutes obscenity outside the protection of the First Amendment. Yet the "price" of the exceptional vocational privilege of academic freedom, in Van Alstyne's elegant phrase, is the "cost" of "a

139

professional standard of care." Professors can be disciplined for professional misconduct, such as falsification of data or plagiarism, even if that misconduct does not violate any law or provoke a reaction from the governing board.[2] Grossly inaccurate speech denying the Holocaust could be cause for dismissing a historian for incompetence, but not for taking any adverse action against a citizen or a professor of engineering writing a letter to the newspaper or speaking in a public space. The expert speech of a professor is held to academic standards that do not apply to other employees or to the public speech of citizens, including professors who express themselves as citizens about subjects outside their expertise.

The added protection for academic freedom, like the protection for free speech generally, is not absolute. As Matthew Finkin and Robert Post observe, "academic research is not a license to commit harm." The definition and the probability of harm can be contentious, but it would be legitimate to regulate research with toxins or radioactive substances.[3] Implicitly invoking the famous statement by Justice Holmes in *Schenck v. United States* that "the most stringent protection of freedom of speech would not protect a man in falsely shouting fire in a theatre and causing a panic," Van Alstyne acknowledged that "the false shouting of fire in a crowded theater may not immunize a professor of psychology from having to answer for the consequences of the ensuing panic, even assuming that he did so in order to observe crowd reaction firsthand and solely to advance the general enlightenment we may otherwise possess of how people act under great and sudden stress." The expression of a faculty member for a legitimate academic purpose, and thus protected by academic freedom, may be outweighed by the public interest in preventing a panic.[4]

Connecting Academic Freedom to the First Amendment

Just as the focus on the expert academic expression of professors differentiates academic freedom from free speech generally, academic freedom fits within major themes in general First Amendment law. Academic freedom is an example of the frequent emphasis on institutional context in First Amendment interpretation. By protecting the production and dissemination of knowledge, it also advances an important First Amendment value recognized in a wide variety of cases. Many argue that it also promotes democratic citizenship, the most central First Amendment value throughout

its history, though I am skeptical that this theoretically appealing argument
has been confirmed in practice.

In one of its earliest decisions recognizing the significance of institutional
context, the Supreme Court asserted that the First Amendment rights of
students and teachers must be "applied in light of the special characteristics of the school environment."[5] While upholding the First Amendment
right of students to wear black armbands in school to protest American involvement in the Vietnam war, the Court stressed that the First Amendment did not preclude public school officials from punishing speech that
interferes with educational functions.[6] Judicial decisions have repeatedly
observed that the different purposes of institutions affect the scope of First
Amendment rights within them. They have limited First Amendment protection on military bases and in prisons.[7] Justices have cited the "inculcative" functions of public schools and the lower "level of maturity" of their
students to justify less First Amendment protection than in universities.[8]

These decisions interpreting the First Amendment in institutional context should alleviate concerns that recognizing a distinctive First Amendment right of academic freedom would be inconsistent with the core First
Amendment commitment to equal free speech rights for all citizens. When
the government acts as sovereign, citizens have equal First Amendment
rights. But institutional context, like government employment, can affect
the application of First Amendment rights. People have fewer First Amendment rights on a military base or in a prison than they do in a university or
a public library. In this sense, they do not have equal rights to free speech.
Nor do public employees have the same free speech rights as citizens. The
government as an employer has legitimate interests in efficiency that justify limiting the speech of its employees that do not apply when the government as sovereign attempts to limit the speech of its citizens.[9] These
government interests as an employer vary with the purpose of the government program.

Many Supreme Court decisions explore how expression within various
institutions contributes to fundamental First Amendment interests in the
production and dissemination of information and effective participation
in a democratic society. They often link these two interests, emphasizing
that effective participation in a democratic society depends on public access to information. For example, in the landmark 1971 "Pentagon Papers"
case affirming the First Amendment right of newspapers to publish classified

documents about the war in Vietnam, Justice Stewart maintained that a free press "most vitally serves the basic purpose of the First Amendment" by contributing to "an informed and critical public opinion," which is necessary to "protect the values of democratic government."[10] Succinctly capturing points made in many cases about higher education, Justice Marshall, without referring to academic freedom, observed the importance of the First Amendment in protecting the "dual responsibility" of the university to "advance the frontiers of knowledge through unfettered inquiry and debate" and "to produce a citizenry willing and able to involve itself in the governance of the polity."[11]

First Amendment decisions that do not examine institutional context similarly emphasize the link between the production and dissemination of information and the effective exercise of democratic citizenship. When the Supreme Court initially granted limited First Amendment protection to commercial speech in the 1970s after previously treating it as an unprotected category of expression, it stressed that the "free flow of commercial information is indispensable" both to the "proper allocation of resources in a free enterprise system" and to "the formation of intelligent opinions as to how that system ought to be regulated or altered."[12] I do not agree that purely commercial speech generally contributes to the discussion of broader issues of public concern in a democracy. As Justice Rehnquist wrote in dissent, the First Amendment is designed to protect public discussion of political and social issues, not commercial information that may help a consumer decide to purchase a particular brand of shampoo.[13] But the commercial speech cases, precisely because they stretch the plausibility of the link between commercial speech and democratic citizenship, underline how broadly the Supreme Court has interpreted speech as contributing to citizenship.

Other Supreme Court decisions have focused on the First Amendment interest in the production and dissemination of information and ideas. Pointing out the compatibility of the copyright clause of the Constitution and the First Amendment, decisions maintained that "copyright's purpose is to *promote* the creation and publication of free expression" by supplying "the economic incentive to create and disseminate ideas."[14] Particularly in cases about journalists and broadcasters, Supreme Court decisions have specified the First Amendment interests of professional employees in gathering information and conveying it to the public.[15] These interests include determining the content of the material published or broadcast.[16] Just as the Supreme Court recognized that journalists and broadcasters must make judgments about what information the public should receive, it quoted approvingly from books asserting that the "librarian's responsibility . . . is to separate out the gold from the garbage," to serve as "the selector to give the public, not everything it wants but the best that it will read or use to advantage."[17]

Some of these decisions have used terms analogous to academic freedom in discussing the First Amendment interests of journalists, variously referring to journalistic freedom, the journalistic role, journalistic judgment, journalistic discretion, journalistic independence, editorial discretion, and editorial judgment. A dissent by Justice Stevens asserted that the discretion to select the content of library collections "is comparable" to the freedom to make decisions on academic grounds in universities, quoting Frankfurter's concurrence in *Sweezy*.[18] Yet none of these opinions maintained that journalists or librarians have special First Amendment rights.

As some scholars have advocated, it may make sense to develop distinctive bodies of First Amendment law—such as "freedom of the press," "librarian's freedom," and "curatorial freedom"—analogous to academic freedom but tailored to the functions of other professionals and the institutions in which they work.[19] Journalists, librarians, and museum curators all use their professional expertise to gather information and convey it to the public, but they do so in different ways that may require distinctive First Amendment rules. The function of professors in the production and dissemination of knowledge in some respects resembles the work of these other professional employees, but there are crucial differences as well. For example, journalists, librarians, and curators deploy their professional expertise to gather and give the public access to information from sources other than themselves. Professors, by contrast, serve the public by using their expertise to develop and share their own and their colleagues' academic knowledge and judgments. Instead of developing additional distinctive First Amendment rights, applying or modifying general First Amendment doctrines might be adequate in other professional settings. The theory of academic freedom as a distinctive subset of First Amendment law, though focused on professors and universities, may provide guidance in choosing among these alternatives. And for readers who ultimately may not be convinced by my arguments for treating academic freedom as a distinctive subset of First Amendment law, arguments I make while developing this position, such as the importance of collective faculty judgment in evaluating academic expression and in formulating educational policies, could inform the application of general First Amendment law in the university context.

Scholarship and Teaching

General commentary about academic freedom as a professional norm, echoing themes in the 1915 Declaration as well as in judicial interpretation of the First Amendment, often justifies it as protecting the function of scholarship and teaching in the production and dissemination of knowledge and in fostering democratic citizenship. In my opinion, the contribution of academic freedom to the production and dissemination of knowledge is substantially greater than its contribution to democratic citizenship.

The Production and Dissemination of Knowledge

The assumption that the production and dissemination of knowledge is itself a substantial benefit to the entire society provides the strongest justification for treating academic freedom as a distinctive First Amendment right. The search for knowledge presumes that it is a continuous process in which existing understandings must be questioned and often revised through the exchange of frequently conflicting ideas.[20] Knowledge based on expertise that meets the standards of the scholarly community is particularly reliable.[21] Evidence that the search for knowledge subordinated scholarly standards to pressures by others on professors or to the ideological commitments of professors themselves undermines confidence in its validity.[22]

Academic freedom protects the function of professors in the production and dissemination of knowledge. It enables them to examine received learning critically and to pursue knowledge wherever it may lead and however much it may disturb people outside or inside the university, including those who administer and provide support for universities and the students enrolled in them.[23] Professors should not be subject to discipline for the content of their scholarship and teaching if it meets academic standards, a determination that should be made by faculty peers who have the necessary expertise.[24] The pursuit of knowledge by professors should extend to the determination of the topics to investigate within their fields of inquiry.[25]

Just as academic freedom protects the production of knowledge through research, it protects the dissemination of knowledge through teaching. In their teaching, the primary functions of college professors are to convey the results of scholarly research to their students and to train them in the methods of scholarly inquiry.[26] As the 1915 Declaration stressed, professors cannot perform these functions unless students have confidence in their intellectual integrity.[27]

In 1883, during the emergence of the American research university and decades before the development of the concept of academic freedom in the 1915 Declaration, Josiah Royce, the eminent American philosopher, provided a powerful justification for academic freedom in university teaching by differentiating the functions of professors from those of schoolteachers. Whereas schoolteachers convey important and well-known facts about elementary subjects, Royce maintained, the subject matter of higher education consists of endlessly disputed concepts. Rather than teach "a set of dogmas," the university professor must teach students how to investigate conflicting views before making judgments about them, often withholding judgment pending further inquiry. The professor must help students understand areas of doubt and demonstrate the hard work necessary to investigate them in the search for truth.[28] "Mind," Royce insisted, "is activity." And "to teach activity, the teacher must show activity." Foreshadowing the concept of academic freedom, he asked, "of what use is the show unless the activity is certainly free?" The activity is not free, he observed, if the professor is prevented from investigating subjects within his expertise or may not present his frank opinions about them. He concluded that the college professor "should be free to teach what doctrines he has been led freely to accept, and that as a model investigator of his subject he should set the example of untrammeled investigation." Royce maintained that professors should be appointed for their competence and then be allowed to teach without interference.[29]

Making similar points, Arthur Lovejoy's influential 1930 essay on academic freedom stressed the function of professors in initiating students into intellectual life by teaching them the diversity of views among scholarly specialists.[30] Recent scholars have emphasized that professors train students to think independently and critically and to evaluate competing ideas while remaining open to new ones.[31] Essential for students who will become scholars themselves,[32] these intellectual skills help all students navigate their adult lives.

The Challenge of Antirealism

The 1915 Declaration assumed that academic research would make continuous progress in discovering objective knowledge about an external reality. I think the overwhelming majority of the public and a significant majority of professors in most disciplines continue to share this assumption. Yet many professors in recent years, particularly in the humanities, have controversially rejected it. In response, others assert that this rejection undermines the justification for academic freedom. If scholarship cannot provide objective knowledge about an external reality, they ask, why should the public support the academic freedom of professors? Similarly, one could argue, the rejection of the conception of knowledge in the 1915 Declaration undermines the primary justification for a theory of academic freedom as a distinctive First Amendment right of professors.

A wide spectrum of views exists among professors who do not fully accept the theory of knowledge underlying the 1915 Declaration. Some maintain that by following traditional academic standards of competence and honesty, professors can gain meaningful knowledge even if they cannot discover transcendent truths about an external reality. Many fewer believe that professors should use their scholarship and teaching to advance their political and ideological goals. I agree with those who conclude that the justification for academic freedom does not require adherence to the position that reality can be progressively discovered. So long as professors adhere to academic standards, they can produce and disseminate knowledge that benefits society and justifies the protection of academic freedom.

As several scholars have observed, challenges to the epistemological assumptions in the 1915 Declaration did not begin in the late twentieth century. Many professors in the generation that produced the 1915 Declaration did not believe that research could eventually discover final truths and governing laws. They treated inquiry as inevitably constrained by the historical and social position of the scholar.[33] Indeed, John Dewey himself, the president of the AAUP who appointed the committee that wrote the 1915 Declaration, often challenged traditional assumptions about truth and knowledge. He asserted that the pursuit of permanent truths was misguided because unattainable, and that it reflected immature psychological needs that should be outgrown. As a leading scholar of pragmatism, he stressed that knowledge should improve society. He treated traditional distinctions between subjectivity and objectivity and between relative and absolute as obsolete distractions from this pragmatic goal. Yet in his own essay on academic freedom, published in 1902, Dewey seemed to agree with the traditional understanding of knowledge in the 1915 Declaration.[34] As Richard Rorty observes, such inconsistency was typical of Dewey, who often took different positions in addressing different audiences.[35]

Some scholars maintain that a convincing justification of academic freedom requires at least some commitment to realism. In a sophisticated presentation of this position, Thomas Haskell acknowledges that there are many versions of realism, including moderate ones that reject the possibility of final truths about reality while exhibiting humility about human limitations in fully grasping it. Haskell believes that moderate realists can still claim the protection of academic freedom. But for him, the denial of realism entirely undermines the justification for academic freedom.[36]

Others maintain that academic freedom and antirealism are compatible if antirealists adhere to academic standards. Skepticism about the existence of external or transcendental foundations, they stress, does not require the conclusion that the production of knowledge is simply a political struggle over ideological goals.[37] Citing himself as an example, Richard Rorty asserts that it is possible to believe that truth is based on intersubjective agreement among scholars rather than correspondence to reality and still follow the practices associated with academic freedom.[38]

Antirealists often assert their commitment to shared standards of academic competence while observing that those standards must be subject to continuous debate and possible revision.[39] They stress that scholars must support arguments with reasons and evidence,[40] and must be honest, as in accurately reporting findings in archives, and not misleadingly quoting out of context. They also frequently condemn those who invoke antirealism to achieve political goals. Richard Rorty maintains that both realist and antirealist philosophers are much more committed to traditional academic standards than to their different views about the correspondence of academic research to an independent reality. But he acknowledges that the "bad guys" who deny these standards in favor of political goals tend to be antirealists.[41]

In my opinion, the essential function of academic freedom in the production and dissemination of knowledge, the primary justification for its protection in the 1915 Declaration and for treating it as a distinctive First Amendment right, does not depend on the conception of knowledge in the 1915 Declaration. I agree with those who assert that meaningful knowledge that benefits society can be developed by scholars with different views about their ability to grasp external reality. Academic freedom should extend to all scholars who respect traditional academic standards of inquiry. But when scholars deviate from those standards, including by subordinating the search for knowledge to political values, they lose the protection of academic freedom.

Critical Thinking and Democratic Citizenship

Echoing the First Amendment emphasis on the function of free speech in promoting democratic values, some commentators have stressed that the critical thinking and open-mindedness learned in the university classroom produce better citizens. In her influential 1987 book, Democratic Education, Amy Gutmann maintains that both schoolteachers and university professors prepare students for participation in a democratic society but do so in different ways. She believes that schoolteachers appropriately try to inculcate fundamental values as character traits, including toleration, respect for truth, and nonviolence. But she thinks that it is harder to inculcate these values in more mature college students and that, apart from this practical difficulty, inculcation is inconsistent with the free inquiry that should prevail in university classrooms. As the 1915 Declaration stressed, the function of the college professor is not to inculcate students but to encourage independent thinking.[42] Observing that college professors teach students how to think critically and to discuss their views with others who disagree, Gutmann approvingly calls this instruction moral education for democratic life because it can be applied to political issues.[43] Citing Gutmann for support, J. Peter Byrne maintains that learning these intellectual skills in university classrooms prepares students for citizenship and leadership in a democracy.[44]

These arguments provide a powerful basis for extending the First Amendment to academic freedom in teaching. The contribution of free expression to democratic government has been a core justification for First Amendment protection since its initial framing and ratification, when many commentators stressed that a government based on popular sovereignty requires freedom of citizens to criticize the elected representatives who are their agents. Justice Frankfurter stressed this connection in his 1952 concurrence in *Wieman,* one of the first Supreme Court opinions that referred to academic freedom and associated it with the First Amendment.

He regarded teachers as "the priests of our democracy" whose "special task" is "to foster those habits of open-mindedness and critical inquiry which alone make for responsible citizens." Making the same point as Royce without citing him, Frankfurter maintained that teachers must demonstrate these habits if they are to teach them.[45] Robert Post appropriately quotes Frankfurter's opinion at length as a convincing sketch of an argument for applying the First Amendment to academic freedom in teaching.[46] In his pathbreaking paragraph on academic freedom in his plurality opinion in *Sweezy* five years after *Wieman,* Chief Justice Warren much more briefly emphasized "the vital role in a democracy of those who guide and train our youth."[47] While identifying academic freedom as "a special concern of the First Amendment" in his 1967 opinion for the majority in *Keyishian,* Justice Brennan did not refer explicitly to democracy. But he similarly stressed that the "Nation's future depends upon leaders trained through wide exposure to" the "robust exchange of ideas."[48]

Although I find assertions of the relationship between university teaching and democratic citizenship theoretically persuasive, I am not convinced that people who are college graduates are better democratic citizens and leaders than those who are not. I do not see substantial evidence of their superiority in public life. David Halberstam convincingly used the term "the best and the brightest" ironically while demonstrating how extremely well-educated Americans, often reflecting an arrogance that might have been fostered in part by their elite college educations, made terrible decisions about American policy in Vietnam that led to substantial loss of human life and undermined democracy at home and abroad.[49] Perhaps the benefits of learning critical thinking and toleration of dissent are often offset by the reinforcement of an elitism and sense of entitlement that undermines democratic values.

Even if university teaching enables students to become better citizens, I think the primary function of both scholarship and teaching is academic. The production and dissemination of knowledge often has pragmatic societal benefits as well. It can contribute to health and safety and to the development of public policy. I think that these pragmatic benefits reinforce rather than underlie the fundamental justification for academic freedom. Knowledge itself is a great value to society even when it does not produce additional benefits.[50] The necessity of free speech in a democracy based on popular sovereignty may be the most long-standing and fundamental First Amendment value. But the First Amendment value of encouraging the production and dissemination of knowledge corresponds more closely to the primary function of professors in scholarship and teaching.

The Paradox of Peer Review

The emphasis in the 1915 Declaration on the role of peer review in determining the boundaries of academic freedom has been reinforced by over a century of practice. As the 1915 Declaration recommended in its concluding "practical proposals," the regulations of American universities overwhelmingly recognize the role of the faculty in making decisions about the appointment and dismissal of professors.[51] Yet peer review presents a paradox. Academic freedom protects individual professors when expert expression meets academic standards as defined by committees of faculty peers. The existence of these standards provides a bulwark for academic freedom. Yet academic freedom, while dependent on these standards, does not insulate professors from the results of contests about defining and applying them. It does not give professors a right to deviate from the standards established by the community of scholars. Ironically, Joan Scott observes, the critic of orthodoxy "must find legitimation in the very discipline whose orthodoxy he or she challenges." As a paradoxical result, "if academic freedom is to remain an effective protection for individual critical scholarly inquiry, it cannot be invoked in most of the battles about the rules and standards that underwrite the individual scholar's open-ended pursuit of understanding."[52] Professors who lose battles over disciplinary standards have limitations on their scholarly freedom, but those limitations do not constitute violations of academic freedom.[53]

As scholars have stressed, and as legal decisions have occasionally observed, the collective interpretation of academic standards changes over time.[54] The faculties of many American law schools, which initially resisted interdisciplinary scholarship, have over the past few decades preferred it to the doctrinal scholarship that previously prevailed. History departments have become more interested in social history than in intellectual history, departments of political science have placed more emphasis on quantitative studies than on political thought, and English departments have favored postmodern analysis over more traditional literary studies. Similar examples could easily be identified in virtually any field of intellectual inquiry. More generally, the assertion in the 1915 Declaration that scholars should state their conclusions "with dignity, courtesy, and temperateness of language" would be rejected by most scholars today as an anachronistic standard that unduly constrains the expression of academic views.[55]

Disciplinary standards in psychiatry and psychology were rapidly changing around the time the Michigan judge assumed that it was obviously within the bounds of legitimate academic discussion to call homosexuality a disease.[56] The American Psychiatric Association and the American Psychological Association, which for decades had listed homosexuality as a disease, had only recently changed their positions. The assertion that homosexuality is a disease, the overwhelming majority of psychiatrists and psychologists today might believe, lacks any plausible academic support, the equivalent of an astronomer claiming that the sun revolves around the earth. If so, it would not violate academic freedom to deny tenure to a psychology professor whose publications asserted that homosexuality is a disease, just as it would not have violated academic freedom a generation earlier to deny tenure to a psychology professor whose publications asserted presciently that homosexuality is not a disease at a time when the overwhelming consensus of the field maintained that it is.

Academic standards that dominate at a particular time may be deemed in retrospect to have denied recognition to promising scholarship. The early scholarship of future Nobel Prize winners was ignored or rejected by their professional peers. Barbara McClintock's work on transposable genetic elements in maize, which won the Nobel Prize in 1983, received little academic interest when she initially presented it in the early 1950s.[57] Professional peers repeatedly denied the grant applications of James Watson to support research that led to his Nobel Prize in 1962 for his role in discovering the structure of DNA.[58] Katalin Karikó, the winner of the 2023 Nobel Prize in Physiology or Medicine, previously had been demoted with a pay cut by the University of Pennsylvania after years of unsuccessful applications for grant funding, lost her lab space, and was told that she was "not of faculty quality."[59] These examples indicate that some new ideas are difficult to assimilate within the existing conceptual framework of a discipline, though they may prevail as that framework changes over time.[60]

Yet the solution to retrospective mistakes is not to abandon peer review and allow people without expertise to determine the merits of academic work.[61] Rather, these examples suggest that professors within a discipline should be generous while considering new ideas, giving them a chance to become accepted over time. They should also be generous in protecting formerly dominant ideas in a field that are no longer popular. In addition to "an intellectual experiment station, where new ideas may germinate," the 1915 Declaration maintained, a university should be the "conservator of all genuine elements of value in the past thought and life of mankind which are not in the fashion of the moment."[62] The judge who protected advocacy of vaginal delivery as an exercise of academic freedom appropriately noted that the medical use of leeches, only recently considered "the height of medieval superstition," has "made its comeback" in modern microsurgery.[63]

Just as the collective decisions of an academic discipline can define academic standards, they can determine what areas of expertise a department may prefer. An AAUP report published in 1986 pointed out that departments have limited resources. "The principles of academic freedom," it concluded, "do not assume that every tributary and rivulet from a disciplinary stream has per se a right to be represented within any given department; it is accordingly not a violation of academic freedom that some candidates be ruled out of consideration on ground of area of interest." The report encouraged departments to include different subjects and methods and asserted that disputes over their value are a healthy sign. It urged departments to avoid basing their decisions on conventional wisdom or prevailing orthodoxy. But it did not recognize a right of professors to assert that these decisions violated their academic freedom.[64]

The restrictions on individual academic freedom imposed by the collective judgments of academic disciplines is mitigated in part by disciplinary norms of tolerance for divergent opinions.[65] Judith Butler urges the recognition of "good work that adheres to modes of inquiry and methods that we do not share." Insight into the contestability and instability of professional norms, she adds, should produce humility in applying them and reluctance to efface the diversity of a field by legislating a particular norm.[66] Joan Scott calls academic freedom "an ethical practice" because it recognizes the contestability of disciplinary standards, the possibility of their transformation, and the danger of consolidating around a particular conception of truth, including the conception of truth itself.[67]

The deference to peer review in the analysis of academic freedom is not unlimited. If evidence exists that decisions by peer review committees justified on academic grounds were made carelessly, in bad faith, or in violation of law, administrators and judges should overturn them.[68] Despite the admonitions of the 1915 Declaration that faculty peers must demonstrate "the capacity for impersonal judgment" and exercise appropriate "judicial severity" when evaluating their colleagues, they do not always do so. Personal friendship or animosity, professional jealousy, reluctance to harm a colleague's career or the collegiality of a department, reliance on political rather than scholarly criteria, and discrimination can interfere with the appropriate exercise of peer review.[69] The 1966 Statement on Government of Colleges and Universities, jointly formulated by the AAUP, the American Council of Education, and the Association of Governing Boards of Colleges and Universities, recognizes that faculty have primary responsibility over academic matters, but "in exceptional circumstances" appropriately justifies reversals of faculty decisions by administrators "for compelling reasons which should be stated in detail."[70] Deviations by professors from academic standards in peer review provide such compelling reasons, for judges as well as for administrators.

Though not perfect, peer review is the best way to identify and protect the boundaries of academic freedom. No better alternative has ever been proposed.[71] Recent investigations and critiques of peer review in tenure decisions,[72] in the selection of articles for scholarly journals,[73] and the award of federal grants to researchers[74] support reform rather than abolition. Suggestions include more diversity among reviewers and more due process for rejected candidates, including written statements of reasons and opportunities to rebut them. As one study observed, peer review is often compared with Winston Churchill's reflection about democracy: "a system full of problems but the least worst we have."[75]

Intramural Speech

The justification of academic freedom as necessary to protect the functions of professors in the production and dissemination of knowledge applies most clearly to their scholarship and teaching. Does this justification extend to intramural speech by professors about university affairs more generally? My answer is yes, but only to the extent that intramural speech addresses educational issues. This question has substantial practical significance because both the experience of the AAUP and the evidence of case law reveal how many disputes between professors and universities have arisen over alleged retaliation for intramural speech.[76] Much, perhaps most, controversial speech by professors fits within this category.

Professors have greatest expertise about subjects within their academic specialties. But their expertise also extends to more general educational issues. The resolution of these issues influences how knowledge is produced and disseminated to an extent that justifies the protection of speech about them through the distinctive First Amendment right of academic freedom.

As with scholarship and teaching, policy positions of the AAUP support including intramural speech within the scope of this right. Speech during the process of peer review is the category of intramural speech most clearly related to academic freedom. Although the 1915 Declaration did not explicitly address intramural speech, its repeated emphasis on the centrality of peer review by expert colleagues to the protection of academic freedom in scholarship and teaching surely contemplates that academic freedom extends to expression in peer review.

Statements in AAUP documents since the 1915 Declaration and scattered comments in judicial decisions support extending the First Amendment right of academic freedom to other intramural speech about educational issues. The 1966 Statement on Government addresses the relative roles of the governing board, the president, and the faculty in university governance. It is particularly influential within the academic world because it is jointly formulated by organizations of universities and trustees as well as by the AAUP. "The faculty," it declares, "has primary responsibility for such fundamental areas as curriculum, subject matter and methods of instruction, research, faculty status, and those aspects of student life which relate to the educational process." The 1966 Statement bases this primary responsibility on the "fact" that faculty "judgment is central to general educational policy." It asserts that "scholars in a particular field or activity have the chief competence for judging the work of their colleagues," but also recognizes "the more general competence of experienced faculty personnel committees having a broader charge." It did not further define this general competence or explore its relation to other areas of primary faculty responsibility. Although focused on the distribution of responsibility in university governance rather than on rights of expression, the 1966 Statement refers to the "means of communication" among the faculty, administration, and governing board, including circulation of memoranda and various meetings and committees.[77] The rationale of this statement supports the application of academic freedom to speech by professors about the educational issues that are their primary responsibility.

In a 1994 document, "On the Relationship of Faculty Governance to Academic Freedom," the AAUP provided stronger support for extending academic freedom to intramural speech. The document recognized that the

AAUP had not previously made this relationship clear. It asserted that a strong system of faculty governance protects the exercise of academic freedom and that, correspondingly, professors must have academic freedom to address issues of institutional governance without fear of retribution. Like the 1966 Statement, it maintained that faculty expertise extends beyond disciplinary competencies to the climate in which teaching and research takes place. Whereas the 1966 Statement referred only to faculty personnel committees in discussing the general expertise of professors, the 1996 document asserted more specifically that this broader expertise should be exercised, and protected, in addressing other issues of governance.[78]

Yet much intramural speech by faculty is not related to either specialized disciplinary or general educational expertise. A First Amendment theory of academic freedom based on the contribution of the expertise of professors to the production and dissemination of knowledge does not extend to such speech, though much of it might be protected by other First Amendment principles covering speech by citizens and public employees. The 1966 Statement helps define the scope of educational policy by differentiating the faculty's primary responsibility in this area from the responsibilities of the governing board and the president. The governing board, for example, has a central role in managing the endowment, obtaining capital and operating funds, and in assessing how to use the predictable resources of the university to meet its future needs. The president is largely responsible for maintaining and creating institutional resources and for many nonacademic activities. The 1966 Statement appropriately encourages joint effort, including the exchange of information and views, among the governing board, the president, and the faculty about all matters of importance to the university. But faculty expression on economic and administrative matters within the primary responsibility and expertise of the governing board and the president is more difficult to translate convincingly into a claim of academic freedom than intramural speech about educational matters within the primary responsibility of the faculty.

Extramural Political Speech

Under the theory that the societal value of expert academic speech in the production and dissemination of knowledge justifies a distinctive First Amendment right of academic freedom, the extramural political speech of professors raises issues of academic freedom only if it addresses matters within their expertise. Just as the general First Amendment law of free speech and employee-speech jurisprudence govern the extramural political speech of other university employees, they govern the extramural political speech of professors unrelated to their expertise.

Contrary to this analysis, significant commentary, including from the AAUP itself, does not differentiate academic freedom from political expression. Although the AAUP has provided no theoretical justification for its extension of academic freedom to extramural political speech, some commentators have defended this broad conception. Advocating a "general theory" of academic freedom, John Searle claims that it includes the right of professors "not to suffer academic penalties through the exercise of their rights as citizens."[79] Joan Scott ascribes a similar position to her father, who lost his tenured job as a high school teacher in New York City in the early years of the Cold War. For him, academic freedom meant the "right not to be judged by any criteria but the quality of his teaching or scholarship." Scott's father was dismissed for his refusal to discuss his political beliefs and affiliations.[80] Searle also defends his general theory of academic freedom by reasoning that "the university is an institutional embodiment of the general social values of free inquiry and free expression together with a theory of specialized scholarly competence."[81] Denial of general rights of free speech on campus, Searle seems to assert, violates academic freedom whether or not the speech relates to an academic issue.

Other justifications for extending academic freedom to extramural political speech are more closely tied to the distinctively academic functions of professors. Some have maintained that uncertainty about the border between academic and political expression would inhibit faculty speech even on topics that should be considered within their academic expertise. The reports of AAUP committees appointed to investigate claimed violations of academic freedom at universities often make this point.[82] Some worry that the extramural political speech of professors could be used as a pretext to dismiss them for their scholarly views, the argument made by Arthur Lovejoy in 1916 immediately after the AAUP adopted the 1915 Declaration. Some believe that if universities punish extramural political expression of any kind they create a general atmosphere of suppression, inhibiting academic expression by professors in scholarship and teaching by prompting understandable concern that universities would punish it as well.[83] Most broadly, some assert that professors are able to apply to general issues of public concern the distinctive scholarly standards of critical judgment they acquire through disciplinary training.[84]

I do not find these arguments convincing. All university employees, not just professors, should be able to engage in extramural political expression without suffering penalties at work. The contribution to knowledge derived from the expert academic speech of professors justifies distinctive protection, but there is no convincing basis for giving professors greater employment security than other employees for general political expression. If professors should not be judged by criteria other than their scholarship and teaching, all university employees should not be judged by criteria unrelated to their job functions. Similarly, if the university is the institutional embodiment of a general societal commitment to free inquiry and free expression, the entire university community, not just professors, should enjoy those freedoms. Universities should protect rights of political expression on campus and, as President Lowell of Harvard argued during World War I, should not allow political expression off campus to become the basis for institutional discipline.[85] General principles of free speech under the First Amendment accomplish these goals. Principles of academic freedom do not because they give professors rights that others cannot claim.

I doubt that the scholarly training and expertise of professors equips them to make better contributions than other citizens to general political discourse. Even if it did, I would not grant more protection to their extramural political expression. Traditionally and appropriately, both popular and constitutional discourse in the United States have treated political expression as an equal right of all citizens in a democracy, as some judges have observed in rejecting a distinctive First Amendment right of academic freedom for professors.[86] A democratic society should not depart from this fundamental principle of equality even in the unlikely event of convincing evidence that some identifiable subset of citizens has better judgment about public affairs than others.

It is plausible that the expert academic speech of professors could be deterred by threats to their expression about other issues. Professors concerned about where others would draw the line between scholarship and general political expression might avoid taking positions on subjects they consider within their academic expertise. Political statements could be invoked as a pretext to dismiss professors for their scholarly views. The suppression of extramural political expression could inhibit academic expression as well. Yet granting professors added protection for speech on general matters as a prophylactic to protect their academic speech is an inappropriate response to these concerns in a society committed to the equal protection of political expression. Instead, general First Amendment rights of free speech should be vigorously enforced, the potential use of pretexts should be carefully monitored, and the scope of speech meriting the protection of academic freedom should be generously construed.

The extension of First Amendment academic freedom to extramural political expression, moreover, may weaken the general First Amendment rights of professors. As professor Van Alstyne pointed out in his article "The Specific Theory of Academic Freedom and the General Issue of Civil Liberty," the added protections for academic expression provided by academic freedom come with the added responsibilities of having to meet "a professional standard of care."[87] He warned that this professional standard could be applied to the political expression of professors if the First Amendment right of academic freedom were construed to cover it. Indeed, he observed that many reports of AAUP committees investigating alleged violations of academic freedom had documented instances when universities invoked this higher professional standard to discipline professors for political expression. If the professional standard were applied, professors would have less freedom of political expression than other citizens would have under the general First Amendment law of free speech.[88] And while employee-speech jurisprudence allows the government to balance its interests as an employer against the free speech interests of its employees, it precludes the government from restricting their First Amendment rights when its interests as an employer are not implicated. The professional standard of care for the political expression of professors would impose an additional restriction on professors that does not apply to other government employees. The federal court decision that differentiated the political from the academic speech of professors, while rejecting university attempts to invoke a higher professional standard in applying the First Amendment to the political expression of a professor as a citizen, illustrates the danger of including extramural political expression within the scope of the First Amendment right of academic freedom.[89]

Sometimes the extramural political speech of professors does relate to academic expertise and, therefore, can raise issues of academic freedom. If a professor of economics rather than an astronomer spoke about the protective tariff, or if a twentieth-century European historian rather than an engineer denied the Holocaust, academic freedom could be implicated. The professor of engineering who made critical comments to the media after Hurricane Katrina about the US Army Corps of Engineers provides another example. Interestingly, the professor did not raise an academic freedom claim in his lawsuit. Rather, the court protected his comments under employee-speech jurisprudence by deciding that it addressed a matter of public concern and that talking to the media did not fall within his official duties.[90]

Judith Butler has offered some useful contemporary examples of expression at the blurred border of the academic and the political: a Straussian political philosopher who publishes articles in the Weekly Standard relating his academic views to current foreign policy issues; a professor of health medicine who makes public statements about the work of Doctors Without Borders; an anthropologist who works in Sudan and writes essays criticizing his own country's policies for their impact on the genocide there; and a professor of constitutional law who writes briefs challenging the legality of the war tribunals established to adjudicate the status of detainees in Guantanamo. Butler observes that professors who list these kinds of writings as part of their professional work, especially when submitted during consideration for promotion and tenure, make them seem more like academic publications. Other professors, by contrast, try to differentiate their political from their scholarly writings, as she herself does by not including some of her publications on her professional record. Butler points out as well that professors can develop academic expertise through activities that began as political commitments outside their disciplinary training. As her example she cities Noam Chomsky, a linguist who arguably developed expertise in American foreign policy though his political activities opposing American involvement in Vietnam.[91]

Despite borderline cases, the distinction between academic speech based on expertise and political expression as a citizen makes sense and in most contexts is clear, as Wigmore concluded a century ago in his debate with Lovejoy during the final stages of drafting the 1915 Declaration and as recent scholars have reiterated.[92] Even Pound's relatively broad and convincing conception of academic expertise that includes relating one's own academic expertise to other areas of knowledge would not extend to most extramural political expression by professors. While Pound's sociological jurisprudence connected law to the social sciences and pragmatic philosophy to address pressing societal problems, extramural political expression by professors more typically resembles Lowell's astronomer speaking about the protective tariff, where no relationship to one's own expertise exists.

It is important to emphasize as well that a significant amount of extramural political speech on subjects within a professor's academic expertise should not be treated as scholarly expression and, therefore, should not be subject to the constraints on it that are part of the justification for academic freedom. A law professor who represents a client in a lawsuit pertaining to the professor's area of expertise has a duty to represent the client vigorously within the ethical standards that apply to lawyers, standards that would permit, or perhaps even require, legal arguments in the client's interest that would not meet scholarly standards of accuracy. Indeed, official comments on the American Bar Association's Model Rules of Professional Conduct maintain that a "lawyer acting as an advocate in an adjudicative proceeding has an obligation to present the client's case with persuasive force" and "is not required to present an impartial exposition of the law or to vouch for the evidence submitted in a cause." The comments do place some limitations on advocates, who "must not allow the tribunal to be misled by false statements of law or fact or evidence that the lawyer knows to be false." Yet in most situations "an advocate has the limited responsibility of presenting one side of the matters that a tribunal should consider in reaching a decision; the conflicting position is expected to be presented by the opposing party."[93]

Other disciplines provide additional examples of speech related to expertise that should be considered outside the realm of scholarly expression covered by academic freedom. A political scientist running for public office might make statements about an opponent's voting record that could not withstand scholarly scrutiny. A professor whose scholarship includes the Israeli-Palestinian conflict might make public statements about it that are not scholarly in substance or in tone. A good example is the tweet: "Zionists, take responsibility: if your dream of an ethnocratic Israel is worth the murder of children, just f**king own it."[94] In neither of these examples is the professor intending to speak, or would be understood by others to be speaking, as a scholar.

Some extramural speech by professors on subjects within their expertise seems closer to the border of scholarly expression. A scientist speaking at a public rally in support of more government regulation to combat global warming might make exaggerated claims about the extent of its danger that could not be substantiated by empirical evidence necessary to convince peer reviewers for an academic journal. An economist who writes an op-ed article for a major newspaper objecting to government regulation of banks that are "too big to fail" might similarly make statements that would not satisfy peer review. A professor of psychiatry could claim that a candidate for president is mentally ill without following the procedures required by the American Psychiatric Association for making this diagnosis.[95] What if the engineer who criticized the US Army Corps of Engineers after Hurricane Katrina made inaccurate statements to the media about standards of engineering safety? When expression by a professor is at the blurred border of the academic and the political, whether or not the professor represents the expression as academic should be a significant factor. In many of the borderline examples provided by Professor Butler, a professor who places an article on a list of scholarly publications should be subjected to scholarly standards that should not otherwise apply.

In many contexts, by contrast, professors are clearly speaking as scholars when they make extramural public statements about matters within their expertise. Presenting a paper at an academic conference away from a professor's own campus is the most obvious example. Professors are also speaking as scholars when they rely on their academic knowledge in commenting on proposed laws before legislative committees or in testifying as expert witnesses at trials. Unlike a professor who represents a client, a professor who signs a "scholars" amicus brief on the meaning of the right to bear arms in the Second Amendment or a "scholars" letter to Congress about the meaning of the impeachment clause of the Constitution is invoking scholarly expertise to strengthen the persuasiveness of the position advocated and should be judged by academic standards that do not apply to citizens generally or to practicing lawyers.[96]

Procedural Protections

A substantive First Amendment right of academic freedom should incorporate procedural protections. Scholars and judges have observed as a general matter that the value of substantive constitutional rights depends on the procedures available to protect them. More particularly, they have maintained that the First Amendment itself requires procedural due process designed to protect freedom of expression. The details of due process, they add, appropriately vary with the context of the First Amendment claim. Supreme Court decisions in the 1960s required notice and a hearing before the state could seize allegedly obscene material or enjoin public rallies or meetings. In 1972, however, a divided Supreme Court reversed lower-court holdings that a public university must offer a pretermination hearing to a nontenured professor who claimed that his constitutionally protected expression was the cause of its decision not to renew his appointment. In my opinion, that decision was incorrect.

Just as substantive interpretation of the First Amendment should differentiate academic freedom from free speech generally, distinctive forms of due process can best protect the substantive right of academic freedom. The 1915 Declaration convincingly incorporated peer review within its conception of academic freedom by emphasizing that only faculty members possess the expertise to assess whether speech meets the academic standards that justify the protection of academic freedom. Though the First Amendment right of academic freedom applies most clearly to the substantive expert expression that contributes to the production and dissemination of knowledge, it should similarly include rights of pretermination due process through peer review.

Advocates of "First Amendment 'due process'" have taken as their starting point the observation by Justice Frankfurter that the "history of liberty has largely been the history of observance of procedural standards."[97] Frankfurter made this point in a case involving criminal procedure, but it applies to all liberties, including those protected by the First Amendment. Two important articles published in 1970 approvingly noticed that the courts had increasingly identified the First Amendment, in addition to the due process clause of the Fourteenth Amendment, as an independent source of procedural rights.[98] The articles maintained that the substantive goals of the First Amendment should guide the details of the due process emanating from it.[99] Henry Monaghan, who came up with the felicitous phrase "First Amendment 'due process,'" wrote: "Like the substantive rules themselves, insensitive procedures can 'chill' the right of free expression."[100] While recognizing that the precise procedural rules should vary in different First Amendment contexts,[101] the articles emphasized that in many circumstances procedural protections for First Amendment rights can be effective only if they occur before the government action that affects speech.[102] Prospective relief prior to the ultimate resolution of the free speech claim, moreover, may be necessary to protect the free speech right.[103]

In the university context, the threat of job loss for a professor or of expulsion for a student can easily deter speech. Even the temporary suspension of a professor or a student can have a significant impact on the ability to exercise First Amendment rights. When a professor or a student claims that a university decision to dismiss, expel, or suspend was motivated by speech protected by the First Amendment, pretermination procedures should be required to safeguard this constitutional right before a potential violation occurs.[104] Subsequent litigation to vindicate First Amendment rights presents numerous difficulties, including the delay and expense of litigation, the possibility of negative publicity, and the danger that reinstatement might not be a feasible remedy even if a court ultimately finds a violation of First Amendment rights.[105] By the time of the judicial decision, the professor often has had to find alternative employment, sometimes reluctantly outside higher education and even unrelated to his professional training and expertise, and sometimes in a new location. Loss of contact with students and colleagues during judicial review exacerbates the difficulties of resuming the position from which the professor was unconstitutionally dismissed. The experience of the AAUP underlines these difficulties. Even when the efforts of the AAUP eventually persuade a university to make an offer of reinstatement, it is frequently not feasible for the professor to accept it. I lack similar direct knowledge about students, but I assume that they, perhaps more than faculty, find it difficult as a practical matter to return to a university when a court, often years after their expulsion, determines that the university had violated their First Amendment rights.

Sensitivity to context suggests that it would not make sense to impose the same pretermination due process requirements on all university decisions affecting speech.[106] But at a minimum a professor or student who alleges retaliation for expression protected by the First Amendment should be entitled to a statement of reasons from the university and the opportunity for a hearing to contest them. In the case reversed by the Supreme Court, the district court judge convincingly reasoned that the substantive First Amendment protection for a nontenured professor denied reappointment "is useless without procedural safeguards." The professor alleged that his criticism of the administration and board of regents had prompted his nonrenewal, and the judge held that he was entitled to minimum standards of due process. He defined those standards as including a statement of reasons for the decision and a hearing at which the professor could submit relevant evidence while maintaining the burden of going forward and the burden of proof. Only if the professor demonstrates that the stated reasons are wholly inappropriate or without factual basis, the judge added, would the university have to defend them.[107]

A divided panel of the court of appeals affirmed. The majority observed that in cases with a background of controversial speech, the due process required by the district judge constitutes a prophylactic against retaliation for the exercise of First Amendment rights.[108] Procedural due process, the dissenting judge asserted by contrast, is totally separate from the substantive protection of constitutional rights.[109]

While reversing and holding that the nontenured professor did not have a constitutional right to due process before termination, the Supreme Court majority, unlike the dissenting judge on the court of appeals, did not entirely dissociate substance from procedure. It noted that sometimes the Supreme Court had afforded procedural protections before determining the substantive First Amendment right. As examples, it cited the prior cases about public rallies and meetings and the seizure of allegedly obscene material, adding a reference to Monaghan's article, "First Amendment 'Due Process.'" But the majority ignored Monaghan's conclusion that this due process should apply as well to professors facing dismissal. Rather, it claimed that the prior decisions involved situations in which the state action would directly affect First Amendment interests. "Whatever may be a teacher's rights of free speech," it observed in concluding that there was no direct impact in this case, "holding a teaching job at a state university, *simpliciter*, is not itself a free speech interest."[110] Yet the argument for procedural rights was not that a teaching job is itself a free speech interest, but that the danger of losing the job as a result of constitutionally protected speech is a free speech interest meriting pretermination due process. As an AAUP amicus brief maintained, without procedural safeguards a summary termination could easily conceal a clear First Amendment violation.[111] This argument, which the Supreme Court majority did not address, is convincing.

Pretermination peer review within the university, moreover, minimizes the danger of inappropriate judicial intrusion if a professor challenges a university decision on First Amendment grounds. An initial determination by expert professional peers, the AAUP emphasized, would alleviate pressure on the courts to evaluate academic matters themselves. Rather than intruding the judiciary into the internal academic decisions of universities, as some judges have asserted, interpreting procedural due process to require peer review before termination of a faculty appointment should help ensure that the internal decision would be made correctly.[112]

The greater procedural protection for tenured than for nontenured faculty set forth in AAUP recommended institutional regulations, which have become the widespread norm throughout American universities, illustrates two general themes central to the constitutional relationship between procedure and substance: the extent to which substantive rights depend on the procedures available to safeguard them, and the relevance of context in determining the specific form of due process. The regulations of most universities contain separate provisions for tenured and untenured faculty that are derived from the AAUP recommendations. The provisions governing tenured faculty preclude the university from dismissing a tenured professor unless it initiates a proceeding and provides a formal hearing before faculty peers at which it bears the burden of proving adequate cause. The provisions governing nontenured faculty, by contrast, place the burden on the professor who receives notice of nonrenewal to allege that the university violated his academic freedom. They do not require a formal hearing unless a faculty committee so recommends after reviewing the evidence submitted by the professor and the university. Even if the faculty committee recommends a formal hearing, the untenured professor has the burden of proving a violation of academic freedom.[113]

These greater procedural protections for tenured faculty members make it harder for a university to dismiss them for any reason, including for reasons that might violate their academic freedom. Tenured professors, therefore, are more secure in expressing their scholarly views than their nontenured colleagues and, to this significant extent, have more academic freedom. The distinction between tenured and nontenured faculty dates from the 1915 Declaration itself and was reinforced by the 1940 Statement of the AAUP and the Association of American Colleges. Yet the 1915 Declaration maintains that the expert academic speech of all professors should be protected by academic freedom. "During the probationary period" before the tenure decision, the 1940 Statement asserts more specifically, "a teacher should have the academic freedom that all other members of the faculty have."[114] In response to the tremendous growth of part-time faculty appointments in recent decades, the AAUP has added a recommended institutional regulation recognizing their academic freedom and granting them procedural rights to claim violations analogous to the rights of probationary professors on the tenure track.[115] In practice, however, the differences in procedural protections allow more academic freedom for tenured professors. The 1940 Statement asserts that tenure is a "means" to the end of academic freedom.[116] Because nontenured professors lack this "means," they do not have the same academic freedom as "all other members of the faculty."

The different treatment of tenured and nontenured professors, though not explained in these documents themselves, can be justified by the function of academic expertise that underlies academic freedom. The probationary period of nontenured appointment gives the university time to assess a professor. The decision to award tenure reflects the university's judgment that the professor has demonstrated sufficient academic quality to justify shifting to the university the burden of demonstrating cause for dismissal.[117] Knowing that it will bear this burden arguably makes the university more rigorous in its review of the candidate for tenure, which promotes the public interest in assuring the value of academic expertise.[118] After a professor has received the presumption of professional quality conferred by tenure, moreover, it is more likely that an attempt to dismiss is not related to fitness but may instead be motivated by reasons that violate academic freedom.[119] While originating independently of any legal considerations, this analysis also makes sense as a matter of constitutional interpretation, supporting different forms of due process for tenured than for nontenured professors.

The extent to which First Amendment due process should require particular procedures can be developed over time. The AAUP's recommended procedures cover many issues at a level of detail that need not be imposed as a matter of constitutional law. Examples include the number of challenges to potential members of a peer review committee without stated cause and the number of days of notice prior to a hearing. Perhaps some more significant issues should also be left to institutional discretion, such as whether the peer review committee should be bound by strict rules of legal evidence or, as the AAUP recommends, should admit any evidence that may have probative value.[120] In a dispute raising issues of academic freedom, First Amendment due process at a minimum should require a statement of reasons on request and access to peer review.

Structural Protections

Substantive rights depend on structure as well as procedure, though no court has maintained that the First Amendment imposes structural requirements on universities. Just as the substance of academic freedom depends on the process of peer review, so the process of peer review depends on a structure, typically a committee, in which peer review occurs. The theory of academic freedom as a distinctive First Amendment right should require the structure that provides peer review. Should it also require other structural protection for the exercise of academic freedom? Arguably, for example, the effective presentation of faculty views on matters of educational policy depends on meaningful structures of faculty governance, as many universities have recognized by voluntarily establishing them. If the distinctive First Amendment right of academic freedom should include the substantive right of intramural expression by professors on matters of educational policy, should it also mandate structures of faculty governance to facilitate this expression?

In contrast to the strong argument for including protection of peer review within the distinctive First Amendment right of academic freedom, I think it is plausible and desirable but not essential to interpret this right as requiring access to structures of faculty governance. Organizations representing faculty, universities, and governing boards agreed in the 1966 Statement on Government about the importance of those structures. More specifically linking faculty governance to academic freedom, a subsequent AAUP statement asserted that "allocation of authority to the faculty in the areas of its responsibility is a necessary condition for the protection of academic freedom within the institution."[121]

Some scholarly commentary on academic freedom as a First Amendment right has emphasized the importance of structures of faculty governance but has also concluded that they are not constitutionally required. While defending an institutional right of academic freedom under the First Amendment, Peter Byrne argued that it should not extend to institutions that fail to recognize any role for faculty governance. Yet he also maintained that the First Amendment cannot impose an ideal structure of authority on universities.[122] In focusing on the "governance dimension of academic freedom" as a First Amendment right, Judith Areen asserted that if a university could demonstrate that the faculty or a duly established faculty committee agreed with an institutional decision in a dispute with a professor, "courts should presume that the matter was decided on academic grounds and defer to it." If the university had not consulted or had overruled the faculty, by contrast, she would place on the institution the burden of proving legitimate academic grounds. While providing this strong incentive for universities to establish and defer to faculty committees, she did not maintain that the First Amendment should be interpreted to require their existence. Such an unprecedented extension of the First Amendment, she feared, would jeopardize the institutional diversity that has been the traditional strength of American higher education.[123] Writing about freedom of intramural expression from a professional rather than a constitutional perspective, Matthew Finkin and Robert Post observed that although it "does not entitle faculty to participate in actual institutional decision making, such an entitlement would be the logical outgrowth of the idea of institutional citizenship on which this aspect of academic freedom rests."[124] Frustratingly, Finkin and Post did not elaborate this statement.

In analyzing academic freedom as a distinctive First Amendment right, I think it is a logical outgrowth of protection for intramural speech on matters of educational policy to require a structure of faculty governance that effectively enables it. As long as the university provides a meaningful structure of governance, its details need not be subject to First Amendment scrutiny, just as the details of due process can be left to university discretion. Minimal procedural requirements in peer review do not significantly threaten a university's ability to determine the substantive standards for appointment and tenure.[125] Similarly, minimal structural requirements do not significantly constrain its substantive educational decisions. The constitutional imposition of minimal procedural and structural standards would not be a major intrusion into university autonomy or to the healthy diversity of American higher education.

Yet the argument for extending First Amendment academic freedom to the structure of governance is not as strong as extending it to peer review. The core substantive right of academic freedom in scholarship and teaching depends on peer review. Formal structures of faculty governance facilitate the communication of faculty views on matters of educational policy, but other, less formal, methods of faculty communication with administrators and trustees are available. I would prefer an interpretation of the First Amendment right of academic freedom that would require some minimal structural protection for faculty expression about educational policy while allowing substantial university autonomy in determining its details. Yet I would not consider it a grave error if courts refused to provide even this minimal First Amendment protection for faculty governance. Structures providing peer review are essential to the protection of academic freedom; faculty senates and similar structures of university governance are not.

Conclusion

The distinctive First Amendment theory of academic freedom I propose is justified by the societal value of protecting the expert academic speech of professors whose boundaries are determined through peer review. This justification differentiates academic freedom from the general right of free speech while connecting it to the fundamental First Amendment interest in promoting the production and dissemination of knowledge. It also connects the most comprehensive and influential justification for academic freedom within the academic community, the AAUP's 1915 Declaration, with First Amendment analysis of its meaning. Yet contrary to the position of the 1915 Declaration, this justification does not extend to expression by professors outside their expertise, to which the First Amendment right of academic freedom should not apply. This conclusion should mitigate understandable concerns that a distinctive First Amendment right of academic freedom would undermine the basic First Amendment principle of equal rights in a democracy to expression about politics and other matters of public concern.

Academic freedom most clearly applies to scholarship and teaching. In addition to protecting the content of ideas, academic freedom should enable professors to conduct their scholarship and teaching in ways that promote the production and dissemination of knowledge. In scholarship, it should protect the interests of professors in access to research material, in confidentiality for research sources and unpublished data and drafts, and in publishing without prior approval of funding agencies. In teaching, it should protect classroom discussion from the inhibiting threat of external scrutiny and should allow professors substantial discretion to decide what and how to teach.

It is plausible to extend the First Amendment right of academic freedom beyond scholarship and teaching. Because academic freedom only attaches to expression that meets academic standards as determined by faculty peers, expression during peer review should also be covered. Other intramural expression about university affairs within the expertise of faculty, which includes their general competence as educators as well as subjects within their scholarly specialties, is sufficiently related to the production and dissemination of knowledge to qualify for protection. The general principle of "First Amendment due process," which recognizes that the value of substantive First Amendment rights depends on the adequacy of procedures available to protect them, applies to the distinctive First Amendment right of academic freedom. First Amendment due process for academic freedom at a minimum should include rights to a statement of reasons for discipline or discharge and access to peer review. It is also persuasive to require structural as well as procedural protections of the substantive First

Amendment right of academic freedom. The crucial role of peer review in the analysis of academic freedom highlights the importance of a structure in which it occurs. And if First Amendment academic freedom protects broader intramural speech within faculty educational expertise, it is plausible, though less compelling than for peer review, to require structures of faculty governance to enable its expression.

Having addressed academic freedom as a First Amendment right of professors, I proceed to explore its meaning as a First Amendment right of universities. Chapter 7 analyzes the judicial development of institutional academic freedom. Chapter 8 proposes a theory of institutional academic freedom as a distinctive First Amendment right of universities.

7

The Development of Institutional Academic Freedom as a First Amendment Right of Universities

THE SUPREME COURT initially recognized academic freedom as a First Amendment right of professors in cases between professors and the government in the 1950s and 1960s. Beginning in the late 1970s, it eventually extended the First Amendment protection of academic freedom to universities as institutions. Opinions often invoked the language of the South African statement on academic freedom, quoted by Justice Frankfurter in his concurrence in *Sweezy*, that identified "the four essential freedoms of a university—to determine for itself on academic grounds who may teach, what may be taught, how it shall be taught, and who may be admitted to study."[1] The *Sweezy* decision protected a lecturer, but it was a small step to invoke these four freedoms as constituting a First Amendment right of institutional academic freedom. By stressing the importance of judicial deference to the academic decisions of universities, justices associated with the First Amendment a position their predecessors had made in numerous other doctrinal contexts since the *Dartmouth College* case in the early nineteenth century.

In contrast to its decisions about professors, some Supreme Court decisions about universities clearly identified academic freedom as a First Amendment right and applied it to determine the outcome. And while Supreme Court decisions about universities continued to invoke general First Amendment principles in cases that raised issues of academic freedom, two important concurring opinions differentiated academic freedom as a distinctive First Amendment right that general First Amendment principles could undermine. One of these concurring opinions recognized the possibility of conflicting academic freedom claims between professors and universities, and some lower-court decisions had to resolve these conflicts.

Lower-court decisions about institutional academic freedom share many of the characteristics of lower-court decisions about the individual academic freedom of professors. Many more cases arose in in the lower courts than in the Supreme Court. The greater number of cases presented a correspondingly greater variety of academic freedom claims. In resolving these claims, judges elaborated the scope of the First Amendment right. But as judges themselves sometimes acknowledged, their decisions barely explored the meaning of this right and provided little justification for it. As in Chapters 3 through 6 regarding the academic freedom of professors, in Chapters 7 through 9 I organize and classify the case law regarding institutional academic freedom before presenting my own theoretical analysis. The case law indicates issues the theory should address and provides realistic contexts for illustrating how the theory would operate in practice. The cases discussed in this chapter reveal that universities have asserted their institutional academic freedom to evaluate students and faculty, to regulate scholarship and teaching, and to resist interference from the state.

Supreme Court Decisions

Supreme Court decisions attached the First Amendment right of academic freedom to universities while upholding institutional decisions to implement affirmative action in student admissions and to dismiss students for failing to meet academic standards. Concurring opinions maintained that this right extends to university decisions about student extracurricular activities. Other decisions rejected university assertions of a First Amendment right of institutional academic freedom. One unanimous decision denied that this right allows a university to resist disclosure of confidential peer review material to the Equal Employment Opportunity Commission (EEOC) during an investigation of a faculty claim of employment discrimination. Another unanimous decision maintained that it did not invalidate a law that prohibited federal funding for universities whose nondiscrimination policies excluded military recruiters. Its application to university rules limiting access to campus by members of the public was thoroughly briefed but not decided when the Court held that the underlying case had become moot. As with individual academic freedom, some justices relied on institutional academic freedom in cases where others ignored it.

Whereas none of the Supreme Court cases recognizing academic freedom as a First Amendment right of professors relied on it as the doctrinal basis for the decision, in some cases the First Amendment right of institutional academic freedom determined the result. Justices identified governing boards, administrators, and faculty bodies as exercising institutional academic freedom without differentiating their roles. They recognized that the individual academic freedom of a professor could conflict with the institutional academic freedom of a university, though no Supreme Court case directly presented this issue. Just as cases about individual academic freedom exhibited ambiguity and confusion about the relationship between academic freedom and free speech, cases about institutional academic freedom exhibited ambiguity and confusion about the relationship between academic freedom and institutional autonomy. The institutional cases resembled the individual cases in other ways. They occasionally maintained that general First Amendment principles are inapplicable to, or even inconsistent with, the First Amendment protection of academic freedom. And while extending institutional academic freedom beyond the core areas of scholarship and teaching to broader issues of educational policy, they also recognized government interests that could outweigh interests in academic freedom.

Affirmative Action

Justice Powell's dispositive opinion in *University of California v. Bakke,* the 1978 landmark affirmative action case at the medical school of the University of California, Davis, was the first time that a Supreme Court justice explicitly applied the First Amendment right of academic freedom to an institutional decision made by a university. Although Powell wrote only for himself and none of the other eight justices addressed the First Amendment or academic freedom, twenty-five years later the Supreme Court majority asserted that it endorsed his analysis. When the Supreme Court majority subsequently invalidated the affirmative action programs at Harvard and the University of North Carolina in 2023, it reviewed these prior cases. Repeating without questioning the earlier identification of institutional academic freedom as a First Amendment right, the Court based its analysis on the equal protection clause of the Fourteenth Amendment.

Four justices in *Bakke* interpreted the equal protection clause of the Fourteenth Amendment as allowing affirmative action based on race to remedy past discrimination. Four other justices opposed the affirmative action program on statutory grounds. Disagreeing with both positions, Justice

Powell provided the fifth vote for invalidating the program but also for permitting the use of race under certain circumstances.[2] According to Justice Powell, a university's First Amendment right of academic freedom can constitute the compelling state interest that is necessary to justify racial classifications otherwise prohibited by the equal protection clause.[3]

Quoting key passages from *Sweezy* and *Keyishian* for support, Powell crisply placed academic freedom within the purview of the First Amendment. "Academic freedom," he wrote, "though not a specifically enumerated constitutional right, long has been viewed as a special concern of the First Amendment." He derived his analysis from the sentence of the South African statement, quoted at length by Frankfurter in his *Sweezy* concurrence, that identified "the four essential freedoms of a university." Powell cited Frankfurter as the source of this sentence, not the South African statement itself, which was written as a protest by senior scholars and administrators of their government's introduction of apartheid to exclude Black students from their universities. Powell, by contrast, invoked this language to justify racial preferences that promote "a diverse student body." Yet his application of the South African statement to an institutional decision involving student admissions and race was much closer to its original context than its initial quotation by Frankfurter in *Sweezy* to protect a lecturer from a government investigation into subversive activities in the United States during the Cold War of the 1950s.[4]

Powell relied on the fourth of the freedoms identified in the South African statement, "who may be admitted to study," to assert that the "freedom of a university to make its own judgments as to education includes the selection of its student body." The creation of a diverse student body for educational reasons, Powell concluded, "clearly is a constitutionally permissible goal." Powell had rejected the university's other three justifications for its affirmative action program: (1) increasing the number of historically disfavored minorities in the medical profession, (2) remedying the effects of past societal discrimination, and (3) increasing the number of physicians practicing in underserved communities.[5] His recognition of a First Amendment right of institutional academic freedom was the only legal basis for his support of affirmative action by universities.

Powell elaborated the educational value of a diverse student body by associating it with passages he quoted from *Sweezy* and *Keyishian*. Student diversity, he maintained, promotes the atmosphere of "speculation, experiment and creation" identified as "the business of a university" in the South

African statement quoted by Frankfurter in *Sweezy*. He added that it also contributes to the "wide exposure" to the "robust exchange of ideas" emphasized in the paragraph on academic freedom in *Keyishian*. The educational benefits of student diversity, Powell observed, extend beyond the purely academic. He quoted in a footnote two paragraphs from a defense of affirmative action by the president of Princeton University, who stressed how much learning occurs informally, not just in the classroom but also in conversations with roommates and through participation in sports and student government. In discussing medical education, the specific context of *Bakke*, Powell pointed out that exposure to a diverse student body would better equip future physicians to serve the heterogeneous population of the United States. Yet he stressed that the educational interest in diversity protected by institutional academic freedom can only be a compelling state interest when many different characteristics are considered. The affirmative action plan at Davis, he concluded, did not meet this standard because it "focused *solely* on ethnic diversity."[6]

The amicus brief filed jointly by Columbia, Harvard, Stanford, and the University of Pennsylvania contributed significantly to Powell's analysis in *Bakke*. Scores of other amicus briefs and the parties themselves focused on the meaning of the equal protection clause of the Fourteenth Amendment. The brief of these four universities, by contrast, related student diversity to the First Amendment and academic freedom. Indeed, the brief contained a lengthy appendix describing the Harvard College admission program, which Powell included as an appendix to his opinion, to illustrate, in contrast to the program at Davis, the permissible use of race as one diversity factor among many. Yet the brief focused much more on the general educational value of student diversity and the need for judicial deference to the academic judgments of universities than on the First Amendment and academic freedom. It did not refer to the First Amendment or academic freedom until late in the brief, and then did so very much in passing.[7] Although Powell was alerted by this brief to the potential use of the First Amendment and academic freedom to defend affirmative action, he made these connections much more explicitly than the brief itself.[8]

Powell had hoped that the Supreme Court majority would agree with his analysis in *Bakke*. A lengthy memorandum from one of his law clerks months before the decision reasoned that this approach offered the "best opportunity for taking a middle course" in resolving the case because it would limit to universities the use of diversity as a compelling state interest.[9]

The memorandum observed that diversity is fundamental to the educational mission of universities, whereas for other state institutions, such as the federal Department of Housing and Urban Development, diversity is simply one means of furthering an "unrelated administrative mission."[10] By the time he wrote an outline of a possible opinion just a month before the official publication of the *Bakke* decision, Powell realized that four justices favored justifications for affirmative action that he rejected and, unlike Powell, were committed to upholding the constitutionality of the affirmative action program at the medical school. Yet Powell expected that those four justices, while writing separately to express their broader defense of affirmative action, would also endorse his analysis of "Diversity / First Amendment Concerns."[11] Although these justices joined portions of Powell's opinion, none joined his analysis of diversity.[12]

In *Grutter v. Bollinger,* a case arising at the University of Michigan twenty-five years after *Bakke,* the Supreme Court issued its next major decision about affirmative action in university admissions. Observing that *Bakke* was a fractured decision, the five-person majority, in an opinion written by Justice O'Connor, announced that "we endorse Justice Powell's view that student body diversity is a compelling state interest that can justify the use of race in university admissions." Powell, O'Connor pointed out, "grounded his analysis in the academic freedom that 'long has been viewed as a special concern of the First Amendment.'"[13] She asserted later in her opinion that Powell's opinion "invoked our cases recognizing a constitutional dimension, grounded in the First Amendment, of educational autonomy." Is it significant that O'Connor referred to "educational autonomy" instead of "academic freedom"? While citing *Sweezy* and *Keyishian,* she did not refer to their discussions of academic freedom. Rather, she cited them to support a more general conclusion. The Supreme Court, she maintained, has "long recognized that, given the important purpose of public education and the expansive freedoms of speech and thought associated with the university environment, universities occupy a special niche in our constitutional tradition."[14]

Justice O'Connor provided other indications that academic freedom did not play a central role in her analysis. She agreed with the district court's conclusion that a diverse student body promotes cross-racial understanding, which improves classroom discussion. She also cited numerous studies showing the relationship between student diversity and learning outcomes. Yet she did not associate these benefits with academic freedom. She then focused on the role of diversity in preparing students to work in an increasingly diverse society, relying on briefs by major American businesses and by retired officers and civilian leaders of the United States military. Whereas Justice Powell in *Bakke* explicitly tied student diversity to the educational benefits of academic freedom identified in *Sweezy* and *Keyishian,* the business briefs referred to the compelling state interest in training students to compete globally and the military brief referred to the compelling state interest in national security fostered by a diverse officer corps that is recruited from universities. Further shifting the focus from the educational benefits of academic freedom, Justice O'Connor observed that universities provide the training ground for future leaders and stressed the need for those leaders to be accepted by the general public. "In order to cultivate a set of leaders with legitimacy in the eyes of the citizenry," she declared, "it is necessary that the path to leadership be visibly open to talented and qualified individuals of every race and ethnicity."[15] Social legitimacy, however valuable, is not an educational benefit.

These important eventual secondary effects of a diverse student body do not fit comfortably within the educational justification for affirmative action that had enabled Powell to analyze it under a First Amendment theory of institutional academic freedom. Perhaps Justice O'Connor believed that the educational benefits of affirmative action enabled these more general contributions, but she did not assert this connection in her opinion. Rather than revisit potential justifications for affirmative action, which could have included these business, military, and societal factors, the majority in *Grutter* endorsed Powell's approach in *Bakke.* I suspect that if *Grutter* had been the Court's first encounter with affirmative action in higher education, the majority might have developed a different rationale that would have reflected its views more closely.

Justice Thomas's dissent in *Grutter* raises additional doubts about the meaning of institutional academic freedom. After quoting O'Connor's reference to educational autonomy grounded in the First Amendment, Thomas proceeded to review how academic freedom became a First Amendment right, apparently equating "educational autonomy" with "academic freedom." Thomas dated this process from Frankfurter's concurrence in *Sweezy* without referring to Warren's plurality opinion, which recognized Sweezy's own academic freedom. After relying on the First Amendment right of academic freedom to prohibit the government's investigation of Sweezy, Thomas accurately asserted, Frankfurter devoted much of his rhetoric to Sweezy's free speech rights. While recognizing that Frankfurter worried about "governmental intrusions into the independence of universities," Thomas doubted that "he was thinking of the Constitution's ban on racial discrimination." Thomas himself maintained that the First Amendment does not "authorize a university to do what would otherwise violate the Equal Protection Clause."[16]

Further undermining the majority's claimed deference to university decisions, Thomas pointed out that in 1996 the Court refused to defer to the policy of the Virginia Military Institute not to admit women, even while accepting VMI's claim that doing so would require changing its "adversative" educational method. The Court reached this decision, he observed, without even mentioning academic freedom. Emphasizing that sex discrimination is subject only to intermediate judicial scrutiny whereas race discrimination is subject to strict scrutiny, Thomas underlined the irony that the Court deferred to a university decision that affected race but not to one that affected sex. Apparently, he sardonically concluded, the Court was willing to defer to "the elite establishment," but not to "a less fashionable Southern military institution."[17] More likely, I think, the majority was not convinced that the admission of women would undermine the "adversative" method, a point emphasized by Justice Ginsburg in her majority opinion.

While challenging the majority's reliance on institutional academic freedom, Thomas criticized its focus on the value of diversity. The "devotees" of diversity, he claimed, used it as a "fashionable catchphrase" to produce an "aesthetic" of black faces. He stressed that affirmative action harms the minority students admitted to attain the diversity pleasing to whites. It "tantalizes unprepared" and "overmatched" students, who "take the bait, only to find that they cannot succeed in the cauldron of competition." As a result of affirmative action, moreover, all minority students "are tarred as undeserving," including those "who would succeed without discrimination" in their favor.[18]

In a 2016 decision reaffirming the constitutionality of affirmative action in selecting a diverse student body, the Court did not refer to the First Amendment or academic freedom. It focused on the details of the challenged affirmative action program and emphasized the general importance of judicial deference to the educational decisions of universities.[19] The Supreme Court majority's interpretation of the equal protection clause of the Fourteenth Amendment in 2023, which invalidated the affirmative action programs at Harvard and the University of North Carolina, makes it clear that the Court no longer conceives of any context in which the First Amendment right of institutional academic freedom could provide a compelling state interest that justifies racial classifications otherwise prohibited by the equal protection clause.[20]

Student Dismissal

Since the *Bakke* decision in 1978, Supreme Court decisions outside the context of affirmative action have addressed academic freedom as a First Amendment right of universities. Writing for a unanimous Court in the 1985 case *Regents of the University of Michigan v. Ewing*, Justice Stevens treated the decision of a faculty committee to dismiss a student on academic grounds as a legitimate exercise of the university's academic freedom. "When judges are asked to review the substance of a genuinely academic decision," Stevens wrote, "they should show great respect for the faculty's professional judgment." A faculty decision, Stevens maintained, should be upheld "unless it is such a substantial departure from accepted academic norms as to demonstrate that the person or committee responsible did not actually exercise professional judgment."[21]

Emphasizing the judicial reluctance to interfere with universities, Stevens referred specifically to "our responsibility to safeguard their academic freedom, 'a special concern of the First Amendment.'" He elaborated this sentence in an important and frequently cited footnote that recognized both individual and institutional First Amendment rights to academic freedom and indicated the potential tension between them. "Academic freedom thrives not only on the independent and uninhibited exchange of ideas among teachers and students," he wrote, "but also, and somewhat inconsistently, on autonomous decision making by the academy itself." He cited *Keyishian* and Warren's plurality opinion in *Sweezy* to support the first clause and Powell's opinion in *Bakke* and Frankfurter's concurrence in *Sweezy* to support the second.[22] Echoing Justice Story's regret a century and a half earlier that the Supreme Court had to decide a dispute at Bowdoin College, Justice Powell wrote a concurrence explaining his dismay that the case was litigated at all. He reiterated that judges should rarely review the academic decisions of universities.[23]

The AAUP filed an amicus brief that approved Justice Powell's identification of institutional academic freedom in *Bakke*, although the AAUP brief in *Bakke* itself did not refer to academic freedom. The academic freedom of a university to select its student body, the brief observed, clearly includes the right to determine whether admitted students meet academic standards. Unsurprisingly, the AAUP stressed that academic judgments about student fitness are best made by faculty with the requisite expertise.[24]

Yet the AAUP warned that some judicial fears of intervention in university affairs may be misplaced. It pointed out that a court is constitutionally obligated to intervene if it finds evidence that the dismissal of a student by a faculty committee was motivated by racial animus or retaliation for a student's exercise of First Amendment rights. Anticipating that universities might invoke their own rights of academic freedom to oppose any judicial requirement that they articulate sound academic reasons for dismissing students, the AAUP disagreed with this position. Providing reasons to students, the brief maintained, constitutes part of the professional commitment of faculty, and being legally obliged to do so as a matter of procedural due process should not be considered a violation of academic freedom. While stressing the limits of institutional academic freedom, the brief noted complaints to the AAUP about administrators who changed the grades that faculty gave students. The note maintained that the professor teaching a course, not administrators, has the expertise to assign grades.[25]

The Court did not respond directly to many of the points made in the AAUP brief. But the assertion by Justice Stevens that faculty decisions must be based on professional judgment recognized a meaningful judicial role in reviewing possible unprofessional considerations that could be illegal. By noting the potential tension between individual and institutional rights of academic freedom, moreover, Stevens acknowledged but did not resolve the issue identified by the AAUP.

Differentiating Institutional Academic Freedom from General First Amendment Doctrines

Concurring opinions by Justices Stevens and Souter made significant analytical contributions by differentiating institutional academic freedom from the general First Amendment doctrines relied on by the majority. Even in previous Supreme Court decisions that clearly identified academic freedom as a First Amendment right of professors and universities, opinions had not indicated how this right relates to general First Amendment doctrines. Some treated academic freedom and general First Amendment law interchangeably. Justices Stevens and Souter stressed that the application of general First Amendment doctrines to universities could undermine academic freedom.

In the 1981 decision *Widmar v. Vincent,* the majority held that a public university violated the First Amendment rights of freedom of speech and assembly by denying a student organization of evangelical Christians access to university facilities that were available to other student organizations. The university maintained, and a lower court agreed, that allowing the evangelical organization to use university meeting rooms for religious worship and religious discussion would have the primary effect of advancing religion, a factor that prior decisions had identified as indicating a violation of the First Amendment's prohibition against laws "respecting an establishment of religion." Complying with the establishment clause, the Supreme Court acknowledged, constitutes a compelling state interest that could justify restrictions on speech. But it argued that allowing a student religious organization equal access to a public forum used by other student organizations would have only an incidental religious benefit, which under existing precedent would not violate the establishment clause. The decision observed that allowing students to use university facilities does not constitute state approval, whatever the content of the group's expression. It also observed that the more than one hundred registered student organizations at the university included both nonreligious and religious speakers.[26]

Rather than a violation of the establishment clause, the majority held, the denial of equal access to a forum created by the university and generally open to student groups was an exclusion of religious speech, which violated the fundamental First Amendment principle that state regulation of speech must be content neutral. Having allowed student groups to use its facilities, the university could not exclude any of those groups based on the content of their speech, including religious speech. While reaching this conclusion, the majority, without referring to academic freedom, quoted Frankfurter's concurrence in *Sweezy* and cited Powell's opinion in *Bakke* to stress that it was not questioning the university's right to make academic judgments. And while noting that a public university campus resembles a public forum, at least for its students, the majority acknowledged that a campus differs significantly from other public forums, such as streets or parks or municipal theaters. In furthering its educational mission, the majority maintained, a university should be able to impose reasonable restrictions on the use of its campus and need not provide equal access to nonstudents.[27]

These concessions to university authority did not satisfy Justice Stevens. The application of general First Amendment doctrines, he maintained, "may needlessly undermine the academic freedom of public universities." Selecting the professors to appoint and reward, developing the curriculum, choosing the books to purchase for the library, and allocating scarce university resources and facilities among student groups, he observed, all require evaluations of the content of expression. Illustrating his point with a vivid example, he assumed that two student groups, one wanting to watch Mickey Mouse movies and the other wanting to rehearse a production of Hamlet, sought to reserve a university facility at the same time. Stevens maintained that "a university ought to be allowed to decide for itself whether a program that illuminates the genius of Walt Disney should be given precedence over one that may duplicate material adequately covered in the classroom." Quoting Frankfurter's opinion in *Sweezy* and Powell's opinion in *Bakke,* he maintained that universities rather than federal judges should make these decisions. He recognized that general First Amendment law properly forbids a police chief from regulating the content of soapbox orators, but he maintained that the First Amendment right of institutional academic freedom should allow a university to determine that some subjects advance its educational mission more than others. Yet Stevens concurred with the majority because he agreed that the university had not asserted a sufficient educational reason for excluding the student evangelical organization.[28]

Concurring in the *Southworth* decision in 2000, which held that a mandatory student activity fee did not violate First Amendment prohibitions against compelled speech, Justice Souter, joined by Justices Stevens and Breyer, invoked the university's First Amendment right of academic freedom to justify departures for educational reasons from viewpoint as well as from content neutrality. "The University," the majority concluded without referring to academic freedom, "may determine that its mission is well served if students have the means to engage in dynamic discussions of philosophical, religious, scientific, social, and political subjects in their extracurricular campus life outside the lecture hall." But the majority also maintained that the First Amendment required the distribution of the fee to be viewpoint neutral.[29] Souter disagreed, relying in part on the "First Amendment and related cases grouped under the umbrella of academic freedom." After quoting the statement in the *Student Organization Handbook* that the activities of student groups constitute a second curriculum, Souter reviewed many of the Court's previous decisions about the meaning of academic freedom as a First Amendment right. These decisions, he observed, recognized liberty from restraints on expression within the university, but also the freedom of the university to decide what and how to teach.[30] Just as institutional academic freedom allows universities to make decisions about teaching that use tuition to support views some students find offensive, Souter reasoned, it should allow universities to make educational decisions that distribute mandatory student activity fees to extracurricular organizations whose views some students find offensive. Souter maintained that in both of these situations universities should not be constrained by requirements of viewpoint neutrality.[31]

Souter noted that prior Court decisions about academic freedom at universities addressed external restrictions on speech by professors rather than university assertions of academic freedom. He observed that Justice Frankfurter's discussion in *Sweezy* of the four essential freedoms of a university was neither rejected nor adopted by the Court majority. While previous decisions protected the academic freedom to determine the subjects taught and viewpoints expressed in the classroom, he added, they never held that universities are immune from students assertions of their First Amendment rights. Souter then noted without further comment that the South African statement on academic freedom quoted by Frankfurter "might be thought even to sanction student speech codes in public universities."[32] Both because the previous decisions did not control the analysis of the student activity fee and because the university had not invoked academic freedom in litigating the case, Souter did not undertake a more detailed analysis of its meaning. Like Stevens in *Widmar,* Souter highlighted but did not elaborate the differentiation of academic freedom from other First Amendment rights.

Rejecting Claims of Institutional Academic Freedom

While extending the First Amendment right of academic freedom to universities, as in recognizing it as a right of individual professors, the Supreme Court in other cases rejected assertions that it applied. In its most explicit and resounding denial of a claim by a university, the Court unanimously rejected in 1990 the University of Pennsylvania's argument that its First

Amendment right of academic freedom provided a privilege against disclosing confidential peer review materials to the Equal Employment Opportunity Commission (EEOC).

Previous lower-court cases had reached conflicting decisions about whether the individual academic freedom of professors or the institutional academic freedom of universities required such a privilege. Addressing the tension between the importance of confidentiality in promoting candid reviews and the legal obligation to remedy employment discrimination, the second circuit recognized a qualified privilege for professors and the seventh circuit recognized a qualified privilege for universities. By contrast, the fifth circuit rejected any privilege for professors and the third circuit rejected any privilege for universities.

The second circuit relied on the AAUP's policy statement on judicially compelled disclosure, which maintained that individual votes should be protected by a qualified privilege if the unsuccessful candidate receives a meaningful written statement of reasons from the peer review committee and is afforded proper intramural grievance procedures.[33] Observing that "AAUP policy statements have assisted the courts in the past in resolving a wide range of educational controversies," the court concluded that the AAUP's position appropriately balances academic freedom and individual rights. The court reasoned that a rule of absolute disclosure would chill frank discussion, but that a rule of absolute privilege would make it too hard to prove the intent necessary to establish a case of discrimination.[34]

Similarly balancing these competing interests, the seventh circuit took a somewhat different approach. It allowed the university to redact from the files sought by the EEOC various identifying features of the professors who wrote evaluations of the tenure candidate. But it also required the university to provide unredacted files to the judge. If the judge determined that the redactions are reasonably necessary to protect confidentiality, the redacted files should be turned over to the EEOC. If the EEOC determined that it needed more information from the unredacted files, it could try to convince the court. The seventh circuit anticipated that the identity of evaluators would only be released in the rare circumstance when an evaluation did not contain nondiscriminatory reasons or when evidence indicated that an evaluator may have had racial animus against the candidate.[35]

In rejecting any qualified privilege for professors, the fifth circuit stressed that the concern about suppressing ideas, which animated the Supreme Court decisions that recognized academic freedom as a First Amendment right of professors, applies as much to the denial of tenure as to the regulation of teaching. It warned that a privilege against disclosing votes and discussions by members of tenure review committees could shield denials of tenure based on ideological rather than academic grounds, presenting a much greater danger to academic freedom than compelled discovery.[36] The third circuit acknowledged that the First Amendment protects the university's academic freedom to determine who may teach, in which confidential peer review is central. It also acknowledged that the disclosure to the EEOC of confidential material gathered through peer review could burden this process. But the court stressed that in 1972 Congress deleted the exemption of universities from the Civil Rights Act of 1964 without indicating any intention to provide special treatment for universities under investigation for discrimination. The dissenting judge, by contrast, found no support in the legislative history of the 1972 amendments that Congress intended a "blunderbuss" and factually unsupported allegation of discriminatory treatment to allow unfettered access to confidential personnel files.[37]

In the case that reached the Supreme Court, the EEOC sought confidential material generated through peer review as part of its investigation of a complaint by a professor that she had been denied tenure based on her sex and national origin. Disclosure, the University of Pennsylvania maintained, would impair its ability to make educational decisions about appointments and curriculum by undermining the integrity of tenure review. Asking only that its First Amendment right of academic freedom be given some weight, the university conceded that its interest in confidentiality could be outweighed if the EEOC provided a specific reason for needing the documents.[38]

Supported by amicus briefs from the American Council of Education (ACE) and many universities, the University of Pennsylvania stressed that the institutional academic freedom of the university supports the individual academic freedom of professors. Making some of the same points in a nonaligned amicus brief, the AAUP emphasized that the case did not present any tension between individual and institutional academic freedom while highlighting the shared interests of the faculty and the university in effective peer review.[39]

Writing for a unanimous Supreme Court, Justice Blackmun rejected these arguments in a tone that bordered on ridicule, indicating much less solicitude for the university's concerns than lower-court decisions that reached the same result. He observed that in the Supreme Court's previous "so-called academic-freedom cases," the government had attempted to regulate the content of speech and the infringement on speech was direct.[40] In this case, by contrast, the university made no claim that the EEOC was influencing the subjects or viewpoints of speech at universities, and the alleged infringement was "extremely attenuated." Blackmun characterized the claim for an "expanded" right of academic freedom in a way that emphasized "how far the burden is from the asserted right." The university, he maintained, "argues that the First Amendment is infringed by disclosure of peer review materials because disclosure undermines the confidentiality which is central to the peer review process, and this in turn is central to the tenure process, which in turn is the means by which petitioner seeks to exercise its asserted academic-freedom right of choosing who will teach."[41]

Underlining his rejection of the university's argument, Blackmun compared the claimed need to preserve the confidentiality of peer review materials in tenure decisions to other possible claims about generally applicable government regulations that may make it harder to exercise First Amendment rights. He pointed out that laws subjecting universities to taxation, though depriving them of money that could be used to attract professors, are not violations of the First Amendment. He doubted that peer review was more important than money in determining who may teach. He then turned more directly to the peer review process itself and maintained that the university's claim was speculative as well as remote and attenuated. Questioning the importance of confidentiality in peer review while seeming to mock the university, he asserted that the justices were not as inclined as the university itself "to assume the worst about those in the academic community." "Not all academics," he maintained, "will hesitate to stand up and be counted when they evaluate their peers," even if they know that their evaluations eventually might be disclosed during an EEOC investigation of alleged employment discrimination in a tenure denial.[42] Prompted by Justice Brennan, Blackmun deleted from his original draft language that questioned the existence of academic freedom as a "special" First Amendment right.[43]

Ignoring Claims of Institutional Academic Freedom

In other cases, the Supreme Court ignored institutional claims to academic freedom. A 2006 decision, *Rumsfeld v. Forum for Academic & Institutional Rights,* did not address the academic freedom arguments raised by an association of law schools and law faculties organized to challenge a federal law that denied federal funds to universities whose policies restricted access of military recruiters to campus. Law schools had imposed these restrictions because the government's prohibition of homosexuals from serving in the military violated their rules against discrimination based on sexual orientation.

While raising numerous First Amendment arguments, the association suggested in its brief that the First Amendment right of academic freedom may give universities broader First Amendment rights than other kinds of private institutions.[44] Amicus briefs from a group of elite private universities, a group of Yale law professors, and the AAUP also invoked the First Amendment right of academic freedom in challenging the law. The universities asserted that when conditions on government funding implicate academic freedom, they must be subject to especially strict judicial scrutiny. If the government could deny all research funds to a university based on its antidiscrimination policies, the brief declared without convincing elaboration, it could also deny universities control over the curriculum, the admission of students, and the hiring of faculty.[45] Relying on the First Amendment right of academic freedom of professors rather than of universities, the Yale law professors maintained that by forcing them to acquiesce in the military's discrimination, the law undermined their efforts to create an inclusive and tolerant classroom atmosphere in which all students could express themselves freely without fear of becoming marginalized.[46]

In contrast to the focus in the other briefs on the academic freedom of law schools, universities, or individual faculty members, the AAUP amicus brief stressed that the First Amendment right of academic freedom extends to the formulation of educational policies by the faculty. Beyond setting the criteria for admitting and evaluating students, it asserted, these policies include modeling professional values students need after graduation. A faculty's decision that employment should be based on merit, the brief observed in a questionable overstatement, is as much an academic judgment as its decision that grades should be based on merit. After observing that academic freedom obviously would be implicated if the government conditioned funding to universities on their agreement that military officers could accompany professors to teach classes or to co-author research, the AAUP boldly claimed that the context of military recruitment was no different.[47] Forcing professors to teach and conduct research with military officers surely is a much more substantial threat to academic freedom than forcing them to allow recruitment by the military in a law school's placement office. Even if this decision about recruitment constitutes an academic judgment that should be protected by the First Amendment right of academic freedom, the AAUP's analogy is extremely farfetched.[48]

Despite these varied arguments in the briefs based on the First Amendment right of academic freedom, neither the oral argument nor the decision mentioned it at all. Writing for a unanimous Court, Chief Justice Roberts concluded that those challenging the law had "attempted to stretch a number of First Amendment doctrines well beyond the sort of activities these doctrines protect."[49]

A large group of Yale law faculty filed a subsequent lawsuit that reiterated their academic freedom claims, asserting that they had not been addressed by the Supreme Court decision. The circuit court disagreed, quoting the statement by Roberts about stretching the First Amendment as evidence that the Supreme Court had already denied them. Pointing out how extensively the Supreme Court briefs had focused on academic freedom, the court added that it would "defy reason" to think that the Supreme Court had not considered it. The court proceeded to provide its own view that the academic freedom arguments in this case, like those explicitly rejected by the Supreme Court in the case between the University of Pennsylvania and the EEOC, were too attenuated and speculative to be convincing.[50]

The Unresolved Debate about Institutional Academic Freedom in *Princeton University v. Schmid*

Whereas the Supreme Court may have implicitly rejected the academic freedom claim in the military recruitment case, it did not address the debate over the meaning of institutional academic freedom in a highly visible 1981 case, *Princeton University v. Schmid*. The Court ultimately held that new university regulations rendered the original dispute moot. Yet the debate between the AAUP and Princeton in this case merits attention. It provides insight into the range of views about the emerging First Amendment right of institutional academic freedom and highlights the tension between this right and the individual academic freedom of professors that the Supreme Court previously included within the First Amendment.

The case arose when Chris Schmid, a member of the United States Labor Party who had no affiliation with Princeton, distributed and sold on the campus material dealing with the Party and the mayoral campaign in nearby

Newark. Existing Princeton regulations prohibited any person without a university connection or sponsorship from entering the campus to solicit support or contributions. Schmid was arrested and convicted of trespass.

In overturning Schmid's conviction, the New Jersey Supreme Court relied on the free speech provision of the state constitution, which it acknowledged to be more protective than the First Amendment. It developed a multi-faceted test to determine when owners of private property must allow freedom of expression. The test focused on three factors: (1) the purposes and normal use of the property, (2) the extent to which the property is open to the public, and (3) the purpose of the expressive activity by a member of the public. The court concluded that the distribution of political literature was not incompatible with the normal use of the Princeton campus for educational purposes and had not violated university regulations prohibiting disruption of its operations or infringements on the rights of others.[51]

The court took pains to highlight the importance of substantial judicial deference to the autonomy of private universities in fulfilling their educational goals. This autonomy, the court asserted, justifies a university in controlling access to its campus. The court also recognized that institutional autonomy implicates academic freedom, though it did not associate academic freedom with a constitutional right. Yet it reversed the conviction because Princeton's regulations did not contain sufficient standards for governing freedom of expression on campus.[52]

In appealing this decision to the US Supreme Court, Princeton relied on its institutional right of academic freedom as a "special concern" of the First Amendment and quoted Justice Frankfurter's emphasis in *Sweezy* on "the exclusion of governmental intervention in the intellectual life of a university." The state constitutional standard established by the New Jersey Supreme Court, Princeton protested, violated the First Amendment because it required courts to determine whether a university regulation over expression by strangers on campus is "consonant" or "discordant" with its educational philosophy, a judgment for Princeton alone to make without judicial intrusion. The court's standard of "discordant" and "incompatible," the brief added, violated the First Amendment's prohibition against vagueness.[53]

The focus of the AAUP's amicus brief urging the Supreme Court to affirm the decision of the New Jersey Supreme Court, by contrast, highlighted and attacked Princeton's invocation of academic freedom. The AAUP agreed with Princeton that the First Amendment right of academic freedom protects universities as institutions as well as professors, but it stressed that nothing in the decision by the New Jersey Supreme Court affected Princeton's academic freedom. Indeed, the AAUP approved the standard of review announced by the court,[54] and indicated throughout its brief that the court had been impressively attentive to concerns about academic freedom.

The AAUP asserted that Princeton's "novel and sweeping claims" combining institutional autonomy and academic freedom, if accepted, would effectively insulate private universities from any government scrutiny.[55] It emphasized that academic freedom and institutional autonomy, though related, are essentially different concepts. Institutional autonomy can be derived from academic freedom in the sense that university autonomy from external control may be necessary to protect its educational functions, including the functions of professors covered by academic freedom. But institutional autonomy also relates to the general control of private property, traditionally protected by the due process clause of the Fourteenth Amendment. Only when a university's claims of institutional autonomy relate to its educational functions, the AAUP maintained, is academic freedom at stake. But Princeton never provided the slightest clue as to how the material Schmid distributed and sold could interfere with its goals. Princeton asserted only that any judicial review of the relationship between institutional policies and educational objectives itself violates the institutional academic freedom protected by the First Amendment. The AAUP disagreed, observing that the free exercise of religion, also protected by the First Amendment, does not prevent the courts from inquiring into the nature and authenticity of religious belief. The AAUP also gave examples of appropriate state scrutiny of the educational affairs of universities. States traditionally, and without controversy, examine the quality of faculty and educational programs to protect the public against fraud. The enforcement of laws prohibiting employment discrimination requires courts to assess whether educational reasons given by universities in decisions about faculty selection, retention, and promotion are unfounded or pretextual.[56]

The AAUP warned that Princeton's broad claim of institutional academic freedom would effectively preclude judicial review of institutional decisions even in cases where faculty challenge administrative actions. Faculty complaints of employment discrimination or of breaches of contractual protection for academic freedom and tenure, the AAUP observed, relate much more closely to institutional educational policies than did Schmid's distribution and sale of political literature. The conception of institutional academic freedom Princeton invoked against Schmid would apply even more strongly against these faculty complaints.[57]

During oral argument at the Supreme Court, justices pressed Princeton's attorney on some of these points. The attorney conceded the legitimacy of state requirements of minimal educational standards to prevent fraud, though he did not differentiate this intrusion from the one imposed by the decision of the New Jersey Supreme Court.[58] When pressed by Justice Stevens about how the speech by the outsider at Princeton posed "any conflict whatsoever with any expressive policy of the University," the lawyer did not answer directly but indicated that Princeton should be able to forbid members of the American Nazi Party from proselytizing on campus because their views "would be highly offensive to the great majority of students." Ultimately, the lawyer stressed Princeton's major point: any state regulation that forces a university to give reasons for its policies governing access of outsiders to campus violates the First Amendment.[59] Neither the justices nor the lawyer mentioned academic freedom during oral argument. By declaring in a short opinion that it was dismissing the case because Princeton had subsequently adopted new regulations governing expressive activity on campus, the Supreme Court left unexamined the most extensive arguments ever presented to it about the meaning of institutional academic freedom as a First Amendment right.[60]

Lower-Court Decisions

The substantially larger number and variety of lower-court decisions reinforced the Supreme Court's extension of the First Amendment right of academic freedom to universities, just as lower-court decisions reinforced the Supreme Court's initial recognition of academic freedom as a First Amendment right of professors. Like their counterparts about individual academic freedom, they recognized the existence of a First Amendment right of institutional academic freedom even when they indicated its limits or found that competing interests outweighed it. In addressing institutional academic freedom, lower courts frequently provided additional support for the First Amendment right of individual academic freedom by presuming its existence as well. While Supreme Court briefs and decisions recognized the possibility of conflicting claims of academic freedom between universities and professors, some lower-court cases directly presented and resolved them. Yet universities occasionally asserted their own institutional academic freedom to protect the academic freedom of professors.

Like the Supreme Court, lower courts ascribed institutional academic freedom to the determinations of faculty bodies evaluating the quality of professors and students. Also like the Supreme Court, lower courts did not differentiate the roles of the governing board, administration, and faculty bodies in making decisions for the university. They recognized greater interests in institutional academic freedom in the substance of decisions about appointment and tenure than in nondisclosure of confidential information used to make these decisions. Though overwhelmingly deferential to university decisions about appointment and tenure, lower courts occasionally overturned them based on findings that they were not made on the academic grounds that justify the protection of institutional academic freedom. Lower courts applied institutional academic freedom to university decisions about scholarship and teaching, which often limited the rights of individual professors but sometimes protected them. Yet lower courts often rejected university claims that institutional academic freedom precluded the application of state statutory and contract law.

The lower-court cases about institutional academic freedom raised many of the same issues as the ones about individual academic freedom. They addressed requests to produce information and the regulation of campus speech. Some limited academic freedom to the content of expression, but more also applied it to protect against the inhibition or interference with the process of scholarship and teaching, to support participation in peer review, and to cover other academic activities. Some resisted the use of academic freedom to give universities and professors greater protection than the First Amendment affords other institutions and employees. And some commented on the lingering lack of clarity about the meaning of academic freedom as a First Amendment right.

Evaluating Student Quality

Following the lead of Justice Stevens in *Ewing*, lower courts have recognized the institutional academic freedom of universities to evaluate the academic quality of students. One interesting case addressed academic eligibility for admission, but most, like *Ewing* itself, upheld student discipline for poor academic performance.

Quoting Justice Stevens on the importance of judicial deference to a faculty's professional judgment regarding genuine academic decisions, a judge upheld as an exercise of institutional academic freedom the University of California's determination that various courses taught by Christian high schools did not meet its admissions requirements.[61] The judge emphasized that the university had relied on the professional judgment of its faculty about the academic merits of these courses, not on any opposition to the religious viewpoints of the Christian schools, which would have been unconstitutional. For example, the university's faculty experts maintained that the English course contained anthologies rather than full-length works and insisted on specific interpretations of texts; the history course focused on the Bible as an unerring source for analysis of historical events and failed to teach modern historical methods; and the biology course rejected scientific evidence and methodology deemed inconsistent with the Bible.[62]

Many other courts upheld university assertions that the First Amendment right of institutional academic freedom justifies actions against students for failing to meet academic standards. One state appellate court observed that many courts since *Ewing* had followed the Supreme Court's "mandate" of deferring to the professional judgment of a faculty committee unless it is such a substantial departure from accepted academic norms as to indicate that the committee acted for other reasons. Even if there is some evidence of arbitrary behavior by the faculty committee, the court maintained while going beyond the reasoning of other decisions, a judge must uphold the faculty's decision whenever there is "*any*" evidence of "some rational academic basis" for it.[63]

Decisions have identified student failure to meet the standards of the field for which they are training as a reason for disciplining them that is protected by institutional academic freedom. In one case, the student was enrolled in a mortuary science program, which required students to follow the statutory code of conduct for mortuary science professionals in the state. The code mandated treating the deceased "with dignity and respect." Faculty maintained that the student's Facebook posts violated the code by giving the human cadaver she was dissecting a name derived from a comedy film about a corpse, and by commenting about playing with the cadaver and taking out her aggression against it. The court rejected the student's argument that her Facebook posts were merely satirical literary expression unrelated to her course work and protected by her First Amendment right of free speech.[64]

Another court upheld a university's institutional academic freedom to determine that speech by an applicant to a teacher training program violated professional standards. The applicant had stated that "it would be fine" for a twelve-year old girl to have a "consensual" sexual relationship with her teacher. He had also characterized special education students as "fakers" and asserted that secondary school teachers should not be expected to teach students with learning disabilities. The court emphasized that professional standards prohibited sexual conduct between teachers and students or minors and required teachers to adapt their instruction to the different needs of students. The court concluded that the university made an "academic decision" to the deny the application, observing that a decision based on "professional disposition" rather than "intellectual aptitude does not strip it of its academic character."[65]

In judging the applicability of state labor law to universities, courts have also upheld the right of institutional academic freedom to discipline students for failing to meet academic standards. A New Jersey state court held that institutional academic freedom protected a university teaching hospital from an order to arbitrate its dismissal of a resident for intentionally positioning a stent improperly. After the state Public Employment Relations Commission decided that the university's action was not arbitrable, the union representing the resident argued that arbitration would not interfere with the university's ability to make academic judgments about whether dismissal was appropriate under the facts alleged. The union maintained that arbitration would only determine whether the facts supported the allegation. Allowing an arbitrator to determine the underlying facts, the court concluded in rejecting this argument, "would usurp the university's academic and medical judgment, and intrude on its academic freedom."[66]

Even in denying a medical school's claim in a previous case, the New Jersey Supreme Court went out of its way to stress that institutional academic freedom restricts the application of labor law. The Public Employment Relations Commission had concluded that state labor law guaranteed an intern a right to union representation at an interview about potential discipline for alleged incompetence. On appeal, the court observed that it would have easily affirmed the Commission's decision if the case had not arisen at a university teaching hospital. But the termination of an intern from a university teaching hospital for alleged failure to meet medical standards, the court added, "triggers a concern for academic freedom that might temper the rights provided" in the state labor law. Although it recognized the existence of a First Amendment right of institutional academic freedom that could limit the application of state labor law in certain circumstances, the court upheld the enforcement of the Commission's order.

The presence of a union representative at an investigatory interview, it reasoned, would not have precluded the university from making an academic decision. Giving an example of a situation in which the university's academic freedom could outweigh state labor law, the court stated that a university would have a valid academic freedom claim if a law allowed a union to veto an institutional decision to dismiss a professor.[67]

Courts have held that institutional academic freedom gives universities discretion over procedure as well as substance in student dismissals. Judge Posner relied on a university's institutional academic freedom in concluding that an undergraduate did not have a right to counsel in disciplinary proceedings that led to his expulsion for a fight outside a bar. Recognizing a right to counsel, he reasoned, would transform student disciplinary proceedings into adversary litigation, adding to the "bureaucratization" of higher education. Conceding that a student facing dismissal has a right to contest it, Posner did not decide when due process limits the informality of campus disciplinary procedures.[68]

Appointment and Tenure

Universities have often relied on the First Amendment right of institutional academic freedom to resist judicial review of their decisions about appointment and tenure. Many of these cases arose when professors filed suits claiming that universities violated the prohibitions against employment discrimination in Title VII of the federal Civil Rights Act. Between the 1972 amendments of Title VII, which removed the exemption of universities in the original 1964 Act, and 1978, when Justice Powell's opinion in *Bakke* identified academic freedom as a First Amendment right of universities, judges often stressed the importance of university independence from judicial review without referring to the First Amendment. After Powell's opinion in *Bakke,* universities relied explicitly on their First Amendment right of institutional academic freedom, often but not always successfully.

In a 1974 decision applying Title VII to universities, a second circuit panel reflected the prevailing approach. "Of all fields, which the federal courts should hesitate to invade and take over," it asserted in *Faro v. New York University,* "education and faculty appointments are probably the least suited for federal court supervision."[69] Four years later, another second circuit decision, *Powell v. Syracuse University,* distanced itself from *Faro* even as it denied a Title VII challenge by a professor whose appointment was not renewed. The court observed that many judges, often citing *Faro,* had adapted its "anti-interventionist policy." As a result, universities had become "virtually immune to charges of employment bias, at least when that bias is not expressed overtly." Dissociating itself from this view, the court stressed that in 1972 Congress had removed the original exemption for educational institutions based on extensive testimony about the "truly appalling," "gross," and "blatant" evidence disclosing the "pervasive nature of discriminatory university employment practices." Referring to academic freedom without describing it as a First Amendment right, the court, in a memorable phrase frequently quoted in subsequent decisions, denied that "academic freedom embraces the freedom to discriminate."[70]

While rejecting the Title VII claim of a woman denied tenure, Judge Posner asserted decades later that a university's interest in institutional academic freedom is stronger in insulating the actual result of the tenure decision than in protecting the confidential peer review material used to make it. After acknowledging that the legal standard for proving employment discrimination under Title VII is the same for all employees, he stressed how often courts, in deferring to determinations within universities, had observed the extent to which many subjective academic judgments are necessary to make a tenure decision. The institutional academic freedom to make these determinations on academic grounds, he believed, should limit judicial review of Title VII cases, though he realized that this deference made challenges to denials of tenure "an uphill fight."[71]

In one of the few cases finding that a university violated Title VII in denying appointment or tenure, the first circuit rejected the argument by Boston University that the award of tenure as a remedy infringed its First Amendment right of academic freedom to determine for itself who may teach. Even after a finding of discrimination, the university maintained, a court could only award tenure without violating the First Amendment if there was no underlying dispute over the professor's qualifications. While agreeing with the general proposition that judges should be wary about intruding into tenure decisions, the court reasoned that the award of tenure is an appropriate remedy for findings of sex discrimination in its denial. Quoting the Supreme Court, it stressed that the purpose of Title VII requires "making persons whole for injuries suffered through past discrimination." The frequently quoted language in Frankfurter's *Sweezy* concurrence from the South African statement, the court emphasized, stated that the academic freedom of a university covers determinations made "*on academic grounds.*" "Academic freedom," the Court asserted while citing *Powell v. Syracuse University,* "does not include the freedom to discriminate against tenure candidates on the basis of sex or other impermissible grounds."[72]

Scholarship and Teaching

Lower courts have recognized that institutional as well as individual academic freedom protects decisions about scholarship and teaching. In a frequently cited decision that analyzed an administration's removal of controversial art from a faculty exhibit, Judge Posner observed the "equivocal" meaning of academic freedom as a First Amendment right. "It is used to denote both the freedom of the academy to pursue its ends without interference from the government . . . and the freedom of the individual teacher (or in some versions—indeed in most cases—the student) to pursue his ends without interference from the academy." The controversial art consisted of stained-glass windows that depicted naked brown women in various sexually explicit poses. Its display on the main floor of the college's principal building provoked complaints from students, cleaning women, and black clergymen. Posner acknowledged the administration's concern that the display would offend potential applicants and thus make it harder to recruit students, particularly black and female students. While upholding the university's academic freedom to move the windows from their original location to a less conspicuous place on campus, he assumed that the professor's own academic freedom precluded the university from denying him the right to display at all.[73]

Quoting Judge Posner on the tension between individual and institutional academic freedom, one district court held that a professor's academic freedom includes the right to assign grades, but that a university's academic freedom includes the right to change them.[74] Most cases about grading, by contrast, simply identified it as an institutional rather than an individual right of academic freedom.[75] Other lower courts recognized the institutional academic freedom of universities to impose requirements on professors in the classroom. In response to a professor's assertion that an administrator abridged her academic freedom by requiring her to communicate more closely with her students after she gave most of them incompletes for substandard work, a circuit court maintained that these facts did not even implicate, let alone violate, her constitutional rights. Yet the court did think that the case implicated the institutional academic freedom of the university. "The freedom of a university to decide what may be taught and how it shall be taught," the court reasoned, "would be meaningless if a professor were entitled to refuse to comply with university requirements whenever they conflict with his or her teaching philosophy." Emphasizing the university's minimal intrusion, the court observed that the administrator only instructed the professor to communicate her expectations and did not place any limitations on what those expectations should be.[76] Another court concluded that institutional academic freedom encompasses the evaluation of teachers, rejecting a professor's claim that the university violated her academic freedom by requiring the distribution of standardized student evaluation forms. As in the case involving the communication of course expectations, the court stressed the minimal impact of this requirement on the professor. It pointed out that the evaluations were unrelated to class content and that the professor remained free to criticize the university's policy of using the standardized forms.[77]

The exercise of institutional academic freedom could protect as well as limit a professor's own academic freedom. The University of Minnesota successfully invoked institutional academic freedom on behalf of the professor who directed its Center for Holocaust and Genocide Studies. The Turkish Coalition of America asserted that by listing its website as "unreliable" and urging students not to use it, the Center had engaged in unconstitutional viewpoint discrimination, favoring the Center's viewpoint that the massacre of Armenians during World War I was a genocide while dismissing the Coalition's viewpoint that a genocide charge could not be sustained. The judge maintained that the Center's viewpoint was within the university's academic freedom in teaching to determine whether assertions meet academic standards.[78]

Rejecting Institutional Academic Freedom as a Defense against State Law

In other cases, lower courts rejected university claims that institutional academic freedom precluded the application of state law. They repeatedly denied university assertions that they should be exempt from state freedom of information and public records laws. They upheld state laws regulating educational standards and extending free speech rights to students at private universities. And they required universities to adhere to their contracts with faculty.

Disputes about professors doing research with animals prompted several of the cases under state public records laws. In one of them, the Progressive Animal Welfare Society (PAWS) used the state public records act to ask that the University of Washington provide a copy of an unfunded grant proposal to the National Institutes of Health (NIH). The NIH itself did not disclose unfunded grant proposals or the formal written evaluations of them by scientists who participate in the confidential peer review. It also warned that breaches of confidentiality could result in the filing of scientific misconduct charges.[79] The Washington Supreme Court relied on the Supreme Court's decision in *University of Pennsylvania v. Equal Employment Opportunity Commission* to reject the university's "putative constitutional privilege of academic freedom." As in the University of Pennsylvania case, the court stressed that the law did not restrict the content of speech and criticized the university for seeking an expanded First Amendment right of academic freedom that could not be justified. Echoing a point made by the fourth circuit majority in *Urofsky,* the court stressed that the employees of a public university do not have greater speech rights than other state employees. The court acknowledged the traditional judicial reluctance to intrude into universities. But it stressed that the public records act was enacted by popular initiative and that the legislature had frequently amended it without providing an exception for universities or for professors.[80] Nor was a court reluctant to enforce a freedom of information act to require the production of teaching materials used in a course titled "Family Life and Human Sexuality." The court concluded that the college's academic freedom to determine curriculum and pedagogy is not infringed by respecting the public's right to know what is being taught.[81]

In a particularly interesting case, Nova University maintained that the Educational Institution Licensure Commission of the District of Columbia violated its academic freedom by denying its application for a license to offer degree courses. The Commission found that Nova had not complied with licensing requirements because it did not have adequate library resources and because it had no resident faculty in the District of Columbia. Conceding that the Commission could regulate fraudulent educational institutions, Nova insisted that this attempt to regulate the quality of higher education infringed its academic freedom.[82]

Citing *Bakke, Sweezy,* and *Keyishian,* the District of Columbia Court of Appeals recognized that universities as well as professors have a First Amendment right of academic freedom but rejected Nova's reliance on it. "Not every limit on institutional autonomy," the court observed, "also implicates academic freedom." The court recognized that meeting licensing requirements would place financial and administrative burdens on the university, thereby limiting its institutional prerogatives, but concluded that these constraints did not violate its institutional academic freedom.[83]

To support its rejection of the academic freedom claim, the court stressed that the statute and the Commission's enforcement of it were content neutral. In contrast to *Sweezy* and *Keyishian,* where the government was motivated by hostility to political views, in passing the law enforced by the Commission the sole interest of Congress was to protect the public by making sure that educational institutions met minimal academic standards. The court emphasized the lack of any evidence that the Commission denied a license to Nova based on the subjects taught, the books assigned, or the views of professors. The First Amendment, the court concluded, cannot shield substandard universities.[84]

Nor was a court persuaded that institutional academic freedom precludes application of a state law governing expression at private universities. Just as Princeton relied on institutional academic freedom in the Supreme Court to resist the free speech provision of the New Jersey constitution, Stanford relied on it to challenge a California law that extended First Amendment protections for speech to students at private universities. In addition to asserting that its speech code was consistent with the First Amendment, Stanford maintained that its institutional academic freedom allowed it to develop its own rules about expression on its campus without adhering to the First Amendment. Using reasoning resembling *Doe v. University of Michigan* and other decisions invalidating campus speech codes, the district judge concluded that the Stanford code violated the First Amendment.

Characterizing Stanford's argument as incorrectly suggesting that its academic freedom provides unlimited discretion, the court observed that *Bakke* and *Sweezy,* on which Stanford relied, addressed the academic freedom to make academic decisions. The speech code, the court reasoned by contrast, did not relate to any of the four elements of academic freedom established in those cases. Stanford remained free to control course content and student admissions.[85] Although Stanford decided not to appeal, Gerhard Casper, its president and a former law professor and dean at the University of Chicago, issued a statement to the Stanford Faculty Senate that criticized the judge's reasoning. A speech code that establishes standards of civil discourse, Casper maintained, is an educational policy that implicates all four of the academic freedoms quoted by Frankfurter in his *Sweezy* concurrence.[86]

Courts also rejected university reliance on institutional academic freedom to escape contractual obligations to professors. In one case, the majority concluded that a private university's response to a blog post by a tenured professor of political science violated his contractual right to academic freedom. The post criticized an instructor for an interchange with one of the students in her course titled "Theory of Ethics." It asserted that the student challenged the instructor's classroom statement that gay rights need not be discussed because everyone agrees about them. According to the post, the instructor responded that "some opinions are not appropriate in class," including "homophobic comments," and invited the student to drop the course. The post accused the instructor of employing "a tactic typical among liberals now," treating opinions with which they disagree not merely as wrong, and subject to debate on the merits, but as offensive and necessary to censor.[87]

The dean suspended the political science professor for writing the post, informing him that the university would bring formal dismissal proceedings against him. The faculty hearing committee that conducted the disciplinary proceedings concluded that the university had not established a sufficient justification for dismissal. But the committee did conclude that the lesser penalty of suspension without pay for one or two semesters was warranted. The president accepted the committee's recommendation, adding that the professor's resumption of duties after the suspension would be conditioned on his written acknowledgment, in a letter to the president to be shared with the instructor, that his blog post was reckless, that it violated the mission and values of the university, and that he deeply regretted the harm the instructor suffered. The political science professor refused to write this letter.[88]

In objecting to the majority's conclusion that the university had breached its contract with the professor by requiring him to write this letter, the dissent relied heavily on the university's First Amendment right of academic freedom. After acknowledging that no court had clearly defined this right, it asserted that the case implicated who may teach, the first of the four essential academic freedoms identified by Frankfurter's concurrence in *Sweezy*.[89] While agreeing with the dissent that the First Amendment protection for academic freedom extends to universities as well as professors, the majority stressed that institutional academic freedom is a shield against the government, not a sword to violate contracts with faculty.[90]

Conclusion

More than twenty years elapsed between 1957, when the Supreme Court recognized academic freedom as a First Amendment right of professors in *Sweezy*, and 1978, when Justice Powell extended it to the institutional decisions of universities in *Bakke*. Powell relied on the prior cases about professors while more clearly identifying academic freedom as a First Amendment right. The many more lower-court decisions about institutional academic freedom, like those about the academic freedom of professors, arose in a broader range of contexts than the Supreme Court decisions and helped illustrate the scope of the right. Cases about both areas of academic freedom addressed some similar issues, such as the relationship between academic freedom and other First Amendment rights, and the extent to which its protection extends beyond the content of scholarship and teaching. Cases about institutional academic freedom also raised conflicting claims of academic freedom between professors and universities and ambiguities about who can act on behalf of the university. Some important considerations about institutional academic freedom have not even been presented in the case law. For example, plausible arguments can be made that the state has more authority to regulate public universities than private ones, leaving public universities with less institutional academic freedom. The generally undeveloped law demonstrates that institutional academic freedom requires more theoretical analysis as a distinctive First Amendment right, analogous to the theory of individual academic freedom discussed in Chapter 6. I undertake this analysis in Chapter 8, again using the facts of decided cases to illustrate the theory while indicating when it would lead to different results.

8

A Theory of Institutional Academic Freedom as a Distinctive First Amendment Right of Universities

ALTHOUGH THE FUNCTION of academic freedom in protecting the expert speech of professors is the fundamental justification for its recognition as a distinctive First Amendment right, this right also convincingly applies to safeguard the university's freedom to make educational decisions. For universities, as for professors, a convincing theory must differentiate academic freedom from other First Amendment rights while explaining why it fits within the First Amendment. It is conceptually more difficult to apply the First Amendment to institutions than to individuals. Individuals obviously speak. Institutions do not speak in the same direct way. Yet courts, recognizing that institutions such as universities, newspapers, and libraries are devoted to expression, have applied the First Amendment to protect this interest.[1] In cases about commercial speech and campaign finance, moreover, courts have extended First Amendment rights to corporations generally, often less convincingly than to institutions themselves devoted to expressive interests. These decisions bring universities as institutions within the ambit of the First Amendment.

Just as there are good reasons to differentiate a distinctive First Amendment right of academic freedom for professors from more general First Amendment rights of free speech, there are good reasons to differentiate a distinctive First Amendment right of academic freedom for universities from the general application of the First Amendment to institutions. Just as the expert academic speech by professors should not be evaluated by First Amendment doctrines defining matters of public concern or the official duties of public employees, the educational decisions of universities should not be evaluated by First Amendment doctrines of content and viewpoint neutrality. For universities, as for professors, the fundamental First

Amendment commitment to the production and dissemination of knowledge provides the justification for a distinctive First Amendment theory of academic freedom.

Yet this justification also defines the boundaries of academic freedom. Just as it does not extend to speech by professors unrelated to their expertise, it does not extend beyond the educational decisions of universities.[2] Peer review is often essential to determining these boundaries for universities as well as for professors. For universities, as for professors, more general First Amendment rights may be available for securing interests outside the scope of academic freedom. Just as the First Amendment right of free speech may protect the nonacademic expression of professors, the First Amendment right of institutional autonomy may protect university decisions that are not primarily educational. Religious institutions are also protected from government interference by the free exercise clause of the First Amendment.

Institutions defined as "proprietary" by the AAUP's 1915 Declaration would not qualify for the protection of institutional academic freedom because they are established to propagate an ideology rather than to advance knowledge.[3] As examples of proprietary institutions, the 1915 Declaration identified universities devoted to promoting religious faith, socialist doctrine, or the protective tariff. The 1915 Declaration observed that proprietary institutions of all kinds, religious and secular, were becoming increasingly rare in the United States. It also observed that most religious universities were not proprietary because they did not limit the search for knowledge by demanding adherence to doctrines of faith.[4] Decades later, Supreme Court decisions in the 1970s relied on the adoption by religiously affiliated universities of the AAUP-AAC 1940 Statement of Principles on Academic Freedom and Tenure as evidence that they were not devoted to religious indoctrination.[5]

Contrary to the apparent expectation of the 1915 Declaration, some religiously affiliated universities are proprietary a century later. Indeed, since the 1970s, theological developments, perhaps especially within the Roman Catholic Church and some Protestant evangelical denominations, have produced a greater, though still relatively small, number of institutions in which religious doctrine limits academic freedom.[6] I am unaware of any current counterparts to the secular proprietary institutions identified in the 1915 Declarations. But the implementation of current arguments for restricting scholarship and teaching would create proprietary institutions. Examples include requiring laudatory interpretations of American history, forbidding the teaching of critical race theory or other academic views that challenge such laudatory interpretations, and denying protection to knowledge that is perceived as rationalizing racism or undermining democracy.

As the history of the American university illustrates, institutional functions may change over time. In his classic work *Academic Freedom in the Age of the University*, Walter Metzger describes the emergence of the modern American university in the generation after the Civil War as an educational revolution in which the function of the university shifted from conserving to searching for knowledge.[7] The 1915 Declaration itself contrasted early universities, whose chief concern was "to diffuse the already accepted knowledge," from the modern university, which was dedicated to discovering new knowledge.[8] It is conceivable that another educational revolution could again transform the American university. If the university no longer seeks the production and dissemination of knowledge, it loses the primary justification for its academic freedom. But unless pervasive evidence exists that universities have abandoned this function, which would be a dramatic transformation from the contemporary situation, judges should recognize institutional academic freedom, deferring to universities when they act within its proper scope.

In this chapter I examine what decisions should be covered by the First Amendment right of institutional academic freedom, who within the university has the authority to make those decisions, and how the distinction between public and private universities should influence the extent of institutional academic freedom from the state. For institutions, as for professors, the 1915 Declaration and other AAUP documents provide insights that help justify the treatment of academic freedom as a distinctive First Amendment right.

The Scope of Institutional Academic Freedom

Determining what constitutes an educational decision is as crucial to defining the scope of institutional academic freedom as determining what constitutes expert academic speech by a professor is to the scope of individual academic freedom. The distinction between educational and other institutional decisions is often clear, but sometimes the assessment of whether a decision is educational can be difficult and contested.

. Institutional academic freedom comes closest to the traditional justification for academic freedom when it protects professors from external intrusion. The 1915 Declaration identifies pressures on universities from both trustees and state legislators to infringe the academic freedom of professors. It stresses that universities must preserve their intellectual independence from these pressures, although it does not expand the language of academic freedom to encompass this institutional need. Yet the relationship between the intellectual independence of the university and the production and dissemination of knowledge justifies referring to this independence as institutional academic freedom and incorporating it within the First Amendment.

In a much more recent discussion of academic freedom unrelated to its legal meaning, Amy Gutmann, a political philosopher who subsequently became president of the University of Pennsylvania, asserted that "universities dedicated to free scholarly inquiry can legitimately assert an institutional right to academic freedom, consistent with (indeed derived from) the right of their faculty to academic freedom." She focused on the institutional role of universities in protecting faculty from government regulations that threaten scholarship and teaching.[9] Legal scholarship advocating a First Amendment right of institutional academic freedom similarly emphasizes its role in protecting the scholarship and teaching that occurs within the university.[10]

Beyond their capacity to protect the academic freedom of faculty from external intrusion, universities make many educational decisions that should be protected by institutional academic freedom because they promote the production and dissemination of knowledge. Examples include but should not be limited to decisions about the selection of faculty and students, curriculum, and pedagogy, the elements of institutional academic freedom identified in the South African statement quoted by Frankfurter in his frequently cited concurrence in *Sweezy*.

In matters of appointment and tenure, I agree with Judge Posner that university interests in institutional academic freedom are stronger in making the decision itself than in maintaining the confidentiality of the peer review process. Lack of confidentiality in peer review does not prevent universities from selecting who may teach. Yet the Supreme Court's refusal to recognize any right of institutional academic freedom to protect confidentiality in peer review is unconvincing. I disagree with its assertion that the relationship between confidentiality in peer review and the right to select professors is "extremely attenuated." Administrators and professors over-whelmingly agree, and many lower-court judges have recognized, that confidentiality promotes frankness. The interests of candidates in enforcing their First Amendment rights and statutory protections against employment discrimination may sometimes require disclosure of confidential peer review material. But as lower-court decisions demonstrated before the issue reached the Supreme Court, it is possible to balance these interests against interests in confidentiality through a qualified privilege against disclosure that could be overcome in certain circumstances. The AAUP's policy on judicially compelled disclosure, relied on by the second circuit, provides useful examples of factors that could be weighed in determining whether to recognize a privilege: the adequacy of the university's procedures in making the decision, the quality of the reasons for the decision provided by the university, statistical evidence supporting an inference of discrimination, statements or incidents indicating bias against the candidate, the availability of the information sought from nonconfidential sources, and the importance of the information sought.

The institutional academic freedom to make appointment and tenure decisions, though stronger than its interest in confidentiality during the peer review process, must be based on the academic grounds required by the South African statement. As I elaborate in Chapter 10, evidence that a decision was not made on academic grounds can include indications of political or discriminatory motivation as well as lack of appropriate peer review, administrative or board reversals of overwhelmingly positive recommendations by peer review committees, unsupported or unconvincing reasons for adverse decisions, inconsistent application of university standards, statements by decision makers, and statistical evidence comparing candidates.

Institutional academic freedom to make decisions about students should extend beyond "who may be admitted to study," the language of the South African statement. Following the lead of the Supreme Court, lower courts have correctly concluded that it should protect decisions by appropriate university bodies to dismiss students for failing to meet academic standards.[11] Judge Posner persuasively maintained that the institutional academic freedom to make these decisions can justify more informality in dismissal proceedings than in civil and criminal litigation. While observing that too much informality could violate the due process clause of the Fourteenth Amendment, Posner concluded that this clause does not provide students with a right to counsel who could perform all the functions of a trial lawyer. Such a right, he warned, would impose the model of adversary litigation on the university, adding to the "bureaucratization" of education as well as to the cost of conducting a hearing.[12] Yet some claims of institutional academic freedom in student dismissal proceedings are unconvincing. I agree with the judge who decided that the presence of a union representative at an investigatory interview of a student subject to possible dismissal did not interfere with the university's discretion to make its decision on academic grounds and, therefore, did not violate its academic freedom.[13] In general, judges should give more deference to university procedures in cases about academic issues, where the distinctive educational context is most relevant.

Educational decisions about student extracurricular activities should also fall within the scope of institutional academic freedom. Several justices have appropriately highlighted the educational value of extracurricular activities while recognizing the First Amendment right of institutional academic freedom. In his landmark opinion relying on this right to support affirmative action in student admissions, Justice Powell, quoting the president of Princeton University, noted that the educational value of student diversity extends beyond the classroom to informal extracurricular learning. Justice Stevens observed that a university could legitimately conclude that some extracurricular activities have more educational value than others. Justice Souter agreed, quoting approvingly from a university handbook that described extracurricular activities as a "second curriculum." And Justice Ginsburg concluded that extracurricular activities are "essential parts of the educational process" while upholding the constitutionality of a law school's policy requiring all registered student organizations to comply with its nondiscrimination policy.[14] Institutional academic freedom should include this second curriculum as well as the classroom curriculum. I agree with Justices Stevens and Souter that the exercise of institutional academic freedom in making educational decisions should not be confined by general First Amendment doctrines of content and viewpoint neutrality. Universities should be able to decide that some extracurricular activities, like some courses, have more educational value than others.

University decisions may be based on institutional commitments to societal rather than educational values, such as denying recruitment facilities on campus to organizations whose employment or environmental policies contradict standards established by the university. These decisions are outside the scope of institutional academic freedom. An affirmative action plan justified by the educational value of diversity would fit within institutional academic freedom, but an affirmative action plan justified by the societal value of a more integrated or economically mobile society would not.

The Supreme Court cases on affirmative action in higher education reveal the differences between educational and broader societal justifications. Justice Powell indicated that he conceived the educational value of diversity to be much broader than its contribution to "speculation" and "the exchange of ideas," the language he quoted from *Sweezy* and *Keyishian*. Among the student "qualities more likely to promote beneficial educational pluralism," Powell identified "exceptional personal talents, unique work or service experience, leadership potential, maturity, demonstrated compassion, a history of overcoming disadvantage, [and] ability to communicate with the poor." These qualities are impressive. Some and perhaps all of them may make people better doctors and, therefore, should be considered in deciding which applicants to admit to medical school. But Powell did not explain how they "promote beneficial educational pluralism" that comes within the rubric of academic freedom. Although Justice O'Connor confused the relationship between institutional academic freedom and general institutional autonomy in *Grutter* while endorsing Powell's analysis in *Bakke,* her opinion provides good examples of justifications for affirmative action that do and do not relate to academic freedom. Claims that student diversity leads to "cross-cultural understanding" that improves classroom discussion and "learning outcomes" clearly relate to academic freedom. Claims that it produces a workforce that contributes to American competitiveness in a global marketplace, a military officer corps that increases national security, and a path to leadership the public perceives as legitimate do not.

Regulation of gun possession on campus presents another example of an issue whose connection to academic freedom may depend on the university's justification, as a case decided by the Utah Supreme Court illustrates. The University of Utah adopted a policy that prohibited students, faculty, and staff from carrying guns on campus. After the state legislature passed a law allowing gun possession on campus, the university asserted that its autonomy over academic matters guaranteed by the state constitution precluded this legislation. The majority upheld the law, rejecting the university's interpretation of the state constitution.[15] But a dissenting judge examined whether the university relied on educational considerations in adopting its policy. If the policy simply reflected a social or political judgment about the relationship between carrying firearms and crime, the judge reasoned, the state constitutional provision would not afford any protection against the legislation because the university has no more expertise than the legislature. But the judge found that the university based its judgment on an evaluation of how gun possession on campus would affect its educational environment, an issue within its academic expertise. He, therefore, concluded that the state constitution prohibited the legislature from interfering with the university's policy.[16] This persuasive analysis, though in a dissent, applies to claims based on institutional academic freedom as well as on state constitutional guarantees. Similarly, if Princeton had provided educational reasons for excluding the public from its property instead of relying on a more expansive right of autonomy from state intervention, its claim of institutional academic freedom would have been more persuasive.

Should institutional academic freedom apply to a university's decision to ban fraternities or to bar military recruiters from campus for refusing to sign the university's required pledge not to discriminate based on sexual orientation? Banning fraternities can encourage a more intellectually serious student body committed to the pursuit of knowledge, a point that universities have emphasized in doing so and that the Supreme Court seemed to recognize in a 1915 decision upholding a state law that prohibited them. Rejecting claims of a fraternity member that the law violated his Fourteenth Amendment rights to equal protection and the pursuit of happiness, the Court observed that fraternities "could distract from the singleness of purpose which the state desired to exist in its public educational institutions."[17] If a university made the same argument as the state, institutional academic freedom would plausibly protect the ban.

Barring military recruiters from campus because military policies on hiring homosexuals are inconsistent with university rules against discrimination presents a more difficult context for extending institutional academic freedom. A majority of the voting members of the Yale law faculty maintained that this policy furthered the law school's educational mission of inculcating the value of equal justice and is, therefore, within the academic freedom protected by the First Amendment. In rejecting the faculty's claim, the judge conceded that allowing military recruiters on campus could incidentally detract from this mission. Perhaps this incidental impact is sufficient to come within a very capacious interpretation of institutional academic freedom. But I agree with the judge that the context of recruitment by potential employers is quite remote from the core educational concerns protected by institutional academic freedom.[18]

Even less convincing is reliance on institutional academic freedom as a justification for an educational exemption from taxation of a university golf course. Yet a California state court upheld this exemption for Stanford. The educational exemption, the court maintained, is based on the academic freedom of universities to remain independent of government control so that they can "fulfill their role as independent critics of government action." Freedom from taxation of university property seems remote from the institutional academic freedom to formulate and implement educational policy. More specifically, a golf course, especially one used more by alumni than students, does not seem related to the educational functions of a university.[19] There may be good policy reasons for exempting university property from taxation, but protecting academic freedom is not one of them. Universities whose golf courses are subject to taxation remain free "to fulfill their role as independent critics of government action." More convincing is the decision of the Alaska Supreme Court that legislation allowing a private developer to reroute a road on state university property, while requiring compensation to the university, did not have any adverse impact on the university's academic freedom.[20]

Who Exercises Institutional Academic Freedom?

The persuasiveness of institutional claims to academic freedom depends on the locus as well as the subject of the decision. Just as only some decisions by universities are within the scope of institutional academic freedom, only some people and groups within universities are competent to make these decisions. The 1966 Statement on Government, jointly formulated by the AAUP, the American Council on Education, and the Association of Governing Boards of Colleges and Universities, helps identify who within the university should make various educational decisions. Judicial decisions and historical controversies provide additional examples.

The 1966 Statement's grant of "primary responsibility" to the faculty covers matters within its academic expertise, such as decisions about appointment and tenure.[21] As Robert Post persuasively maintains, university administrators do not possess the capacity to assess the academic quality of professors. Effectively invoking the landmark *Sweezy* case to illustrate this point, Post observes that the result should not have been different if "lay administrators" rather than the state attorney general "had sought to dictate or determine relevant economic truth and to regulate Paul Sweezy's lectures on that basis."[22] Proof by lay administrators that they made their determination of economic truth in good faith cannot overcome their lack of capacity to make that determination at all on the academic grounds that justify institutional academic freedom.

While maintaining that the administration and governing board "should concur with the faculty judgment" in areas of primary faculty responsibility, the 1966 Statement recognizes that they have the power to review and reverse faculty decisions in exceptional circumstances for compelling reasons. Such reversals would be a legitimate exercise of institutional academic freedom.[23] The 1966 Statement does not specify what constitutes "exceptional circumstances" or "compelling reasons," but they are generally understood to include convincing evidence that the faculty did not exercise or deviated from academic standards in making its decisions.

Although it acknowledges primary faculty responsibility for many academic decisions by a university, subject to administrative and board review, the 1966 Statement identifies a greater role for governing boards and administrators regarding some academic matters. It views the development of "general educational policy" as a "joint effort" in which the governing board actively participates. Only after the establishment of an educational goal does the faculty assume the primary responsibility to determine the curriculum and pedagogy. More specifically, it encourages joint participation of the governing board, administration, and faculty before any decisions are made regarding "the size or composition of the student body and the relative emphasis to be given to the various elements of the educational and research programs." In discussing the role of the president, the 1966 Statement identifies functions that directly relate to academic issues. The president has "a special obligation to innovate and initiate," and "must at times, with or without faculty support, infuse new life into a department," which can include "working within the concept of tenure, to solve problems of obsolescence."[24]

The reasoning of the 1966 Statement helps identify specific examples of educational decisions within the proper locus of the governing board and administration. Some are matters of very general institutional policy. A university may have an institutional commitment to a traditional classical education, such as St. Johns, or to experiential learning, such as Antioch. A university may decide to become coeducational, as many did in the late

1960s and early 1970s, or to remain single sex, as have several women's colleges. Universities place varying emphasis on the mix of scholarship, teaching, and service expected of faculty. They may have educational reasons for adopting policies on affirmative action, prohibiting gun possession on campus, banning fraternities, enacting a code governing campus speech, regulating student extracurricular activities, and restricting access to campus by the general public. They make financial decisions with clear educational implications, such as building a new medical school, or giving more money to an emerging field or less to fields with long term declines in enrollment. It is appropriate for administrators and governing boards to make these decisions, though, as the 1966 Statement provides, faculty advice about them is often useful and should be sought.

Illustrations from Judicial Decisions

The facts, though not always the holdings, of judicial decisions illustrate the relationship between the locus of a university's decision and its claims to institutional academic freedom. Many cases involve issues of faculty status requiring assessments of academic competence that should be made by faculty peers. In responding to challenges by professors denied reappointment or tenure, courts have overwhelmingly and appropriately deferred to the academic judgment of faculty committees acting on behalf of the university. They have occasionally and accurately recognized the primary faculty role by pointing out that the decision by the peer review committee is typically decisive rather than merely advisory and that, therefore, a statement of reasons for a negative decision from the president to the candidate would not provide sufficient information.[25] Reflecting the prevalence of peer review in decisions about reappointment and tenure, I am unaware of any case in which it did not occur. In such a case, the decision should not be protected by institutional academic freedom because neither administrators nor the governing board have the requisite competence to act for the university.

Courts have also recognized that faculty committees make decisions for the university when they assess the qualifications of students. In his majority opinion upholding the decision of a faculty committee that dismissed a student for academic deficiencies, Justice Stevens treated the committee as acting on behalf of the university and deferred to "the faculty's professional judgment."[26] A circuit court specifically attached institutional academic freedom to the decision by a faculty committee that a student dissertation did not meet the university's academic standards.[27] In the context of student admissions, a district court, quoting Justice Stevens, similarly based its recognition of institutional academic freedom on the academic expertise of the faculty. The university's determination that various courses taught by Christian high schools did not meet its requirements for adequate preparation, the court emphasized, was based on faculty assessments of their quality.[28]

Faculty should be the locus of institutional academic freedom for other decisions by universities that depend on assessments of academic competence, including the pedagogical relevance of classroom speech, and the extent to which writing or speech by faculty is professional, unprofessional, or unrelated to academic matters. In contrast to reappointment and tenure, where peer review is well established, administrators, including people who had never been faculty members, often make these decisions for universities, and judges often defer to them or make their own determinations without requiring any peer review. In some of these cases, judges convincingly relied on administrative enforcement of collective faculty judgments about appropriate pedagogy to reject claims by professors that these judgments violated their individual academic freedom. Examples include requiring the teaching of upper-level Spanish courses in Spanish and limiting the ability of students to select their own assignments and organize class time. Yet the courts deferred to the administrators rather than to the collective determination of the faculty, which the administrators enforced.[29]

Judicial decisions similarly misplaced the locus of institutional academic freedom in holdings that applied it to decisions of administrators who changed grades assigned by faculty. Grading is an expert academic judgment whose potential abuse should be assessed by peers, not administrators. It is hard to imagine a legitimate institutional interest that justifies a university president ordering a professor to change an F to an incomplete for a student who attended only three of fifteen class sessions in a "practicum" course designed to give students supervised practical experience.[30]

Some legal decisions illustrate the increase of administrators without academic backgrounds who have authority to regulate and discipline academic speech without any role for peer review. In one case, the vice president of student services reprimanded and threatened disciplinary proceedings against a professor for classroom comments asserting that homosexuality is a disease and for assigning religious texts to provide a moral perspective.[31] In another, the administrator of complaints of discriminatory behavior in the Office of the Vice President of Student Services had discretion over enforcement of the university's Policy on Discrimination and Discriminatory Harassment of Students in the University Environment. The judge observed that in three internal proceedings involving allegations of harassing statements by students made during classroom discussions, the administrator ignored issues of free speech and academic freedom.[32]

Recent interpretations and applications of Title IX, enacted by Congress in 1972 to address discrimination that affects educational opportunities for women, reinforce concerns that nonacademic administrators are making unilateral decisions that implicate academic freedom, particularly in treating expression by professors as prohibited sexual harassment. A 2016 Report of the AAUP, "The History, Uses, and Abuses of Title IX," pointed out that the current interpretation of sexual harassment under Title IX covers speech that creates a "hostile environment."[33] The report included examples of Title IX administrators at various campuses who have sat in classes unannounced, challenged a professor's pedagogy, urged that professors issue "trigger warnings" about especially sensitive or disturbing curricular content that might distress students who have suffered past trauma, and investigated a professor based on an article she published in the *Chronicle of Higher Education* entitled "Sexual Paranoia Strikes Academia." It observed that these administrators often lack faculty standing, work in human resources departments or offices of equity and inclusion, and are insulated from professors and from systems of shared governance within universities. As a result, the report stressed, the Title IX administrators have not considered potential concerns about academic freedom. It urged faculty participation in the creation and implementation of policies that "define proscribed conduct and speech while protecting academic freedom and free expression" and that incorporate peer review.[34] As in other matters raising issues about the extent and limits of expert academic speech, the faculty should be the primary locus of the institutional decisions about whether speech alleged to violate university policies is protected by academic freedom.

In other cases, by contrast, courts have appropriately identified administrators as the proper locus for the exercise of institutional academic freedom. Unlike decisions about the competence of professors, university requirements that professors convey course expectations to students at the beginning of the semester and distribute standardized course evaluation forms at the end do not depend on specialized faculty expertise and seem within the legitimate range of administrative judgment.[35] Although faculty expertise would be helpful in determining the contents of the course evaluation forms, I do not think the fact that administrators or trustees developed them should necessarily undermine the claim to institutional academic freedom. Though administrators do not have the academic expertise to evaluate individual grades, they should be able to enforce a general grading policy, designed to implement the university's decision to educate a broad rather than an elite student body, over the academic freedom of a professor to assign his own grades reflecting higher standards. The determination of a university's mission is a matter of broad educational policy for the institution, and the dispute over grading did not turn on professional competence to evaluate a student's performance.[36]

Another case, consistent with the 1966 Statement and the AAUP's Recommended Institutional Regulations on academic freedom and tenure, recognized the appropriate division of responsibility between the faculty and the governing board in a dismissal proceeding.[37] The faculty hearing committee found a professor guilty of unethical conduct and recommended that he be placed on probation for three years. The board of trustees confirmed that finding, but it rejected the recommendation regarding probation and directed the faculty committee to reconsider the issue of punishment. Upon reconsideration, the faculty committee reversed its prior determination and recommended dismissal. The board accepted this revised recommendation and fired the faculty member.[38]

Historical Controversies Raising Close Questions

Although judicial decisions provide good examples of who within the university should exercise institutional academic freedom, two historically important controversies indicate that the proper locus of institutional authority can be unclear and debatable. A dispute at Harvard, featuring key figures in the history of academic freedom, arose in 1937 when instructors in the Economics Department received notice that their appointments would not be renewed. Newspapers in Boston published articles intimating that the radical views of two instructors prompted their dismissals. Harvard responded with a press release stating that it had made its decisions "solely on grounds of teaching capacity and scholarly ability." Over a hundred members of the Harvard faculty below the rank of full professor wrote a memorandum to nine senior professors expressing concerns about the dismissals and requesting an inquiry into them. The senior professors transmitted the memorandum to President Conant, who then asked them to conduct the inquiry. Paul Sweezy, who twenty years later was the plaintiff in the first Supreme Court case that identified academic freedom as a First Amendment right, was one of the dismissed instructors. Felix Frankfurter, then a law professor at Harvard and subsequently the author of the influential concurring opinion in *Sweezy* that became the foundation for First Amendment protection of institutional academic freedom, was one of the senior professors on the committee that conducted the inquiry. Arthur Lovejoy, a key author of the AAUP's 1915 Declaration, wrote a review in the AAUP's journal of the committee's lengthy report.[39]

The report found that the university had not violated the academic freedom of the dismissed instructors, but that a misunderstanding between the president and the Department of Economics had unintentionally caused injustice to them.[40] It also recommended general criteria that should govern decisions about retention and promotion. It maintained that it is at least arguable that great teachers should receive permanent appointments even if they are not creative scholars, and worried about giving young professors in undergraduate colleges the impression that teaching can be neglected. It opposed using volume of publication as the sole measure of scholarly capacity, pointing out that the most promising young scholars often need time to make original and important conclusions. It urged every academic department to identify emerging new areas within its field of learning and to provide instruction and research in them, citing labor problems as an example in economics. Beyond including new areas within a field, the report emphasized the "need for diversity of method, attitude and point of view" within a department's faculty, especially in a field, like economics, where many traditional assumptions had become "open questions on which trained and competent scholars are divided." Asserting that "a university can not live in isolation from the society in which it is embedded," it maintained that many departments should have members who "are directly in contact with social movements and economic activities outside the universities." In studying industrial relations, for example, departments should include both people who are not participants in the labor movement, who can have a "detached" perspective on it, and participants "who can learn something of the movement from the inside."[41]

These subjects addressed by the report clearly involve matters of educational policy within the expertise of faculty. Yet in contrast to the evaluation of the merits of scholarship or pedagogy, which requires competence that the faculty uniquely possess, they are matters about which academic administrators also have informed views and raise broad issues of general educational policy arguably within the purview of the governing board.

Another difficult issue about the locus of institutional authority arose during the Cold War following World War II, when people disagreed about whether membership or past membership in the Communist Party provided grounds for dismissing professors. While arguing in his debate with Alexander Meiklejohn that the act of joining the Communist Party constitutes a renunciation of academic freedom justifying dismissal, Sidney Hook maintained that this determination should be made by the faculty at each university. He reasoned persuasively that the faculty is less subject than administrators and trustees to improper pressure from external groups.[42] It is plausible, moreover, that professors are in the best position to assess the impact of Communist Party membership on the ability of a professor to engage in free academic inquiry. Yet unlike assessing the quality of a professor's research, this assessment does not depend on specialized academic knowledge. Although it may fit within the more general competence of the faculty identified by the 1966 Statement, it was a major issue of public controversy throughout the country during the Cold War about which many people who had no connections to universities had informed and intelligent opinions. I incline to Hook's view that the relationship between Communist Party membership and academic freedom is best assessed by the faculty even as I disagree with his own assessment. But I do not think the First Amendment protection for academic freedom should preclude placing this decision with the administration and governing board.

It is also useful to remember that during the Cold War professors as well as administrators and trustees often favored the dismissal of professors who had joined the Communist Party. Hook, himself a professor, quoted the declaration of the graduate faculty of the New School of Social Research that "no member of the faculty can be a member of any political Party or group which asserts the right to dictate in matters of science or scientific opinion."[43] And sometimes, administrators opposed taking any adverse action against professors who were members of the Communist Party. Meiklejohn himself, though a professor when he wrote his article disagreeing with Hook, had been the president of Amherst College decades before.[44]

The Distinction between Public and Private Universities

Ever since the *Dartmouth College* decision in 1819 interpreting the "impairment of contracts" clause, the distinction between public and private universities has influenced judicial review, often prompting courts to allow more state regulation of public than of private universities. Should institutional academic freedom depend on this distinction? The answer to this question is complicated. In many contexts, whether a university is public or private should make no difference in the extent to which it is either protected from or subject to state interference. Yet on many matters that have educational implications, the state arguably has more legitimate control over its own universities than over private ones, leaving public universities with less institutional academic freedom.

Legislative designation of an institution as a university, I believe, entails acceptance of the widespread societal understanding that universities are committed to the production and dissemination of knowledge, functions that require academic freedom. Some institutions funded by the state are established as vehicles for conveying government viewpoints, but universities are not. Justice Rehnquist recognized this point while declaring that the general right of the state to regulate the content of speech in its own institutions does not extend to state universities.[45] The contrast between a solicitor general's office and a university law school provides a good illustration. The solicitor general, whose function is to support government positions in the courts, should be able to condition continued employment of staff attorneys on their advocacy of legal arguments that conform to government policy. By contrast, a state university, whose function is to promote critical inquiry, should not be able to condition continued employment of law professors on their advocacy of legal arguments favored by the state legislature or university administrators.

Yet state legislators often fund various institutions of higher education with quite different goals and programs, including research universities, community colleges, agricultural universities, and medical schools. Insufficient legislative funding can lead to the elimination of faculty positions, and legislatures can decide to end funding entirely for institutions of higher education they previously established. These legislative decisions clearly limit the freedom of state colleges and universities to determine "who may teach," "what may be taught," and "who may be admitted to study." Yet no one has ever maintained that they violate a public university's institutional academic freedom, and it is difficult to imagine convincing arguments that they do. A legislature's determination of the kinds of institutions of higher education and the extent of their funding seems clearly within its legitimate power. These arguments for legislative authority do not apply to private universities, whose decisions about their educational goals and programs should be protected by institutional academic freedom from state interference.

Similar Treatment of Public and Private Universities

Institutional academic freedom should protect public as well as private universities from legislation that investigates or regulates the content of scholarship and teaching. Court cases that identified academic freedom as a First Amendment right arose at state universities. They convincingly asserted that it prohibits legislation requiring disclosure of the contents of a classroom lecture or interfering with the assignment and classroom discussion of controversial views.[46] It is in this context that Justice Frankfurter lay the foundation in *Sweezy* for the First Amendment right to institutional academic freedom recognized by Justice Powell in *Bakke*, another case arising at a public university. Frankfurter emphasized "the dependence of a free society on free universities," which requires "the exclusion of governmental intervention in the intellectual life of a university."[47] *Sweezy* and the other early cases identifying academic freedom as a First Amendment right involved teaching about Marxism during the Cold War. Legislation prohibiting universities from teaching evolution or requiring them to teach "creation science" should similarly be deemed violations of institutional academic freedom at both public and private universities because they preempt the expertise of peer review in determining whether a theory meets academic standards. Though a former law professor, Justice Scalia ignored the central relationship between peer review and academic freedom by maintaining in a dissenting opinion that a legislature should be able to decide what constitutes "scientific evidence" regarding the origins of life and to impose its view on professors who disagree.[48] Legislation that conditions research grants to universities on the right of government officials to approve publication also violates institutional academic freedom. The federal case that raised this issue arose at Stanford, a private university, but the result should not be different at the public University of California.

A flurry of recent bills and laws illustrates the persistence of legislative intrusion that violates institutional academic freedom.[49] A highly publicized Florida law governing public universities in the state, frequently referred to as the "Stop WOKE Act," is a particularly good example. It defines as unlawful discrimination instruction that "espouses, promotes, advances, inculcates or compels" a student "to believe" in eight listed concepts. One concept is that an individual's "moral character or status" is "determined" by "race, color, sex, or national origins." Others are that an individual, by virtue of these characteristics, should receive "adverse treatment" based on "past actions" by members of the same group, or to "achieve diversity, equity or inclusion." Similarly prohibited is the concept that "such virtues as merit, excellence, hard work, fairness, neutrality, objectivity, and racial colorblindness are racist or sexist" or created to "oppress."[50] The law also provides that discussion is not prohibited if the instruction "is given in an objective manner without endorsement of the concepts."[51] In significant respects, this law is more intrusive than the one declared unconstitutional in *Sweezy*. Whereas the attorney general of New Hampshire invoked the state law to ask about the contents of Sweezy's lecture, the Florida law directly interferes with instruction, the academic freedom of the university "to determine for itself on academic grounds" both "what may be taught" and "how it shall be taught."[52]

The judge who granted a preliminary injunction against enforcement of this law pointed out how it could interfere with instruction by the professors at various state universities who challenged it. A law professor uses a casebook that "explains how racism is embedded in the criminal justice system." A professor of education assigns articles that "discuss white privilege and critique the concept of colorblindness" in a course in critical race studies. A professor of political science teaches courses in which she "endorses critical race theory and assigns reading materials that advocate for affirmative action." A professor of philosophy "teaches that merit, objectivity, and colorblindness function to solidify systems of oppression as foundational truths rather than academic theories." A professor of communications includes sections on "whiteness" and "race discrimination in academia." And a professor of measurement and statistics "encourages students to consider systemic discrimination when evaluating the effects of race in statistical models" and discusses "his own white privilege."[53]

As in many cases, the judge focused on general First Amendment issues in analyzing facts that raise clear issues of academic freedom. He stressed that the law constitutes viewpoint discrimination prohibited by the First Amendment, banning "disfavored viewpoints in university classrooms while permitting unfettered expression of the opposite viewpoint." Yet he did refer to academic freedom in elaborating his conclusion about viewpoint discrimination. The defendants, he observed, argue that under the act "professors enjoy 'academic freedom' so long as they express only those viewpoints of which the State approves." Using affirmative action as an example, the judge observed that a professor could discuss it as a fact or condemn it as a failed policy but could not endorse its benefits.[54]

In addition to safeguarding scholarship and teaching, institutional academic freedom should protect the right of public as well as private universities to select faculty on academic grounds without state interference. Just as he ignored the role of peer review in determining what shall be taught, Justice Scalia questioned its function in decisions about faculty hiring and retention. "I guess somebody has a right to say who may teach," he mused during oral argument of the University of Pennsylvania case involving the disclosure of confidential tenure files, "but does it have to be the faculty?" Wondering "what is the principle that . . . members of a faculty have a constitutional right to . . . replicate themselves," he asked the university's lawyer if the right to hire faculty in a state university could be reserved to a legislative committee or the governor. The university attorney emphasized the faculty's traditional role in making these decisions, but he seemed to concede that the alternatives posed by Justice Scalia did not raise constitutional problems.[55] A more convincing answer would have stressed that this traditional role derives from the faculty's expertise in determining the academic merits of professors and that involvement by others would not only lack expertise but would increase the danger that violations of academic freedom might influence the decision. This reasoning applies equally to public and private universities.

Just as First Amendment academic freedom should protect some core educational functions of both public and private universities from state interference, some state interests are substantial enough to justify laws that constrain both public and private universities even though educational functions may be affected. State interests in national security may justify laws that restrict dissemination of academic research that would reveal the details of military operations during wartime or how to produce dangerous weapons. They may also justify laws that prohibit federal funding for universities that refuse access to military recruiters, even if those laws impede the ability of law schools to model professional values that are violated by military discrimination against homosexuals. State interests in public health may justify laws that restrict research involving toxic chemicals or endangering human subjects. State interests in public safety may justify laws allowing or preventing possession of weapons on campus. State interests in preventing discrimination may justify laws that limit university discretion over student admissions and faculty employment. State interests in protecting peaceful expression or in preventing incitement to unlawful violence may justify laws regulating campus speech. State interests in preventing fraud and maintaining academic standards may justify state scrutiny of the educational claims and programs of universities. These state interests apply to private as well as public universities.

Different Treatment of Public and Private Universities

Other state interests seem within the state's authority to regulate public but not private universities, often by analogy to the right of the state to determine what kinds of universities to establish. After World War II, for example, the California legislature extended engineering education into the less selective state college system despite the resistance of administrators from the University of California. The administrators argued that instruction in engineering should be focused within the University of California because it had better faculty and students.[56] Whatever the educational merits of this claim, the legislature's decision seems clearly within its authority and should not be considered a violation of the university's academic freedom.

Similarly, a state legislature should be able to establish a state university designed to promote progressive or conservative educational values. And if a state legislature can establish such universities, it should be able to transform a progressive or conservative university into its opposite, accomplishing by legislation what Governor DeSantis achieved in Florida by appointing new trustees who want to turn traditionally progressive New College into a state counterpart to the conservative private Hillsdale College.[57] On the other hand, a private university should be able to invoke its institutional academic freedom to determine its educational goals, such as traditional classical education at St. Johns College and experiential learning at Antioch College.

A legislative decision that a particular state university should serve a broad or elite student body is not that different from a legislative decision to establish a community college or a research university. A lower court has indicated that institutional academic freedom protects a decision by university administrators to serve an "average" student population while rejecting a professor's claim that they had violated his own academic freedom by changing his grades to higher ones.[58] But what if the state legislature had made the determination that the university should serve average students and had restricted attempts by the university faculty, administration, and trustees to raise academic standards? While institutional academic freedom might protect the university against a faculty member when grading implicates broad issues of educational policy, I do not think it should protect the university against the legislature in the context of determining the university's fundamental mission. Arguably, legislative imposition of a grading curve on the university to help average students may be so significant or specific an intrusion into academic life that it violates institutional academic freedom. But I do not think institutional academic freedom should be available to resist legislative interference if a public university established to serve a broad student population significantly raises its admissions standards or devotes substantial resources to an "honors college" open only to a select minority of the best students. Yet the state interest in serving a broad student body is not strong enough to justify imposing it on private universities whose goals may include educating students with the highest possible academic credentials and potential. Similarly, state regulation of faculty workload to encourage more attention to teaching than to scholarship seems justified for public but not for private universities, which should be able to make their own determinations about the relative weight of teaching and scholarship.[59]

Requiring that public universities enroll at least a designated percentage of state residents in each entering class of students similarly seems a legitimate legislative regulation even though it constrains the university's ability to select its student body on academic grounds. The state has a strong interest in spending its money to educate its own residents, an interest that does not apply to privately funded universities within the state. In my opinion, this state interest outweighs a public university's interest in the educational benefits of a more geographically diverse and potentially more accomplished student body. Legislatures have also passed laws requiring state universities to admit a fixed percentage of each entering class based on class rank in high school, often to increase the number of minority students when courts or referenda have prohibited the use of affirmative action. In considering whether such laws violate academic freedom, Peter Byrne suggests that they do not so long as the percentage is relatively low, but that they do above a relatively high percentage which would interfere too much with a university's ability to establish its own educational goals.[60] While I recognize his concern, I do not think the constitutional analysis should change with the percentage of automatic admits established by the state. The legislative interest in admitting students above a particular class rank may be less than its interest in admitting state residents, but in both cases I think it is sufficient to outweigh the institutional academic freedom of public universities.

Some states require that certain courses be taught in their public universities. The Texas education code, for example, provides that all its public universities must offer a course covering the United States and Texas constitutions and a course in American or Texas history.[61] Imposing these course requirements clearly affects "what may be taught." But just as the legislative designation of an agricultural university affects what may be taught without violating institutional academic freedom, I think the imposition of particular courses to promote the public interest in civic education is a legitimate interest of a state legislature that does not violate the institutional academic freedom of a state university. The state interest in civic education, by contrast, seems weaker with respect to private universities, which should have more discretion in determining for themselves the values they wish to promote. Even in a public university, issues of academic freedom would arise if the legislature, as arguably in *Keyishian* and clearly in the Florida "Stop WOKE Act," attempted to regulate how the state university taught the required courses. Institutional academic freedom should protect against legislative interference with the ability of professors at public as well as private universities to express their expert views about the subject matter, to assign class readings, and to make pedagogical decisions about teaching techniques.

Should a legislature be able to force professors to teach "scientific critiques of prevailing scientific theories"? The majority in *Epperson* assumed that it would be permissible while holding that a law requiring instruction in "creation science" violated the establishment clause. The legislative interest in civic education in a democracy is greater than its interest in the details of the science curriculum. Mandating course content with this degree of specificity, moreover, seems inconsistent with the majority's own recognition of the academic freedom of professors to "teach what they will" based on their expert views of what constitutes "effective and comprehensive science instruction." Yet so long as the legislation allows academic experts within the university to determine what critiques are "scientific," I do not think it violates the institutional academic freedom of a public university, even if it is an unwise intrusion into educational matters that are better decided by the university itself. Private universities, by contrast, should have the institutional academic freedom to determine their science curriculum without state interference.

Private universities should also have more institutional academic freedom to regulate public access to campus. Under general First Amendment law, the public has greater rights of access to public than to private property, and legislatures might want to further specify these rights. Public as well as private universities should be able to invoke institutional academic freedom to limit public access that interferes with educational functions, such as noise from demonstrations on campus that makes it hard to hear in class or the need to reserve certain areas on campus for the many student groups that seek to use them. But the greater public rights of access to public property could outweigh some claims of institutional academic freedom by public universities. As I discuss in Chapter 9, general concerns of public universities that the presence of outsiders on campus detracts from the environment for education, for example, might not outweigh the individual rights of members of the general public to campaign for political candidates or to protest university policies.

Concerns about Educational Misjudgments by Universities

State legislators, like members of the public, have expressed concerns that universities have made educational misjudgments. What if legislators receive evidence that the popularity of postmodernism has precluded the appointment or tenure of highly competent professors with more conventional intellectual orientations, that adherents of law and economics or critical legal studies have supplanted law professors who taught the details of legal doctrine that are much more useful to students studying to be practicing lawyers, that courses focusing on sex, race, and class have crowded out more traditional analysis of literature and history, or that new offerings under the heading "science and society" have replaced courses in the basic sciences? Conversely, what if legislators receive evidence that faculty had remained stuck in academic orthodoxies that disserve their students by denying them access to these exciting new trends in scholarship?

Ronald Dworkin asserted without elaboration that it would be a violation of academic freedom as a "social institution" for a legislature to forbid an English department from becoming entirely dominated by a "trendy new form of criticism" even if that would be "silly" as a matter of academic policy. He also believed that academic freedom as a social institution should inform its constitutional definition. Yet he did not indicate his own opinion about whether a constitutional definition of academic freedom should include this particular social meaning.[62]

In his innovative book analyzing the application of the First Amendment to expert knowledge, Robert Post concluded that state regulation of disciplinary speech is not inherently unconstitutional. "Government may properly seek to regulate professional disciplinary speech whenever experts resist needed change out of inertia or self-interest," he reasoned, "or whenever political control is required to render professions responsive to contemporary needs and values." As his example, he noted the famous argument by Milton and Rose Friedman that licensure enabled the medical profession in its economic self-interest to restrict technological and organizational changes that could have improved the delivery of medical care. Yet he also recognized "the danger of state overreaching" for political and ideological reasons and maintains that the First Amendment "puts the state to its proof whenever it seeks to manipulate the creation and diffusion of disciplinary knowledge."[63] In another book, he and Matthew Finkin convincingly observed that requiring a professor to be balanced or neutral would violate academic freedom if it forced the inclusion of views that had no scholarly merit.[64] Post did not see any "general theoretical solution" for determining the proper balance between state authority to regulate and the First Amendment protection of practices based on expert knowledge. Instead, he envisaged "an endless process of adjustment" that recognizes the need "to negotiate" this "continuous tension." He provided only one specific guideline: "The more divided the community of disciplinary expertise, the greater the leeway for political control."[65] If the state acts contrary to the overwhelming consensus of professional opinion, he persuasively suggested, the odds are great that it is acting for illegitimate reasons.

Debate over the proposed "International Studies in Higher Education Act," passed by the House of Representatives in 2003 but never ratified by the Senate, provides a revealing example in the context of public funding of the issues posed by legislative regulation of academic balance within universities. The act would have amended Title VI of the Higher Education Act of 1965, which funded international education programs at both public and private institutions, by creating an advisory board to the secretary of education and Congress. The advisory board was instructed to make recommendations to promote programs "that will reflect diverse perspectives and the full range of views on world regions, foreign languages, and international affairs." The act authorized the advisory board to monitor and evaluate a sample of the programs funded by Congress as a basis for making recommendations, but not "to mandate, direct, or control an institution of higher education's specific instructional content, curriculum, or program of instruction."[66]

Alleged bias within centers for Middle East studies provided much of the impetus for this legislation. A letter from American Jewish organizations urging that the Senate enact similar language reflects the views of its proponents. The letter asserted that many of these centers "rather than encouraging academic objectivity—follow a political agenda, with scholars uncritically promoting a positive image of Palestinians, Arabs, and the Islamic world, while ignoring or denigrating Israel." Research, it claimed, had documented that these centers frequently "exclude scholars with other perspectives—thereby stifling discourse on critical issues." "Far from stifling academic freedom," the letter concluded, the House legislation "seeks to enhance intellectual freedom and debate in international studies."[67]

While this letter emphasized that scholars had faulted these centers for excluding unpopular academic perspectives, members of Congress who supported the advisory board relied on ideological rather than scholarly considerations. One congressman, for example, associated the "lack of balance" in Middle East studies programs funded by Title VI with "anti-American bias" that is "at odds with our national interest." He concluded without any elaboration that the establishment of the board did not impinge on academic freedom.[68]

Universities and professors raised significant concerns about this legislation. The American Council on Education, on behalf of numerous organizations representing universities, observed that the powers of the advisory board made it more of an investigative than an advisory body. It worried that the board "could intrude into the academic conduct and content of higher education and impinge on institutional decisions about curriculum and activities."[69] The AAUP and the National Coalition Against Censorship asserted without much elaboration that the very establishment of the board would undermine both academic freedom and First Amendment principles. They also highlighted the extent to which proponents of the legislation were driven by political considerations.[70]

In my opinion, state overreaching in academic affairs poses a much greater danger than university abuse of institutional academic freedom. From the investigations of subversive activities in universities during the Cold War to more recent attempts to regulate the teaching of evolution and critical race theory, legislation has frequently threatened academic freedom. Universities generally adhere to academic values and, as many commentators have observed, contests within universities about the relative merits of different intellectual approaches, though yielding temporary winners and losers, are in constant flux. Professors continuously redefine the contours of disciplinary knowledge and create entirely new disciplines. At least over the intermediate and long term, the dominance of intellectual orientations shift.[71]

Even if the problem of university abuse is limited and the danger of state intervention is great, it is difficult to argue that the First Amendment right of academic freedom should preclude a state legislature from any right to intervene when it concludes that universities it has established and funded have made serious educational misjudgments. In order to justify legislative intervention without violating the university's institutional academic freedom, I would require proof that that the university has not followed academic norms in reaching its educational decisions or that the problems perceived by the legislature have persisted for so long that that the typical process of self-correction within universities has failed. These conditions rarely occur. Even when they do, the lack of legislative expertise in educational affairs and the danger that legislative action would be counterproductive should caution against intervention. But subject to these significant constraints, legislative intervention in state universities, even if not prudent, should not always be unconstitutional. The legislature has substantially less legitimate interest in the internal educational decisions of universities it does not fund. I would interpret the institutional academic freedom of private universities to preclude legislative intervention in these decisions, except in programs funded by the government itself, such as the international educational programs under Title VI.

Conclusion

Although the initial emergence of academic freedom as a First Amendment right, like the dominant professional conception of academic freedom developed in the AAUP's 1915 Declaration, attached it to individual professors, the subsequent extension of the First Amendment protection of academic freedom to universities as institutions makes sense. Through numerous decisions about educational issues as well as by protecting the academic freedom of their faculties, universities foster the production and dissemination of knowledge and the education in democratic citizenship that justify First Amendment protection for academic freedom. To qualify for the protection of institutional academic freedom, universities must demonstrate that they have based a decision on educational considerations related to these First Amendment interests. This demonstration depends on convincing evidence that the person or group assessing educational considerations on behalf of the university has sufficient expertise to do so. Assessment of academic quality is the primary responsibility of faculty, whereas the administration and governing board have a major role in the development of general educational policies. With respect to some but far from all issues that have educational implications, the state may have more legitimate interests in regulating public universities than private ones. To this extent, public universities have less institutional academic freedom.

The institutional academic freedom of universities can be invoked to limit general rights to free speech on university campuses. Chapter 9 addresses restrictions on offensive speech that may undermine a healthy learning environment, and exclusions of the public from university property.

9

Can Institutional Academic Freedom Limit Free Speech?

UNIVERSITIES HAVE OFTEN asserted educational interests that could be protected by institutional academic freedom to justify restrictions on the free speech of members of the university community and of the public. In this chapter, I highlight two important and controversial areas in which universities have claimed educational purposes for limiting speech. They have relied on their interest in preserving a healthy educational environment to regulate and punish various forms of offensive speech, and to exclude the public from university property. The theory of institutional academic freedom as a First Amendment right of universities suggests that current First Amendment analysis should be revised in both areas. Universities should be able to regulate more offensive speech, but they should also be required to allow more access by members of the public who want to speak on campus.

Regulating Offensive Speech on Educational Grounds

The institutional academic freedom to make educational decisions provides convincing grounds for restricting more offensive speech on campus than general First Amendment law allows in the public sphere.[1] In the educational interest of maintaining a healthy learning environment, a university should be able to prohibit some offensive speech that is currently protected by the First Amendment so long as it does not punish ideas for their offensiveness. This educational interest applies most to classroom expression, less to speech elsewhere on campus, and least but still to some extent to speech off campus.

Judicial decisions, particularly while invalidating campus "speech codes" that prohibit and punish various categories of offensive speech, have applied general First Amendment law without modification in the university context. The decision in *Doe v. University of Michigan* is an influential example. The judge observed that the Supreme Court had identified a few categories of expression that are unprotected by the First Amendment, such as obscenity, words inciting imminent lawless action, certain kinds of libel and slander, credible "threats of violence or property damage made with specific intent to harass or intimidate," and "fighting words," defined as "those which by their very utterance inflict injury or tend to incite an immediate breach of peace." Yet he emphasized that those unprotected categories did not allow the university to "proscribe speech simply because it was found to be offensive, even gravely so, by large numbers of people." The general prohibition against punishing offensive speech, he added citing *Sweezy* and *Keyishian,* "acquires a special significance in the university setting, where the free and unfiltered interplay of competing views is essential to the university's mission."[2] The unprotected categories identified by the judge are extremely narrow and often require direct expression to a particular individual. And even a substantial amount of offensive speech directed at individuals does not fit within these unprotected categories.

In declaring that the speech code at the University of Wisconsin violated the First Amendment, for example, the court emphasized that the proposed limiting construction by the board of regents did not protect speech that is "(1) is discriminatory; (2) is directed at an individual; (3) demeans the race, sex, religion, etc. of that person; (4) creates an intimidating, hostile or demeaning environment and lacks an intellectual basis." Much speech within this construction, the court observed, "is unlikely to cause an immediate breach of the peace" and, therefore, does not constitute unprotected "fighting words." To illustrate, the court observed that "the comment 'you're just a dumb black, woman, or homosexual,' does not necessarily tend to incite violent reaction even if it demeans the addressee and creates an intimidating, hostile or demeaning environment."[3] I believe that the institutional academic freedom of a university should enable it to prohibit this comment and other speech that creates a hostile environment for education, even if that speech does not constitute "fighting words" or some other category of expression excluded from general First Amendment protection.

Justifications for protecting offensive speech in the public sphere are less convincing in the university context. In a landmark 1971 opinion addressing the general First Amendment right of free speech, Justice Harlan emphasized that expression often "conveys not only ideas capable of relatively precise, detached explication, but otherwise inexpressible emotions as well." He observed that "words are often chosen as much for their emotive as their cognitive force" and that the "emotive function of speech" may be more important to the speaker than its "cognitive content."[4] He, therefore, concluded that the First Amendment protects the right of an opponent of American involvement in Vietnam to wear a jacket with the words "Fuck the Draft" in the corridor of a courthouse. Reinforcing this conclusion, he quoted an earlier opinion by Justice Frankfurter that described American citizenship as including "the right to criticize public men and measures—and that means not only informed and responsible criticism but the freedom to speak foolishly and without moderation."[5] Harlan also rejected "the facile assumption that one can forbid particular words without also running a substantial risk of suppressing ideas in the process." Upholding the First Amendment right of *Hustler* magazine to publish a parody in which the evangelical minister and political activist, Jerry Falwell, stated that his "first time" was during a drunken rendezvous with his mother in an outhouse, Chief Justice Rehnquist, writing for a unanimous Court, reasoned that it impossible to develop a principled standard that could differentiate degrees of outrageousness. Giving examples from the history of the political cartoon, including the portrayal of George Washington as an ass, Rehnquist observed that in public debate about public figures outrageousness "has an inherent subjectiveness about it which would allow a jury to impose liability on the basis of the jurors' tastes or views, or perhaps on the basis of their dislike of a particular expression."[6]

I agree with these decisions. But the educational functions of a university bring different considerations into play. The university's commitment to the production and dissemination of knowledge supports placing more value on cognitive content and informed and responsible criticism than on emotive force or speech that is foolish or immoderate. The parody of Falwell, as Rehnquist observed, suggests that he is a hypocrite in his public statements about morality and that he should not be taken seriously by the public. By contrast, no point relevant to public debate was raised by an allegedly homophobic limerick during a public-speaking exercise in class that ridiculed a well-known student athlete for his presumed sexual orientation, even if he could plausibly be considered a public figure within the university. The limerick, moreover, could predictably affect the emotional health of the student-athlete in ways that could impede his education.[7] Although the judge in the *Doe* case assumed that the First Amendment protected the student who used this limerick, I think that the First Amendment right of institutional academic freedom should allow the university to prohibit the limerick and punish its utterance.

Regulation of Classroom Speech

Institutional academic freedom should permit greater regulation of classroom speech than of speech elsewhere on campus. Classroom speech is limited by the subject of the course and is evaluated by academic standards of quality that do not apply to interactions in dormitories, cafeterias, extra-curricular activities, and elsewhere on campus. In the classroom, professors should be able to encourage and reward student speech that is rational, thoughtful, and critical and to discourage and prohibit speech that is abusive, vulgar, obscene, or even merely foolish. Wearing a jacket with the words "Fuck the Draft" should be protected in a demonstration on campus as well as in the corridor of a courthouse, but a professor in a course covering the relative merits of a draft or a volunteer army should be able to tell his students that this phrase does not contribute to classroom discussion and should not be used. And wearing that jacket in class may be more disruptive to the learning environment, and therefore more subject to regulation, than the black armbands protesting the war in Vietnam that the Supreme Court protected as a First Amendment right of students in public schools.[8]

Case law provides good examples of classroom speech by professors that a university should be able to regulate as an exercise of institutional academic freedom. Calling comments by students "bullshit" and other gratuitous use of profanity, referring to the professor's own sexual experiences, telling a homosexual student that the professor would pray for him, making obscene gestures to students, telling a student she's like "a middle-aged woman who isn't getting any," and humping his desk to simulate sex should be grounds for punishing professors even if this language does not come within any of the exceptions to the general First Amendment protection of offensive speech.[9]

Although universities should be able to discipline some offensive speech that would be protected in the public sphere, institutional academic freedom should not encompass a right to regulate expression based on the offensive content of ideas, whether expressed in class or elsewhere on campus. Exposure to ideas, including ones that may be so offensive that they make it harder for some students to learn, is a fundamental part of the educational process. Whether an idea is harmful and whether the harm causes significant impediments to the learning process, moreover, are extremely subjective determinations. The distinction between ideas that are harmful and ones that are only offensive or unpopular is often unclear and contested. Broad constructions of harm and impediments to learning could eliminate ideas that many would not consider within those categories.

Just as case law illustrates offensive speech that should be subject to regulation, it provides examples of discussion of offensive ideas that should be beyond the power of the university to forbid. The graduate student who challenged the speech code at the University of Michigan should be able to discuss in his course on comparative animal behavior controversial scholarly theories that biological differences between males and females in performing spatially related tasks may account for the prevalence of men in engineering.[10] Nor should students in a course on constitutional law be punished for opposition to affirmative action similar to the views expressed by Justice Thomas in his dissent in the *Grutter* case.[11]

In recent years, many have argued that any use of the word "nigger" in class should be prohibited as harmful offensive speech, and university administrators have sometimes suspended or dismissed professors who have used it. While institutional academic freedom should enable a university to prohibit its use as an epithet, even if it is protected under general First Amendment law, speaking the word is sometimes pedagogically appropriate in discussing class material. *The Adventures of Huckleberry Finn,* the classic American novel by Mark Twain, repeatedly refers to its central Black character as "Nigger Jim." In discussing this novel in class, professors and students should be able to read passages from the novel and analyze them, including discussing why Twain used the word "nigger," without having to substitute "N-word" for "nigger." *Brandenburg v. Ohio,* the 1969 Supreme Court decision that established an important new principle in First Amendment interpretation, quoted the language for which a leader of the Ku Klux Klan was convicted. It included the sentence: "Personally, I believe the nigger should be returned to Africa, the Jew returned to Israel."[12] Professors and students should be able to quote this sentence while discussing whether it is protected by the First Amendment principle announced in the case. As a judge properly concluded, a professor should be able to conduct a classroom exercise in a course on social communication that encourages students to suggest words used to oppress minorities, and students should be able to say "faggot," "nigger," and "bitch" in response.[13] Another court appropriately held that administrators could not cancel a drama class because the professor had selected a play depicting "a Black New York City police officer who, in the course of a routine arrest of a White suspect, is subjected to a flurry of racial slurs and epithets."[14] Similarly, professors and students should be able to quote the "Fuck the Draft" language in the Supreme Court opinion that describes the speech at issue in the case even though using this phrase in a general discussion of the merits of the draft could be prohibited. The major analytic point of the case was that the First Amendment protects the emotive as well as the cognitive content of expression and saying "Fuck" demonstrates the power of emotive speech more than substituting the "F-word."[15]

Classroom discussion of the law of rape provides another recent example of the limits of institutional academic freedom in regulating speech. Law professors report student complaints that the discussion of the role of consent and coercion in the context of rape, and even any discussion of rape in class, can create traumatic emotional injuries.[16] Covering these issues as part of the discussion of class materials should be protected by the academic freedom of professors and should be beyond the scope of university regulation under its institutional academic freedom, even if this discussion makes it harder for some students to learn and may possibly cause traumatic emotional injuries. Universities should provide counseling services for students harmed by such speech and the Americans with Disabilities Act allows reasonable accommodations on an individual basis for students subject to its provisions. But a university should not be able to restrict the academic freedom of professors and students to discuss these topics.

Regulation of Campus Speech

Though some justifications for regulating classroom speech do not apply elsewhere on campus, institutional academic freedom should permit more regulation of campus speech than general First Amendment law allows in the public sphere. The incidents that prompted the enactment of the speech codes at Michigan and Wisconsin provide good examples of expression a university should be able to discipline as an exercise of institutional academic freedom. The background events at Michigan included the distribution of a flier declaring "open season" on Blacks, referred to as "saucer lips, porch monkeys, and jigaboos," broadcasting racist jokes on the campus radio station, and displaying a Ku Klux Klan uniform from a dormitory window during a demonstration protesting racism on campus.[17] At Wisconsin, a fraternity held what it called a "slave auction" during which pledges performed skits in blackface. Institutional academic freedom should also protect the University of Wisconsin's right to regulate speech for which it disciplined students under the code that the court invalidated as violating the First Amendment. A student, after entering another student's bedroom without an invitation, called the student a "Shakazulu." During an argument, a student called a Black female student a "fat-ass nigger." A student angrily told an Asian-American student, "It's people like you—that's the reason this country is screwed up," adding, "You don't belong here." A student impersonating an immigration officer demanded to see the immigration documents of a Turkish-American student.[18]

Other incidents that were not litigated further illustrate offensive campus speech that should be subject to university regulation. A fraternity at Yale required pledges to march blindfolded around campus, chanting "My name is Jack, I'm a necrophiliac, I fuck dead women" and "No means yes, yes means anal."[19] During the Spring 2017 semester several posters and fliers were distributed on the campus of the University of Texas at Austin. One poster suggested that people should "imagine a Muslim-Free America."[20] Another, titled "Ethical Lessons to Chinese," claimed that in Chinese culture it isn't bad to steal another's work or lie on job applications, and described a fake course in ethics to teach integrity to Chinese students.[21] After a Black male student was taken into custody following a stabbing incident on campus that led to the death of another student, fliers depicted a caricature of a Black man holding a knife alongside the words "Around blacks . . . never relax."[22]

Yet as with classroom speech, institutional academic freedom should not allow universities to discipline the expression of offensive ideas on campus by members of the university community. A professor should not be disciplined for emails objecting to the celebration of an ethnic holiday on campus and asserting the superiority of Western civilization or for using public bulletin boards on campus to protest abortion.[23]

Although lower courts overwhelmingly have resisted treating offensive speech on campus differently than in the public sphere, one Supreme Court decision invoked the educational mission of secondary schools to limit offensive sexual innuendo in a speech by a high school student that would be protected if uttered in public by an adult. The decision focused on the relative immaturity of high school students, but the educational mission of the university to provide a healthy learning environment could provide a different plausible argument for limiting vulgar and offensive speech. Justice Stevens dissented because he felt that the students had not received sufficient notice of the prohibited language and the consequences of a violation. But he agreed that high school administrators could prohibit expletives in classroom discussion and extracurricular activities. Indicating the applicability of his reasoning to the university as well, he followed this statement with a footnote quoting from his earlier opinion that invoked the academic freedom of public universities to justify content-based regulations of student extracurricular activities.[24] Justice Souter's speculation that institutional academic freedom could justify student speech codes, though in an unelaborated footnote of a concurring opinion, provides further support for limiting offensive speech on university campuses.[25]

Regulation of Extramural Speech

Does institutional academic freedom allow a university to regulate off campus as well as on campus offensive speech that is otherwise protected by the First Amendment? In my opinion, institutional academic freedom should allow universities to regulate some offensive extramural expression directed at members of the university community. But the arguments against extending institutional academic freedom to the regulation of offensive ideas on campus that would otherwise be protected by the First Amendment apply even more forcefully when those ideas are expressed off campus.

The offensive speech that can be regulated on campus could occur off campus and should similarly be subject to regulation because it undermines the learning environment at the university. Whether a fraternity is located on or off campus should not affect the institutional academic freedom of a university to discipline it for holding a "slave auction" in blackface. If a university can discipline students for comments or distributing pamphlets to other students on campus that use racist epithets or claim that ethnic or religious groups do not belong in America, it should not be prevented from doing so if those interactions among students occur off campus. A court properly allowed a university to discipline a professor who made ribald, vulgar, and off-color comments to graduate students at an academic conference away from campus. The judge concluded that the professor's comments were not protected by the First Amendment because they addressed matters of private concern, but the university's institutional academic freedom to protect its learning environment could have provided an alternative justification.[26]

By contrast, some offensive off-campus speech that could undermine the learning environment should not be subject to university regulation even if it refers to members of the university community. In controversial and highly publicized comments during an interview off campus, Amy Wax, a professor at the University of Pennsylvania Law School, stated "I don't think I've ever seen a black student graduate in the top quarter of the [Penn Law School] class and rarely, rarely in the top half," and "I can think of one or two students who've graduated in the top half of my required first-year course."[27] Wax's comments damaged the academic reputations of her former students and could predictably cause other Black students to worry that she might not treat them fairly in class. But this information about her students was directly relevant to explaining her opposition to the highly contested and socially important policy of affirmative action. As a private institution, the University of Pennsylvania is not bound by the First Amendment. But I don't think Pennsylvania State University, a public university, could legitimately assert its institutional academic freedom to justify disciplining a professor for these extramural comments that are clearly protected by the First Amendment right to speak on matters of public concern.

Yet if these comments about her students were false, I think the institutional academic freedom of a public university in maintaining the learning environment would justify disciplinary action, even though the First Amendment protects false statements about public concerns so long as they are not made with actual malice. A professor speaking about the academic performance of her own students in connection with a matter of public concern should be subject to standards of accuracy that do not apply to the public generally. Similarly, if Wax, as charged by her dean, made the false assertion that the law review at the University of Pennsylvania had a racial diversity mandate, institutional academic freedom would justify disciplinary action. Wax's alleged public comments that students at her law school "are ignorant" and "know nothing" present a closer question.[28] Though not personally directed at individual students, they are arguably unprofessional and are less connected to the expression of an idea about an important matter of public policy than her comments about student performance while discussing affirmative action.

The institutional academic freedom to maintain a healthy educational environment should not extend to review of general extramural utterance as a citizen that is unrelated to the university and is otherwise protected by the First Amendment. In these circumstances, the general First Amendment interest in free speech is strongest, the potential impact on the university's educational environment is attenuated, and a member of the university community should not have fewer First Amendment rights than other citizens.

I disagree with Michael Berubé and Jennifer Ruth, who maintain in a recent book that universities should be able to discipline professors as unfit if their extramural speech expresses views outside the range of "legitimate political disagreement." Berubé and Ruth place advocacy against affirmative action and for limitations on immigration within "legitimate political disagreement," but exclude defenses of colonialism and theories of white supremacy because they "have no intellectual legitimacy whatsoever." And they would exclude advocacy against affirmative action and for limitations on immigration if it is "demonstrably grounded in white nationalism or western-civilization chauvinism."[29] Determining what counts as legitimate political disagreement is difficult and ideologically freighted, as Berubé and Ruth illustrate by only identifying scholars on the right as expressing illegitimate views.[30] More fundamentally, the very attempt to make this distinction violates the most basic First Amendment principle that the government should not decide what ideas are legitimate.

In reviewing the extramural expression of the philosophy professor who asserted that the lower IQs of Blacks demonstrated the futility of affirmative action, a faculty committee referred to the "clearly established" fact that a teacher's low expectations can frequently have a negative impact on student performance. While conceding that the professor had not expressed these views in class, had taught in a highly professional manner, and had been fair in his treatment of students, the dean of the college expressed similar concerns that knowledge of the professor's views would cause "psychic damage" to his students and impair their ability to learn. These concerns are plausible, but I do not think that institutional academic freedom should allow the university to discipline the professor for making this extramural statement, which, as the judge correctly determined, was clearly protected by the First Amendment because it addressed a matter of public importance.[31]

Many of the public statements by Professor Wax cited by the Dean Ruger as justifications for a major sanction similarly involved offensive comments that did not refer to members of the university community. According to Ruger, Wax's "public commentary espousing derogatory and hateful stereotypes has led students to reasonably conclude that she is unable to evaluate them fairly based on their individualized merit." Among other public comments, she allegedly asserted that women are less intellectual than men, that Blacks are not evenly distributed among all occupations because they have "different average IQs than non-Blacks," that Asians have an "indifference to liberty," that Ashkenazi Jews are "diluting" their brand by intermarrying, that "diversity, equity, and inclusion initiatives are poisoning the scientific establishment," and that some cultures are "not equal in preparing people to be productive in an advanced economy."[32] Without evidence that Wax unfairly evaluated students, I do not think that institutional academic freedom should allow a university to discipline her for these derogatory stereotypes in reference to highly contested issues of public concern.[33] Yet if independent evidence indicated that she did evaluate students unfairly, I think a university could legitimately cite these extramural comments as corroboration.

A recent Supreme Court opinion addressing the suspension of a high school student for off-campus expression indirectly supports the distinctions I have made about university regulation of extramural speech. After not making the high school cheerleading team, the student posted a photo on Snapshot of herself and a friend with their middle fingers raised and the caption: "Fuck school fuck softball fuck cheer fuck everything." The authority of the school to regulate student speech that substantially interferes with its educational functions, the majority of the lower-court panel maintained, does not extend to "off-campus speech." The Supreme Court, by contrast, believed that in certain limited circumstances schools could also regulate off-campus speech by students, such as serious bullying, harassment, and threats aimed at particular students or teachers.[34] But the Supreme Court stressed that a school has much less interest in regulating student speech off campus than on campus, and it did not find a sufficient interest in disciplining the student who posted the photo even though it had some adverse effect on team morale and generated a few minutes of discussion in an algebra class. It pointed out that the post, while using vulgar language to criticize school activities, did not identify the school or target any member of the school community. While protecting off-campus student speech that related to the school, the Supreme Court made it clear that the school would have an even heavier burden to justify regulation of student political or religious speech. Citing previous decisions, it invoked the general principle that the First Amendment protects "even hurtful speech on public issues to ensure that we do not stifle public debate."[35]

The Problem of Subjective Standards

Even if courts were willing to concede that universities could prohibit some offensive speech that is protected in the public sphere, it remains difficult to develop a principled standard that would identify degrees of offensiveness that would differentiate protected from unprotected speech, as Chief Justice Rehnquist recognized in the *Hustler* case.[36] The overwhelming majority of campus speech codes that have been challenged in court have been declared unconstitutional on First Amendment grounds, often because judges found that the language in the codes characterizing prohibited speech was too vague or broad. I often agree, including, for example, the "stigmatizes and victimizes" standard in the University of Michigan code.[37] But courts have struck down narrower codes, such as the one at the University of Wisconsin, which limited the prohibited category to speech directed at an individual that "creates an intimidating, hostile or demeaning environment."[38]

I do not think that there is an easy solution to the problem of vague, broad, and subjective standards. Yet current First Amendment law contains many such standards. The distinction between matters of public and private concern is extremely subjective, with many cases reaching different conclusions based on almost identical facts. The concept of pedagogical relevance has similarly led to different conclusions in cases that are difficult to distinguish on their facts. Claims of vagueness and subjectivity have also arisen in the university context when tenured professors have challenged their dismissals for cause as violating the due process clause of the Fourteenth Amendment. In upholding the dismissal of a tenured professor for engaging in sexual misconduct with students, a court rejected his assertion that the university's regulations prohibiting "exploitation of students" for a professor's "private advantage" did not refer explicitly to sexual misconduct and, therefore, did not give him the adequate notice required by the Fourteenth Amendment. "As is the case with other laws, codes and regulations covering conduct," the court maintained, it is not reasonable to assume that the drafters of the university's regulations "could and must specifically delineate each and every type of conduct (including deviant conduct) constituting a violation." The court added that the professor's academic peers on the faculty hearing committee were well-qualified to interpret the regulations and, more generally, to determine what constitutes acceptable faculty conduct.[39] Relying on this decision, a court subsequently rejected a tenured professor's claim that his university had not relied on sufficiently ascertainable standards in firing him for incompetence because its regulations did not list incompetence as grounds for dismissal. The court stressed it was not feasible to include all grounds for dismissal.[40]

I agree with these decisions and would also allow some imprecision in defining prohibited speech by members of the university community. Universities can mitigate concerns about imprecision by providing examples of prohibited speech in their policies. Even more powerfully, universities could adopt regulations that do not punish people for an initial violation of policies on prohibited speech. They could simply identify the speech as unprotected and warn that a second violation could lead to punishment. The warning would provide clear notice of what is prohibited, and the interests of those whose education is jeopardized by the expression would be recognized through the warning and possible subsequent punishment. Warnings rather than initial discipline, moreover, seem consistent with the educational functions of a university.

I make these suggestions very tentatively. Universities have often cited the interest in protecting the educational environment from offensive speech while egregiously violating the First Amendment rights of students and faculty. Sometimes universities seem to be asserting this justification in good faith, but they often seem to invoke it as a pretext for punishing unpopular ideas. I do not think it is an exaggeration to maintain that a significant portion of American universities have clearly disregarded judicial precedents protecting campus speech, just as a significant portion of American primary and secondary schools have clearly disregarded judicial prohibitions against school prayer and judicial orders to desegregate. Laws that would allow more regulation of offensive speech, as I propose, might encourage additional suppression of speech I think should be protected. But they might seem more reasonable to universities than the current law, and for that reason encourage at least some universities that currently flout the law to respect it, which would protect some speech that now is illegally punished. Apart from these practical considerations about the influence of law on behavior, I think there is independent value in formulating legal rules that make sense.

Access to University Property

The institutional academic freedom to make educational decisions should extend to regulation of access to university property to engage in expression. The Supreme Court did not address Princeton's assertion of institutional academic freedom to exclude members of the public from its campus. To my knowledge, no other university has invoked institutional academic freedom for this purpose. But several public universities, without referring to institutional academic freedom, have made a similar argument by asserting that the educational mission of a university makes it an enclave from the rest of society and precludes treating any of its property as a public forum under general First Amendment law.[41]

In this context, as in others, claims of institutional academic freedom are convincing only to the extent that they rely on educational justifications. The institutional academic freedom to regulate gun possession on campus must be based on its impact on the learning environment rather than on general considerations of public safety.[42] So, too, the institutional academic freedom to restrict access to campus must be based on preserving the university's educational mission and not on general claims of institutional autonomy. Just as the New Jersey Supreme Court required Princeton to provide educational justifications for limiting the state constitutional right of access to private property, courts should require state universities to provide educational justifications for limiting the federal First Amendment right of access to public property.[43]

The Supreme Court has differentiated three basic categories of public property, each with its own First Amendment rules. The first category, the traditional public forum, consists of public property that has historically been used by the public for assembly and discussion. In traditional public forums, such as streets and parks, the government cannot prohibit all expression, though it can enforce neutral time, place, and manner regulations. The second category consists of public property that the government has voluntarily designated as a public forum, which may be limited to use by specific groups or to discussion of specific subjects. As examples, the Supreme Court has referred to a public university that limits meeting rooms on campus to student groups and to a school board that limits meetings to school board business. Though not required to open the property as a public forum, once it has done so the government must follow the same standards as in traditional public forums. The third and largest category consists of all other public property, on which there is no First Amendment right of expression by the public.[44]

Most university property, like the property of most government institutions, falls within the third category of nonpublic forum. While many universities have designated portions of their campuses as public forums or as limited public forums, many others have not. In analyzing the conflict between the institutional academic freedom of the university and the First Amendment rights of members of the public to speak on university property, the key issue is whether any university property is a traditional public forum. Can a public university prohibit all public expression in streets and parklike spaces within the boundaries of its campus even though the First Amendment precludes the municipality in which the university is located from similarly prohibiting expression in streets and parks elsewhere in the community?

In recognizing the right of a student group of evangelical Christians to use campus facilities open to other student organizations, the Supreme Court included a footnote that could be read to suggest that some university property is a traditional public forum. After noting that "the campus of a public university, at least for its students, possesses many of the characteristics of a public forum," the Court quoted its frequent statement that First Amendment rights must be analyzed "in light of the special characteristics of the school environment." A university has the authority, the court added, to impose reasonable regulations on the use of its campus compatible with its educational mission. No prior Supreme Court decision had held "that a campus must make all of its facilities equally available to students and non-students alike, or that a university must grant free access to all of its grounds or buildings."[45] By concluding that a university need not make all of its grounds or buildings available to nonstudents, the Court left open the possibility, and arguably even indicated, that some university property is open to the public and is not just a limited public forum for students or other members of the university community.

Yet lower courts have overwhelmingly denied that any property within the campus of a public university constitutes a traditional public forum where the public has inherent rights of expression. In contrast to the New

Jersey Supreme Court's interpretation of state constitutional law in the Princeton case, the lower federal courts have not required public universities to explain the relationship between their educational mission and the denial of rights to expression by the public.[46] A few decisions have recognized that some spaces on university campuses resemble the streets, sidewalks and parks that are generally deemed traditional public forums. But they have stressed that the physical characteristics of public property do not in themselves determine whether they are traditional public forums, pointing out that the distinctive function of the government entity located on the property is another important factor. Just as the Supreme Court held that the unique role of military bases precludes its sidewalks and streets from being characterized as traditional public forums,[47] lower courts have reasoned, so do the "special characteristics of the school environment" highlighted by the Supreme Court in *Tinker* justify universities in limiting expression in areas within its boundaries that would be considered traditional public forums elsewhere.[48]

A rare decision that identified a traditional public forum on property owned by a university emphasized the uniqueness of the facts and the narrowness of its holding. The case involved the Special Events Center at the University of Texas at Austin. It was surrounded by public streets and used for events sponsored by groups unaffiliated with the university as well as by university academic and athletic organizations. The Austin Chamber of Commerce hosted a reception at the Special Events Center. Members of the Austin Greens political party who were not affiliated with the University of Texas were forced to leave adjacent university property while attempting to distribute leaflets to delegates as they entered the reception. The fifth circuit described this property as a gravel area extending from the Center's public entrance to the city sidewalk. There was no indication of where the university property ended and the city sidewalk began. Based on these "very specific facts," "a unique piece of university property that is, for all constitutional purposes, indistinguishable from the Austin city sidewalk," the fifth circuit upheld the district court's judgment that the university property was a traditional public forum. Yet it also indicated that university grounds typically are not public forums.[49]

Emphasizing how much the fifth circuit limited its holding to the specific property at issue, a district court subsequently rejected the claim that the streets, sidewalks, parks, and pedestrian malls of another branch of the University of Texas should be characterized as traditional public forums.

In contrast to the university property outside the Special Events Center in Austin, the judge reasoned, there was no indication that these areas on the campus of the University of Texas at Arlington were "indistinguishable from the City of Arlington's streets, sidewalks, parks, and pedestrian areas." The judge accurately observed that "no court has found a university's campus to be a traditional public forum."[50]

These lower-court cases are unconvincing in relying on the educational mission of the university to exempt university property resembling traditional public forums from that category. Their occasional citation of the Supreme Court decision holding that the sidewalks and streets of military bases are not public forums is inapt because the mission of the military is so different. Many American universities, both public and private, have institutional policies that endorse the educational value of an open campus and encourage contact between students and the public. Supreme Court decisions similarly assert the educational value of exposing students to a wide variety of different ideas, including from outside speakers and through extracurricular activities that engage the broader community. Though these decisions do not directly address the specific issue of access to the campus by outsiders, they recognize that interaction between students and the public promotes rather than undermines the university's educational mission. In addition, the campuses of public universities have historically been places where the public as well as members of the university community have debated major issues of national policy, as one lower-court decision observed while finding that a university had designated various outdoor areas on campus to be public forums. A concurring judge convincingly pointed out that this historic public use provides good reasons for characterizing these areas as traditional public forums, not simply as designated ones. He persuasively maintained that the public, which pays taxes to support state universities, should have rights to use the streets, sidewalks, and parks on their campuses.[51]

The lower-court cases that invoke the educational mission of the university to deny that its streets, sidewalks, and parks are traditional public forums rarely elaborate how public access interferes with education. They occasionally refer vaguely to "protecting the educational experience of students" and "ensuring public safety" on campus.[52] They sometimes more specifically cite university interests in maintaining a quiet environment for study, preventing campus congestion, and enabling sufficient access to scarce public spaces on campus by the diverse student community, which could be compromised by allowing their use by the public as well.[53] University requirements that outside speakers are only permitted on campus if they are sponsored by student organizations, one court observed, serves the educational purpose of connecting speech by visitors to the actual interests of students.[54]

Yet many of these concerns can easily be addressed through "time, place, and manner" restrictions that are constitutionally permitted in regulating access to public forums generally. As a concurring opinion observed, the educational mission of a university might permit greater and different restrictions on the use of traditional public forums within a university campus, but it does not justify treating these spaces as a different category of property.[55] Cases treating public spaces on campus as designated public forums illustrate effective time, place, and manner regulations that could apply to traditional public forums as well. Requiring a permit and advance notice before an outsider can speak on campus promotes university interests in public safety.[56] Universities can preclude external access to public forums on campus during the "dead days" of the final exam period, when the need for students to study in quiet is particularly great.[57] Although a decision held that a university regulation imposing a cap on outside speakers of five days per semester violated the First Amendment because there is no reason to exclude if space is available, it stated that more narrowly tailored rules to achieve a diversity of views on campus would survive constitutional scrutiny. For example, it would be permissible for a university to give preferences to speakers who had not already spoken five times, or to provide that speakers could only obtain a limited number of permits at a single time.[58] Another decision upheld university regulations limiting outside speakers not sponsored by student organizations to an hour and a half per month and declared that a university may give priority to its own students in using public forums on campus.[59]

Yet in some circumstances time, place, and manner restrictions may not be sufficient to protect a university's institutional academic freedom. For example, a university's institutional academic freedom to maintain standards of civil discourse that contribute to a healthy learning environment could justify denying access to public forums on campus to people who have engaged in forms of hate speech that could not be regulated by the state in other public forums.

Whereas the educational functions of universities do not justify a complete exception from the general First Amendment right of the public to speak on streets, parks, and other traditional public forums, the individual interest in exercising this right on campus as well as in other public forums can be substantial. The individual interest is greatest in addressing issues involving the university itself, such as requirements for admission, the cost of an education, the implementation of affirmative action, university investment policies, allegations of discrimination, regulation of gun possession on campus, the exhibition of statues of controversial figures, and the content and implementation of campus speech codes. The expression of views about campus issues is likely to be more effective on the campus itself than elsewhere. As many of the cases indicate, members of the public are also interested in addressing more general issues with campus audiences, including political campaigners, religious preachers, and advocates of causes such as vegetarianism.[60] Members of the campus community and outsiders might want to join together to demonstrate their shared views about issues of public concern.

Conclusion

The theory of academic freedom as a First Amendment right of universities helps define the boundaries of institutional authority to regulate offensive speech and public access to campus for expressive purposes. The theory suggests different approaches than prevail under current First Amendment analysis. It would allow more university regulation of offensive speech that undermines the learning environment while still forbidding regulation of offensive ideas. And it would allow less university regulation of public access to campus by requiring universities to provide educational justifications for denying access to parks, streets, sidewalks, and other areas on campus that fit within the category of traditional public forums.

Having justified and indicated the scope of a distinctive First Amendment right of academic freedom for both professors and universities, I analyze in Chapter 10 situations in which the academic freedom claims of professors and universities conflict. In response to judges who often assert their lack of competence to assess these conflicting claims, I maintain that standard techniques of judicial review often enable judges to resolve them. When academic expertise is necessary, I urge judges to defer to the conclusions of peer review committees within universities.

10

Judicial Review of Conflicting Academic Freedom Claims between Professors and Universities

As JUDGES have occasionally observed, the recognition of a First Amendment right of academic freedom for both professors and universities means that they can raise conflicting claims of academic freedom against each other.[1] Case law demonstrates that universities have occasionally asserted their institutional academic freedom to protect the academic freedom of professors against external threats, sometimes successfully and sometimes not. For example, a university successfully invoked its institutional academic freedom to protect a professor's right to discourage his students from using the "unreliable" website of the Turkish Coalition of America.[2] Other courts rejected claims of institutional academic freedom by universities that tried to protect the confidentiality of professors who engaged in research using animals and who resisted public disclosure of their teaching materials.[3] But much more frequently universities have asserted their institutional interests to resist claims against them by professors. The cases were, or could have been, litigated as conflicts between the institutional academic freedom of universities and the individual academic freedom of professors.

The theoretical analysis developed in previous chapters should help judges resolve many of these conflicts. It provides guidance in determining if a claim by a professor or a university presents an issue of academic freedom. Settling this underlying issue would frequently enable a judge to decide a case, as in determining that speech by a professor is clearly unrelated to his expertise or that a decision by a university is clearly unrelated to educational matters.

In this chapter I address additional issues posed by conflicting claims of academic freedom between professors and universities. In some cases, both professors and universities present plausible claims of academic freedom, and a judge must decide which claim is stronger. The strength of a university claim may depend on whether the faculty, administration, or trustees made the decision.[4] More difficult cases raise conflicting claims between professors and universities about the academic merits of a professor's research or teaching. Judges lack the competence to assess academic quality, complicating judicial review. Yet they are often able to resolve these cases without analyzing the academic merits by using standard judicial techniques for determining whether a decision was made in good faith or was justified on pretextual grounds. And in cases that do depend on an assessment of academic merits, judges should generally defer to the conclusions of peer review committees. These committees, unlike judges or university administrators or trustees, have the expertise to evaluate academic quality. Disputes over university regulation of external funding, "trigger warnings" from professors to students about potentially traumatic or disturbing subjects, and "diversity statements" in which candidates for appointment and tenure address their commitment to diversity pose additional tension between the academic freedom of professors and universities.

Reviewing the Strength of Competing Claims

Case law provides good evidence of the relative strength of competing claims by universities and professors. It also indicates that some university interests should not be balanced against the academic freedom of professors.

Universities have convincingly asserted institutional interests in educational policy to restrict pedagogical decisions by individual professors. A department of foreign languages can legitimately decide that all professors in the department should not teach upper-level courses in English.[5] A university concerned about the relatively unsophisticated background of the student body can restrict the discretion of a professor to use unorthodox teaching methods.[6] The same concern justifies a university's limits on a professor's admittedly "abrasive" teaching style even though it was effective for some students. The balance tilts more heavily to the university because it only required the professor to warn students about his teaching style and attend a sexual harassment seminar rather than taking disciplinary action against him or even requiring him to change his teaching style.[7] University requirements that professors communicate course expectations to students and distribute standardized evaluation forms in class are justifiable on educational grounds and place only the most modest limitations on a professor's academic freedom in pedagogy.[8]

Cases alleging disruptive speech by professors, though often decided through employee-speech jurisprudence, provide good examples of when either an institutional or an individual claim of academic freedom should prevail. Universities have institutional interests in preventing disruptions on campus that could outweigh faculty interests in academic freedom. University interests could legitimately prevail when faculty expression about academic controversies has "degenerated into name-calling and shouting matches" exhibiting "great personal animosity" that disrupted the department or when a professor constantly makes "vitriolic attacks" against administrators.[9] The claim by an administrator that a professor's speech made her feel "threatened and harassed," which "clearly impaired her ability to run the accounting department," could outweigh the professor's academic freedom.[10] So could the conclusion of a faculty dismissal committee that a professor had engaged in "defamatory charges" and "personal threats."[11]

In some cases, the university's evidence did not support balancing in its favor. A university's desire "to conduct its affairs without constant disruptions due to factionalism" should not outweigh a professor's interest in "fomenting a hostile faction (the lunch bunch)" of "dissident faculty members" whose meetings criticized and displayed "intense hostility" toward the dean and department chair.[12] Hostility toward administrators expressed at a lunch meeting of dissident faculty does not constitute "disruption." I also doubt that a professor's "habit of copying multiple members of the accounting department on his lengthy insubordinate emails surely interfered with other professors' abilities to do their jobs."[13] Though a professor's claim that the administration had disregarded faculty governance prompted his colleagues to walk out of a faculty meeting, I think the professor's interest in making the claim outweighs the university's interest in preventing the disruption.[14]

The importance of the issue raised by the professor should influence the balance. The claim of a professor at a historically Black university that grade inflation and easy courses had undermined its reputation for educational quality, for example, was an exercise of academic freedom that could outweigh the university's legitimate concerns about the "name-calling and shouting-matches" that disrupted his department as a result.[15] Speech about less important subjects, even if covered by academic freedom, might not prevail over this university interest.

Cases applying the First Amendment law of employee-speech jurisprudence identify interests that universities should not be able to assert against professors. Several concluded that a university cannot balance the loss of funding or other support from a state legislature, alumni, or the public against a professor's controversial expression on matters of public concern.[16] Nor should a university be able to balance these harms against controversial expression by a professor protected by the distinctive First Amendment right of academic freedom. With respect to academic freedom as well as free speech, allowing the university to assert these interests in the balance would undermine the underlying individual First Amendment right.

Creatively, but ultimately unconvincingly, Judge Posner attempted to reconcile conflicting academic freedom claims by upholding the university's removal of a professor's controversial art from a faculty exhibit in a main building to a less conspicuous place on campus.[17] I believe that Posner underestimated the professor's interest and overestimated the university's interest. Protection from adverse reactions to expert academic expression is a major function of academic freedom for professors. Institutional academic freedom should not include the right to limit this expert academic expression because the reaction to it by others may harm the interests of the university. Neither the reduction of financial support by alumni or legislators offended by academic ideas, nor reduction in applicants by students offended by art, justifies restrictions on a professor's academic freedom. Forced removal of art from a highly visible faculty exhibition to a remote place on campus, though not censorship, is a significant impairment of a professor's academic freedom. The impact of the offensive art on the university's institutional academic freedom to select its student body, by contrast, is much more speculative and much less direct. A more convincing decision would have required the university to continue to display the controversial art in the faculty exhibition but would have also acknowledged the relatively minor impact on institutional academic freedom.

In the case evaluating the classroom exercise that resulted in students saying the words "nigger" and "bitch" as examples of words used to marginalize minorities, the court concluded that the professor's academic freedom outweighed the university's concern about the comments of a local minister and civil rights leader, who said that he would urge African American students not to attend the university unless it prevented their use in class. The court stressed that the university could not rely on its "undifferentiated fear and apprehension" about loss of enrollment.[18] Even if the university had strong evidence beyond "undifferentiated fear and apprehension" that its enrollment of minority students would be significantly affected by the continuation of pedagogically defensible class exercises, I believe that this interest should not be weighed against the professor's interest in academic freedom.

Judicial Competence to Review Academic Merits

Some academic commentators cite the lack of judicial competence to assess academic quality as the basis for arguing that the First Amendment right of academic freedom should be limited to universities as institutions. Recognizing an individual First Amendment right of academic freedom for professors, they warn, would require "ill-equipped" judges who "lack sufficient understanding of the academic enterprise" "to find their way among the labyrinths of academic decision-making" and "make judgments about what academic speech should be protected and what speech should be subject to regulation."[19] Judicial review of academic freedom claims by professors against universities "would inevitably restrict the *academic* autonomy of the institution itself."[20] Peter Byrne acknowledges that judges are competent to resolve some of these cases, as when a board of regents relies on the "political direction" of a professor's scholarship to overturn a favorable recommendation by an academic department. But such cases, he asserts, are "extremely rare." He dramatically concludes that judicial review of academic disputes between professors and universities "would put the department or school into intellectual receivership, with the court determining the appropriate paradigms of thought."[21] Less ominously, Frederick Schauer maintains that institutional academic freedom "may require limiting the scope and strength of individual academic freedom rights, for it is a necessary component of such rights that they are typically enforced by a judicial evaluation of, and potential interference with, an academic judgment by an academic institution."[22] As many legal cases and AAUP investigations reveal, universities often violate the academic freedom of professors. Precluding judicial review in these cases would deny these professors any legal remedies.

I agree that judges often are not competent to assess the quality of scholarship and teaching. But I believe that traditional techniques of judicial analysis at the core of their own expertise enable them to resolve conflicting claims about academic merit between professors and universities without jeopardizing institutional academic freedom. Judges often do not need academic expertise to determine whether universities acted in good faith on academic grounds or relied on them as a pretext. When cases do require judicial assessment of academic merits, judges should defer to the decisions of peer review committees or seek them if the university had not relied on peer review, unless there is compelling evidence that the peer review committees themselves deviated from academic standards or violated the law. Legal decisions provide good illustrations of how judges can resolve disputes over academic merits.

Determinations of Good Faith or Pretext

Even when universities rely on academic justifications for actions against professors, judges often do not have to evaluate their merits. In some of these cases, judges can determine that the university made its decision in good faith and, therefore, uphold it. In others, judges can determine that the academic justification was a pretext for illegal behavior and, therefore, reverse the university decision.

While expressing concerns about excessive judicial deference to university decisions in Title VII cases and stressing that academic freedom does not include "the freedom to discriminate," the second circuit nevertheless found that the university's denial of tenure to a Black woman was made in good faith for legitimate reasons. The tenure committee cited the candidate's inadequate background in the courses she taught and the poor performance of her students. The court's independent review of the trial court record confirmed that the tenure committee had actually relied on these factors and did not disclose any evidence of overt or covert discrimination.[23]

In another Title VII case, a judge held that the dean's reversal of the favorable though divided tenure vote by the English Department did not constitute discrimination based on sex. The judge found that the dean refused to give credit for the candidate's "works of feminist criticism, not because of their feminist bent, but because they had not been published or accepted for publication" at the time of the tenure decision. Concluding that this was a "nondiscriminatory academic judgment," the judge was not persuaded that the dean used it as a pretext to obscure discriminatory intent.[24]

Upholding the unanimous decision of the faculty tenure committee that a professor did not meet the university's standards for scholarship, a judge rejected claims by the professor that the committee penalized him for his participation in protests against the government and the university. The professor opposed government policies about Vietnam and about various domestic racial and economic issues. He also advocated a greater role for students in university governance. The judge found that the tenure committee disregarded these beliefs and activities and did not rely even in part on his exercise of protected First Amendment rights.[25]

Other decisions rejected the university's stated academic reasons as pretexts by relying on evidence that could be evaluated without any academic expertise. In a particularly thorough opinion, a judge explained why the university's evidence of a professor's weaknesses as a teacher did not convince him that it denied reappointment for this reason. The judge pointed out that the university had never advised the professor of serious dissatisfaction with his teaching, had previously evaluated his teaching as average or superior in every category, had never seriously investigated the vague and undocumented complaints by students, and did not provide evidence to support its assertion that the professor failed to cover the subject matter of his courses. Nor had the university ever denied reappointment or dismissed any other professor for any reason. The timing of the university's decision provided particularly strong grounds for concluding that the university's stated reason was a pretext. The university denied reappointment soon after the professor announced that he was a communist and a member of the Progressive Labor Party, prompting widespread newspaper coverage and a lawsuit against the university by members of the state legislature. The chancellor of the university then called a meeting with the professor that focused on his political beliefs. These facts convinced the judge that the university substantially based its decision on violations of the professor's First Amendment rights and that it otherwise would have reappointed him. The "paucity" of evidence to support the university's stated reasons for its decision, the judge maintained, indicated that they were "hastily prepared" and "makeweight" rather than reflections of "true motivation."[26]

Recognizing the crucial role of peer review in university tenure decisions, courts have cited unanimous or near unanimous votes of faculty tenure committees as grounds for upholding their decisions, whether the votes were positive or negative and whether the administration affirmed or reversed them. In the case of the Black woman denied tenure based on university claims about her inadequate background and the poor performance of her students, the court stressed that all eight members of the tenure committee had relied on these factors in voting against her.[27] In one of the few cases in which courts have awarded tenure as a remedy for a violation of Title VII, the court emphasized that the administration had reversed the unanimous 22–0 favorable vote of the candidate's department, the unanimous favorable vote of the peer review committee of the College of Liberal Arts, the 9–2 favorable vote of the university-wide peer review committee, and the subsequent unanimous vote of the university-wide committee. While acknowledging "the risk of improperly substituting a judicial tenure decision for a university one," the court concluded that these votes constituted compelling evidence "going beyond a mere difference in judgment" between the faculty committees and the administration.[28]

Biased statements have provided another source of evidence for courts to evaluate appointment and tenure decisions without having to assess the academic reasons asserted by the university. In the same case in which the court cited the overwhelming favorable votes of the faculty committees, it quoted as evidence of possible sex discrimination statements by the president who reversed these recommendations. The president referred to the candidate's department as "a damn matriarchy" and to her husband as an economic "parachute," making unnecessary any worry about her job security.[29] Another court cited a statement indicating possible political bias while reversing the summary judgment against a woman who alleged that a law school violated her First Amendment rights by refusing to offer her a position in its writing program. The law school claimed that the faculty voted against her because she "did not understand the analysis portion" of the writing program. But the court relied on a professor's reference to the candidate's conservative views during the faculty meeting considering her appointment as part of the evidence indicating that the decision was motivated at least in part by opposition to her Republican politics and work on behalf of socially conservative organizations. It also cited evidence that only one of the fifty members of the law school faculty was a registered Republican.[30] A jury subsequently rejected the claim of political discrimination.[31]

Nor have judges needed academic expertise to evaluate claims by professors denied appointment or tenure that the university illegally applied different standards to them than to successful candidates. In reversing the dismissal of a Title VII claim and remanding for further review, a circuit court concluded that the plaintiff had established a prima facie case by providing detailed data demonstrating that she had the same background as professors who had received tenure.[32] The court that upheld the finding of discrimination and awarded tenure cited evidence that the woman candidate had been "held to a stricter standard than her male peers." It noted that the university required her to write a second book before receiving tenure, whereas during the prior six years none of the candidates for tenure in her department had published a second book. She was the only candidate in the department denied tenure after publishing a book and having it reviewed, and a male professor in the same department who received tenure soon after her denial had not written a single book. In addition, she received substantially higher favorable votes from the faculty peer review committees than some males who received tenure.[33] The court that reversed the summary judgment against the woman who applied for the position in the law school writing program observed that the law school hired others who had less teaching experience and low student evaluations.[34] And a court concluded that a white professor denied reappointment established a prima facie case of unlawful discrimination by providing evidence that the university retained and promoted Blacks "with comparable or lesser qualifications."[35]

In another case, by contrast, the court found that the university adequately explained why it treated a woman denied tenure differently than men who received it. The woman had significantly fewer publications than the men. The dean did not defer to the departmental recommendation in her case as he had in recommendations for four men because he had evidence that the department had lowered its publication requirements in evaluating her. And the dean credited the writings of a Black professor of philosophy on Black philosophy but not her writings on women's studies because the philosophy professor's writings were about an area of specialization within his discipline, whereas her writings on women's studies dealt mainly with administrative rather than substantive aspects of the field. In addition, she was being considered for tenure in the English Department, which required demonstrated competence in English literature, not women's studies.[36]

The Role of Peer Review

Although judges have often been able to rely on evidence of motivation to assess the validity of a university's academic justification for a decision, other cases require evaluation of the merits of the decision itself. In those cases, judges should defer to the expert determinations by peer review committees unless the university administration or governing board provides compelling reasons for rejecting them. Judges have properly observed that their role is not to determine whether an academic decision is correct, which is beyond their competence, but whether it violates the law.[37] Two Title VII cases alleging sex discrimination well illustrate this point.

In one case, a Religion Department maintained that it had denied reappointment to a woman who specialized in Sanskrit because she "was unable to relate" this specialized area of scholarship "to the broader issues of the study of religion." The university's grievance committee rejected this explanation, concluding that it was a pretext for sex discrimination. The grievance committee emphasized that the Religion Department had "an admitted history of discrimination against women" and had hired the woman denied reappointment, its first female faculty member, "with a narrowly defined and clearly understood specialty for her teaching and research." It recommended that the Religion Department reconsider and offer reappointment without tenure. But the department, after several additional meetings, adhered to its original position. After a lengthy review of the department's deliberations, the court concluded that its assessment of her scholarly weaknesses was made in good faith and was not a pretext for discrimination that would violate Title VII. It, therefore, upheld the denial of reappointment. It concluded that no evidence in the record contradicted the department's justification for its decision or indicated that other faculty had similar weaknesses or were judged by different standards.[38]

Another Title VII case was more complicated because the academic merits of "women's studies" was the subject of dispute. Denying the validity of women's studies as a field may be more likely to reflect sex discrimination than the claim that a professor is unable to relate specialized studies in Sanskrit to broader issues in religious studies. Reviewing the claim of sex discrimination by a specialist in medieval French literature who was denied tenure, the district court judge found that the lack of enthusiasm for her candidacy from both faculty and administrators may have stemmed from their view that her scholarly focus on the role of women was an "unworthy topic." Yet this hostility to "women's studies," the judge concluded, was not evidence of sex discrimination because a male professor pursuing women's studies could be subject to the same criticism. The judge emphasized more broadly that for him to "tell a university 'you cannot deny tenure on the grounds that you do not like the scholar's subject of study' is the equivalent of ordering that the tenure committee must exercise its professional scholarly judgment in a particular way." Such judicial intervention, he concluded, "gets very near a First Amendment problem."[39]

On appeal, the circuit court panel disagreed with this analysis. "A disdain for women's studies, and a diminished opinion of those who concentrate on those issues," the court asserted, "is evidence of a discriminatory attitude toward women."[40] The court noted that it was "sensitive to the problems related to judicial examination of issues like the importance of women's studies, and to the need for courts to refrain from substituting their judgment for that of educators in areas affecting the content of curricula." Yet it did not add much about why it overcame its sensitivity. It asserted without elaboration that its decision was "narrow." It also observed that Title VII compels relief when decisions about academic employment "are motivated by discriminatory attitudes" or are "rooted in concepts which reflect such discriminatory attitudes, however subtly."[41] The possibility that opposition to women's studies as a field reflects a general "discriminatory attitude toward women" is plausible enough to justify the court's decision to remand the case for further proceedings to gather additional evidence. But unless independent evidence of sex discrimination is uncovered, academic reservations about women's studies as a field by a peer review committee should not itself constitute proof of discrimination. A history of departmental discrimination against women, as in the Religion Department that denied reappointment, could provide such independent evidence.

While judges should defer to peer review in evaluating the academic merits of conflicts between professors and universities, the judicial responsibility to interpret and apply the law requires them to overturn peer review decisions that rely on illegal considerations. Refusing to defer to the recommendation of a peer review committee to terminate a professor's tenure, a court appropriately pointed out that the committee could not base its recommendation on speech protected by the First Amendment. Citing evidence that the president and board of trustees took into account protected speech that was not considered by the committee, the court convincingly added that its review of the termination must extend beyond the record the committee compiled.[42] After determining that the contract between a professor and a university protected the speech for which a peer review committee recommended the professor's suspension without pay, another court properly invalidated the suspension.[43]

In other cases, by contrast, judges have inappropriately decided the academic merits on their own without reference to peer review. Evaluating the content of academic speech, the judge who invalidated the speech code at the University of Michigan assumed that academic freedom protects classroom speech declaring that homosexuality is a disease and teaching theories that males are better than females in some spatially related mental tasks.[44] He did not refer to academic support for these assumptions. The judge who stressed that a medical school professor's advocacy of vaginal delivery instead of unnecessary cesarean procedures was "well within the range of accepted medical opinion" did not address how he reached this conclusion.[45] The judges in these cases should have deferred to the evaluations of peer review committees, ordering them if they had not already occurred.

Academic expertise is also generally necessary to determine the legitimacy of pedagogical techniques. Judges should not have reached their own differing conclusions about whether a professor's tolerance of student use of vulgarities during a classroom exercise reflected a lack of academic judgment that justified his dismissal by the administration. Instead, they should have sought the views of the professor's faculty peers, who, in contrast to both the judges and the administrators, had the professional competence to make this determination.[46] Similarly, professors of political science, not a federal judge, should determine if discussion of union activities on campus is relevant to the contents of a course in political science.[47] In some extreme cases, pedagogical relevance or irrelevance may be so clear that an expert academic evaluation is not needed. A judge, for example, could determine without the benefit of peer review that the distribution of religious pamphlets on the sinfulness of homosexuality had nothing to do with teaching cosmetology or that teaching James Joyce's *Ulysses* is inappropriate in a chemistry class.[48] But most disputes about pedagogical value raise more complicated issues that should be resolved by experts in the field. In contrast to the cosmetology class, a professor of health sciences plausibly asserted that his assignment of the Bible and other religious texts provides a valuable "moral perspective" on the subject. Faculty peers should evaluate this pedagogical claim, not the vice president of student services who reprimanded him or a federal judge.[49]

Judicial review of the merits of academic decisions can become more complicated when the administration or governing board reverses the recommendation of a faculty peer review body. Even though the administration and governing board lack the expertise of the faculty, there may be occasions when judges should defer to legitimate justifications for reversing faculty determinations of academic merit.

Some issues seem on the border between matters of general educational policy within the scope of administrative and board authority and the evaluation of academic merit within the scope of faculty authority. A history department may decide on the academic merits to grant tenure to a social historian and an American historian while denying tenure to an intellectual historian and a historian of Latin America. A decision by the administration and board to reverse these decisions based on their view of the proper balance of specialties within the department seems within the scope of institutional academic freedom, especially if the department' s own review indicates that the differences in quality among these candidates are not substantial. The administration and governing board would have even stronger grounds to reverse if the department had frequently favored and disfavored these specialties, providing more evidence of imbalance.

Decisions about the relative weight of scholarship and teaching in making a tenure decision is another issue of general educational policy within the scope of administrative and board authority that may conflict with a department' s evaluation of academic merit. The faculty committee appointed by the president of Harvard in the 1930s to investigate tenure decisions in the Department of Economics concluded that it was "at least arguable" that great teachers who are not creative scholars should receive tenure.[50] If the Department of Economics voted to tenure such a professor, I think the president and governing board legitimately could have reversed this decision had they believed that all tenured professors should be creative scholars. I am personally familiar with a tenure review in which the administration asked the faculty to reconsider its recommendation to tenure an excellent scholar who had extremely low teaching evaluations from both students and colleagues. The faculty reversed its vote, but I think the administration legitimately could have rejected another favorable recommendation from the faculty if it believed that all tenured professors, no matter how outstanding their scholarship, should be effective teachers.

The general oversight responsibilities of the administration and governing board could also justify rejecting the recommendation of a peer review committee based on disagreement over whether to depart from traditional measures in determining tenure. A peer review committee recommended that a candidate with a weak scholarly record who is not a "traditional academic" should be granted tenure because his "life experiences" contributed to a "rounded account of his accomplishments" that would be "an exciting, valuable, and not replaceable resource to Africana Studies, students, and the university community." The committee conceded that much of the professor's "expertise has not been written down," but observed that few people in the Western world had been as heavily involved in African affairs.[51] If the administration reversed the department because it wanted to tenure only traditional academics with strong scholarly records, that would have been a legitimate exercise of its authority to which a judge should defer. On the other hand, if the professor could prove his claim that the reversal was based on pressure from state officials and Jewish organizations outraged by his course equating Zionism with racism, which a faculty committee unanimously concluded was taught "within the bounds of academic freedom," the court should invalidate it as a violation of the professor's First Amendment right of academic freedom. What if the peer review committee had recommended against tenure, citing the professor's weak scholarship, and the administration and governing board had reversed, citing the contributions he could make based on his life experiences? While administrators and judges should defer to faculty evaluations of academic merit, it is plausible that the institutional academic freedom of the university encompasses the determination by the administration that the educational value of a professor's life experiences justifies occasional departures from strict reliance on the traditional measures of academic merit.

Even with respect to disputes over academic merits that do not raise broader issues, administrators and governing boards may have legitimate grounds to reverse a peer review committee. Evidence that departments were not sufficiently rigorous in applying academic standards justifies reversal. It would be permissible as well for the administration and governing board to cite evidence of a department's declining academic reputation among scholars at other institutions as grounds for giving less deference to its evaluations of academic merit.[52] In these cases, judges should not simply require proof that administrative reversals were made in good faith on academic grounds.[53] Judges should not uphold them "except in rare instances and for compelling reasons which should be stated in detail." This is the standard of the 1966 Statement on Government. It should also be the standard for judicial review in these cases.

In addition, judges should consider which administrators reversed the decision by a faculty committee. Administrative expertise varies. Some administrators have lengthy previous experience as professors; others have no background in scholarship and teaching. Even among administrators who had been professors, the higher the position in the administrative hierarchy, the less likely the administrator has expertise about the subject of dispute. It may make more sense for a judge to defer to a chair who disagrees with the department's peer review committee about the academic merits than to the dean, provost, or president, particularly if they were trained in other fields.

An arbitration decision in 1984 by Clyde Summers, an eminent professor of labor law at the University of Pennsylvania, provides an excellent model for judicial review of peer review committees. His sensitive analysis of the role of the arbitrator in reviewing the reversal of a peer review committee by the administration and governing board applies to judicial review as well.

Throughout his decision, Summers focused on the distinctive role of peer review in appointment and dismissal decisions at universities. The university context, he emphasized, "significantly changes the arbitrator's function and the questions which he must decide." "The dominant principle, which is widely accepted in colleges and universities, is that faculty members are to be judged by their peers."[54] The language of the collective bargaining agreement he was interpreting, derived from the 1966 Statement on Government, provided that the president and the governing board should reverse recommendations from peer review committees "only for compelling reasons, stated in detail." Summers interpreted this language to mean that a faculty committee's judgment of the appropriate sanction for academic misconduct should be given a "strong presumption of correctness." It should not be overruled unless it is "plainly unreasonable or irresponsible," as indicated by evidence of "intolerance, bias or indifference." He maintained that the faculty is in the best position to judge the seriousness of the offense and the appropriateness of sanctions.[55]

The three-person majority of the faculty peer review committee in this case found that the professor had committed "grave academic misconduct" by failing to acknowledge the contribution to his own work of a seminar paper by one of his graduate students. It concluded that the professor "attempted plagiarism" in submitting one article to a scholarly journal that he subsequently withdrew following complaints from the student, and that he committed plagiarism by publishing another article. It recommended sanctions that included public corrections by the professor, withdrawing his name from the articles and acknowledging the student as the author of them, and a public censure of the professor by the faculty senate. Under the heading "mitigation," the majority emphasized that the professor previously had never been accused of misconduct and that he had the potential to make future contributions to his field. Two members of the committee did not agree that the professor had attempted plagiarism.[56]

After reviewing the report of the peer review committee, the president determined that the recommended sanctions were too lenient and requested further review by the board of trustees. In his memorandum to the board, the president maintained that a professor who plagiarizes a student's work should always be dismissed. The board agreed with the president and asked the faculty committee to reconsider the sanction. The faculty committee responded by recommending the additional sanctions of reduction of rank and benefits for the professor, but it did not recommend what it called "the extreme sanction of dismissal." The board of trustees rejected the new recommendation of the faculty committee and voted to dismiss the professor.[57]

In his arbitration award, Professor Summers rescinded the dismissal and ordered reinstatement as a full professor. In contrast to a typical arbitration of a dismissal case, in which the arbitrator decides "whether the charges are proven and whether the sanction imposed is reasonable," Summers maintained that in a case arising in a university, the "underlying institutional procedure, which is built upon peer judgment by a faculty committee with limited review by the President and Board of Trustees, defines the function of the arbitration." The arbitrator must first decide "whether each of the decision-making bodies or individuals properly performed their prescribed function." More specifically in this case "the question is whether the President and the Board of Trustees gave the required deference to the recommendations of the Faculty Hearing Committee."[58]

Summers found that president and board simply disagreed with the faculty committee about the appropriate sanction and substituted their own judgment. This different judgment, Summers emphasized, did not constitute the evidence of unreasonableness that could provide the necessary compelling reason to overcome the strong presumption of deference to the determination of the faculty committee built into the system of peer review. A reasonable recommendation by a peer review committee, Summers indicated, must be upheld even if the president and governing board have equally reasonable reasons for rejecting it. Although not required by his own analysis, Summers proceeded at some length to argue that the faculty recommendation proceeded from premises about the nature of plagiarism that were more reasonable than those of the president and board of trustees. He did not enforce the faculty committee's revised recommendation on reconsideration to reduce the professor's rank and benefits because it "did not represent their judgment but a proposed alternative to dismissal."[59]

Professor Summers's analysis in this arbitration decision provides useful guidance for judges reviewing reversals by the administration or governing board of peer review recommendations about matters within the primary expertise of the faculty. By deferring to the faculty recommendation unless the administration or governing board provides "compelling evidence" that it was unreasonable, judges reinforce the system of peer review that both protects and defines the limits of academic freedom. Judicial deference to peer review committees, moreover, addresses concerns about the competence of the judiciary to evaluate academic disputes by insuring that the primary evaluation of the academic merits is made by the faculty itself. When universities explicitly adopt the "compelling reasons" standard of the 1966 Statement, as many do, the argument for judicial deference to peer review is particularly strong. But the structural importance of peer review in protecting the First Amendment right of academic freedom justifies this standard of judicial review for all universities.

University Regulation of External Funding

University regulation of external funding of research by professors has raised additional competing claims of academic freedom. These competing claims have not prompted litigation but may do so. The institutional academic freedom of universities justifies the prohibition of grants from external funders that limit the academic freedom of professors, even if professors themselves are willing to accept those limitations. But it does not justify relying on the activities or ideology of external funders to forbid professors from accepting grants to support scholarship and teaching that meets academic standards. Judges do not need academic expertise to differentiate these two contexts.

The AAUP has issued recommended principles about external funding that provide useful guidance for judges. Universities should prohibit faculty from accepting money from external sources who ghostwrite articles for professors to sign and publish under their own names.[60] Nor should universities allow professors to receive money conditioned on the right of external funders to alter the design of the project after the initial agreement has been signed, revise the resulting article, insert their own statistical analyses, or require professors to obtain permission prior to presenting findings at professional meetings or otherwise disseminating research results.[61] University regulations prohibiting these conditions on faculty research, like those prohibiting plagiarism and the falsification of data, do not violate the individual academic freedom of professors. They identify unprofessional behavior by professors that is inconsistent with the exercise of academic freedom in research and publication. To protect against possible abuse, it also seems legitimate for universities to require that professors disclose the sources of their outside research funding. The campus climate change committee at the University of California, San Diego, has proposed such a policy for funding from the fossil fuel industry.[62] Demands that universities contribute substantial resources to a project or evidence that potential donors had a history of not honoring prior commitments provide other legitimate reasons for rejecting external funding.[63]

It is also legitimate for universities to restrict external funding of research that must remain confidential or classified.[64] These restrictions serve the same purposes as academic freedom: fostering the discussion of ideas and the dissemination of knowledge. Professors who accept conditions on research that prevent open inquiry and publication undermine rather than exercise academic freedom. Many universities allow brief delays in publication to provide external funders an opportunity to protect their intellectual property interests, giving them time to file provisional patent claims or to review drafts that might contain sensitive proprietary information revealing trade secrets. Some universities allow classified research on campus for reasons of national security during wartime.[65] These exceptions to general restrictions on confidential and classified research seem reasonable and within the general institutional prerogatives of universities.

Two controversies addressed by the AAUP, by contrast, illustrate improper university restrictions on external funding. A university's faculty committee on research and development determined that a professor had received funding from a foundation with a history of supporting research that promoted theories of racial inferiority. Allowing a professor to accept funding from this source, the committee concluded, would be inconsistent with the university's commitment to racial equality and diversity. It therefore urged the university to disallow the grant. "Denying a faculty member the opportunity to receive requisite funding," the AAUP convincingly observed in commenting on this incident, "improperly curtails the researcher's academic freedom no less than if the university took direct steps to halt research that it considered unpalatable."[66]

Decisions by universities to ban professors from accepting funding from the tobacco industry raised similar issues. Some advocates of these bans differentiated the tobacco industry from other corporate support of academic research, pointing out that it had manipulated scientific research about the dangers of smoking and had used aggressive legal tactics to harass professors and universities. Yet the AAUP reiterated the position it took in opposing the ban on funding from the foundation alleged to promote theories of racial inferiority, adding that in practice it would be impossible to develop a principled policy that could differentiate among degrees of corporate wrongdoing in determining when to accept or reject external funding.[67] Similarly, the academic senate of the University of California passed a resolution maintaining that restrictions based on moral or political judgments about the source of the funding, the propriety of the research, or speculation about the possible uses of the results would impermissibly interfere with the academic freedom of a professor to determine a research program.[68] A subsequent legal decision finding overwhelming evidence of fraudulent and false statements by the tobacco industry lent substantial support to those who claimed it had engaged in uniquely bad behavior. The judge concluded that for decades it had undermined independent scholarly research about the health hazards from smoking, funded and controlled research that generated results favorable to its own interests, and suppressed adverse research results. Its research program funded studies that explored the basic processes of disease but did not deal with the dangers of smoking itself.[69]

The findings of the judge in the tobacco case suggest a convincing resolution of disputes over restrictions on external funding. Whatever the motives of the funding agency, the academic freedom of a professor should protect accepting research funds so long as the project meets academic standards. If a research project that studies the basic processes of lung cancer can meet academic standards without also investigating how smoking might have contributed to the onset of the disease, it should be protected by academic freedom, whether or not the funder is motivated by interests in diverting attention from the impact of smoking. But if divorcing the study of the processes of cancer from smoking, rather than a plausible limitation on the scope of a study, cannot be justified on academic grounds as determined by a peer review committee, the restriction on funding should be permissible.

Institutional regulation of external funding can extend to teaching as well as research. Some grants require that professors teach specific books or teach courses designed by the granting agency, such as *Atlas Shrugged* by Ayn Rand or a course devoted to libertarian theory.[70] Though some believe that universities should prohibit all grants containing conditions on teaching, I think a peer review committee should determine if the conditions require the professor to teach material that does not meet the standards of knowledge in a discipline. If the conditions cannot meet these standards, the grant should be prohibited. But if they can, I think the university's denial of the grant would violate the academic freedom of the professor.

Universities have legitimate institutional interests in determining the range of courses included in the curriculum, coordinating coverage in different sections of the same course, and preventing overlapping coverage in different courses. Subject to these constraints, academic freedom generally allows a professor to determine reading assignments and course coverage within the scope of accepted academic discourse. The availability of external funding should not determine the validity of a professor's choice of reading assignments and course coverage that meet disciplinary standards of knowledge any more than it should determine the validity of a professor's decision to pursue one academically defensible research project rather than another. It is appropriate for peer review committees to evaluate the academic value of books by Ayn Rand or of libertarian theory. But an otherwise academically defensible decision should not be rendered indefensible because it was influenced by the availability of outside funding, just as an academically indefensible decision should not be rendered defensible because a professor made it independently. A grant conditioned on the professor's adherence to the donor's views about a particular subject, by contrast, would violate academic freedom. Even if the professor who received the grant agreed with the donor, the condition would limit free inquiry by preventing the professor from reaching different conclusions during the process of research and teaching. A grant could legitimately be limited to the subject of libertarian or socialist theory, but not to views about its strengths and weaknesses.

As chair of the AAUP's Committee of Academic Freedom in 1920, Arthur Lovejoy addressed this issue in response to the acceptance of an endowed "professorship of civil rights" by Lafayette College. The deed of gift provided that its purpose was to provide instruction "in the civil rights of individuals, meaning thereby all those absolute rights of persons, such as the right of personal security, the right of personal liberty, and the right to acquire property as regulated and protected by law, to the end that individual initiative and effort may be encouraged and promoted and protected, and may receive its just reward, and that the fallacies of socialism and kindred theories and practices which tend to hamper and discourage and throttle individual efforts, and individual energy, may be exposed and avoided." Commenting that this language "is doubtless not a masterpiece of drafting" and that "a quibbling lawyer might be able to find in it justifications for the teaching of doctrines probably not contemplated by the donor," Lovejoy maintained that the real purpose of the donor was clearly to propagate a social philosophy opposed to socialism. Lovejoy concluded that universities should be able to accept gifts to study identified subjects so long as the faculty determines that these subjects are plausible fields for academic inquiry, but not gifts to promote or attack "any particular *ism*."[71] A court followed Lovejoy's approach decades later by construing a will to require a course in conservative political philosophy but not to require one that assigns the donor's books and teaches his ideas, which would abridge academic freedom.[72]

Trigger Warnings and Diversity Statements

Highly publicized recent controversies about trigger warnings and diversity statements pose additional conflicting academic freedom claims between professors and universities. Trigger warnings are signals from professors to students that class assignments and discussion include potentially traumatic or otherwise unsettling material. Diversity statements are submitted by candidates for appointment and tenure to address their commitment to promoting diversity. In this section, I describe the operation of trigger warnings and diversity statements at American universities, summarize policy arguments for and against them, and present my own views. I then turn to the conflicting academic freedom claims. I address trigger warnings first because disputes over them arose earlier.

My views about the merits of trigger warnings and diversity statements as a matter of policy differ from my views about how the First Amendment right of academic freedom should apply to them. I oppose mandatory trigger warnings and diversity statements, though I believe that individual professors should have discretion to provide trigger warnings and that universities should be able to use diversity as a factor in evaluating candidates for appointment and tenure. In interpreting the First Amendment right of academic freedom, I observe that universities can legitimately assert the right of institutional academic freedom when trigger warnings and diversity statements are justified on educational grounds. But I also observe that the academic freedom of professors to make expert decisions about pedagogy and the topics of research can support the refusal to give trigger warnings or to submit diversity statements. Because trigger warnings are part of the content of classroom speech, I believe that they are a greater constraint than diversity statements on a professor's academic freedom.

In assessing these conflicting claims, I conclude that the academic freedom of individual professors should prevail if universities require trigger warnings but not if they encourage them. Reluctantly, I also conclude that the institutional academic freedom of universities should prevail if mandatory diversity statements are implemented with the approval of the faculty, evaluate contributions to diversity rather than viewpoints about it, and are used to assess these contributions as one factor among many in making an employment decision. Most current policies that require diversity statements do not meet these standards. They are often justified and evaluated based on social rather than educational goals, imposed by administrators, and used to exclude professors, whatever their academic merits, for disfavored views.

Trigger Warnings

Trigger warnings initially alerted students to potentially traumatizing material. They subsequently expanded to include material that might be enraging, troubling, or upsetting.[73] A study finding that 70 percent of college students report experiencing at least one traumatic event indicates that even the narrower definition could cover many students.[74] Some policies list many subjects that could be triggering and appropriate for warnings.[75] The guide to trigger warnings at the University of Michigan provides examples of triggering subjects that might be listed on a syllabus, including "death or dying," "pregnancy/childbirth," "miscarriages/abortion," "blood," "eating disorders," "body hatred," and "fat phobia." It also states that professors should consider asking students to suggest additional subjects for trigger warnings. Very few universities require that professors give trigger warnings, but some "advise" or "urge" them as a matter of official institutional policy.[76] Institutional and individual policies vary in their treatment of student responses to triggering material. Some allow students not to attend class and to complete alternative assignments, but others do not.[77]

Proponents maintain that trigger warnings prevent or mitigate student reactions to emotionally challenging material that could interfere with their ability to learn. By preparing students in advance, they believe, the warnings foster productive engagement with this material. They fear that without trigger warnings, students might disengage from the class, the entire course, or even leave the university.[78] Rather than stifling expression, some view trigger warnings as "more speech," which demonstrates a professor's sensitivity to student concerns and makes it more likely that students will express their own views about the triggering material.[79] Even opponents of trigger warnings share concerns that exposure to emotionally challenging material could interfere with the ability of students to learn. "Assaulting students with difficult materials without interpretive tools," one argued, "is not education."[80]

Rather than endorsing the establishment of official university policies, some proponents of trigger warnings encourage professors, at their own discretion, to provide students with general comments about potentially disturbing material in a course. They treat trigger warnings as a "heads up" from the professor indicating sensitivity to student concerns, sometimes avoiding the term itself as overly simplistic.[81] One professor, for example, includes a "course content note" in his syllabus stating that the class "will be discussing historical events that may be disturbing, even traumatizing, to some students," and encouraging students to discuss their "personal reactions to this material" with him.[82]

Opponents of trigger warnings point out that broad definitions of potentially triggering material allow professors to identify material they consider ideologically objectionable even if it is not potentially harmful.[83] They maintain that trigger warnings are inevitably ideological because they convey that the material identified as triggering is particularly important.[84] They believe that trigger warnings themselves may unnecessarily distress students and prompt them to avoid emotional challenging material rather than prepare them to engage it.[85] They worry that professors would delete potentially triggering material from their courses.[86] Although they recognize that some students have mental health issues for which accommodations should be made, they assert that these issues should be addressed through procedures provided by the Americans with Disabilities Act, counseling services on campus, or other special arrangements, not through trigger warnings for all students that inappropriately treat pedagogy as an aspect of psychological care.[87]

Some opponents rely on empirical studies concluding that trigger warnings rarely make any difference. To the extent trigger warnings do have any effects, these studies find, they mostly harm the students they are intended to protect. They increase rather than reduce the anticipated negative responses to the triggering material and prompt avoidance of it, leading to additional anxiety and distress. They also reinforce negative memories of prior stressful events while making them more central to the student's identity.[88] Any positive effects were "so small as to lack practical significance" and "at best trivially helpful."[89]

In a 2014 statement, "On Trigger Warnings," the AAUP characterized trigger warnings as "infantilizing and anti-intellectual" because they presume that students "need to be protected rather than challenged in the classroom." It observed that trigger warnings stifle the thought of both teachers and students, who fear discussing controversial subjects that might make others feel uncomfortable, such as sex, race, class, capitalism, and colonialism. By directing attention to the potentially triggering aspects of classroom material, they "signal an expected response to the content (e.g., dismay, distress, disapproval), and eliminate the element of surprise and spontaneity that can enrich the reading experience and provide critical thought." As an example, it observed that if students receive trigger warnings that novels such as *The House of Mirth* and *Anna Karenina* deal with suicide, "they might overlook the other questions about wealth, love, deception, and existential anxiety that are what those books are actually about."[90] Making a similar point, Keith Whittington worried that concern about potential harm to students might divert class discussion from the most important intellectual issues in the assigned texts.[91]

As a matter of policy, I generally agree with the arguments against mandatory trigger warnings. Yet I think it is plausible to assert that they come within the First Amendment institutional academic freedom of universities to make educational decisions. Universities defend trigger warnings as promoting student interests in learning, a clear educational interest that should be recognized even by people who believe that trigger warnings do not achieve, and often impede, this intended goal. Because trigger warnings implicate pedagogy, a subject within the primary responsibility of the faculty, a legitimate exercise of institutional academic freedom would require action by a faculty body rather than the administration or board of trustees.[92]

But even if a faculty body mandates trigger warnings for pedagogical reasons, thereby making them a legitimate exercise of institutional academic freedom, I think that individual professors who object to their use have a stronger First Amendment right of academic freedom to refuse to provide them. Mandatory trigger warnings directly interfere with the fundamental academic freedom of individual professors to make pedagogical decisions and to present their own expert views on the content of class materials.[93] Unlike required teaching in a foreign language, for example, mandatory trigger warnings often force professors to convey positions about the substance of the course that they do not hold.

University policies that encourage rather than require trigger warnings, while putting pressure on faculty to use them, do not seem sufficiently intrusive to constitute a violation of a professor's academic freedom.[94] But any adverse action against professors for not following institutional recommendations to use trigger warnings would violate their academic freedom.

Diversity Statements

In recent years, many American universities have included diversity, equity, and inclusion as criteria for appointing, promoting, and granting tenure to professors. In contrast to trigger warnings, which are rarely required, a study found that in 2020, 19 percent of positions advertised at all universities and 34 percent of positions advertised at elite universities required applicants to submit diversity statements.[95] The history and content of diversity statements in the University of California system have received most attention.[96]

A revision to the system-wide Academic Personnel Model at the University of California that took effect in 2006 instructed campus committees evaluating professors for appointment, promotion, and tenure to give credit for contributions to diversity in teaching, research, and service.[97] The following year, the regents of the University of California adopted a policy statement that described diversity as "integral to the University's achievement of excellence" and part of its "core mission."[98] In 2019 the academic council of the University of California recommended that all campuses of the system require diversity statements from all candidates for faculty positions.[99] During the 2018–2019 academic year, several campuses adopted pilot programs that used diversity statements as an "initial barrier step" for further consideration. Only candidates who met a "high standard" at this initial stage would be considered for further review.[100] Guidance for evaluating these diversity statements provided that low scores should be given to candidates who state that they will "ignore the varying backgrounds of their students and 'treat everyone the same,'" who only describe activities that are known expectations of the institution, who do not seem to "feel any personal responsibility for helping to eliminate barriers," or who regard required diversity in faculty hiring "as antithetical to academic freedom or the university's research mission."[101] These pilot programs produced substantial increases in the number of applicants, finalists, and appointments from underrepresented minorities and from women.[102]

Proponents of diversity statements maintain that they support the commitment to diversity identified by many universities as an important aspect of their mission.[103] They often emphasize that attention to diversity promotes an effective learning environment, particularly for students from underrepresented backgrounds. The chancellor and the vice chancellor for diversity, equity and inclusion at the University of California, Davis, jointly wrote that "using inclusionary practices to engage students from different backgrounds is part of the skill set we expect from faculty" and maintained that diversity statements help universities assess this skill.[104] Similarly emphasizing the importance of skills in teaching a diverse student body, the chancellor of University of California, Santa Cruz, pointed out that this campus serves many minority and first-generation college students.[105] Others commend diversity statements as a way to engage the entire faculty in the hard work of creating and maintaining an equitable and inclusive learning environment, which would alleviate the current burden disproportionately performed by professors from underrepresented backgrounds.[106]

Because diversity statements are implemented to serve the institutional mission of universities, proponents claim, they should not be treated as a general attempt to impose ideological tests on professors.[107] Proponents assert that assessing the views expressed in diversity statements is similar to assessing other views of professors related to teaching and scholarship. Just as a university could refuse to hire scientists who believe the earth is flat or deny tenure to professors who misunderstand or misrepresent the work of leading figures in their fields, it should be able to deny appointment or tenure to professors who lack sufficient competence in advancing university interests in effectively teaching a diverse student body and in expanding the diversity of scholarship.[108] And just as history departments could favor social history over intellectual history and English departments could favor postmodern analysis over more traditional literary studies, departments could favor teaching and research sensitive to the experience of previously underrepresented minorities.[109] Requiring professors to provide information about how they would address issues of diversity in teaching and scholarship, some observe, are similar to long-standing requirements that professors provide general statements about their teaching and scholarly interests. All these statements may be a bother and a distraction from the actual work of teaching and scholarship, but proponents maintain that they are justifiable requirements.[110]

Acknowledging that it is easier in some fields than in others to expand the subjects of teaching and research to underrepresented minorities, some proponents of diversity statements propose that they should be tailored to the different specialties of professors.[111] The guide to the diversity, equity, and inclusion policy at the University of Illinois, while asserting that all faculty can contribute to these goals, recognizes that they will be more central for some. Professors whose specialties do not easily encompass issues of diversity, the guide indicates, can support diversity in other ways, for example through participation in programs that encourage minorities to study the field or that apply research in ways that benefit minority communities.[112] Some who defend eliciting views on diversity that they deem relevant to job performance nevertheless believe that diversity statements are most defensible when they focus on past actions and future plans rather than on viewpoints.[113]

Opponents of diversity statements often claim that they are ideological tests unrelated to legitimate educational goals, sometimes comparing them to the anticommunist loyalty oaths during the Cold War and to the religious tests imposed by Oxford and Cambridge in the nineteenth century.[114] The Academic Freedom Alliance, an organization of professors who have a broad range of political views, maintains that the "demand for diversity statements enlists academics into a political movement, erasing the distinction between academic expertise and ideological conformity."[115] Critics assert that they "have nothing to do with the core professional duties of the faculty" and that they improperly conflate social and political goals with professional qualifications.[116] Some oppose diversity statements as viewpoint discrimination forbidden by the First Amendment.[117] Others question why diversity should be favored over other values, such as mitigating climate change, curing diseases, or concepts of social justice that challenge the value of diversity itself. Success by the left in advancing its ideological values through mandatory diversity statements, they maintain, can serve as a blueprint for the right to impose its very different ideological values, including required statements detailing a candidate's commitment to colorblindness.[118]

Critics observe the irony that diversity statements reduce the diversity of views among professors, including views about diversity itself. The rubric developed at the University of California, Berkeley, assigns low scores to a statement that defines "diversity only in terms of different areas of study or different nationalities, but doesn't discuss gender or ethnicity / race."[119] Abigail Thompson complained that this rubric eliminates "classical liberals," who believe that every person should be treated as a unique individual.[120] Brian Leiter reads the Berkeley rubric as conditioning employment on agreement with Justice Powell's view in *Bakke* that diversity, rather than remediating past discrimination, provides the best defense of affirmative action.[121] Before submitting to the central administration the diversity statement of a law professor at the University of California, Davis, the law school deleted her description of her white, rural, and working class background and references to her scholarship about rural poverty.[122] Beyond limiting views about diversity, critics maintain that the evaluation of diversity statements could exclude professors whose scholarship maintains that free markets reduce poverty or that affirmative action harms minorities.[123]

Perhaps most broadly, opponents of diversity statements often complain that they detract from the educational mission of a university by replacing traditional measures of academic excellence.[124] Some differentiate traditional peer review of the relative academic value of different subjects and intellectual orientations within a field from the focus on diversity, which interjects a mandatory "political dimension in teaching and research," placing both "under the impress of an ideological end."[125] Critics also deny that the expertise of faculty peers extends beyond their disciplines to analyzing the value of diversity and the methods to achieve it.[126] In institutions where diversity statements are used as initial screening devices, critics complain, applicants who may have outstanding records or potential as teachers and scholars could be eliminated from further scrutiny. Reporting that at a pilot program at UC Berkeley, 76 percent of qualified applicants in the life sciences were rejected at the initial screening, a commentator observed that those rejected applicants could have included the next Albert Einstein or Jonas Salk.[127]

Some opponents of diversity statements assert that they cannot even achieve their intended purposes. They question whether effective diversity statements correlate with teaching and research that meaningfully promotes diversity in practice, observing the absence of any meaningful studies.[128] They stress that required diversity statements encourage insincere commitments to diversity by applicants seeking to advance their prospects.[129] And they maintain that there are many ways to promote diversity in teaching and research without requiring diversity statements, including through traditional statements about teaching and research interests that could include diversity as part of a holistic review.[130]

I generally agree with the opponents. Though I recognize the educational benefits of diversity, I believe they can be achieved without diversity statements, which are often used to impose ideological tests on professors. Yet critics are unconvincing in asserting that all diversity statements are unrelated to the academic work of faculty and, therefore, subsume educational to political or other ideological considerations. As their proponents maintain, attention to diversity can promote effective teaching and research. And sometimes the same goal can be educational as well as ideological. One can believe, for example, that diversity improves educational outcomes and, more generally, that diversity should be a key factor in organizing society. By contrast, the loyalty oaths of the McCarthy era, to which critics often compare diversity statements, were justified by concerns about national security rather than by educational considerations.

Apart from considerations of policy, mandatory diversity statements, like mandatory trigger warnings, raise tensions between the individual academic freedom of professors and the institutional academic freedom of universities. Universities can plausibly maintain that their imposition of diversity statements, like their imposition of trigger warnings, is protected by institutional academic freedom. Indeed, in an analogous context, the Supreme Court recognized academic freedom as a First Amendment right of universities while highlighting the educational benefits of a diverse student body. In its 2023 decision invalidating the affirmative action programs at Harvard and the University of North Carolina, the Court did not question this analysis of institutional academic freedom, relying instead on a transformed interpretation of the equal protection clause of the Fourteenth

Amendment. Attention to issues of diversity in teaching, like the existence of a diverse student body, can contribute to the learning environment. And more attention to diversity in scholarship can contribute to the university's educational mission of producing and disseminating knowledge.

But if a university justifies diversity statements without reference to educational values or uses them to suppress unpopular or controversial ideas, it should not be covered by institutional academic freedom. Many defenses of diversity do not cite educational considerations. Even Justice Powell's decisive opinion in *Bakke,* which relied on the educational value of diversity in upholding a university's First Amendment right of institutional academic freedom to use affirmative action in student admissions, did not explain how the impressive range of qualities he identified in a diverse student body would contribute to the learning environment. More strikingly, Justice O'Connor's subsequent defense of student diversity focused on its contribution to the broad societal goals of economic competitiveness and national defense, not on its educational benefits within the university. I believe that many universities after *Bakke* invoked the educational benefits of diversity pretextually, as a constitutionally protected justification for affirmative action, though they primarily implemented it to remedy past discrimination, a justification rejected by the majority of the Supreme Court in *Bakke,* including Justice Powell. As the guidelines used by the University of California make clear, mandatory diversity statements are being used to favor or eliminate people with specific views about diversity, not to measure how candidates have effectively included attention to diversity in their teaching and scholarship. Without the educational judgment that justifies deference to the First Amendment right of institutional academic freedom, diversity statements should be evaluated by general First Amendment standards, including the prohibition against viewpoint discrimination.

If a university does provide plausible educational reasons for requiring diversity statements, it should be protected by institutional academic freedom even if professors also have plausible educational reasons for disagreeing. In determining the validity of an institutional decision to require diversity statements for educational reasons, a distinction should be made between general policy and implementation. Whether to use diversity statements is the kind of general educational policy that comes within the broad authority of the governing board and administration, analogous to decisions about the factors to be considered in selecting students or about the resources allotted to different areas of the curriculum. Yet the implementation of this general policy depends on assessments of how diversity contributes to teaching and scholarship, which may vary by discipline. Consideration of diversity might be more relevant in history or literature than in mathematics or physics. Determining the educational value of diversity in different disciplines depends on academic expertise within the competence of the faculty, analogous to developing the curriculum and evaluating the academic merits of candidates for appointment and tenure after general decisions about the resources allocated to various departments have been made.[131]

Although mandatory diversity statements implemented for educational purposes and with appropriate faculty involvement are justifiable exercises of institutional academic freedom, they constrain the academic freedom of professors to make their own expert judgments about teaching and scholarship by putting enormous pressure on them to place great weight on diversity. Because they encompass scholarship as well as teaching, mandatory diversity statements have a broader impact on the academic freedom of professors than mandatory trigger warnings about class assignments and discussions. Yet mandatory trigger warnings interfere much more directly with a professor's pedagogical decisions than mandatory diversity statements, which do not force professors to take specific actions in the classroom and give professors some discretion in formulating how they would include attention to diversity in their teaching and scholarship. I oppose mandatory diversity statements on policy grounds and recognize that they threaten and often violate the academic freedom of professors. But in analyzing the First Amendment right of academic freedom, I regretfully reach the uncomfortable conclusion that the academic freedom of a university could outweigh the academic freedom of professors when universities present plausible educational reasons for requiring them, follow faculty determinations about how they should be adapted for different disciplines, and do not use them as an ideological test that treats a professor's views about diversity as a basis for denying appointment. The failure of most mandatory diversity statements to meet these standards, especially the strong evidence that they are being used to promote a broad ideological agenda beyond the educational value of diversity, should prompt intensive judicial review of their use.

Conclusion

In cases presenting conflicting claims of academic freedom between professors and universities, judges can often decide by determining whether the facts actually raise this issue. If both the professor and the university present legitimate academic freedom claims, judges must evaluate their relative strength. Some of these cases dispute the academic merits of professors. In response to a professor who claims that the university has violated his academic freedom, the university asserts that the decision was an exercise of its institutional academic freedom to act against a professor who failed to meet academic standards. Although judges are not themselves qualified to assess academic merits, they can often decide these cases by determining whether the asserted reliance on them by universities was in good faith or pretextual. In cases that do require evaluation of academic merits, judges should generally defer to those who do have the requisite expertise, faculty peers within the university.

Informed by my theoretical analysis of academic freedom as a distinctive First Amendment right of professors and universities, I explore in Chapter 11 the plausibility of similar First Amendment protection for students. Though student interests in academic freedom differ substantially from the interests of professors and universities, I conclude that student academic freedom should also be recognized as a distinctive First Amendment right.

11

Student Academic Freedom

A First Amendment theory of academic freedom for students, like a First Amendment theory of academic freedom for faculty or for universities, must differentiate academic freedom from general rights of free speech while explaining why the distinctive right of academic freedom merits First Amendment protection. The societal value of the student interest in learning provides a plausible justification for a distinctive theory of student academic freedom. The student interest in learning, while different from general rights of free speech, promotes the broadly recognized First Amendment values of disseminating knowledge and promoting democratic citizenship.

Since the 1960s, many judicial decisions have applied general First Amendment principles and doctrines to student speech. Just as the Supreme Court's 1968 decision in *Pickering* held that teachers retain their First Amendment rights as citizens, its 1969 decision in *Tinker* held that students as well as teachers "do not shed their constitutional rights at the schoolhouse gate." And just as the *Pickering* decision added that the state has interests as an employer that justify more regulation of the speech of its employees than of citizens generally, the *Tinker* decision added that the First Amendment rights of students must be "applied in light of the special characteristics of the school environment."[1] Courts have frequently enforced the First Amendment rights of students to speak and associate on campus. But in contrast to the many judicial decisions that address academic freedom as a First Amendment right of professors and universities, only a few have alluded to student academic freedom, and fewer still have explicitly identified it as a First Amendment right. Yet these few decisions indicate that student academic freedom can be incorporated within the First Amendment. After reviewing them, I examine the analysis of student academic freedom within the academic community and explore its potential scope as a distinctive First Amendment right.

Student academic freedom must be contrasted with faculty academic freedom both in differentiating academic freedom from general rights of free speech and in justifying its protection through the First Amendment. The expertise of the faculty justifies First Amendment protection for their academic freedom in scholarship and teaching and is the basis for much of the institutional academic freedom of universities to make educational decisions through faculty bodies. Students lack academic expertise. The most fundamental justification for faculty academic freedom does not apply to them. Indeed, the academic freedom of professors entails substantial control over student expression. Professors appropriately evaluate the academic speech and writing of students, and decisions by professors about course content, pedagogy, and assignments appropriately restrict the scope of student expression. Yet students have stronger claims than faculty that their academic freedom includes rights of political expression. Whereas the protection of expert speech that justifies academic freedom for faculty does not extend to political expression beyond this expertise, the exercise of political speech by students in extracurricular activities contributes to the learning process that justifies their academic freedom.

In significant respects, the academic freedom of professors itself advances the student interest in learning. Students learn most effectively when professors can convey their expert knowledge without interference. The limits on the academic freedom of professors also safeguard the student interest in learning. Unprofessional speech by professors is not protected by their academic freedom. Indoctrination, harassment, expression that reflects incompetence, and other unprofessional speech that interferes with the ability of students to learn is subject to university discipline. Yet the rights and limitations of faculty academic freedom provide only uncertain and partial protection of the student's interest in learning.

Beyond access to academically competent speech from professors and freedom from indoctrination or harassment, students should be able to present ideas related to the subject matter of the course and to be evaluated fairly, even if they reach different conclusions than their professors. Student learning at universities occurs beyond the classroom, through informal interchanges with each other and through expression as members of student organizations. Student academic freedom plausibly covers all this classroom and extracurricular expression. And for students, as for faculty, procedural and structural protections may be necessary to ensure the substantive right of academic freedom.

The differences in how faculty and student academic freedom contrast from general rights of free speech and connect to First Amendment values should not obscure a fundamental similarity. Whereas faculty academic freedom is grounded in the societal value of the expert speech of professors and student academic freedom is grounded in the societal value of the student interest in learning, they both invoke the educational functions of the university as the justification for distinctive First Amendment protections.

Supportive Judicial Decisions

Some judicial decisions provide support for recognizing a First Amendment right of student academic freedom. Early Supreme Court decisions about academic freedom as a right of professors maintained that students must also "remain free to inquire, to study and to evaluate"[2] and referred to "learning-freedom" as a constitutionally protected "corollary" of "academic-teaching freedom."[3] While elaborating the meaning of institutional academic freedom, Justices Stevens and Souter also observed that academic freedom encompasses "the independent and uninhibited exchange of ideas among teachers and students."[4] When Louisiana asserted that the promotion of academic freedom, rather than an unconstitutional establishment of religion, was the purpose of its law requiring "balanced treatment" of "creation science" and evolution, Justices Powell and Scalia considered the meaning of student academic freedom as they reached opposite conclusions about the statutory purpose. Whereas the majority's treatment of academic freedom focused on the right of faculty to determine what should be taught, Scalia's dissent asserted that it means "*students'* freedom from *indoctrination*" and Powell's concurrence identified both the academic freedom of professors to "present information" and of students "to receive it."[5]

In a case upholding the First Amendment rights of students, Justice Powell made a brief reference to academic freedom without indicating how, if at all, it functioned in his analysis. Student members of a local chapter of Students for a Democratic Society (SDS) challenged on general First Amendment grounds the college's decision to deny it official recognition, which precluded it from meeting on campus. In justifying this decision, the college president claimed that SDS, through its commitment to disruption and violence, itself repudiated the academic freedom on which a university depends. Justice Powell's majority opinion asserted that "we break no new constitutional ground in reaffirming this Nation's dedication to academic freedom." Yet he did not refer to academic freedom in rejecting the president's own justification based on it. He relied instead on general First Amendment principles prohibiting discrimination based on viewpoint and forbidding the "guilt by association" of ascribing an organization's philosophy to its members without evidence that they had a specific intent to further the organization's unlawful goals. Throughout his opinion, Powell focused on the First Amendment protection for the political and associational rights of the students. He never connected these rights to concerns about academic freedom, or even mentioned academic freedom beyond his initial endorsement of it. The Court remanded the case for a determination of whether the local SDS chapter was willing to abide by reasonable campus rules, not for any reason having to do with academic freedom. At one point, Powell observed that the denial of official recognition impeded the ability of students "to participate in the intellectual give and take of campus debate," but he did not follow up on the possible link between this "intellectual" impact and academic freedom.[6]

None of these Supreme Court cases involved a student assertion of a First Amendment right to academic freedom. In a 1964 case, students did make this assertion when they joined a challenge to oaths the state required of professors. The Supreme Court did not address the student academic freedom claim. Yet it did seem to lend the claim some support by observing that "the interests of the students at the University in academic freedom are fully protected" by its decision holding the oaths unconstitutional.[7]

A few lower-court decisions provide additional support for a First Amendment right of student academic freedom. Invoking the overbreadth doctrine to invalidate a campus harassment policy that could punish student speech in private conversations and in the classroom about the role of women in the military, a court maintained that free speech on campus "is the lifeblood of academic freedom." The court stressed that the expression of adult students on college campuses should not be evaluated by the more restrictive standards applicable in high schools,[8] but other cases also recognized academic freedom for high school students. While relying mostly on the establishment clause to declare unconstitutional a state law requiring balanced treatment of creation science, a court also observed that it violated the academic freedom of high school students as well as teachers because it deprived them of competent science instruction.[9] In another case arising in secondary schools, a court recognized the First Amendment protection for student academic freedom while associating it with the more general First Amendment right to hear, but emphasized that it is more "bounded" than for college students.[10]

These cases indicate that judges are open to applying the First Amendment protection of academic freedom to students. To my knowledge, no decision has rejected the concept of student academic freedom, further indicating the possibility of judicial receptivity to it. A fuller justification for student academic freedom might promote more widespread recognition of its status as a First Amendment right.

Consideration of Student Academic Freedom within the Academic Community

Although few legal decisions have addressed student academic freedom, it has received more attention from the AAUP and from leading academic commentators. Discussion within the academic community about student academic freedom, like the discussion of faculty academic freedom in the AAUP's 1915 Declaration and subsequent documents, helpfully informs its meaning for First Amendment analysis as well. The 1967 "Joint Statement on Rights and Freedoms of Students," which was endorsed by many organizations, including the AAUP and the Association of American Colleges, the two organizations that wrote the 1940 Statement, is an important example. So are articles by Sidney Hook and William Van Alstyne in the 1960s, and an AAUP statement on trigger warnings in 2014.

The classic early documents of the AAUP gave scant attention to student academic freedom. But the AAUP began treating it seriously in the 1960s. The AAUP continues to recognize and address student interests in academic freedom, as in its statement opposing trigger warnings about classroom materials that might produce difficult emotional reactions.

Although the 1915 Declaration stated in its opening sentences that it would not address student academic freedom, it did provide some indirect protection for the student interest in learning through its assertion that the right of faculty academic freedom entails "correlative obligations." "Above all," the 1915 Declaration maintained, a professor should "remember that his business is not to provide his students with ready-made conclusions, but to train them to think for themselves, and to provide them access to those materials which they need if they are to think intelligently."[11]

The 1940 Statement of Principles on Academic Freedom and Tenure contained a brief reference to students in one of its introductory paragraphs. "Academic freedom in its teaching aspect," it maintained, "is fundamental for the protection of the rights of the teacher in teaching and of the student to freedom in learning."[12] Yet its elaboration of academic freedom focused entirely on the academic freedom of professors without mentioning students at all. It leaves the impression that the academic freedom of professors in teaching protects the student "freedom in learning," not that students themselves have a right to academic freedom.

Two decades later, the AAUP did address student academic freedom in significant detail. In his report for 1960–1961, the chair of the AAUP's Committee on Academic Freedom and Tenure stated that recent events, particularly in the South, directed the committee's attention to this issue. He included a long list of topics that could raise issues of student academic freedom, including censorship of the student press, the functioning of student government and other student associations, meetings in university facilities, invitations to outside speakers, various forms of discrimination, and institutional punishment for student participation in off-campus activities opposing segregation, such as sit-ins, demonstrations, and picketing. The breadth and complexity of these issues prompted the committee to recommend the creation of a new Committee on Faculty Responsibility for the Academic Freedom of Students.[13] The AAUP established this committee, which produced two statements on "the academic freedom of students."[14] These AAUP statements led to the 1967 "Joint Statement on Rights and Freedoms of Students."[15] The 1967 Statement is not nearly as comprehensive or as theoretically sophisticated as the 1915 Declaration and has not been nearly as influential within the academic world. Yet many universities incorporated it into their student codes of conduct.[16]

"Freedom to teach and freedom to learn," the preamble of the Joint Statement declared, "are inseparable facets of academic freedom." Frustratingly, the Joint Statement provided no elaboration about why or how these freedoms are inseparable. The preamble maintained that "students should be encouraged to develop the capacity for critical judgment and to engage in a sustained and independent search for truth." The student freedom to learn, it added, encompasses the campus and the community outside the university as well as the classroom.[17]

In the classroom itself, students should be able to take "reasoned exception" to their professors and should be protected from unfair evaluation. While making these points, the Joint Statement observed that students must learn the content and maintain academic standards in their courses. Student freedom in the classroom, it also maintained, should include protection against improper disclosure of their views and political associations by professors.[18]

On the campus more generally, students should be free to form associations to express their views, including about educational policy, to invite speakers, and to have editorial freedom in student publications subject to journalistic standards. Throughout these activities, students should make it clear that they are not speaking for the university or the entire student body.[19]

Off-campus, students should have the same rights of speech, assembly, and petition as other citizens, subject to their obligations as members of the university community. The Joint Statement did not explain how off-campus expression contributes to the student freedom to learn. Nor did it explain why membership in the university community imposes obligations that restrain off-campus expression by students, or specify these obligations and restraints.[20]

In addition to identifying rights of student expression, the Joint Statement urged procedural and structural protections for them. These protections seem analogous to those asserted by the AAUP for faculty academic freedom. The Joint Statement contained a lengthy section on procedural standards in disciplinary proceedings against students and maintained that procedures should be available for students to challenge the fairness of their academic evaluation. The freedom of students to express themselves about issues of institutional policy, it asserted, should extend to the structural right to participate in the development of institutional policy. It assumed the existence of student government and stated that its role should be clearly specified.[21]

The Joint Statement also included a section on "freedom of access to higher education" without relating it to the academic freedom of students identified in the preamble. This section provided that a university should be open to all students who meet its admissions standards and specifically condemned using race as a basis for denying admission. Just as some argue that the academic freedom of faculty should preclude consideration of any factors that unfairly impede scholarship or teaching, this section might have reflected the view that the academic freedom of students should preclude denial of access to higher education based on discriminatory or other irrelevant factors.[22]

Although the Joint Statement did not elaborate its assertion that freedom to teach and freedom to learn "are inseparable facets of academic freedom," Sidney Hook and William Van Alstyne analyzed the relationship among freedom to learn, academic freedom, and free speech in thoughtful detail in articles published during the 1960s. Both Hook and Van Alstyne maintained that student freedom to learn should be protected as a distinctive right. But while Hook differentiated student freedom to learn from both academic freedom and general rights of free speech, Van Alstyne treated it as an aspect of academic freedom and included general rights of political expression on campus within it.

Writing in 1965, at the height of the "free speech movement" at the University of California, Berkeley, that provoked national debate about student rights of expression, Hook rejected the assertion that "freedom to teach and freedom to learn are indivisible" as "simply false both in logic and in fact." The traditional definition of academic freedom, Hook observed, applies primarily to the teaching and research of professors. "Strictly speaking," he concluded, "it makes no sense to talk of 'academic freedom' for students. Students have a right to freedom to learn." While differentiating faculty "academic freedom" from student "freedom to learn," Hook stressed their relationship. "The best guarantee of freedom to learn," he succinctly stated, "is academic freedom for those who teach them."[23]

Anticipating Van Alstyne's classic article on "The Specific Theory of Academic Freedom and the General Issue of Civil Liberty," Hook maintained that a professor who is dismissed for incompetence is not deprived of free speech. "As a citizen he can talk nonsense." But as a professor, he is subject to peer review of his professional competence. Similarly, a student's freedom of speech as a citizen is not subject to the "educational standards" that govern "the freedom to learn." If a university wants to restrict the freedom of speech of students beyond the limitations that apply to citizens generally, Hook maintained, it must provide educational justifications for doing so.[24]

Student organization of political groups on campus and student invitations to controversial outside speakers, Hook concluded, are justified on educational rather than political grounds. He maintained that the educational process extends beyond the campus. Students should be able to pursue controversial social issues on their own initiative as part of their education. He similarly concluded that publication of student newspapers and magazines has educational value. This extracurricular student freedom to learn, Hook observed, is not absolute. It does not protect expression that disrupts student meetings or publications that violate journalistic norms. Hook stressed that the faculty should have the primary responsibility for determining whether a student's expression meets academic standards of competence.[25] Thus, while distinguishing faculty academic freedom from student "freedom to learn," Hook treated both as different from the general rights of all citizens to freedom of speech and as subject to the educational judgments of faculty.

Disagreeing with Hook in an article written later in 1965, William Van Alstyne asserted that academic freedom applies to the student freedom to learn as well as to professors. The recent attention to student academic freedom by the AAUP and other organizations, he observed, "revived" the German concept of learning freedom (*Lehrnfreiheit*) that the 1915 Declaration had excised from its analysis of academic freedom. He defined student academic freedom as the right to "the orderly pursuit of knowledge" and maintained that it can be limited only by rules "reasonably related to the protection of the opportunity of others to learn." Invoking the developing law that the government cannot condition benefits on the surrender of constitutional rights, he added that a university can only restrict the rights of students as citizens if their exercise would substantially "impair the legitimate purposes for which a university is established." As examples of student rights as citizens, he cited political speech, signing petitions, participating in orderly demonstrations, exercising religious liberties, associating with others, and reading whatever interests them.[26]

In a 1968 article detecting a "judicial trend toward student academic freedom," Van Alstyne cited decisions that recognized the First Amendment rights of students to political expression on campus, including the right to invite controversial speakers, though these decisions themselves did not explicitly refer to academic freedom.[27] In contrast to his subsequent 1975 article differentiating faculty academic freedom from general rights of political speech and limiting it to the expression of academic expertise, he incorporated student extracurricular political speech within student academic freedom. Yet unlike the Joint Statement, he did not extend student academic freedom to off-campus political speech. Van Alstyne did not explain these conclusions. But he might have agreed with Hook that student learning extends beyond the classroom. He might have believed as well that this extracurricular learning includes lessons from participation in political activities on campus. He might have thought that off-campus political expression by students, precisely because it is away from campus, is insufficiently connected to the learning experience at universities to fall within student academic freedom. As in his initial article on student academic freedom, he probably continued to view off-campus political expression by students as a general First Amendment right of citizens, which universities should not restrict, rather than as a distinctive right of student academic freedom related to the right to learn. Unlike Hook and his own subsequent scholarship on the academic freedom of professors, Van Alstyne did not address the role of the faculty in determining the academic standards that limit the scope of student academic freedom.

Decades later, in 2014, the AAUP's Committee on Academic Freedom and Tenure reinforced its recognition of academic freedom as a right of students while addressing demands for trigger warnings about emotionally difficult subjects. It concluded that trigger warnings "threaten the academic freedom of teachers and students whose classrooms should be open to difficult discussions, whatever form they take."[28]

The academic discussion of student academic freedom is not nearly as comprehensive as the treatment of academic freedom for faculty in the 1915 Declaration and subsequent commentary. But it does demonstrate that many within the academic community, including the AAUP, have extended the concept of academic freedom to students as well as faculty.

Student Academic Freedom as a First Amendment Right

The student right to learn endorsed within the academic community supports recognition of a distinctive First Amendment right of student academic freedom. Hook convincingly observed that the student "freedom to learn" is different from both faculty academic freedom and from general rights of free speech. It is plausible to limit the term academic freedom to professors. Perhaps confusion would have been avoided had the courts done so and used a phrase such as "educational autonomy" instead of "institutional academic freedom" to differentiate the educational decisions of universities both from faculty academic freedom and from "institutional autonomy" more generally. Perhaps student "freedom to learn" might be a better phrase than "student academic freedom" to differentiate the educationally valuable speech of students both from faculty academic freedom and from the free speech of all citizens. But the widespread judicial recognition of a First Amendment right of institutional academic freedom makes it difficult at this point to confine First Amendment academic freedom to professors. And while it is plausible to limit the term "academic freedom" to professors, it is also plausible to use academic freedom more broadly to differentiate expression related to the educational functions of universities from free speech generally. Because First Amendment cases have already extended academic freedom beyond professors to universities as institutions, it makes sense to apply academic freedom to students as well, as a few decisions have done. The separate recognition of faculty, institutional, and student academic freedom helpfully focuses attention on the distinctive First Amendment analysis that should apply to the educational value of speech within universities.

What should be the scope of the First Amendment right of student academic freedom? It should reflect many of the conclusions reached by the AAUP, Hook, and Van Alstyne. Within the classroom, it should include access to knowledge through competent instruction, freedom from indoctrination and harassment, freedom to take reasoned exception to the views of professors, fair evaluation by professors, and expectations that views expressed in class will not be disclosed beyond it. The academic freedom of students, like the academic freedom of professors, should be subject to academic standards determined by expert faculty evaluation. Professors can impose requirements of relevance, quality, and basic civility on student classroom expression.

Beyond the classroom, students should have academic freedom to participate in extracurricular activities that have educational value. These activities encompass student newspapers, radio stations, and other media, and student organizations covering a broad range of interests, including political and ideological activity. The institutional academic freedom of universities should give them substantial discretion in determining which student extracurricular activities have educational value and which among them should be funded by university resources. Because these determinations are based less on specialized academic expertise than is the evaluation of student speech in the classroom, administrators as well as faculty should exercise this institutional academic freedom on behalf of universities, and, as the 1966 Statement on Government suggests, administrators should have the primary responsibility for funding decisions.

The academic standards appropriate to student speech in the classroom should not confine the speech of students in broader extracurricular activities. Advocacy in student extracurricular political organizations, like advocacy in political organizations generally, should not have to meet standards of accuracy and proof that would be appropriate in a political science class. Learning how to engage in effective political advocacy, which may even require departures from academic standards, is part of the educational value of student participation in these extracurricular organizations.

Other extracurricular student organizations, by contrast, are devoted to learning professional standards. A student newspaper or radio station, for example, could be funded by the university to teach students the standards of professional journalism. It would be appropriate for the university to require students to meet those standards, and to discipline them if they do not. Those standards include editorial freedom, so a university should not be able to dictate the editorial positions or coverage of student media organizations as long as the students follow proper journalistic practice. A university should be able to require the student media to verify factual assertions. But it should not be able to censor articles or editorials that criticize or embarrass the administration or governing board, or discipline the students who wrote them.

Speech by students off campus, unless part of the activities of a campus student organization, is not sufficiently connected to the educational functions of universities to qualify for the protection of academic freedom. The off campus political expression of students as well as faculty should be subject to the same general First Amendment doctrines that the state applies to citizens generally.

For students as well as faculty, the substantive right of academic freedom depends on the procedures and structures available to protect it. Students, like professors, should have the "First Amendment due process" of hearings before faculty bodies to review claimed violations of academic freedom, and possibly also the structural right of a student senate, analogous to a faculty senate, to convey student views about educational issues to the university administration. Other claims of student academic freedom, such as the "freedom of access to higher education" asserted in the 1967 Statement, seem too far removed from expressive rights to fall within the coverage of academic freedom.

Specific examples help illustrate the contours of student academic freedom. If biologists overwhelmingly reject "creation science" as a valid scientific theory or if twentieth-century European historians overwhelmingly reject Holocaust denial as a plausible interpretation of events during World War II, students of biology and history should be able to invoke the First Amendment right of student academic freedom to compel elimination of this material from their classes. The right of access to academically competent teaching should also give students the right to compel elimination of clearly irrelevant material from their classes. The academic freedom of professors should give them broad scope in determining relevance. It is plausible, for example, that discussion of European history in a biology class might be relevant to an explanation of the reception of Darwin's ideas, or that discussion of biological concepts of evolution may be relevant to explaining the role of racial theories in the Holocaust. But, to use President Lowell's example, discussion of the protective tariff is unlikely to be relevant in an astronomy class.

Sometimes, however, even the inclusion of material irrelevant to the subject matter of a course may have educational value. My class in introductory chemistry met the morning after the assassination of Dr. Martin Luther King Jr. At the beginning of class, the professor made some brief emotional comments about the tragedy of King's assassination. His comments provoked additional responses to the assassination from students. Some Black students in the class commented on race relations on campus while responding to the assassination, which generated more discussion about campus issues by both Black and white students, often presenting perspectives I had never previously heard. The professor let this discussion continue for the entire class hour, never reaching the class assignment about chemistry. It is difficult to relate this discussion to introductory chemistry, but it was one of the most educationally valuable hours of my undergraduate experience. I do not think that the professor violated the academic freedom of his students in this context. But if he had spent the rest of the semester discussing race relations instead of chemistry, students would have had a valid academic freedom claim to lack of competent instruction.

Student academic freedom to take reasoned exception to the views of their professors and to receive fair evaluation is well illustrated by Sidney Hook's account of his own college experience. In a political science class, he wrote a report defending the controversial thesis of Charles Beard that the Constitution of the United States derived more from the economic interests of wealthy property owners than from commitments to democratic values. He then wrote a second report arguing that in the famous debates between Senator Calhoun of South Carolina and Senator Webster of Massachusetts over the right the Southern states to secede from the Union, Calhoun made the better argument. The professor indicated his clear disapproval of Hook's first report and ejected Hook from the class after the second report. "When you aren't preaching sedition," the professor told Hook, "you are preaching secession!" In describing this incident, Hook convincingly maintained that his right to learn should have protected him against ejection from the class, just as a professor making similar arguments should be protected by academic freedom.[29]

Legal cases decided on other grounds provide additional illustrations of the contours of student academic freedom. A graduate student in a course on comparative animal behavior who teaches scholarly theories asserting that males are better than females at spatial tasks and a student in a constitutional law course who agrees with Justice Thomas's opposition to affirmative action are expressing ideas related to the subject matter of the course.[30] This expression should be protected by student academic freedom, just as it should not be within the university's power to regulate as an exercise of institutional academic freedom. Plaintiffs who challenged a state law restricting abortions asserted that it violated academic freedom because it would prevent state medical schools from teaching abortion procedures. The court declared the law unconstitutional but declined to address the academic freedom claim because there was no evidence that any of the plaintiffs were medical students.[31] A claim to academic freedom by students as well as by professors would be valid if the faculty of the medical school determined that the law denied access to competent instruction. The right of a student in the Speech Department to choose the subject of abortion for her class presentation raises a more complicated issue of academic freedom. Professors in the department maintained that the topic of abortion is so controversial that it would interfere with the focus of the class on the mechanics of the presentation. This pedagogical justification seems plausible, though debatable.[32]

Legal cases arising outside the classroom further illustrate the contours of student academic freedom. Judge Posner upheld the right of students to perform a controversial play portraying Jesus as a homosexual in order to fulfill their course requirements as theater majors. Dismissing the lawsuit brought by citizens who claimed the performance constituted university endorsement of anti-Christian beliefs, Posner rested his decision on the institutional academic freedom of the university.[33] But he could have invoked the academic freedom of students to perform the play as part of their education as theater majors.

Another judge relied on general First Amendment principles in granting a summary judgment to a medical student who was suspended for comments made at a panel discussion of "microaggressions." The student challenged the definition of microaggression used by a professor. Another professor, who had helped organize the panel and attended it, filed a "Professional Concern Card" against the student, which led to the suspension. The card asserted that the student had asked a series of "antagonistic" questions, accused a professor of "contradictory" statements, and revealed a "level of frustration / anger" that "seemed to escalate until another faculty member defused the situation by calling on another student for questions." The professor filing the card was "shocked" that a medical student "would show so little respect toward faculty members" and consequently worried about "how he will do on wards." The judge observed that the student's statements, made during the portion of the panel reserved for questions, "were academic in nature," indicating that they should be protected by student academic freedom.[34]

Many legal decisions have applied general First Amendment principles in addressing the rights of student organizations. The educational value of many extracurricular activities justifies extending the First Amendment right of student academic freedom to expression within them. Student academic freedom should include rights of student journalists to make editorial decisions and rights of student organizations to meet on campus and to invite outside speakers.

Other legal cases provide examples of campus speech unprotected by student academic freedom. Just as the university's institutional academic freedom should allow it to regulate racist, sexist, and other offensive speech that does not contribute to the discussion of ideas and could interfere with the ability of students to learn, student academic freedom should not protect this expression. Student academic freedom should not protect broadcasting racist jokes on the campus radio station, distributing fliers declaring "open season" on Blacks, holding a "slave auction" at a fraternity, telling Asian-American students they do not belong in the United States, or using racial or sexual epithets directed at other students.[35] Nor should student academic freedom protect a graduate student whose dissertation contained an unprofessional "disacknowledgments" section expressing "special *Fuck-Yous*" to various "degenerates" for "being an ever-present hindrance during my graduate career," including the dean and staff of the graduate school.[36]

Conclusion

Academic freedom in the United States traditionally protected the expert academic speech of professors. But it makes sense to extend its First Amendment protection to the student interest in learning. The student interest in learning, like the faculty interest in its expert academic speech, differs from general interests in freedom of expression. It also correlates with the First Amendment values of disseminating knowledge and promoting democratic citizenship.

The First Amendment protection for student academic freedom should cover student interests in access to knowledge, in disagreeing with the views of their professors, and in fair evaluation. It should also extend to the "second curriculum" of extracurricular expression, which contributes to student learning, including preparation for effective participation and leadership in a democratic society. It should protect the classroom expression of all ideas that are relevant to the subject of a course, even if those ideas produce reactions that might impede the ability of some students to learn. Yet student academic freedom should not extend to forms of expression without any educational value that interfere with student learning. Rather, it should protect students from them. Procedural and structural safeguards, moreover, are necessary to protect the substantive right of academic freedom for students as well as for professors.

Conclusion

THE THEORY of academic freedom as a distinctive subset of First Amendment law protects the valuable educational functions of American universities. Derived primarily from the fundamental First Amendment interests in the production and dissemination of knowledge, it is more sensitive to the functions of expression at universities than the general First Amendment law of free speech or employee-speech jurisprudence.

The theory recognizes the central role of the faculty in the production and dissemination of knowledge, the most essential function of a university. In order to perform this function, faculty must have freedom to research, publish, and teach within their academic expertise without interference from the university or the state. Expression must meet academic standards to qualify as the expert academic speech that merits the protection of academic freedom. Because academic expertise is required to determine academic standards, peer review by fellow professors plays an essential role in determining if a violation of academic freedom has occurred. Academic freedom depends on the existence of peer review committees and protects the expression of professors who serve on them. Scholarship requires access to and control over research material, and teaching includes pedagogical decisions about how to present material. Academic freedom protects these aspects of scholarship and teaching as well as expression about the substantive content of academic ideas. Beyond scholarship and teaching, professors contribute to the production and dissemination of knowledge less directly but still meaningfully through their expert expression about matters of educational policy within the university. Academic freedom extends to this intramural expression. But its justification does not extend to the general political expression of professors unrelated to their academic expertise.

The First Amendment right of academic freedom encompasses the educational decisions of universities as well as the academic speech of professors. Institutional academic freedom includes decisions about the appointment and tenure of faculty, the structure of the curriculum, the admission and discipline of students, student extracurricular activities, the regulation of offensive speech, and public access to campus. The validity of a university's exercise of its academic freedom often depends on who makes the decision on its behalf. Many educational decisions by the university require faculty expertise, especially the appointment and tenure of professors and the content of the curriculum. Faculty have the primary responsibility for these decisions, subject to limited oversight by the administration and governing board. Broader issues of educational policy are the primary responsibility of the administration and governing board, though faculty have an advisory role. These broader issues include the allocation of resources among academic departments, determining the size and composition of the student body, the treatment of offensive speech on campus, and the regulation of public access to university property. Although institutional academic freedom provides substantial independence from state interference for both public and private universities, the state has more interests in regulating the public universities it funds. A state legislature, for example, could require a public university but not a private one to offer a course in the history of the state or to enroll a designated percentage of state residents.

Although students lack the expertise that provides the foundation for the academic freedom of professors, their interests in learning justify protection through a distinctive First Amendment right of student academic freedom. This right includes access to competent instruction, freedom from indoctrination by their professors, and freedom to express their own views about course material so long as they meet academic standards. It protects students from harassment and gratuitously harmful speech that is unrelated to the discussion of ideas and that undermines the environment for learning. Student academic freedom extends to the extracurricular activities that provide "a second curriculum." Subject to professional norms, it covers the freedom of student theater groups to select which plays to perform, and the editorial freedom of student journalists. Whereas the justification for faculty academic freedom does not extend to political speech unrelated to academic expertise, the educational value of student participation in extra-curricular political organizations justifies the protection of academic freedom for their political speech in those organizations even if it is unrelated to their studies.

By providing the criteria for determining whether a particular claim raises issues of academic freedom, the theory enables judges to resolve many conflicts. But many cases raise additional complications. Disputes between professors and universities often turn on the merits of academic expression that judges lack the competence to assess. Judges can avoid this difficulty when they find evidence that asserted reliance on the academic merits was a pretext for a decision made on other grounds. If no evidence of pretext exists, they should defer to peer review committees within universities, which have the expertise to assess the merits. If peer review had not occurred, judges should require it before deciding the case. Because administrators generally lack the expertise of peer review committees, judges should not defer to administrative reversals on the academic merits unless the administration can provide convincing evidence that the peer review committee failed to perform its function competently or that broad institutional policies within administrative discretion justified a different result. Some disputes between professors and universities require judges to balance a professor's interest in academic freedom against competing interests of universities in maintaining an effective educational environment, including through standards established by collective faculty decisions.

Since the framing and ratification of the US Constitution, American courts have recognized the societal value of universities in transmitting knowledge and in preparing students for democratic citizenship. They have explored the relationship of constitutional law to the educational functions of a university, initially through the impairment of contracts clause, subsequently through the due process clause of the Fourteenth Amendment, and since the 1950s through the First Amendment. The Supreme Court has identified academic freedom as "a special concern of the First Amendment," a phrase frequently quoted in decisions at all levels of the judicial system. Yet as judges as well as scholars constantly complain, neither the Supreme Court itself nor the hundreds of lower-court cases referring to academic freedom as a First Amendment right have elaborated its meaning. Without a clear understanding of this right, it is difficult to address its relationship to the First Amendment generally. In analyzing similar facts, judges sometimes refer to the First Amendment right of academic freedom, sometimes

to the First Amendment generally, sometimes to employee-speech jurisprudence, and sometimes to all three simultaneously without differentiating
them.

I have attempted in this book to clarify the meaning of a distinctive First
Amendment right of academic freedom as a subset of First Amendment
law. Focusing especially on the role of academic freedom in promoting the
production and dissemination of knowledge, I developed it as a First
Amendment right of professors, universities, and students. Often using the
facts of the decided cases as examples, I suggested how judges should apply
this right. I hope my own views stimulate further reflection about its
meaning and application.

I also hope that this book prompts research on two important related
topics: the application of the First Amendment to other professional employees, and the legal protection of academic freedom without reliance on
the First Amendment. The theory of academic freedom as a distinctive First
Amendment right could help analyze the appropriate First Amendment
protection in other institutions that depend on the expression of professional employees. The unique functions of professors and universities preclude the blanket extension of the First Amendment protection of academic
freedom. But there are sufficient similarities between professors in universities and professional employees in other institutions to suggest that aspects of the theory could have broader implications. It is also important to
recognize that the First Amendment is not the only legal route to protect
academic freedom. The potential of contract law, collective bargaining
agreements, and statutory law is substantial but relatively unexplored.

BIBLIOGRAPHICAL ESSAY

In this bibliographical essay I focus on the prior scholarship most relevant to the central themes in this book. William Van Alstyne's 1972 essay "The Specific Theory of Academic Freedom and the General Issue of Civil Liberty" was the first major scholarly analysis of the meaning of academic freedom as a First Amendment right. Van Alstyne argued that academic freedom must be differentiated from general First Amendment rights of political expression. Writing fifteen years after the Supreme Court initially associated academic freedom with the First Amendment in *Sweezy*, he observed that this differentiation had not occurred. He largely blamed professors, whose "promiscuous usage" of the term "academic freedom" had expanded its original purpose of enabling them "to fulfill the critical functions of their profession" into a vehicle for protecting their general political expression. Expanding academic freedom beyond its "core rationale," Van Alstyne maintained, "has inadvertently delayed" its "specific assimilation" into the First Amendment.[1]

The Supreme Court's references to academic freedom while adjudicating First Amendment cases, Van Alstyne asserted, gave it "highly honorable mention" without clarifying its meaning. He pointed out that since the late 1950s the Supreme Court had interpreted the First Amendment to provide "separate and distinct protection for freedom of association," derived from general First Amendment principles but having a different "character of its own." Academic freedom, by contrast, had not become "an identifiable First Amendment claim, a special subset readily derived from but not simply fungible with freedom-of-speech doctrine in general, or First Amendment doctrine in respect to public employees at large."[2]

Van Alstyne attributed the "promiscuous usage" of academic freedom to the lack of First Amendment protection for political expression by public employees until the 1960s. Without this protection, "'academic freedom' offered itself as a possible way out" for professors, who used it as "any old port in a storm." He criticized the "suspect elitism" of professors, who relied on academic freedom to claim more protection for general political expression than was available to other public employees. The unjustified expansion of academic freedom, moreover, became an example of "crying wolf." Professors made unpersuasive claims of academic freedom so often that the public became indifferent to authentic ones related to their academic functions. Observing the "marvelous irony" that general First Amendment law had changed in the decade before he wrote his essay, Van Alstyne stressed the Supreme Court's recent decisions establishing that public employees retain First Amendment rights of political expression. The "practical reason that provided the incentive (if not a compelling logic)" for the extension of academic freedom to cover general political expression no longer existed.[3]

A specific theory of academic freedom tied to the academic expression of professors, Van Alstyne pointed out, would provide both more and less protection than general First Amendment rights. "The price of an exceptional vocational freedom to speak the truth as one sees it, without penalty for the possible immediate impact upon the economic well-being of the employing institution," he asserted, "is the cost of exceptional care in the representation of that 'truth,' a professional standard of care."[4]

When the Supreme Court started recognizing academic freedom as a First Amendment right of universities as well as professors, scholars turned their attention to this topic, beginning with Matthew Finkin's pioneering 1983 article "On 'Institutional' Academic Freedom." Finkin's article derived from the amicus Supreme Court brief he wrote for the AAUP opposing Princeton's broad assertions of its First Amendment right of institutional academic freedom. Princeton invoked this right as a barrier to judicial review of its decision to exclude anyone without a Princeton connection or sponsorship from entering its campus to solicit political support or contributions. Finkin differentiated the "related but distinct ideas" of institutional academic freedom and institutional autonomy. Institutional academic freedom, he asserted, is based on a university's commitment to scholarship and teaching. Broader institutional rights of autonomy may be based on property interests, but they do not implicate institutional academic freedom.

To prove a violation of institutional academic freedom, a university must demonstrate a connection between an "invasion of autonomy and the institution's capacity to maintain freedom of teaching, research, and publication." Finkin asserted that Princeton failed to recognize this difference by refusing even to provide educational justifications for its policy limiting access to campus property. Princeton's claim that a private university has the right to indoctrinate students in a particular ideology, he added, "cannot be invoked under the head of 'academic freedom' without working a debasement of meaning."[5]

Prior Supreme Court cases, Finkin complained, had not devoted sufficient attention to whether the university based its decisions on concerns about scholarship and teaching that justify the protection of institutional academic freedom. He pointed out, for example, that some university decisions about student admissions or the allocation of university facilities to student groups might consider these concerns, but that others might be based on different factors.[6]

Even when universities invoke concerns about scholarship and teaching in making decisions, Finkin stressed, institutional academic freedom should not preclude judicial review of conflicting academic freedom claims between professors and universities. If a professor claims that administrators violated his academic freedom by denying tenure, judges should not automatically defer to the university's response that the decision was made on valid academic grounds protected by institutional academic freedom. Such deference, he observed, would "constitutionalize the concept of administrative prerogative that the American professoriate struggled against" during the period when the AAUP formulated the 1915 Declaration, "and it would do so, perversely, in the name of academic freedom."[7]

Peter Byrne's important 1989 article, "Academic Freedom: A 'Special Concern of the First Amendment,'" maintained that academic freedom as a First Amendment right should primarily protect universities from the state rather than professors from universities. He pointed out that in the prior decade, Supreme Court decisions about academic freedom had focused on the corporate right of universities to perform their core educational functions without government interference. Yet he recognized that, as in the *Sweezy* and *Keyishian* cases that initially recognized academic freedom as a First Amendment right, this "new turn" to institutional academic freedom "has flowered in dicta and rhetoric more than in holdings and rules." Like Van Alstyne, Byrne differentiated the First Amendment right of academic freedom from general First Amendment rights of free speech. Disagreeing with the widespread assumption that academic freedom encompasses "all First Amendment rights exercisable on a campus or by members of the academic community," Byrne maintained that it "should be reserved for those rights necessary for the preservation of the unique functions of the university, particularly the goals of disinterested scholarship and teaching."[8]

Byrne asserted that First Amendment protection for institutional academic freedom "is justified by the same compelling need to protect inquiry and exchange among trained scholars that underlay the traditional struggle within the university for academic freedom." He believed that institutional academic freedom should protect the tradition of peer review as well as scholarship and teaching. Not only "the canonical procedure" for making the institutional decision about who will teach, peer review "also is the linchpin in the structural compromise over governance that insulates faculty from regular supervision or review by administrators." Byrne stressed that faculty peers have the competence to evaluate the academic performance of their colleagues and are typically dedicated to principles of academic freedom that reject reliance on "exogenous factors." He called peer review the "mechanism by which the professor's scholarly freedom is assured." "Academic freedom," he starkly concluded, "has no meaning without peer review."[9]

Even though Byrne's analysis of peer review stressed the need to insulate professors from administrative supervision or review, he advocated a "very limited judicial role in protecting faculty against their schools." While acknowledging that "the main thrust of the non-legal tradition of academic freedom has been to secure the autonomy of the individual teacher against improper interference by administrators," he viewed judicial intervention in these disputes as itself a form of state intervention in academic affairs that jeopardizes academic freedom. Byrne approved judicial review to determine whether a university punished a professor for political or other ideological views protected by general First Amendment principles. But he asserted that judges are not competent to address conflicting claims of academic freedom between professors and universities. "When presented with claims by faculty members that other academics, usually administrators and department chairs, have violated their rights to academic freedom," Byrne concluded, "courts should only ascertain if the administrators can establish that they in good faith rejected the candidate on academic grounds." Courts should not intervene if faculty bodies and administrators reach different academic judgments in good faith "because the Constitution cannot impose any ideal structure of authority among the constituents of the university." While the AAUP and other "academic organizations" are "entirely justified" in challenging the grounds for academic decisions made by administrators, Byrne asserted, there is no "legal standard or test" that could enable judges to do so.[10]

Yet Byrne did identify a limiting principle on institutional academic freedom that protected the individual academic freedom of professors. Universities should not be granted institutional academic freedom if they "do not respect the academic freedom of professors (understood as the core of the doctrine developed by the AAUP) or the essential intellectual freedom of students (a concept barely developed)." He thought this limitation "may lessen fears that institutional freedom will cloak extensive violations of professors' academic freedom." Similarly seeking to allay concerns about the lack of First Amendment protection for the academic freedom of professors against universities, he contrasted a "dark age of faculty dependence" in the past with the present, "when most universities voluntarily defend the academic freedom of their faculties."[11]

In 1990 I published an article, "A Functional Analysis of 'Individual' and 'Institutional' Academic Freedom under the First Amendment," that addressed some of the topics treated more comprehensively in this book.[12] I pointed out that Supreme Court decisions had recognized First Amendment protection of both individual and institutional academic freedom. Although they initially were viewed as complementary, I observed a trend treating individual and institutional academic freedom as competing claims. Rather than viewing institutional academic freedom as an additional layer of protection for professors against the state, administrators and trustees increasingly invoked it as a bar to judicial review of claims by professors that universities had violated their academic freedom. I maintained that the functions of professors and universities justify the judicial recognition of both individual and institutional academic freedom under the First Amendment. I also tried to demonstrate that judges are often competent to resolve competing academic freedom claims between professors and universities without themselves threatening academic freedom.

In making these points, I criticized Byrne's privileging of institutional over individual academic freedom as a First Amendment right, even as I agreed with much of his analysis of the meaning of academic freedom and the central role of faculty peer review. I particularly challenged his assumption that administrators have comparable academic expertise to professors. I urged more judicial deference to the decisions of faculty peer review committees than to administrative reversals of them. Based on the evidence of legal cases and investigations by the AAUP, I also challenged Byrne's confidence that widespread university defense of the academic freedom of their faculties had superseded the administrative suppression of faculty academic freedom in the past. The evidence demonstrated that many abridgments of individual academic freedom occurred in universities that ordinarily respect it, to which Byrne's "limiting principle" on institutional academic freedom would not apply.[13]

Like Byrne, Frederick Schauer subsequently argued that the First Amendment should protect institutional rather than individual academic freedom. Following a pathbreaking article advocating the development of distinctive First Amendment rights for institutions, Schauer applied his institutional analysis to universities while considering the First Amendment meaning of academic freedom. In his initial 1998 article on institutional First Amendment rights, "Principles, Institutions, and the First Amendment," he complained that in cases presenting the opportunity to elaborate these rights the Supreme Court instead "clung to the wreckage of doctrines designed for the demonstrably different situations of earlier First Amendment controversies." He directed attention to the "government's controls over its own speech-related enterprises—schools, universities, libraries, museums, arts funding, public broadcasting, state publications."[14] His 2005 article, "Towards an Institutional First Amendment," maintained that the First Amendment should cover institutions that "serve important purposes of inquiry and knowledge acquisition."[15]

The following year, Schauer relied on his institutional approach in answering the question posed by his article "Is There a Right to Academic Freedom?" He pointed out that the right of academic freedom "only has bite" if it protects what otherwise would be unprotected outside the academic context. In discussing "the individual side of academic freedom," he expressed doubt that "except in a surprisingly small number of instances, the Supreme Court's references to academic freedom were intended to recognize, or had the effect of recognizing, a genuinely distinct *individual* academic freedom right, as opposed to simply pointing out an important but undifferentiated instantiation of a more general individual right to freedom of speech." Yet he acknowledged that "traces" of a limited right of individual academic freedom can be found in lower court cases. Although he believed that individual academic freedom for professors in teaching and scholarship is "better for the academic enterprise," he ultimately concluded as a "normative" matter that a First Amendment right of individual academic freedom "is almost impossible to imagine in practice."[16]

For Schauer, as for Byrne, the strongest argument against recognizing a First Amendment right of individual academic freedom was that it "would inevitably restrict the academic *autonomy* of the institution itself." He maintained, moreover, "that an institutional understanding of academic freedom, even if it comes at the expense of an individual understanding, is both more faithful to the best account of what academic freedom is all about and more compatible with larger and emerging themes in First Amendment doctrine generally." Like Byrne, Schauer understood institutional academic freedom as an enforceable right of universities "to be protected from external political or bureaucratic interference with its academic judgments," including from courts.[17]

While reiterating that institutional academic freedom "may also be consistent with the absence of academic freedom rights of individual academics against their academic supervisors," Schauer seemed to leave open some room for individual academic freedom. He stated that "recognizing the constitutional dimensions of the institutional autonomy of academic institutions may even require limiting the scope and strength of individual academic freedom rights, for it is a necessary component of such rights that they are typically enforced by a judicial evaluation of, and potential interference with, an academic judgment by an academic institution." Yet "limiting the scope and strength of individual academic freedom rights" does not deny them entirely.[18] Schauer did not explore the possible meaning of individual academic freedom, however limited and weak, and elsewhere in his article he did not recognize it at all.

In an ambitious book published in 2013, *First Amendment Institutions,* Paul Horwitz developed the theory of First Amendment protection for institutions and explored how it would apply to different institutions, including universities.[19] Like Byrne and Schauer, Horwitz maintained that the First Amendment right of academic freedom should protect universities as institutions rather than individual professors. Emphasizing the lack of judicial competence to evaluate academic speech, he warned that if courts follow "the paradigm of the individual speaker against the restrictive state" in applying the First Amendment to universities, decisions "are likely to be both overprotective of the speech of individual academics, even when they violate disciplinary norms, and underprotective of the obligation of university administrators to govern the enterprise according to its academic mission." Judicial intervention on behalf of individual academic freedom, he added, is not needed because traditional university practices of self-regulation protect the teaching and scholarship of individual professors.[20]

While agreeing with other proponents of institutional academic freedom that it should only protect the academic decisions of universities, Horwitz had a much broader conception of what constitutes an academic decision, claiming it should be "loosely defined." He disagreed with Supreme Court decisions that rejected university claims of institutional academic freedom and of rights to regulate speech on campus. Criticizing Byrne's restriction of institutional academic freedom to "the fundamental values of disinterested inquiry, reasoned and critical discourse, and liberal education," Horwitz maintained that it "risks reifying a particular legal definition of academic freedom, and of the university's mission." He argued instead that courts should defer to "what universities say about the scope and boundaries of proper academic judgment." He objected to "a judicially imposed definition of the mission of the university." He even asserted that institutional academic freedom protects the right "to *defy*, rather than advance" antidiscrimination laws so long as the university provides "*academic* reasons" for doing so. Yet he thought such defiance would be rare. Pointing out that universities act within a "tradition of cultural norms and self-regulatory practices," he was confident that if a university engaged in "flagrant racial discrimination in hiring," its "own stakeholders" would resist without the need for judicial intervention.[21]

Asserting that the scholarly literature had overemphasized the tension between individual and institutional academic freedom, Judith Areen's innovative 2008 article, "Government as Educator: A New Understanding of First Amendment Protection of Academic Freedom and Governance," focused instead on the faculty role in university governance to determine the level of First Amendment protection for academic freedom.[22] Contrary to the widespread belief that academic freedom is "simply the university professor's analogy to the citizen's right of free speech," Areen stressed that it is "central to the functioning and governance of colleges and universities." Academic freedom, she maintained, "is not only about faculty research and teaching; it is also about the freedom of faculties to govern their institutions in a way that accords with academic values whether they are approving the curriculum, hiring faculty, or establishing graduation requirements for students." It should protect a professor's "power, as a member of the governing faculty," to "facilitate the core university tasks of producing and disseminating new knowledge."[23]

The increasing judicial use of employee-speech jurisprudence governing public employees generally to resolve disputes over the First Amendment protection of faculty speech, Areen maintained, does not take "adequate account of the distinctive nature of the academic workplace." She observed that "employee criticism that might seem insubordinate in other public agencies may be a necessary part of fulfilling the governance responsibilities of a faculty member in a college or university." Faculty speech about academic matters, she asserted, should be protected even if it does not raise issues of concern to the general public, which is the requirement for First Amendment protection under employee-speech jurisprudence.[24]

Addressing the implications of her conception of academic freedom for judicial review, Areen concluded that in resolving an academic freedom claim by a professor against a university, judges should defer to the determination of a faculty body unless the professor can meet the very high burden of proving that it had deviated from academic standards. But if the administration or governing board had overturned the determination of a faculty body or had made the decision without consulting one at all, judges should place the burden on them to prove that they made the decision on academic grounds. She noted her disagreement with judges who deferred to administrators rather than to faculty bodies about academic decisions and with Byrne's advocacy of judicial deference to universities even when academic decisions are made by administrators rather than faculty bodies. Areen did not argue that the First Amendment right of academic freedom should require faculty participation in university governance, though she observed that under her interpretation of its meaning a collective role for the faculty in making academic decisions would largely insulate universities from judicial scrutiny.[25]

Robert Post's 2012 book, *Democracy, Expertise, Academic Freedom,* placed the First Amendment protection for academic freedom within a broader distinction he creatively developed between the related First Amendment values of "democratic legitimation" and "democratic competence."[26] Democratic legitimation, "the central thrust of the First Amendment," is based on the "egalitarian premise that every person is entitled to communicate his own opinion." It precludes viewpoint and content discrimination. Democratic competence refers to "distinct First Amendment doctrines designed to protect the social practices that produce and distribute disciplinary knowledge." Whereas democratic legitimation treats all persons with "tolerance and equality," democratic competence subjects speech "to a disciplinary authority that distinguishes good ideas from bad ones." Disciplinary methods "are neither democratic nor egalitarian." Yet Post reached the "awkward conclusion" that democratic competence, though "incompatible" with democratic legitimation, is also "required by it."[27]

Attempting to reconcile democratic legitimation with democratic competence, Post observed that "a state that can manipulate the production of disciplinary knowledge can set the terms of its own legitimacy" and "undermine the capacity of citizens to form autonomous and critical opinions." That would "make a mockery" of democratic legitimation. Democratic competence "empowers democratic citizens to demand accountability from their government." Because democratic competence makes this important contribution to democratic legitimation, the production of disciplinary knowledge should "remain at least partially independent from state control." In fostering democratic competence, courts must give First Amendment "status to the disciplinary practices by which expert knowledge is itself created," in effect recognizing "a constitutional sociology of knowledge."[28]

Post argued that the recent emergence of "commercial speech doctrine is best explained as resting on the constitutional value of democratic competence." Though "expert knowledge" also promotes democratic competence, Post acknowledged that courts had not made this connection or otherwise treated it as "a distinct and well recognized branch of First Amendment jurisprudence." He identified academic freedom as an "obvious candidate" for developing First Amendment doctrine that promotes democratic competence through expert knowledge, even as he joined the consensus that the existing First Amendment law of academic freedom "stands in a state of shocking disarray and incoherence." He differentiated academic freedom from the professional speech of lawyers and doctors. Whereas lawyers and doctors are expected to convey existing expert knowledge to clients and patients, scholars are expected to create new knowledge, which requires the academic freedom to challenge existing knowledge.[29]

Post asserted that the AAUP's 1915 Declaration, by justifying academic freedom as protecting the function of professors in "identifying and discovering knowledge," could be "translated into contemporary constitutional terms" because this function "triggers the constitutional value of democratic competence." He maintained that the value of democratic competence could reconcile the tension so often observed by judges and scholars between First Amendment rights of individual and institutional academic freedom. "This value," he stressed, "encompasses *both* the ongoing health of universities as institutions that promote the growth of disciplinary knowledge *and* the capacity of individual scholars to promote and disseminate the results of disciplinary inquiry." Concern about the tension between individual and institutional academic freedom, he concluded, is based on a misunderstanding—the failure to appreciate that the exercise of professional standards does not inhere either in universities or in professors "as such."[30]

Treating academic freedom as an aspect of democratic competence, Post stressed, does not justify the frequent judicial deference to university administrators, who often "possess neither the capacity nor the pretense of exercising professional judgment." If in the landmark *Sweezy* case "lay administrators" rather than state officials had tried to inhibit classroom lectures, a violation of academic freedom would still occur because in both situations the determination would be based on "non-professional, non-scholarly assessments of relevant knowledge." First Amendment coverage should be triggered whenever "disciplinary competence" is not determined by "disciplinary experts." Post recognized that administrators often claim that they rely on professional standards, but he did not give his own opinion about whether or when they may be "disciplinary experts." He did agree with Areen that academic freedom does not apply to university decisions that are unrelated to professional standards.[31]

Post explicitly did not address the application of academic freedom to intramural speech, including about matters of internal governance stressed by Areen, or to "freedom of teaching" beyond rights to disseminate the results of research in class. He did join Areen in criticizing courts for applying employee-speech jurisprudence to the academic expression of professors. "The logic of democratic competence," he maintained, "unmistakably suggests that regulation of faculty research and publication should trigger First Amendment coverage whether or not faculty speech involves matters of public concern."[32]

I mostly relied on scholarship that addressed the relationship of academic freedom to the First Amendment, the main subject of this book. Other scholarship was extremely helpful in analyzing two other important issues: the context of the AAUP's 1915 Declaration, and the tension between the individual academic freedom of professors and the role of academic disciplines in determining the standards that define legitimate academic speech. Walter Metzger's book *Academic Freedom in the Age of the University,* originally published in 1955, was especially useful in understanding the controversies in the late nineteenth and early twentieth centuries that influenced the conception of academic freedom in the 1915 Declaration.[33] Joerg Tiede's 2015 book, *University Reform: The Founding of the American Association of University Professors,* provided fascinating details of the internal deliberations among the founders of the AAUP between 1915 and 1919.[34] Tiede emphasized that the AAUP was not specifically established to be "the primary defender of academic freedom that it subsequently became." Its founders had broader concerns about the weak role of faculty in university governance and about attempts to standardize higher education. Tiede effectively traced the AAUP's "shift in focus to the defense of academic freedom" in the early years of its existence.[35]

In analyzing the paradoxical relationship between individual academic freedom and the limitations on it imposed by disciplinary standards, three essays were particularly valuable: Judith Thomson's "Ideology and Faculty Selection";[36] Joan W. Scott's "Academic Freedom as an Ethical Practice";[37] and Judith Butler's "Academic Norms, Contemporary Challenges: A Reply to Robert Post on Academic Freedom."[38] I also recommend the other essays about academic freedom in these three edited volumes.

NOTES

Introduction

1. Sweezy v. New Hampshire, 354 U.S. 234, 250 (1957). As of 2022, more than 40 percent of national constitutions mention academic freedom. Tom Ginsburg, "Academic Freedom and Democratic Backsliding," *Journal of Legal Education* 71 (2022): 238, 243, and n32. Many documents of international and regional law also identify academic freedom (Ginsburg, 248–257). Eric Barendt, *Academic Freedom and the Law: A Comparative Analysis* (Oxford: Hart, 2010), provides an excellent comparative analysis of academic freedom, focusing especially on the United Kingdom, Germany, and the United States.

2. Keyishian v. Board of Regents, 385 U.S. 589, 603 (1967).

3. Garcetti v. Ceballos, 547 U.S. 410, 419 (2006).

4. William Van Alstyne, "The Specific Theory of Academic Freedom and the General Issue of Civil Liberty," in *The Concept of Academic Freedom*, ed. Edmund L. Pincoffs (Austin: University of Texas Press, 1975): 59–85.

1. Defining Academic Freedom in the AAUP's 1915 Declaration

1. American Association of University Professors, "1915 Declaration of Principles on Academic Freedom and Academic Tenure" (1915) (hereafter cited as 1915 Declaration), reprinted in *Academic Freedom and Tenure*, ed. Louis Joughin (Madison: University of Wisconsin Press, 1969), appendix A.

2. Walter P. Metzger, *Academic Freedom in the Age of the University* (New York: Columbia University Press, 1955).

3. Metzger, *Academic Freedom,* 90.

4. Metzger, *Academic Freedom,* 67–68, 85–86, 89–90, 92.

5. Metzger, *Academic Freedom,* 111–116, 119–122, 130–132.

6. Metzger, *Academic Freedom*, 144–145; Hans-Joerg Tiede, *University Reform: The Founding of the American Association of University Professors* (Baltimore: Johns Hopkins University Press, 2015), 11.

7. Metzger, *Academic Freedom*, 150, 153, 160, 176–177.

8. Metzger, *Academic Freedom*, 162–171; Tiede, *University Reform*, 35–37.

9. "The Dismissal of Professor Ross," Report of Committee of Economists, Feb. 20, 1901, Edward Robert Anderson Seligman Papers, Rare Book & Manuscript Library, Columbia University, box 92, 5, 7.

10. Tiede, *University Reform*, 42–44.

11. Metzger, *Academic Freedom*, 168; Tiede, *University Reform*, 35.

12. "The Case of Professor Mecklin: Report of the Committee of Inquiry of the American Philosophical Association and the American Psychological Association," *Journal of Philosophy, Psychology and Scientific Methods* 11 (Jan. 29, 1914): 67–81.

13. Metzger, *Academic Freedom*, 200–201; Tiede, *University Reform*, 61.

14. Tiede, *University Reform*, 67.

15. "Preliminary Report of the Joint Committee on Academic Freedom and Academic Tenure," *American Economic Review* 5 (March 1915): 316–323.

16. Tiede, *University Reform*, 61–62.

17. Tiede, *University Reform*, 94.

18. "Preliminary Report," 319.

19. "Preliminary Report," 320.

20. "Preliminary Report," 320–321.

21. "Preliminary Report," 321.

22. AAUP, "Report of the Committee of Academic Freedom," AAUP office files, Washington, D.C., 4–5, 18–19. The AAUP office files have been deposited in the Special Collections Research Center at the George Washington University Library, but accessions to this collection have not been processed. I cite the AAUP office files when I have not been able to find the document in the George Washington collection.

23. The *Nation* published articles based on this exchange. John H. Wigmore, "Academic Freedom of Utterance," *The Nation,* Dec. 7, 1916, 538–540; A. O. Lovejoy, "Academic Freedom," letter to the editor, *The Nation,* Dec. 14, 1916, 561.

24. John H. Wigmore, "Academic Freedom in the Light of Judicial Immunity," AAUP office files, 1–7.

25. Wigmore, "Academic Freedom in the Light of Judicial Immunity," 7–8.

26. Wigmore, "Academic Freedom in the Light of Judicial Immunity," 9, 10.

27. Letter from Edwin R. A. Seligman to Richard T. Ely, Dec. 13, 1915, AAUP office files.

28. Letter from Edwin R. A. Seligman to the Members of the Committee of Fifteen, Dec. 16, 1915, AAUP office files.

29. Letter from A. O. Lovejoy to Mr. Wigmore, Dec. 14, 1915, 1–2, AAUP office files, Walter P. Metzger Records of Academic Freedom and Tenure, MS 2369, Special Collections Research Center, George Washington University, quotation at 2.

30. Lovejoy to Mr. Wigmore, 3–4. Henry W. Farnam, another member of the drafting committee, opposed Wigmore's position on practical grounds. He observed that it would eliminate the many alleged violations of academic freedom that do not "relate to strictly professional work." Letter from Henry F. Farnam to E. R. A. Seligman, Dec. 15, 1915, Metzger Records.

31. Letter from Roscoe Pound to E. R. A. Seligman, Dec. 15, 1915, Metzger Records, Box 84.

32. 1915 Declaration, appendix A, 157–158, 162.

33. 1915 Declaration, 169.

34. 1915 Declaration, 173.

35. 1915 Declaration, 169–170.

36. 1915 Declaration, 158–159.

37. 1915 Declaration, 160.

38. 1915 Declaration, 160–163.

39. 1915 Declaration, 167–168.

40. 1915 Declaration, 165.

41. 1915 Declaration, 172.

42. 1915 Declaration, 158.

43. Walter P. Metzger, "Profession and Constitution: Two Definitions of Academic Freedom in America," *Texas Law Review* 66 (1988): 1265, 1276.

44. Arthur O. Lovejoy, "Academic Freedom," in *Encyclopaedia of the Social Sciences*, vol. 1, ed. Edwin R. A. Seligman and Alvin Johnson (New York: Macmillan, 1930), 384, 386.

45. Abbott Lawrence Lowell, quoted in Henry Aaron Yeomans, *Abbott Lawrence Lowell, 1856–1943* (Cambridge, MA: Harvard University Press, 1948), 310.

46. Yeomans, *Abbott Lawrence Lowell*, 311–312, 315–316.

47. 1915 Declaration, 157–158.

48. Metzger, "Profession and Constitution," 1271.

49. Metzger, *Academic Freedom*, 123–124.

50. Letter from Harry Walter Tyler to A. O. Lovejoy, Dec. 31, 1932, AAUP office files.

51. 1915 Declaration, 165.

52. Letter from Charles H. Van Hise to Richard T. Ely, May 18, 1916, AAUP office files.

53. Alexander Meiklejohn, "Freedom of the College," *Atlantic Monthly*, Jan. 1918, 83, 87–88.

54. Metzger, *Academic Freedom*, 205–206; Tiede, *University Reform*, 210–211.

55. "1940 Statement of Principles on Academic Freedom and Tenure," jointly formulated by the AAUP and the AAC (hereafter cited as 1940 Statement of Principles), reprinted in Joughin, *Academic Freedom and Tenure,* 33–39.

56. Hans-Joerg Tiede, "Policies on Academic Freedom, Dismissal for Cause, Financial Exigency, and Program Discontinuance," *AAUP Bulletin* 106 (July 2020): 50–65.

57. 1940 Statement of Principles, 33, 36.

58. 1940 Statement of Principles, 39. Walter Metzger provides a comprehensive account of the background of the 1940 Statement and negotiations about its specific provisions. Walter P. Metzger, "The 1940 Statement of Principles on Academic Freedom and Tenure," *Law and Contemporary Problems* 53, no. 3 (Summer 1990): 3–77.

59. AAUP, "Committee A Statement on Extramural Utterances" (hereafter cited as 1964 Statement on Extramural Utterances), reprinted in Joughin, *Academic Freedom and Tenure,* 64.

60. For historical analysis of the AAUP's position on the relationship between extramural speech and academic freedom, see Hans-Joerg Tiede, "Extramural Speech, Academic Freedom, and the AAUP: A Historical Account," in *Challenges to Academic Freedom,* ed. Joseph C. Hermanowicz (Baltimore: Johns Hopkins University Press, 2021), 104–131; William Van Alstyne, "The Specific Theory of Academic Freedom and the General Issue of Civil Liberty," in *The Concept of Academic Freedom,* ed. Edmund L. Pincoffs (Austin: University of Texas Press, 1975), 59, 81–85.

61. Matthew W. Finkin and Robert C. Post, *For the Common Good: Principles of American Academic Freedom* (New Haven, CT: Yale University Press, 2009), 127–148.

62. Letter from Arthur O. Lovejoy to H. W. Tyler, Jan. 7, 1916, 3, AAUP office files.

63. Metzger, *Academic Freedom,* 216–218. "Model Case Procedure," chap. 2 in Joughin, 11–29, provides a comprehensive overview of the AAUP's case work.

64. Arthur O. Lovejoy, book review, "The Freedom of the Teacher," *Bulletin of the American Association of University Professors* 23, no. 5 (May 1937): 401, 403–404, reviewing Howard K. Beale, *Are American Teachers Free? An Analysis of Restraints upon the Freedom of Teaching in American Schools* (New York: Scribner's, 1936). My own experience as staff counsel for the AAUP from 1976 through 1982 supports the points Lovejoy made forty years earlier.

2. Initial Applications of the Constitution to the University

1. See, for instance, John S. Whitehead and Jurgen Herbst, "How to Think about the Dartmouth College Case," *History of Education Quarterly* 26 (1986): 333–349; Eldon L. Johnson, "The Dartmouth College Case: The Neglected Educational Meaning," *Journal of the Early Republic* 3 (1983): 45–67; George Thomas, "Rethinking the *Dartmouth College* Case in American Political Development: Constituting Public

and Private Educational Institutions," *Studies in American Political Development* 29 (2015): 23–39.

2. Trustees of Dartmouth College v. Woodward, 17 U.S. 518 (1819).

3. See, for instance, Lawrence M. Friedman, *A History of American Law* (New York: Simon and Schuster, 1973), 174–175; Morton J. Horwitz, *The Transformation of American Law, 1780–1860* (Cambridge, MA: Harvard University Press, 1977), 136–137; Morton J. Horwitz, *The Transformation of American Law, 1870–1960* (New York: Oxford University Press, 1992), 11, 67, 106, 206; J. Willard Hurst, *Law and the Conditions of Freedom in the Nineteenth-Century United States* (Madison: University of Wisconsin Press, 1956), 66; William J. Novak, *The People's Welfare: Law and Regulation in Nineteenth-Century America* (Chapel Hill: University of North Carolina Press, 1996), 106–108; G. Edward White, *The Marshall Court and Cultural Change, 1815–1835* (New York: Oxford University Press, 1991), 627–628.

4. Steven J. Novak, "The College in the Dartmouth College Case: A Reinterpretation," *New England Quarterly* 47 (1974): 550, 551.

5. William Gwyer North, "The Political Background of the Dartmouth College Case," *New England Quarterly* 18 (1945): 181, 183–184.

6. Novak, "The College," 550, 556–557, 562–563.

7. North, "The Political Background," 192–193.

8. Thomas, "Rethinking the *Dartmouth College* Case," 31–33.

9. North, "The Political Background," 201–202.

10. Johnson, "The Dartmouth College Case," 47. The legislation is described in Trustees of Dartmouth College v. Woodward, 17 U.S., 626.

11. Thomas, "Rethinking the *Dartmouth College* Case," 33.

12. Thomas, "Rethinking the *Dartmouth College* Case," 32–33.

13. Trustees of Dartmouth College v. Woodward, 1 N.H., 111, 115–117, 132 (1817).

14. Trustees of Dartmouth College v. Woodward, 1 N.H., 119–120, 122.

15. Trustees of Dartmouth College v. Woodward, 1 N.H., 135–136.

16. American Association of University Professors, "Declaration of Principles" (1915), reprinted in *Academic Freedom and Tenure*, ed. Louis Joughin (Madison: University of Wisconsin Press, 1969), appendix A, 157, 160.

17. Trustees of Dartmouth College v. Woodward, 1 N.H., 137.

18. Trustees of Dartmouth College v. Woodward, 17 U.S., 644–646.

19. Trustees of Dartmouth College v. Woodward, 17 U.S., 634, 638–639, 647, 653.

20. Trustees of Dartmouth College v. Woodward, 17 U.S., 648 (Marshall, J.), 666, 676–677 (Story, J., concurring).

21. Trustees of Dartmouth College v. Woodward, 1 N.H., 136.

22. Trustees of Dartmouth College v. Woodward, 1 N.H., 670–672.

23. Trustees of Dartmouth College v. Woodward, 17 U.S. 680, 689, 702, 706–707.

24. Allen v. McKean, 1 F. Cases 489 (C.C.D. Me. 1833); Louisville v. President and Trustees of the University of Louisville, 54 Ky. 642 (1855).

25. State ex rel. Pittman v. Adams, 44 Mo. 570, 581 (1869). A half century later Austin Scott, the great scholar of trust law, acknowledged that college trustees cannot deviate from the purposes of the original trust. But he urged courts to approve changes made by trustees that "are not unreasonable in view of the general purposes of the donors and of the changes that time has brought to pass," such as the elimination of religious requirements. Austin W. Scott, "Education and the Dead Hand," *Harvard Law Review* 34 (1920): 1, 17. He worried that courts would construe the *Dartmouth College* case more rigidly than it required, which would "eventually create an intolerable situation" by obstructing valuable "educational reform." Scott, "Education and the Dead Hand," 19.

26. Head v. Curators of the University of the State of Missouri, 47 Mo. 220, 224–226 (1871).

27. See, for instance, Lewis v. Whittle, 77 Va. 415, 424 (Va. 1883); State v. Knowles, 16 Fla. 577, 596 (1878); University of North Carolina v. Maultsby, 43 N.C. 257, 263–264 (1852). Regarding the agricultural college, see State ex rel. Wyoming Agricultural College v. Irvine, 84 P. 90, 96–97, 108 (1906).

28. State ex rel. Medical College of Alabama v. Sowell, 143 Ala. 494, 500–501 (1905).

29. Regents of the University of Maryland v. Williams, 9 G. & J. 365. 390–391 (54541838).

30. Folz v. Hoge, 54 Cal., 28, 32, 34–35 (1879).

31. Berea College v. Kentucky, 211 U.S. 45, 56 (1908).

32. Berea College v. Kentucky, 53, 57.

33. Berea College v. Kentucky, 58, 67–69 (Harlan, J., dissenting).

34. See Farrington v. Tokushige, 273 U.S. 284 (1927); Pierce v. Society of Sisters, 268 U.S. 510 (1925); Bartels v. Iowa, 262 U.S. 404 (1923); Meyer v. Nebraska, 262 U.S. 404 (1923).

35. Meyer v. Nebraska; Pierce v. Society of Sisters.

36. Gitlow v. New York, 268 U.S. 652, 666 (1925).

37. Institute for Creative Research Graduate School v. Texas Higher Education Coordinating Board, 2010 WL 2522529, 8 (W.D. Texas 2010); Nova University v. Educational Institution Licensure Commission, 483 A.2d 1172, 1185 (DC Ct App. 1984); Shelton College v. State Board of Education, 226 A.2d 612, 618 (NJ 1967).

38. Shelton College v. State Board of Education; Nova University v. Educational Institution Licensure Commission; Institute for Creative Research Graduate School v. Texas Higher Education Coordinating Board.

39. See generally Charles L. Black, "Foreword: 'State Action,' Equal Protection, and California's Proposition 14," *Harvard Law Review* 81 (1967): 69–109.

40. Henry J. Friendly, *The Dartmouth College Case and the Public-Private Penumbra* (Austin, TX: University of Texas Humanities Research Center, 1969), 10–11, 22–23.

41. Friendly, *The Dartmouth College Case,* 12, 20, 22, 25–26.

42. Robert M. O'Neil, "Private Universities and Public Law," *Buffalo Law Review* 19 (1972): 155, 169, see generally 169–188.

43. O'Neil, "Private Universities and Public Law," 170–171, 175–176.

44. Powe v. Miles, 407 F.2d 73, 81 (2d Cir. 1968).

45. O'Neil, "Private Universities and Public Law," 189–190, 192. See also Robert C. Schubert, "State Action and the Private University," *Rutgers Law Review* 24 (1970): 323–352.

46. Guillory v. Tulane University, 203 F. Supp. 855, 858–859 (E.D. La. 1962).

47. Guillory v. Tulane University, 859, 863–864.

48. Guillory v. Tulane University, 212 F. Supp., 674, 679 (E.D. La. 1962).

49. Guillory v. Tulane University, 687.

50. Grafton v. Brooklyn Law School, 478 F.2d 1137, 1141–1142 (2d Cir. 1973).

51. Remy v. Howard University, 55 F. Supp. 2d 27, 28–29 (D.D.C. 1999); Greenya v. George Washington University, 512 F.2d 556, 559–560, and n4 (D.C. Cir. 1975).

52. Greenya v. George Washington University; Grafton v. Brooklyn Law School; Remy v. Howard University.

53. Issacs v. Board of Trustees of Temple University, 385 F. Supp. 473, 493–494 (E.D. Pa. 1974).

54. State v. Schmid, 423 A.2d 615, 626–627 (N.J. 1980). The US Supreme Court dismissed the appeal of this case. Princeton University v. Schmid, 455 U.S. 100 (1982).

55. Corry v. Leland Stanford Jr. University, No. 740309 (Cal. Super. Ct. Feb. 27, 1995).

56. Franklin v. Atkins, 409 F. Supp. 439, 442 (D. Colo. 1976), aff'd, 562 F.2d 1188 (10th Cir. 1977).

3. The Emergence of Academic Freedom as a First Amendment Right of Professors

1. See generally Lucas A. Powe Jr., *The Warren Court and American Politics* (Cambridge, MA: Harvard University Press, 2000), 75–103, 135–156, 310–317; Morton J. Horwitz, *The Warren Court and the Pursuit of Justice* (New York: Hill and Wang, 1998), 52–73; Majorie Heins, *Priests of Our Democracy: The Supreme Court, Academic Freedom, and the Anti-Communist Purge* (New York: NYU Press, 2013).

2. See Victor Navasky, *Naming Names* (New York: Viking Press, 1980).

3. See Ellen Schrecker, *No Ivory Tower: McCarthyism and the Universities* (New York: Oxford University Press, 1986).

4. Schrecker, *No Ivory Tower*, 188–189, 314–316; Walter P. Metzer, "Ralph F. Fuchs and Ralph E. Himstead: A Note on the AAUP in the McCarthy Period," *Academe* 72, no. 6 (1986): 29–35 (on AAUP inaction due to Himstead); "Academic Freedom and Tenure in the Quest for National Security," *AAUP Bulletin* 42, no. 1 (1956): 49–107, 99–100.

5. Keyishian v. Board of Regents, 385 U.S. 589, 603 (1967).

6. Sidney Hook, "Should Communists Be Permitted to Teach?," *New York Times*, Feb. 27, 1949, Sunday Magazine, 7, 22.

7. Hook, "Should Communists Be Permitted to Teach?," 22, 24, 26.

8. Hook, "Should Communists Be Permitted to Teach?," 26, 28.

9. Hook, "Should Communists Be Permitted to Teach?," 29.

10. Alexander Meiklejohn, "Should Communists Be Allowed to Teach?," *New York Times*, March 27, 1949, Sunday Magazine, 10.

11. Meiklejohn, "Should Communists Be Allowed to Teach?," 64–65.

12. Meiklejohn, "Should Communists Be Allowed to Teach?," 66.

13. Meiklejohn, "Should Communists Be Allowed to Teach?," 10.

14. Adler v. Board of Education, 342 U.S. 485, 487n3 (1952).

15. Adler v. Board of Education, 490–491.

16. Appellants' Brief, Adler v. Board of Education, 4, 7.

17. Brief of the State of New York Amicus Curiae, Adler v. Board of Education, 17, 25.

18. Kay v. Board of Higher Education of City of New York, 18 N.Y.S. 2d 821, 829 (Sup. Ct. 1940), aff'd, 20 N.Y.S.2d 1016 (Sup. Ct., App. Div. 1940).

19. Kay v. Board of Higher Education of City of New York, 829, 830–831. The decision provoked an outraged response from John Dewey. See John Dewey and Horace M. Kallen, eds., *The Bertrand Russell Case* (New York: Viking Press, 1941).

20. Brief of the State of New York Amicus Curiae, Adler v. Board of Education, 40.

21. Adler v. Board of Education, 492–494.

22. Adler v. Board of Education, 508–510 (Douglas, J., dissenting).

23. Adler v. Board of Education, 511.

24. Adler v. Board of Education, 497 (Frankfurter, J., dissenting).

25. Felix Frankfurter Papers, Harvard Law School Library, part 1, reel 54, 768–769.

26. Wieman v. Updegraff, 344 U.S. 183 (1952).

27. Wieman v. Updegraff, 186, 191.

28. Wieman v. Updegraff, 194, 196 (Frankfurter, J., concurring).

29. Note from William O. Douglas to Felix Frankfurter, Felix Frankfurter Papers, Harvard Law School Library, part 1, reel 42, 283.

30. Wieman v. Updegraff, 195.

31. Wieman v. Updegraff, 196–197.

32. Sweezy v. New Hampshire, 354 U.S. 234, 250 (1957).

33. Sweezy v. New Hampshire, 255, 267 (Frankfurter, J., concurring).

34. Sweezy v. New Hampshire, 236–238, 239–242.

35. Sweezy v. New Hampshire, 238, 243–244.

36. Brief for Appellant, Sweezy v. New Hampshire, 27, 29n11. See Robert M. MacIver, *Academic Freedom in Our Time* (New York: Columbia University Press, 1955).

37. "Record of Council Meeting," *AAUP Bulletin* 42, no. 2 (1956): 354, 359–360.

38. Robert K. Carr, "Academic Freedom, the American Association of University Professors, and the United States Supreme Court," *AAUP Bulletin* 45, no. 1 (1959): 5, 6, 19, 20.

39. Although the AAUP did not file an amicus brief, its general secretary, Ralph F. Fuchs, corresponded with Emerson about the Sweezy case. Fuchs addressed the possibility of an AAUP amicus brief, the reasons he ultimately opposed filing one, and the complicated legal issues posed by the facts of the case. In Thomas Irwin Emerson Papers, Yale University Archives (hereafter cited as Thomas Irwin Emerson Papers), see letter from Ralph F. Fuchs to Thomas Emerson, July 6, 1956, box 64, folder 886; letter from Ralph F. Fuchs to Thomas Emerson, Nov. 23, 1956, box 64, folder 887; and letter from Ralph F. Fuchs to Thomas Emerson, Feb. 5, 1957, box 64, folder 887. After the Supreme Court published its decision, Fuchs congratulated Emerson for winning "a moral as well as a legal victory" because the opinion had largely accepted Emerson's contentions about the First Amendment. Letter from Ralph F. Fuchs to Thomas Emerson, July 9, 1957, Thomas Irwin Emerson Papers, box 64, folder 888.

40. Sweezy v. New Hampshire, 248–249, 253–255.

41. Letter from Felix Frankfurter to Earl Warren, June 3, 1957, Earl Warren Papers, Library of Congress, box 580, folder containing "Comments by Associate Justices."

42. Memorandum by Mr. Justice Frankfurter, June 4, 1957, Earl Warren Papers, Library of Congress, box 580, folder containing "Comments by Associate Justices."

43. I discuss this investigation in Chapter 8.

44. See draft stamped June 5, 1957, Earl Warren Papers, Library of Congress, box 579, folder 8.

45. Sweezy v. New Hampshire, 250.

46. Sweezy v. New Hampshire, 250.

47. Sweezy v. New Hampshire, 251.

48. Uphaus v. Wyman, 360 U.S. 72, 77 (1959).

49. Leonard Boudin, "Academic Freedom: Should We Look to the Court?," in *Regulating the Intellectuals: Perspectives on Academic Freedom in the 1980s*, ed. Ellen Schrecker and Craig Kaplan (New York: Praeger, 1983), 184–185.

50. Sweezy v. New Hampshire, 250.

51. Sweezy v. New Hampshire, 256 (Frankfurter, J., concurring).

52. Sweezy v. New Hampshire, 261.

53. Felix Frankfurter Papers, Harvard Law School, reel 25, 00673.

54. Sweezy v. New Hampshire, 261–262.

55. Sweezy v. New Hampshire, 262–263.

56. *The Open Universities in South Africa* (Johannesburg: Witwatersrand University Press, 1957), 1, 5.

57. *The Open Universities in South Africa*, 10–12.

58. Letter from Arthur Suzman to Felix Frankfurter, May 15, 1957, Felix Frankfurter Papers, Harvard Law School, part 2, reel 25, 721–722. . See generally David B. Oppenheimer, "The South African Sources of the Diversity Justification for U.S. Affirmative Action," *California Law Review Online* 13 (2022): 32, 47.

59. Albert Centlivres, "Sacred Principles of Academic Freedom," Felix Frankfurter Papers, Harvard Law School, part 2, reel 25, 723–726. This article was published in *The Forum*, March 1957, 16.

60. Letter from Albert Cantlivres to Felix Frankfurter, June 29, 1957, Felix Frankfurter Papers, Harvard Law School, part 2, reel 25, 719–720.

61. Sweezy v. New Hampshire, 262–263.

62. In response to many correspondents who congratulated him after the Supreme Court's decision, Emerson wrote: "The prevailing opinion was a bit of a surprise." Letter from Thomas Emerson to Robert L. Carter June 27, 1957; letter from Thomas Emerson to Mrs. William R. Ginsburg, June 27, 1957; letter from Thomas Emerson to Harold Leventhal, June 27, 1957; letter from Thomas Emerson to Harry I. Rand, June 27, 1957; letter from Thomas Emerson to H. H. Wilson, June 27, 1957, box 64, folder 888; all in Thomas Irwin Emerson Papers.

63. Letter from Thomas Emerson to John P. Frank, March 15, 1957; letter from Thomas Emerson to John T. McTernan, July 8, 1957; letter from Thomas Emerson to Clore Warne, July 8, 1957; letter from Thomas Emerson to Dr. Eason Monroe, July 11, 1957; all in box 64, folder 888, Thomas Irwin Emerson Papers.

64. Carr, "Academic Freedom," 20.

65. Brief of American Association of University Professors as Amicus Curiae, Barenblatt v. United States, 360 U.S. 109 (1959), 7.

66. Brief of American Association of University Professors as Amicus Curiae, 7, 13–14.

67. Brief of American Association of University Professors as Amicus Curiae, 13–14.

68. Brief of American Association of University Professors as Amicus Curiae, 15–17, 26–28.

69. Brief of American Association of University Professors as Amicus Curiae, 24.

70. Barenblatt v. United States, 112.

71. Barenblatt v. United States, 128–129.

72. Barenblatt v. United States, 129, 129n29, 130.

73. Barenblatt v. United States, 134, 144 (Black, J., dissenting).

74. Shelton v. Tucker, 364 U.S. 479, 486 (1960).

75. Shelton v. Tucker, 487.

76. Shelton v. Tucker, 490, 496–497 (Frankfurter, J., dissenting).

77. Baggett v. Bullitt, 215 F. Supp. 439, 447 (W.D. Wash. 1963).

78. Jurisdictional Statement, Baggett v. Bullitt, 377 U.S. 360 (1964), 6, 72–76.

79. Baggett v. Bullitt, 366, 366n5, 369–370 (majority), 380–382 (Clark, J., dissenting).

80. Keyishian v. Board of Regents, 595, 604.

81. Keyishian v. Board of Regents, 605–607.

82. Keyishian v. Board of Regents, 620, 622, 626–627 (Clark, J., dissenting).

83. Brief of the American Association of University Professors, Amicus Curiae, 25–27.

84. Brief of the American Association of University Professors, Amicus Curiae, 18, 28.

85. Keyishian v. Board of Regents, 599–602 (majority), 628 (Clark, J., dissenting).

86. Keyishian v. Board of Regents, 603.

87. Abrams v. United States, 250 U.S. 616, 624, 630 (1919) (Holmes, J., dissenting).

88. Fred P. Graham, "Academic Freedom Is Free Speech," *New York Times,* Jan. 29, 1967, 12E.

4. The Development of Academic Freedom as a First Amendment Right of Professors

1. Rust v. Sullivan, 500 U.S. 173, 200 (1991).

2. Garcetti v. Ceballos, 547 U.S. 410, 425 (2006).

3. Garcetti v. Ceballos, 421.

4. Brief of Amici Curiae the Thomas Jefferson Center for the Protection of Free Expression, and the American Association of University Professors, Garcetti v. Ceballos, 12, 17.

5. Garcetti v. Ceballos, 425.

6. Garcetti v. Ceballos, 427, 438–439 (Souter, J., dissenting).

7. Garcetti v. Ceballos, 425.

8. Board of Regents v. Roth, 408 U.S. 564, 579, 581–582 (1972) (Douglas, J., dissenting).

9. Minnesota State Board of Community Colleges v. Knight, 465 U.S. 271, 287–288 (1984).

10. Minnesota State Board of Community Colleges v. Knight, 295, 296–297 (Brennan, J., dissenting).

11. Epperson v. Arkansas, 393 U.S. 97, 99n3, 100 (1968) (quoting Arkansas court).

12. State v. Epperson, 416 S.W.2d 322 (Ark. 1967).

13. Transcript of Oral Argument, Epperson v. Arkansas, 7, https://www.oyez.org/cases/1968/7.

14. Epperson v. Arkansas, 103–105.

15. Abe Fortas Papers, Yale University Archives (box 77, folder 1638).

16. Epperson v. Arkansas, 106.

17. Epperson v. Arkansas, 109 (majority), 114 (Black, J., concurring).

18. Kleindienst v. Mandel, 408 U.S. 753, 755, 759–760 (1972).

19. Mandel v. Mitchell, 325 F. Supp. 620, 632 (E.D.N.Y. 1971).

20. Kleindienst v. Mandel, 763, 765.

21. Rust v. Sullivan, 500 U.S. 173, 192 (1991).

22. Rust v. Sullivan, 193–194.

23. Letter from David H. Souter to Chief Justice Rehnquist, April 25, 1991, John Paul Stevens Papers, Library of Congress, box 600, *Rust v. Sullivan*, folder 3.

24. Rust v. Sullivan, 200.

25. Letter from William Rehnquist to David Souter, April 29, 1991, Stevens Papers, *Rust v. Sullivan*, folder 3. Indeed, Rehnquist informed Souter that he would have joined the dissenters in *Keyishian*.

26. Edwards v. Aguillard, 482 U.S. 578, 580–581 (1987).

27. See Edwards v. Aguillard, 581 (majority), 610, 627–628 (Scalia, J., dissenting).

28. Edwards v. Aguillard, 586, 586n6, 593. See Brief Amicus Curiae of the American Association of University Professors and the American Council on Education, Edwards v. Aguillard.

29. Roemer v. Board of Public Works of Maryland, 426 U.S. 736, 756 (1976); Tilton v. Richardson, 403 U.S. 672, 681–682 (1971).

30. Tilton v. Richardson, 681.

31. National Labor Relations Board v. Yeshiva University, 444 U.S. 672, 687–688 (1980).

32. National Labor Relations Board v. Yeshiva University 691, 700 (Brennan, J., dissenting).

33. Central State University v. American Association of University Professors, Central State University Chapter, 526 U.S. 124, 128 (1999).

34. Central State University v. American Association of University Professors, Central State University Chapter, 130, 134 (Stevens, J., dissenting).

35. Urofsky v. Gilmore, 216 F.3d 401, 410 (4th Cir. 2000); see also McCready v. O'Malley, 804 F. Supp. 2d 427, 439 (D. Md. 2011) (relying on Urofsky).

36. Urofsky v. Gilmore, 404, 406.

37. Urofsky v. Gilmore, 409n9.

38. Urofsky v. Gilmore, 410–411.

39. Urofsky v. Gilmore, 411nn12–13.

40. Urofsky v. Gilmore, 411–413.

41. Urofsky v. Gilmore, 414–415.

42. Urofsky v. Gilmore, 426, 428 (Wilkinson, J., concurring).

43. Urofsky v. Gilmore, 432–433.

44. Urofsky v. Gilmore, 435, 440–441 (Murnaghan, J., dissenting).

45. Urofsky v. Gilmore, 416, 416–417, 419 (Luttig, J., concurring).

46. Urofsky v. Gilmore, 421–422.

47. Urofsky v. Gilmore, 423.

48. Urofsky v. Gilmore, 424–425.

49. Urofsky v. Gilmore, 425.

50. Russ v. White, 541 F. Supp. 888, 896 (W.D. Ark. 1981) (citing Hostrop v. Board of Junior College District No. 515, 337 F. Supp. 2d 977, 980 (N.D. Ill. 1972)); see also Dixon v. University of Toledo, 842 F. Supp. 2d 1044 (N.D. Ohio 2012).

51. Grimes v. Eastern Illinois University, 710 F.2d 386, 388 (7th Cir. 1983); see also Devine v. Department of Public Institutions, 317 N.W.2d 783 (Neb. 1982) (state psychologist does not have academic freedom similar to a professor).

52. Kerr v. Hurd, 694 F. Supp.2d 817, 844, 844n11 (S.D. Ohio 2010).

53. ONY, Inc. v. Cornerstone Therapeutics, Inc., 720 F.3d 490, 496–498 (2d Cir. 2013).

54. Complaint for Declaratory and Injunctive Relief, Trustees of Indiana University v. Prosecutor of Marion County Indiana, 2016 WL 3031709 (paragraphs 19 and 20).

55. Trustees of Indiana University v. Curry, 918 F.3d 537, 543 (7th Cir. 2019).

56. Emergency Coalition to Defend Educational Travel v. U.S. Department of the Treasury, 545 F.3d 4 (D.C. Cir. 2008); Faculty Senate of Florida International University v. Winn, 477 F. Supp. 2d 1198 (S.D. Fla. 2007).

57. Emergency Coalition to Defend Educational Travel v. U.S. Department of the Treasury, 13; Glass v. Paxton, 2016 WL 8904948, 3 (W.D. Tex. 2016); Faculty Senate of Florida International University v. Winn, 1207.

58. Southern Christian Leadership Conference v. Supreme Court of Louisiana, 61 F. Supp. 2d 499, 509 (E.D. La. 1999).

59. Hardy v. Jefferson Community College, 260 F.3d 671, 674–675 (6th Cir. 2001).

60. Hardy v. Jefferson Community College, 675, 679–680.

61. Axson-Flynn v. Johnson, 356 F.3d 1277, 1280, 1291–1292 (10th Cir. 2004).

62. Silva v. University of New Hampshire, 888 F. Supp. 293, 298–299, 314 (D.N.H. 1984); Mahoney v. Hankin, 593 F. Supp. 1171, 1172, 1174 (S.D.N.Y. 1984).

63. Vega v. Miller, 273 F.3d 460 (2d Cir. 2001), 462–463, 467–468, 471 (majority), 478 (Cabranes, J., dissenting).

64. Bonnell v. Lorenzo, 241 F.3d 800, 803–804, 820, 823–824 (6th Cir. 2001).

65. Piggee v. Carl Sandberg College, 464 F.3d 667, 668–669, 671 (7th Cir. 2006).

66. Mayberry v. Dees, 663 F.2d 502 (4th Cir. 1981), relying on Hetrick v. Martin, 480 F.2d 705 (6th Cir. 1973).

67. Edwards v. California University of Pennsylvania, 156 F.3d 488, 492 (3d Cir. 1998).

68. See Brown v. Armenti, 247 F.3d 69 (3d Cir. 2001); Parate v. Isabor, 868 F.2d 821, 826 (6th Cir. 1989); Lovelace v. Southern Massachusetts University, 793 F.2d 419 (1st Cir. 1986); Hillis v. Stephen F. Austin State University, 665 F. 2d 547 (5th Cir.1982).

69. White v. Davis, 533 P.2d 222, 231, 235 (Cal. 1975).

70. Boikus v. Aspland, 247 N.E.2d 135 (N.Y. 1969), 142 (majority), 145–146 (Fuld, J., concurring).

71. Deitchman v. E. R. Squibb and Sons, Inc., 740 F.2d 556, 559–560 (7th Cir. 1984); United States v. Trustees of Boston College, 831 F. Supp. 2d 435, 457–458 (D. Mass. 2001), affirmed in part and reversed in part, 718 F.3d 13 (1st Cir. 2013); In re Grand Jury Subpoena Dated Jan. 4, 1984, 583 F. Supp. 991, 993 (E.D.N.Y. 1984).

72. Deitchman v. E. R. Squibb and Sons, Inc., 560; In re Grand Jury Subpoena Dated Jan. 4, 1984, 993.

73. Dow Chemical Co. v. Allen, 672 F.2d 1262, 1276 (7th Cir. 1982).

74. In re Grand Jury Subpoena Dated Jan. 4, 1984, 993–994.

75. United States v. Trustees of Boston College, 441. Patrick Radden Keefe, *Say Nothing: A True Story of Murder and Memory in Northern Ireland* (New York: Doubleday, 2019), 3–4, 266–275, 337–339, 352–360, 387–389, 394–396, contains fascinating background information about this case in the larger context of the conflict in Northern Ireland. According to Keefe, some professors at Boston College did not support its reliance on academic freedom to challenge a subpoena seeking disclosure of the confidential interviews. Among other factors, they were disturbed that the interviewers lacked expertise and shared ideological sympathies and sometimes close friendships with the people they interviewed.

76. Deitchman v. E. R. Squibb and Sons, Inc., 559, 564.

77. In re Grand Jury Subpoena Dated Jan. 4, 1984, 992.

78. Dow Chemical Co. v. Allen, 1265–1266; In re Application of American Tobacco Co., 880 F.2d 1520, 1522 (2d Cir. 1989).

79. Agrawal v. University of Cincinnati, 977 F. Supp. 2d 800, 832, 834 (S.D. Ohio 2013), reversed in part and remanded sub nom. Agrawal v. Montemagno, 547 Fed. Appx. 570 (6th Cir. 2014); Radolf v. University of Connecticut, 364 F. Supp. 2d 204, 215–216 (D. Conn. 2005).

80. McElearney v. University of Illinois at Chicago Circle Campus, 612 F.2d 285, 287–288 (7th Cir. 1989).

81. Rosenzweig v. University of Minnesota, 1990 WL 1722, 3 (Minn. Ct. App. 1990); see also Weinstein v. University of Illinois, 628 F. Supp. 862, 866–867 (N.D. Ill. 1986) (insufficient quantity of research).

82. Megill v. Board of Regents of State of Florida, 541 F.2d 1073, 1082 (5th Cir. 1976).

83. Stasny v. Board of Trustees of Central Washington University, 647 P.2d 496, 504 (Wash. Ct. App. 1982).

84. Trimble v. West Virginia Board of Directors, 549 S.E.2d 294, 297, 300 (W.Va. 2001); In re County of Rensselaer, 262 A.D.2d 843, 843–844 (N.Y. App. Div. 1999); Bruce Committee v. Yen, 764 Fed. Appx. 68–69 (2d Cir. 2019); Yarcheski v.

Reiner, 669 N.W.2d 487, 497–498 (S.D. 2003); Carley v. Arizona Board of Regents, 737 P.2d 1099, 1103 (Ariz. Ct. App. 1987).

85. Karetnikova v. Trustees of Emerson College, 725 F. Supp. 73, 75, 81 (D. Mass. 1989); Demers v. Austin, 746 F.3d 402, 411, 414–415 (9th Cir. 2014).

86. Rodriguez v. Maricopa County Community College District, 605 F.3d 703, 705 (9th Cir. 2010).

87. Rodriguez v. Maricopa County Community College District, 709.

88. Clark v. Holmes, 474 F.2d 928, 931 (7th Cir. 1972).

89. Lux v. Board of Regents of New Mexico Highlands University, 622 P.2d 266, 272 (N.M. Ct. App. 1980).

90. Fong v. Purdue University, 672 F. Supp. 930, 951, 957–958 (N.D. Ind. 1988), aff'd, 976 F.2d 735 (7th Cir. 1992).

91. Jew v. University of Iowa, 749 F. Supp. 946, 958, 961 (S.D. Iowa 1990).

92. Board of Regents v. Roth, 579, 581 (Douglas, J., dissenting).

93. Ollman v. Toll, 518 F. Supp. 1196, 1202–1203 (D. Md. 1981); Franklin v. Atkins, 409 F. Supp.439, 445 (D. Colo. 1976), aff'd, 562 F.2d 1188 (10th Cir. 1977).

94. Ollman v. Toll, 1215.

95. Franklin v. Atkins, 446, 452.

96. Wagner v. Jones, 664 F.3d 259, 269 (8th Cir. 2011).

97. See Manning v. Jones, 875 F.3d 408 (8th Cir. 2017).

98. Karetnikova v. Trustees of Emerson College, 81.

5. The Limited Application of Academic Freedom as a First Amendment Right of Professors

1. Doe v. University of Michigan, 721 F. Supp. 852, 853 (E.D. Mich. 1989).

2. Doe v. University of Michigan, 858, 860.

3. Doe v. University of Michigan, 861–863.

4. Doe v. University of Michigan, 863.

5. Doe v. University of Michigan, 866–867.

6. Board of Trustees of Leland Stanford Junior University v. Sullivan, 773 F. Supp. 472, 477n15 (D.D.C. 1991).

7. Board of Trustees of Leland Stanford Junior University v. Sullivan, 473.

8. Board of Trustees of Leland Stanford Junior University v. Sullivan, 477–478, 477n14.

9. Board of Trustees of Leland Stanford Junior University v. Sullivan, 474, 477–478.

10. American Academy of Religion v. Chertoff, 463 F. Supp. 2d 400, 404–407 (S.D.N.Y. 2006).

11. American Academy of Religion v. Chertoff, 406, 408–409.

12. American Academy of Religion v. Chertoff, 414.

13. Kleindienst v. Mandel, 408 U.S. 753, 770 (1972).

14. American Academy of Religion v. Chertoff, 415, 415n17, 418, 422.

15. American Academic of Religion v. Chertoff, 2007 WL 4527504 (S.D.N.Y. 2007).

16. See William Van Alstyne, "The Specific Theory of Academic Freedom and the General Issue of Civil Liberty," in *The Concept of Academic Freedom,* ed. Edmund L. Pincoffs (Austin: University of Texas Press, 1975), 59, 64–65. Writing in the 1970s, Van Alstyne maintained that freedom of association had become a distinctive First Amendment right, derived from the express clauses of the First Amendment but having its own meaning and instrumental features. He lamented that academic freedom had only received "highly honorable mention" by the Supreme Court as a First Amendment right and had not attained the distinctive meaning attached to freedom of association.

17. Keyishian v. Board of Regents, 385 U.S. 589, 607 (1967).

18. Selzer v. Fleisher, 629 F.2d 809, 810 (2d Cir. 1980).

19. Selzer v. Fleisher, 811, 814–815 (Kaufman, J., concurring in part and dissenting in part).

20. Selzer v. Fleisher, 816.

21. Garcetti v. Ceballos, 547 U.S. 410, 419 (2006).

22. Pickering v. Board of Education, 391 U.S. 563, 568 (1968).

23. Connick v. Myers, 461 U.S. 138, 149 (1983).

24. Connick v. Myers, 146–148.

25. Connick v. Myers, 148, 156 (majority), 165 (Brennan, J., dissenting).

26. Garcetti v. Ceballos, 421 (majority), 427–429, 430–431, 434 (Souter, J., dissenting). In his separate dissent, Justice Stevens also rejected this categorical exclusion. Garcetti v. Ceballos, 426, 427 (Stevens, J., dissenting).

27. Garcetti v. Ceballos, 425 (majority), 438–439 (Souter, J., dissenting). See Chapter 4 for more detailed discussion of this exchange in the context of the development of academic freedom as a First Amendment right.

28. Compare Urofsky v. Gilmore, 216 F.3d 401, 428 (4th Cir. 2000) (Wilkinson, J., concurring) with Hall v. Kutztown University of Pennsylvania, 1998 WL 10233, 26 (E.D. Pa. 1998).

29. Urofsky v. Gilmore, 407–409 (Wilkins), 416, 418 (Luttig, J., concurring), 426, 428 (Wilkinson, J., concurring), 435, 438 (Murnaghan, J., dissenting).

30. Meriweather v. Hartop, 992 F.3d 492, 498 (6th Cir. 2021).

31. Meriweather v. Trustees of Shawnee State University, 2019 WL 4222598, 15 (S.D. Ohio 2019). In a brief opinion, the district court affirmed the decision of the magistrate judge. Meriweather v. Trustees of Shawnee State University, 2020 WL 704615 (S.D. Ohio 2020).

32. Meriweather v. Hartop, 509, citing Carol Sanger, "Feminism and Disciplinarity: The Curl of the Petals," *Loyola L.A. Law Review* 27 (1993): 225, 247n87.

33. Meriweather v. Hartop, 507–509.

34. Scallet v. Rosenblum, 911 F. Supp. 999, 1013–1014 (W.D. Va. 1996), aff'd, 1997 WL 33077 (4th Cir. 1997).

35. Levin v. Harleston, 770 F. Supp. 895, 921 (S.D.N.Y. 1991).

36. Blum v. Schlegel, 18 F.3d 1005 (2d Cir. 1994).

37. Hardy v. Jefferson Community College, 260 F.3d 671, 679 (6th Cir. 2001).

38. Kerr v. Hurd, 694 F. Supp. 2d 817, 842 (S.D. Ohio 2010).

39. Clark v. Holmes, 474 F.2d 928 (7th Cir. 1972); Ghosh v. Ohio University, 861 F.2d 720 (6th Cir. 1988); McCready v. O'Malley, 804 F. Supp. 2d 427 (D. Md. 2011); Vance v. Board of Supervisors of Southern University, 124 F.3d 191 (5th Cir.1997).

40. Hentea v. Trustees of Purdue University, 2006 WL 1207911 (N.D. Ind. 2006).

41. Heim v. Daniel, 2022 WL 1472878, 14 (N.D.N.Y. 2022).

42. Singh v. Cordle, 936 F.3d 1022, 1035–1036 (10th Cir. 2019); Colburn v. Trustees of Indiana University, 973 F.3d 581, 587–588 (7th Cir. 1992).

43. Colburn v. Trustees of Indiana University, 586.

44. Howell v. Millersville University of Pennsylvania, 283 F. Supp. 3d 309, 337–338 (E.D. Pa. 2017), aff'd, 749 Fed. Appx. 130 (3d Cir. 2018).

45. Klaasen v. Atkinson, 348 F. Supp. 3d 1106, 1173 (D. Kan. 2018).

46. Hong v. Grant, 516 F. Supp. 2d 1158, 1169 (C.D. Cal. 2007).

47. Urofsky v. Gilmore, 429n4 (Wilkinson, J., concurring).

48. See Chapter 4.

49. Corr v. Mazur, 1988 WL619395, 5 (Va. Cir. Ct. 1988).

50. Hulan v. Yates, 322 F.3d 1229, 1233 (10th Cir.2003).

51. Demers v. Austin, 746 F.3d 402, 416 (9th Cir. 2014).

52. Demers v. Austin, 417. See also Hammond v. Board of Trustees of Southern Illinois University, 1988 WL 95923, 6 (S.D. Ill. 1988) (reorganization of school is a matter of public concern but not if professor had a "personal interest" in the outcome).

53. Demers v. Austin, 406.

54. Demers v. Austin, 729 F.3d 1011 (9th Cir. 2013).

55. Hall v. Kutztown University of Pennsylvania, 25; Scallet v. Rosenblum, 1017–1018.

56. Hall v. Kutztown University of Pennsylvania, 26.

57. Savage v. Gee, 716 F. Supp. 2d 709, 711, 716 (S.D. Ohio 2010).

58. Johnson v. Lincoln University, 776 F.2d 443, 452 (3d Cir. 1985).

59. Wetherbe v. Goebel, 699 Fed. Appx. 297, 300 (5th Cir. 2017).

60. Schrier v. University of Colorado, 527 F.3d 1253, 1263 (10th Cir. 2005); North Central Texas College v. Ledbetter, 566 F. Supp. 2d 547, 554 (E.D. Tex. 2006).

61. Wetherbe v. Goebel, 301; Demers v. Austin, 416; Savage v. Gee, 716; Hammond v. Board of Trustees, 6.

62. Vance v. Board of Supervisors of Southern University, 124; Howell v. Millersville University of Pennsylvania, 338; Hentea v. Trustees of Purdue University 8.

63. Johnson v. Lincoln University, 451; Kerr v. Hurd, 841–843; Hall v. Kutztown University of Pennsylvania, 26; Scallet v. Rosenblum, 1013–1015.

64. Landrum v. Eastern Kentucky University, 578 F. Supp. 241, 246 (E.D. Ky. 1984).

65. Johnson v. Lincoln University, 453 (quoting Trotman v. Board of Trustees, 635 F.2d 216, 230 [3d Cir. 1980]).

66. Franklin v. Atkins, 409 F. Supp. 439, 446 (D. Colo. 1976), aff'd, 562 F.2d 1188 (10th Cir. 1977); Starsky v. Williams, 353 F. Supp. 900, 924 (D. Ariz. 1972), aff'd in part, rev'd in part, 512 F.2d 109 (9th Cir. 1972).

67. Hardy v. Jefferson Community College, 680; see also Meriwether v. Trustees of Shawnee State University, 19 (quoting Hardy approvingly).

68. Hardy v. Jefferson Community College, 681.

69. Meriweather v. Hartop, 510–511.

70. Roseman v. Indiana University of Pennsylvania, 520 F.2d 1364, 1368–1369 (3d Cir. 1975).

71. Starsky v. Williams, 921; see also Adamian v. Jacobsen, 523 F.2d 929, 934 (9th Cir.1975).

72. Klaasen v. Atkinson, 1174–1176.

73. Hong v. Grant, 1162–1163, 1167.

74. Renkin v. Gregory, 541 F.3d 769, 774 (7th Cir. 2008); Klaasen v. Atkinson, 1167; Huang v. Rectors and Visitors of the University of Virginia, 896 F. Supp. 2d 524, 543–545 (W.D. Va. 2012).

75. Kerr v. Hurd, 844.

76. Adams v. University of North Carolina-Wilmington, 640 F.3d 550, 554–555 (4th Cir. 2011).

77. Adams v. University of North Carolina-Wilmington, 557, 562–564.

78. Demers v. Austin, 411.

79. Demers v. Austin, 411, 415.

80. Savage v. Gee, 718; Meyers v. California University of Pennsylvania, 2014 WL 3890357, 14 (W.D. Pa. 2014).

81. Salid v. Vailas, 936 F. Supp. 2d 1207, 1224–1226 (D. Idaho 2013).

82. Ezuma v. City University of New York, 665 F. Supp. 2d 116, 129–130 (E.D.N.Y. 2009); Alberti v. Carlo-Izquierdo, 548 F. App'x 625, 638–639 (1st Cir. 2013).

83. Gorum v. Sessoms, 561 F.3d 179, 183, 185–186 (3d Cir. 2009).

84. Van Heerden v. Board of Supervisors of Louisiana State University, 2011 WL 5008410, 5–7 (M.D. La. 2011).

85. Interestingly, a federal district court judge suggested a similar exception for journalists, observing that the freedom of the press "holds an equally exalted place" as academic freedom "in the First Amendment firmament." Turner v. U.S. Agency for Global Media, 502 F. Supp. 3d 333, 375 (D.D.C. 2020).

86. Bonnell v. Lorenzo, 241 F.2d 800, 822 (6th Cir. 2001); Bishop v. Aranov, 926 F.2d 1066, 1075 (11th Cir. 1991); Axson-Flynn v. Johnson, 356 F.3d 1277, 1292n14 (10th Cir. 2004).

87. Dow Chemical Co. v. Allen, 672 F.2d 1262, 1274, 1277 (7th Cir. 1982).

88. Vega v. State University of New York, 67 F. Supp. 2d 324, 337–338 (S.D.N.Y. 1999).

89. Pigee v. Carl Sandberg College, 464 F.3 667, 671 (7th Cir. 2006).

90. Scallet v. Rosenblum, 1011.

91. Cohen v. San Bernadino Valley College, 883 F. Supp. 1407, 1412, 1414 (C.D. Cal. 1999).

92. Emergency Coalition v. U.S. Department of Treasury, 545 F.3d 4, 14, 15 (D.C. Cir. 2008) (Edwards, J., concurring).

93. Rust v. Sullivan, 500 U.S. 173, 200 (1991).

94. Board of Trustees of Leland Stanford Junior University v. Rust, 773 F. Supp. 472, 477 (D.D.C. 1991).

95. Garcetti v. Ceballos, 425.

6. A Theory of Academic Freedom as a Distinctive First Amendment Right of Professors

1. William Van Alstyne, "The Specific Theory of Academic Freedom and the General Issue of Civil Liberty," in *The Concept of Academic Freedom*, ed. Edmund L. Pincoffs (Austin: University of Texas Press, 1975), 59, 75.

2. Van Alstyne, "The Specific Theory," 76–77.

3. Matthew W. Finkin and Robert C. Post, *For the Common Good: Principles of American Academic Freedom* (New Haven, CT: Yale University Press, 2009), 69–70.

4. Van Alstyne, "The Specific Theory," 78.

5. Tinker v. Des Moines Independent Community School District, 393 U.S. 503, 506 (1969).

6. Tinker v. Des Moines Independent Community School District, 508–509, 513–514; see also Bethel School District v. Fraser, 478 U.S. 675, 685 (1986) (upholding sanctions for "offensively lewd and indecent" speech by student at high school assembly).

7. See Parker v. Levy, 417 U.S. 733, 758 (1974) (military bases); Pell v. Procunier, 417 U.S. 817, 822 (1974) (prisons).

8. Board of Education v. Pico, 457 U.S. 853, 904, 909, 914–915 (1982) (Rehnquist, J., dissenting); Hazelwood School District v. Kuhlmeier, 484 U.S. 260, 271, 272

(1988). Rehnquist contrasted university and public libraries, which are designed for "freewheeling inquiry," from the "inculcative role" of elementary and secondary school libraries. Board of Education v. Pico, 915.

9. Pickering v. Board of Education, 391 U.S. 563, 568 (1968).

10. New York Times Co. v. United States, 403 U.S. 713, 727, 728 (1971) (Stewart, J., concurring).

11. Minnesota State Board of Community Colleges v. Knight, 465 U.S. 271, 292, 293 (1984) (Marshall, J., concurring).

12. Virginia State Board of Pharmacy v. Virginia Citizens Consumer Council, Inc. 425 U.S. 748, 765 (1976). Robert Post relies heavily on the development of commercial speech doctrine in justifying First Amendment protection for academic freedom. Robert C. Post, *Democracy, Expertise, Academic Freedom: A First Amendment Jurisprudence for the Modern State* (New Haven, CT: Yale University Press, 2012). Post asserts that commercial speech doctrine is based on "the constitutional value of democratic competence" (35), a value also promoted by academic freedom (61).

13. Virginia State Board of Pharmacy v. Virginia Citizens Consumer Council, Inc., 781, 787 (Rehnquist, J., dissenting).

14. Elred v. Ashcroft, 537 U.S. 186, 219 (2003); Harper & Row Publishers Inc. v. Nation Enterprises, 471 U.S. 539, 558 (1985).

15. See, for instance, Branzburg v. Hayes, 408 U.S. 665, 681 (1972).

16. See, for instance, Arkansas Educational Television Commission v. Forbes, 523 U.S. 666, 673–674 (1998); Federal Communications Commission v. League of Women Voters, 468 U.S. 364, 402 (1984); Miami Herald Publishing Co. v. Tornillo, 418 U.S. 241, 256, 258–259, 261 (White, J., concurring); Columbia Broadcasting System, Inc. v. Democratic National Committee, 412 U.S. 94, 118, 120–121, 124 (1973).

17. Columbia Broadcasting System, Inc. v. Democratic National Committee, 112 (majority), 191 (Brennan, J., dissenting); United States v. American Library Association, Inc., 539 U.S. 194, 204 (2003).

18. United States v. American Library Association, Inc., 220, 226. See also Harrison v. Coffman, 35 F. Supp. 2d 722, 725–726 (E.D. Ky. 1999) (observing that constitutional protection for the "decisional independence" of an administrative law judge seems "logically and historically compelled under the expansive view of the First Amendment that covers academic freedom").

19. On the press, see David A. Anderson, "Freedom of the Press," *Texas Law Review* 80 (2002): 429–530; Randall P. Bezanson, "The Developing Law of Editorial Judgment," *Nebraska Law Review* 78 (1999): 754–857; Sonja R. West, "Favoring the Press," *California Law Review* 106 (2018): 91–134; Sonja R. West, "Awakening the Press Clause," *UCLA Law Review* 58 (2011): 1025–1070; Potter Stewart, "Or of the Press," *Hastings Law Journal* 26 (1997): 631–637. On librarians, see Rodney A. Smolla, "Freedom of Speech for Libraries and Librarians," *Law Library Journal* 85 (1993):

71–79; Robert M. O'Neil, "Libraries, Librarians and First Amendment Freedoms" (1975), in Articles by Maurer Faculty, 2199, https://www.repository.law.indiana .edu/facpub/2199. On museum curators, see Alfred F. Young, "A Modest Proposal: A Bill of Rights for American Museums," *Public Historian* 14, no. 3 (1992): 67–75.

For critical views on a distinctive freedom of the press, see William W. Van Alstyne, "The First Amendment and the Free Press: A Comment on Some New Trends and Some Old Theories," *Hofstra Law Review* 9 (1980): 1–37; Anthony Lewis, "A Preferred Position for Journalism?," *Hofstra Law Review* 7 (1979): 595–627.

A recent article provided data indicating a dramatic decline in references to freedom of the press in Supreme Court decisions over the past fifty years. RonNell Andersen Jones and Sonja R. West, "The Disappearing Freedom of the Press," *Washington and Lee Law Review* 79 (2022): 1377–1462.

20. Arthur O. Lovejoy, "Academic Freedom," in *Encyclopaedia of the Social Sciences,* vol. 1, ed. Edwin R. A, Seligman (New York: MacMillan, 1930): 384–388. See also Post, *Democracy, Expertise, Academic Freedom,* 64, 73; Keith E. Whittington, *Speak Freely: Why Universities Must Defend Free Speech* (Princeton, NJ: Princeton University Press, 2018), 46; Thomas L. Haskell, "Justifying the Rights of Academic Freedom in the Era of 'Power/Knowledge,'" in *The Future of Academic Freedom,* ed. Louis Menand (Chicago: University of Chicago Press, 1996), 43, 47.

21. Haskell, "Justifying," 53.

22. AAUP, "Declaration of Principles" (1915), reprinted in *Academic Freedom and Tenure,* ed. Louis Joughin (Madison: University of Wisconsin Press, 1969): appendix A, 157, 159–160, 162–163, 169, 170 (hereafter cited as "1915 Declaration"); J. Peter Byrne, "Academic Freedom: A 'Special Concern of the First Amendment,'" *Yale Law Journal* 99 (1989): 251, 334; Van Alstyne, "The Specific Theory," 77; Lovejoy, "Academic Freedom," 385; Walter P. Metzger, *Academic Freedom in the Age of the University* (New York: Columbia University Press, 1955), 92; Metzger, "Profession and Constitution: Two Definitions of Academic Freedom in America," *Texas Law Review* 66 (1988): 1267, 1282.

23. 1915 Declaration, 162–163; Amy Gutmann, *Democratic Education* (Princeton, NJ: Princeton University Press, 1987), 175; Lovejoy, "Academic Freedom, 384; Post, *Democracy, Expertise, Academic Freedom,* 73. Regarding students, see Finkin and Post, *For the Common Good,* 104–111.

24. 1915 Declaration, 169, 173; Gutmann, *Democratic Education,* 175; Van Alstyne, "The Specific Theory," 78.

25. Metzger, *Academic Freedom,* 107; Van Alstyne, "The Specific Theory," 71.

26. 1915 Declaration, 162; Stanley Fish, *Save the World on Your Own Time* (New York: Oxford University Press, 2008), 12–13.

27. 1915 Declaration, 164.

28. Josiah Royce, "The Freedom of Teaching," *Overland Monthly* 2, no. 9 (1883): 235, 236–237.

29. Royce, "The Freedom of Teaching," 237–238, 240.

30. Lovejoy, "Academic Freedom," 385.

31. Finkin and Post, *For the Common Good*, 81–82 (quoting Royce); Byrne, "Academic Freedom," 335, 337; J. Peter Byrne, "Neo-orthodoxy in Academic Freedom," *Texas Law Review* 88 (2009): 143, 158.

32. Fish, *Save the World*, 13; Post, *Democracy, Expertise, Academic Freedom*, 88.

33. Haskell, "Justifying," 57.

34. John Dewey, "Academic Freedom," *Educational Record* 23 (1902): 1–14.

35. Richard Rorty, "Does Academic Freedom Have Philosophical Presuppositions?," in Menand, *The Future of Academic Freedom*, 21, 34–36; see also Louis Menand, "The Limits of Academic Freedom," in Menand, *The Future of Academic Freedom*, 3, 13 (discussing Dewey on academic freedom).

36. Haskell, "Justifying," 70, 73, 89n46. See also Joyce Appleby, Lynn Hunt, and Margaret Jacob, *Telling the Truth about History* (New York: Norton, 1994), 283.

37. Evelyn Fox Keller, "Science and Its Critics," 199, 211; Rorty, "Does Academic Freedom Have Philosophical Presuppositions?," 21–24; Joan W. Scott, "Academic Freedom as an Ethical Practice," 163, 173–175; and Cass R. Sunstein, "Academic Freedom and the Law: Liberalism, Speech Codes, and Related Problems," 93, 114, 116; all in Menand, *The Future of Academic Freedom*.

38. Rorty, "Does Academic Freedom Have Philosophical Presuppositions?," 21, 24; see also Keller, "Science and Its Critics," 211.

39. Stanley Fish, *Versions of Academic Freedom* (Chicago: University of Chicago Press, 2014), 27; Keller, "Science and Its Critics," 205–206; Judith Butler, "Academic Norms, Contemporary Challenges: A Reply to Robert Post on Academic Freedom," in *Academic Freedom after September 11*, ed. Beshara Doumani (Brooklyn, NY: Zone Books, 2006), 107, 128; Scott, "Academic Freedom as an Ethical Practice," 175.

40. Fish, *Versions of Academic Freedom*, 133–134.

41. Rorty, "Does Academic Freedom Have Philosophical Presuppositions?," 26–27, 30–31.

42. 1915 Declaration, 169.

43. Gutmann, *Democratic Education*, 173–174.

44. Byrne, "Academic Freedom," 335, 337; Byrne, "Neo-orthodoxy," 158.

45. Wieman v. Updegraff, 344 U.S. 183, 194, 196 (Frankfurter, J., concurring).

46. Post, *Democracy, Expertise, Academic Freedom*, 86–88.

47. Sweezy v. New Hampshire, 345 U.S. 234, 250 (1957).

48. Keyishian v. Board of Regents, 385 U.S. 589, 603 (1967).

49. David Halberstam, *The Best and the Brightest* (New York: Random House, 1972).

50. See also Metzger, *Academic Freedom,* 107; Fish, *Save the World;* Whittington, *Speak Freely,* 14.

51. 1915 Declaration, 174–175.

52. Scott, "Academic Freedom as an Ethical Practice," 166, 176–177; see Butler, "Academic Norms," 142n4 (in "substantial agreement" with Scott).

53. See Scott, "Academic Freedom as an Ethical Practice," 176.

54. See Butler, "Academic Norms," 112, 120; Scott, "Academic Freedom as an Ethical Practice," 175; Kerr v. Hurd, 694 F. Supp.2d 817, 844n11 (S.D. Ohio 2010); State ex. rel. Pittman v. Adams, 44 Mo. 570, 581 (1869).

55. 1915 Declaration, 169.

56. Doe v. University of Michigan, 721 F. Supp. 852, 865 (E.D. Mich. 1989).

57. Judith Jarvis Thomson, "Ideology and Faculty Selection," *Law and Contemporary Problems* 53, no. 3 (1990): 155, 161.

58. Butler, "Academic Norms," 118.

59. Megan Zahneis, "Penn Demoted Her. Then She Won the Nobel Prize," *Chronicle of Higher Education,* Oct. 5, 2023, https://www.chronicle.com/article/penn-demoted-her-the-she-won-the-nobel-prize.

60. Thomson, "Ideology and Faculty Selection," 160. See generally Thomas S. Kuhn, *The Structure of Scientific Revolutions* (Chicago: University of Chicago Press, 1962).

61. Thomson, "Ideology and Faculty Selection," 161.

62. 1915 Declaration, 168.

63. Kerr v. Hurd, 814n11.

64. AAUP, "Some Observations on Ideology, Competence, and Faculty Selection," *Academe* 72, no. 1 (1986): 1a, 2a. See also, Thomson, "Ideology and Faculty Selection," 164.

65. Post, *Democracy, Expertise, Academic Freedom,* 77.

66. Butler, "Academic Norms," 121–123.

67. Scott, "Academic Freedom as an Ethical Practice," 175–177.

68. See generally Judith Areen, "Government as Educator: A New Understanding of First Amendment Protection of Academic Freedom and Governance," *Georgetown Law Journal* 97 (2009): 945, 1000; Butler, "Academic Norms," 120; Thomson, "Ideology and Faculty Selection," 162.

69. See David M. Rabban, "The Regrettable Underenforcement of Incompetence as Cause to Dismiss Tenured Faculty," *Indiana Law Journal* 91 (2015): 39, 53, 55; Van Alstyne, "The Specific Theory," 75.

70. American Association of University Professors, American Council on Education, and Association of Governing Boards of Colleges and Universities, "Statement on Government of Colleges and Universities" (1966), reprinted in Joughin, *Academic Freedom and Tenure,* 90, 98–99.

71. See William Van Alstyne, "Tenure: A Summary, Explanation, and 'Defense,'" *AAUP Bulletin* 57 (1971): 328, 330; Van Alstyne, "The Specific Theory," 75.

72. Patricia A. Matthew, "Written / Unwritten: The Gap between Theory and Practice," Introduction to Patricia A. Matthew, ed., *Written / Unwritten, Diversity and the Hidden Truths of Tenure* (Chapel Hill: University of North Carolina Press, 2016): 1–24.

73. Kyle Siler, Kirby Lee, and Lisa Bero, "Measuring the Effectiveness of Scientific Gatekeeping," *Proceedings of the National Academy of Sciences (PNAS)* 112, no. 2 (2015): 360–365; Barbara A. Spellman, "A Short (Personal) Future History of Revolution 2.0," *Perspectives on Psychological Science* 10 (6): 886–899; Richard Smith, "Peer Review: A Flawed Process at the Heart of Science and Journals," *Journal of the Royal Society of Medicine* 99 (2006): 178–182; Aaron E. Carroll, "Peer Review: The Worst Way to Judge Research, Except for All the Others," *New York Times*, Nov. 5, 2018, B3.

74. Thomas O. McGarity, "Peer Review in Awarding Federal Grants in the Arts and Sciences," *High Technology Law Journal* 9 (1994): 1–91.

75. Smith, "Peer review," 178.

76. Based on a review of all AAUP investigations published in its official journal through 1953, Walter Metzger concluded that almost two-thirds "were intramural and largely personal," often involving jealousy, conflicting personalities, petty vindictiveness, and presidents who were autocratic and arbitrary. Metzger, *Academic Freedom*, 218. Writing in 1988, Metzger similarly concluded that since the AAUP's founding, its docket of academic freedom cases had been dominated by "charges of hierarchic subordination and coworker friction." Confusingly, Metzger includes these cases within the category of "extramural freedom," differentiating them from disputes over "the content of teaching or research" without identifying a separate category of "intramural speech." Metzger, "Profession and Constitution," 1276.

77. AAUP et al., "Statement on Government," 98–100.

78. "On the Relationship of Faculty Governance to Academic Freedom," *Academe* 80, no. 4 (1994): 47–49. Professors Finkin and Post conclude that the professional understanding of academic freedom should include freedom of intramural speech. Finkin and Post, *For the Common Good*, 113–126, esp. 124. Professor Areen concludes that the First Amendment protection for academic freedom should protect "academic governance speech." Areen, "Government as Educator," 985–1000.

79. John R. Searle, "Two Concepts of Academic Freedom," in Pincoffs, *The Concept of Academic Freedom*, 86, 94.

80. Scott, "Academic Freedom as an Ethical Practice," 164.

81. Searle, "Two Concepts of Academic Freedom," 93.

82. Finkin and Post, *For the Common Good*, 140.

83. Finkin and Post, *For the Common Good*, 139–140.

84. See Robert Post, "The Structure of Academic Freedom," in Doumani, *Academic Freedom after September 11*, 86 (stating and questioning this position).

85. See Butler, "Academic Norms," 125–126 (universities should protect the free speech of professors as citizens as well as their academic freedom).

86. See Urofsky v. Gilmore, 216 F.3d 401, 411n13 (4th Cir. 2000), 424–425 (Luttig, J., concurring).

87. Van Alstyne, "The Specific Theory," 76.

88. Van Alstyne, "The Specific Theory," 60, 68–70.

89. Starsky v. Williams, 353 F. Supp. 900, 920 (D. Ariz. 1972), aff'd in part, rev'd in part, 512 F.2d 109 (9th Cir. 1972).

90. Van Heerden v. Board of Supervisors of Louisiana State University, 2011 WL 5008410, 5–7 (M.D. La. 2011).

91. See Butler, "Academic Norms," 124–125. Finkin and Post, *For the Common Good*, 134 (making the same point about Chomsky).

92. See Finkin and Post, *For the Common Good*, 136.

93. American Bar Association, *Model Rules of Professional Conduct* (2023), Rule 3.3, Comment [2], Comment [14].

94. This quotation is contained in the appendix, "Selection of Professor Salaita's Tweets," which the counsel for the trustees of the University of Illinois at Urbana-Champaign provided to the AAUP. See "Academic Freedom and Tenure: The University of Illinois at Urbana-Champaign," *AAUP Bulletin* (July–August 2015): 20. The federal district court judge who rejected the university's motion to dismiss Professor Salaita's First Amendment claim decided not to quote the tweets verbatim. He stated that "they were critical of Israel's actions and used harsh, often profanity-laden rhetoric." Salaita v. Kennedy, 118 F. Supp. 3d 1068, 1075 (N.D. Ill. 2015).

95. Ryan Quinn, "Yale Professor Who Diagnosed Dershowitz and Trump in Tweet Loses Appeal," *Inside Higher Education*, June 29, 2023.

96. See Ward Farnsworth, "Talking out of School: Notes on the Transmission of Intellectual Capital from the Legal Academic to Public Tribunals," *Boston University Law Review* 81 (2001): 13, 31–35.

97. McNabb v. United States, 318 U.S. 332, 347 (1943). See Henry P. Monaghan, "First Amendment 'Due Process,'" *Harvard Law Review* 83 (1970): 518; William Van Alstyne, "The Constitutional Rights of Teachers and Professors," *Duke Law Journal* 19 (1970): 841, 858.

98. Monaghan, "First Amendment 'Due Process,'" 518–519; Van Alstyne, "The Constitutional Rights," 873.

99. Monaghan, "First Amendment 'Due Process,'" 518–519, 521n13, 548; Van Alstyne, "The Constitutional Rights," 868–869.

100. Monaghan, "First Amendment 'Due Process,'" 519.

101. Van Alstyne, "The Constitutional Rights," 864–869; see Monaghan, "First Amendment 'Due Process,'" 526.

102. Monaghan, "First Amendment 'Due Process,'" 532–534; Van Alstyne, "The Constitutional Rights," 860–861, 864.

103. Monaghan, "First Amendment 'Due Process,'" 547–548.

104. Monaghan, "First Amendment 'Due Process,'" 519n7, 549; Van Alstyne, "The Constitutional Rights," 858–859.

105. Van Alstyne, "The Constitutional Rights," 858–859.

106. Van Alstyne, "The Constitutional Rights," 864–866.

107. Roth v. Board of Regents, 310 F. Supp. 972, 980 (W.D. Wisc. 1970).

108. Roth v. Board of Regents, 446 F.2d 806, 810 (7th Cir. 1971).

109. Roth v. Board of Regents, 810, 812 (Duffy, J., dissenting).

110. Board of Regents v. Roth, 408 U.S. 564, 575n14 (1972).

111. Brief of the American Association of University Professors, Amicus Curiae, Perry v. Sindermann, 408 U.S. 593 (1972), 26.

112. Brief of the American Association of University Professors, Amicus Curiae, Board of Regents v. Roth, 14.

113. AAUP, "Recommended Institutional Regulations on Academic Freedom and Tenure" (2023), Regulation 5, Regulation 10. See generally Van Alstyne, "Tenure," 331–333.

114. AAUP, "1940 Statement of Principles on Academic Freedom and Tenure" (1940), reprinted in Joughin, *Academic Freedom and Tenure,* 33, 38 (3).

115. AAUP, "Recommended Institutional Regulations," Regulation 13. See J. Peter Byrne, "Academic Freedom of Part-Time Faculty," *Journal of College and University Law* 27 (2001): 583–593 (highlighting distinctive threats to the academic freedom of part-time faculty and proposing mechanisms to safeguard it).

116. AAUP, "1940 Statement of Principles," 34.

117. Van Alstyne, "Tenure," 329, 331.

118. Kingman Brewster Jr., "On Tenure," *AAUP Bulletin* 57 (1971): 381, 383.

119. Van Alstyne, "Tenure," 333. I am not persuaded by two other considerations provided by Van Alstyne to justify greater procedural protections for tenured than for nontenured professors: that dismissal is a greater hardship to the more senior tenured professor, and that the added experience of the senior tenured professor is more likely to lead to original academic contributions. Van Alstyne, "Tenure," 332–333.

120. See AAUP, "Recommended Institutional Regulations," 5c, 5c3, 5c13.

121. "On the Relationship of Faculty Governance to Academic Freedom," 48.

122. Byrne, "Academic Freedom," 308n223, 338.

123. Areen, "Government as Educator," 984–985, 999, 1000.

124. Finkin and Post, *For the Common Good,* 8–9, 125.

125. Van Alstyne, "The Constitutional Rights," 871n84; Van Alstyne, "Tenure," 328.

7. The Development of Institutional Academic Freedom as a First Amendment Right of Universities

1. Sweezy v. New Hampshire, 354 U.S. 234, 263 (1957) (Frankfurter, J., concurring).

2. Regents of the University of California v. Bakke, 438 U.S. 265, 325 (1978) (Brennan, White, Marshall, and Blackmun, JJ., concurring in the judgment in part and dissenting in part), 408 (Stevens, Burger, Stewart, and Rehnquist, JJ., concurring in the judgment in part and dissenting in part), 269 (Powell, J., announcing the judgment of the Court).

3. Regents of the University of California v. Bakke, 311–315.

4. Regents of the University of California v. Bakke, 312.

5. Regents of the University of California v. Bakke, 305–312.

6. Regents of the University of California v. Bakke, 312–313n48, 314–315.

7. Brief for Columbia University, Harvard University, Stanford University, and the University of Pennsylvania, as Amici Curiae, Regents of the University of California v. Bakke. The text of this appendix had already appeared in the amicus brief filed on behalf of the President and Fellows of Harvard College in DeFunis v. Odegaard, 416 U.S. 312 (1974), an earlier affirmative action case at the University of Washington that the Supreme Court dismissed as moot. See David B. Oppenheimer, "Archibald Cox and the Diversity Justification for Affirmative Action," *Virginia Journal of Social Policy & the Law* 22 (2018): 158, 172.

8. Interestingly, the amicus brief filed by the AAUP did not refer to the First Amendment or academic freedom at all, largely because the AAUP had not developed an organizational policy on their relevance in the context of affirmative action. Rather, the AAUP brief stressed in very general terms the educational value of student diversity, and particularly the role of the faculty in making educational judgments about the composition of the student body. Brief of the American Association of University Professors, Amicus Curiae, Regents of the University of California v. Bakke.

9. Memorandum for Mr. Justice Powell from Bob Comfort (Aug. 29, 1977), Lewis F. Powell Jr. Papers, Washington and Lee University School of Law (hereafter cited as Powell Papers), file 10-1977, Regents of University of California v. Bakke, 12.

10. Memorandum for Mr. Justice Powell, 55.

11. Powell outline of possible opinion (May 2, 1978), Powell Papers, file 10-1977, 2.

12. Responding to an outline of a draft opinion circulated by Powell a week after he drafted his "possible opinion," Justice Brennan wrote that he would "reserve decision" about "educational diversity" until he completed his own draft. "The reason," Brennan explained, "is that there may be other reasons besides educational diversity that will support competitive consideration of race and ethnic origin." Letter from William J. Brennan to Lewis F. Powell, Jr., May 16, 1978, Powell Papers, file 10-1977.

13. Grutter v. Bollinger, 539 U.S. 306, 324 (2003).

14. Grutter v. Bollinger, 329.

15. Grutter v. Bollinger, 330–332.

16. Grutter v. Bollinger, 349, 362–364 (Thomas, J., concurring in part and dissenting in part).

17. Grutter v. Bollinger, 366, citing United States v. Virginia, 518 U.S. 515 (1996).

18. Grutter v. Bollinger, 354n3, 372–373.

19. Fisher v. University of Texas at Austin, 579 U.S. 365 (2016).

20. Students for Fair Admissions, Inc. v. President and Fellows of Harvard College, 143 S. Ct. 2141 (2023).

21. Regents of the University of Michigan v. Ewing, 474 U.S. 214, 225 (1985).

22. Regents of the University of Michigan v. Ewing, 226, 226n12.

23. Regents of the University of Michigan v. Ewing, 228, 230 (Powell, J. concurring).

24. Brief of the American Association of University Professors as Amicus Curiae, Regents of the University of Michigan v. Ewing, 8.

25. Brief of the American Association of University Professors as Amicus Curiae, Regents of the University of Michigan v. Ewing, 9, 11n19, 12, 15–16.

26. Widmar v. Vincent, 454 U.S. 263, 271–274 (1981).

27. Widmar v. Vincent, 267–269, 276.

28. Widmar v. Vincent, 277, 278–280 (Stevens, J., concurring).

29. Board of Regents of University of Wisconsin v. Southworth, 529 U.S. 217, 233 (2000).

30. Board of Regents of University of Wisconsin v. Southworth, 237 (Souter, J., concurring).

31. Board of Regents of University of Wisconsin v. Southworth, 243.

32. Board of Regents of University of Wisconsin v. Southworth, 238n4, 239, 239n5.

33. AAUP, "A Preliminary Statement on Judicially Compelled Disclosure in the Nonrenewal of Faculty Appointments," *Academe* (Feb.–Mar. 1981): 17.

34. Gray v. Board of Higher Education, City of New York, 692 F.2d 901, 907–908 (2d Cir. 1982); see also Dixon v. Rutgers, 541 A.2d 1046, 1058 (N.J. 1988) (approving AAUP policy statement as useful guidance in determining extent of discovery).

35. E.E.O.C. v. University of Notre Dame Du Lac, 715 F.2d 331, 338–339 (7th Cir. 1983); see also Dixon v. Rutgers, 1051–1060.

36. In re Dinnan, 661 F.2d 426, 430–431 (5th Cir. 1980).

37. E.E.O.C. v. Franklin and Marshall College, 775 F.2d 110, 114–115 (3d Cir. 1985), 117, 119 (Aldisert, J., dissenting).

38. Reply Brief of University of Pennsylvania, University of Pennsylvania v. E.E.O.C., 493 U.S. 182 (1990), 15–17.

39. Brief of the American Association of University Professors, Amicus Curiae, University of Pennsylvania v. E.E.O.C.

40. University of Pennsylvania v. E.E.O.C., 197.

41. University of Pennsylvania v. E.E.O.C., 199–200.

42. University of Pennsylvania v. E.E.O.C., 200–201.

43. Blackmun asserted in his original draft that "in no previous case has a majority of this Court relied upon any special right of academic freedom as a basis for decision." The discussion of academic freedom in previous cases, he asserted, "may have been helpful, but it was not necessary to the ultimate disposition of any of these cases." In a footnote following this passage, he rejected the claim that *Keyishian* "amounted to a holding that teachers and school administrators enjoy some special First Amendment protection." First draft circulated Dec. 19, 1989, Harry A. Blackmun Papers, Library of Congress, container 543, file 4, 13–14.

Conceding that Blackmun "may be technically correct that the discussion of academic freedom was not necessary to the holding in Sweezy or Keyishian," Brennan maintained that a majority of the Court "agreed in both cases that there is a First Amendment right to academic freedom inherent in university teaching." Brennan felt "strongly" that Blackmun's understandable desire to construe the holdings narrowly "may be misconstrued in the future." Memorandum from Bill Brennan to Harry Blackmun, Dec. 21, 1989, container 543, file 4.

Blackmun apparently agreed with his law clerk, who thought Brennan's strong feelings about this issue might lead him to write a separate opinion if the objectionable language was not deleted. Memorandum from Vic (Amar, law clerk) to Mr. Justice Blackmun, container 543, file 4.

44. Brief for the Respondents, Rumsfeld v. Forum for Academic & Institutional Rights, 547 U.S. 47 (2006), 20–21.

45. Brief for Columbia University, Cornell University, Harvard University, New York University, the University of Chicago, the University of Pennsylvania, and Yale University as Amici Curiae, Rumsfeld v. Forum for Academic & Individual Rights, 6–7.

46. Brief Amici Curiae of Robert A. Burt et al., Rumsfeld v. Forum for Academic & Individual Rights, 11.

47. Brief for Amicus Curiae the American Association of University Professors, Rumsfeld v. Forum for Academic & Institutional Rights, 8, 11–12.

48. I served as general counsel of the AAUP when it filed this brief and was one of the lawyers who signed it. I disagreed at the time with the statements in the brief that I criticize in the text. Though not alone, I was in the minority, and I acquiesced in the decision to include them. For a thoughtful criticism of the brief, see J. Peter Byrne, "Constitutional Academic Freedom after *Grutter:* Getting Real about the 'Four Freedoms' of a University," *University of Colorado Law Review* 77 (2006): 929, 946–953.

49. Rumsfeld v. Forum for Academic & Institutional Rights, 70. Without discussing issues of academic freedom, Judge Richard Posner ridiculed the arguments of the law professors who challenged the law, highlighting the "left-liberal domination of elite law school faculty" and the "growing chasm between the professoriat and the judiciary." Richard A. Posner, "A Note on Rumsfeld v. FAIR and the Legal Academy," *Supreme Court Review* 2006, no. 1 (2006): 47, 57.

50. Burt v. Gates, 502 F.3d 183, 190–191 (2d Cir. 2007).

51. State v. Schmid, 423 A.2d 615, 630–631 (N.J. 1980).

52. State v. Schmid, 632–633.

53. Brief of Appellant Princeton University, Princeton University v. Schmid, 455 U.S. 100 (1980), 6–8, 16.

54. Brief Amicus Curiae of the American Association of University Professors, Princeton University v. Schmid, 3.

55. Brief Amicus Curiae of the American Association of University Professors, 1. The text of this and much of the following paragraph was published in David M. Rabban, "A Functional Analysis of 'Individual' and 'Institutional' Academic Freedom under the First Amendment," *Law and Contemporary Problems* 53, no. 3 (1990): 227, 260–261, which contains a more comprehensive account of the litigation.

56. Brief Amicus Curiae of the American Association of University Professors, 2–3, 5, 18–19, 21, 24–25.

57. Brief Amicus Curiae of the American Association of University Professors, 26–28.

58. Transcript of Oral Argument, Princeton University v. Schmid (80-1576), 18–21, https://www.oyez./org/cases/1981/80-1576.

59. Transcript of Oral Argument, Princeton University v. Schmid, 11–12, 16.

60. Princeton University v. Schmid, 103. Interestingly, a draft opinion reached the merits without discussing academic freedom. The draft opinion declared that "Princeton's claim is without substance" because states can grant more protection for expression than required by the First Amendment. John Paul Stevens Papers, Library of Congress, box 215, folder 2, May 14 (1980). Apparently, Justice Rehnquist wrote this draft. Letter from Harry Blackmun to Chief Justice Rehnquist, Nov. 23, 1981, box 215, folder 2.

61. Association of Christian Schools International v. Stearns, 678 F. Supp. 2d 980, 989 (C.D. Cal. 2008).

62. Association of Christian Schools International v. Stearns, 992–994.

63. Eiland v. Wolf, 764 S.W.2d 827, 835 (Tex. App. Houston 1989).

64. Tatro v. University of Minnesota, 816 N.W.2d 509, 522–523 (Minn. 2012).

65. Oyama v. University of Hawaii, 813 F.3d 850, 856–857, 874–875 (9th Cir. 2015).

66. In re Rowan University, 2016 WL 3981802, 6 (N.J. App. Div. 2016).

67. Matter of University of Medicine and Dentistry of New Jersey, 677 A.2d 721, 731–733 (N.J. 1996).

68. Osteen v. Henley, 13 F.3d 221, 225 (7th Cir. 1993). See also Hernandez v. Overlook Hospital, 692 A.2d 971 (N.J. 1997).

69. Faro v. New York University, 502 F.2d 1229, 1231–1232 (2d Cir. 1974).

70. Powell v. Syracuse University, 580 F.2d 1150, 1153–1154 (2d Cir. 1978). See also Lieberman v. Gant, 630 F.2d 60 (2d Cir. 1980).

71. Blasdell v. Northwestern University, 687 F.3d 813, 815–816 (7th Cir. 2012).

72. Brown v. Trustees of Boston University, 891 F.2d 337, 359–360 (1st Cir. 1989).

73. Piarowski v. Illinois Community College District 515, 759 F.2d 625, 627–630 (7th Cir. 1985).

74. Parate v. Isabor, 868 F.2d 821, 826 (6th Cir. 1989).

75. See, for instance, Hillis v. Stephen F. Austin State University, 665 F. 2d 547 (5th Cir.1982); Brown v. Armenti, 247 F.3d 69 (3d Cir. 2001); Lovelace v. Southern Massachusetts University, 793 F.2d 419 (1st Cir. 1986).

76. Johnson-Kurick v. Abu-Absi, 423 F.3d 590, 595 (6th Cir. 2005).

77. Wirsig v. Board of Regents of University of Colorado, 739 F. Supp. 551, 554 (D. Colo. 1990).

78. Turkish Coalition of America, Inc. v. Bruininks, 804 F. Supp. 2d 959, 965–966 (D. Minn. 2011).

79. Progressive Animal Welfare Society v. University of Washington, 884 P.2d 592, 596 (Wash. 1994).

80. Progressive Animal Welfare Society v. University of Washington, 604. See also S.E.T.A., UNC-CH, Inc. v. Huffines, 399 S.E.2d 340 (N.C. Ct. App. 1991); State ex rel. Thomas v. Ohio State University, 643 N.E.2d 216 (Ohio 1994). Some courts ignored university claims of First Amendment academic freedom while agreeing that statutes did not compel disclosure of information. See, for instance, Sussex Commons Associates, LLC v. Rutgers, 46 A.3d 536 (N.J. 2012), reversing, 6 A.3d 983 (N.J. Super. App. Div. 2010); Cuccinelli v. Rector and Visitors of the University of Virginia, 722 S.E.2d 626 (Va. 2012).

81. Russo v. Nassau County Community College, 554 N.Y.S.2d 774, 777–778 (N.Y. Sup. 1990). Relying on its interpretation of the freedom of information act without discussing academic freedom, the state's highest court affirmed this decision after an intermediate appellate court reversed it. Russo v. Nassau County Community College, 623 N.E.2d 15 (N.Y. 1993).

82. Nova University v. Educational Institution Licensure Commission, 483 A.2d 1172, 1179, 1186 (D.C. Ct. App. 1984).

83. Nova University v. Educational Institution Licensure Commission, 1182, 1184.

84. Nova University v. Educational Institution Licensure Commission, 1183, 1183n7, 1186. See also In re Rules of Court of Appeals for the Admission of Attorneys, 274 N.E.2d 440, 442 (N.Y. 1970).

85. Corry v. Leland Stanford Jr. University, No. 740309 (Cal. Super. Ct. Feb. 27, 1995), 35, https://web.archive.org/web/20050419211842/http://www.ithaca.edu/faculty/cduncan/265/corryvstanford.htm.

86. Gerhard Casper, Statement on Corry v. Stanford University (March 9, 1995), https://web.stanford.edu>speeches>950309corry.

87. McAdams v. Marquette University, 914 N.W.2d 708, 713 (Wis. 2018).

88. McAdams v. Marquette University, 714–716.

89. McAdams v. Marquette University, 755, 757 (Bradley, J., dissenting).

90. McAdams v. Marquette University, 737. See also Garner v. Michigan State University, 462 N.W. 2d 832 (Mich. App. 1990).

8. A Theory of Institutional Academic Freedom as a Distinctive First Amendment Right of Universities

1. See generally Paul Horwitz, *First Amendment Institutions* (Cambridge, MA: Harvard University Press, 2013); Frederick Schauer, "Principles, Institutions, and the First Amendment," *Harvard Law Review* 112 (1998): 84–120; Frederick Schauer, "Towards an Institutional First Amendment," *Minnesota Law Review* 89 (2005): 1256–1279.

2. See Matthew W. Finkin, "On 'Institutional' Academic Freedom," *Texas Law Review* 61 (1983): 817, 839–840, 850, 854.

3. American Association of University Professors, "1915 Declaration of Principles on Academic Freedom and Academic Tenure" (1915) (cited as 1915 Declaration), reprinted in *Academic Freedom and Tenure*, ed. Louis Joughin (Madison: University of Wisconsin Press, 1969), appendix A.

4. 1915 Declaration, 157, 159.

5. AAUP, "1940 Statement of Principles on Academic Freedom and Tenure" (1940), reprinted in Joughin, *Academic Freedom and Tenure*, 33–39.

6. See Michael McConnell, "Academic Freedom in Religious Colleges and Universities," *Law and Contemporary Problems* 53, no. 3 (1990): 303, 309.

7. Walter P. Metzger, *Academic Freedom in the Age of the University* (New York: Columbia University Press, 1961), 3, 43.

8. 1915 Declaration, 164.

9. Amy Guttman, *Democratic Education* (Princeton, NJ: Princeton University Press, 1987), 177.

10. J. Peter Byrne, "Academic Freedom: A 'Special Concern of the First Amendment,'" *Yale Law Journal* 99 (1989): 251, 312; Finkin, "On 'Institutional' Academic

Freedom," 850; Schauer, "Principles," 116–20; Schauer, "Towards an Institutional First Amendment," 1274–1275, 1278–1279.

11. Regents of the University of Michigan v. Ewing, 474 U.S. 214 (1985); Tatro v. University of Minnesota, 816 N.W.2d 909 (Minn. 2012); In re Rowan University, 2016 WL 3981802 (N.J. App. Div. 2016); Eiland v. Wolf, 764 S.W.2d 827 (Tex. App. Houston 1989).

12. Osteen v. Henley, 13 F.3d 221, 225–226 (7th Cir. 1993).

13. Matter of University of Medicine and Dentistry of New Jersey, 677 A.2d 721 (N.J. 1996).

14. Christian Legal Society of the University of California, Hastings College of the Law v. Martinez, 561 U.S. 661, 686 (2010).

15. University of Utah v. Shurtleff, 144 P.3d 1109 (Utah 2006).

16. University of Utah v. Shurtleff, 1122, 1127–1128 (Durham, C.J., dissenting).

17. Waugh v. Board of Trustees of the University of Mississippi, 237 U.S. 589, 597 (1915).

18. Burt v. Gates, 502 F.3d 183, 191–192 (2d Cir. 2007).

19. Board of Trustees of the Leland Stanford Junior University v. County of Santa Clara, 150 Cal. Rptr. 109, 112–113 (Ct. App., 1st Dist. 1978).

20. State v. University of Alaska, 624 P.2d 807, 815 (AK 1981).

21. American Association of University Professors, American Council on Education, and Association of Governing Boards of Colleges and Universities, "Statement on Government of Colleges and Universities" (1966) (hereafter cited as 1966 Statement on Government), reprinted in Joughin, *Academic Freedom and Tenure*, 90, 98.

22. Robert C. Post, *Democracy, Expertise, Academic Freedom: A First Amendment Jurisprudence for the Modern State* (New Haven, CT: Yale University Press, 2012), 88.

23. 1966 Statement on Government, 98–99.

24. 1966 Statement on Government, 92–93, 97.

25. Haimowitz v. University of Nevada, 579 F.2d 526, 530 (9th Cir. 1978); Gray v. Board of Higher Education, City of New York, 692 F.2d 901, 906n9 (2d Cir. 1982).

26. Regents of the University of Michigan v. Ewing, 474 U.S. 214, 225 (1985).

27. Brown v. Li, 299 F.3d 1092, 1104–1105 (9th Cir. 2002).

28. Association of Christian Schools International v. Stearns, 678 F. Supp. 2d 980, 989–994 (C.D. Cal. 2008).

29. Mayberry v. Dees, 663 F.2d 502 (4th Cir. 1981); Hetrick v. Martin, 480 F.2d 705 (6th Cir. 1973).

30. Brown v. Armenti, 247 F.3d 69, 72 (3d Cir. 2001).

31. Lopez v. Fresno City College, 2012 WL 844911, 2–4 (E.D. Cal. 2012).

32. Doe v. University of Michigan, 721 F. Supp. 852, 857, 865–866 (E.D. Mich. 1989).

33. AAUP, "The History, Uses, and Abuses of Title IX," *AAUP Bulletin* (June 2016), 69.

34. AAUP, "History, Uses, and Abuses," 82–83, 85, 87–88.

35. Johnson-Kurick v. Abu-Absi, 423 F.3d 590 (6th Cir. 2005); Wirsig v. Board of Regents of University of Colorado, 739 F. Supp. 551 (D. Colo. 1990).

36. See Lovelace v. Southeastern Massachusetts University, 793 F.2d 419 (1st Cir. 1986).

37. "AAUP Recommended Institutional Regulations," in AAUP, *Policy Documents and Reports,* 11th ed. (Baltimore: Johns Hopkins University Press, 2015), 79–90.

38. Korf v. Ball State University, 726 F. 2d 1222, 1224–1225 (7th Cir. 1984).

39. Arthur O. Lovejoy, "Harvard University and Drs. Walsh and Sweezy," *Bulletin of the American Association of University Professors* 24, no. 7 (1938): 598–608.

40. Lovejoy, "Harvard University," 600–602.

41. Lovejoy, "Harvard University," 604–605.

42. Sidney Hook, "Should Communists Be Permitted to Teach?," *New York Times,* Feb. 27, 1949, Sunday Magazine, 7, 29.

43. Hook, "Should Communists Be Permitted to Teach?," 22.

44. Ellen W. Schrecker, *No Ivory Tower* (New York: Oxford University Press, 1986), 109–110.

45. Rust v. Sullivan, 500 U.S. 173, 200 (1991).

46. Sweezy v. New Hampshire, 354 U.S. 234 (1957); Keyishian v. Board of Regents, 385 U.S. 589 (1967).

47. Sweezy v. New Hampshire, 262 (Frankfurter, J., concurring).

48. Edwards v. Aguillard, 482 U.S. 578, 610, 629–635 (Scalia, J., dissenting).

49. Keith E. Whittington, "Professorial Speech, the First Amendment, and Legislative Restrictions on Classroom Discussions," *Wake Forest Law Review* 58 (2023): 463, 467–477, provides an excellent survey of these bills and laws.

50. Florida Statute Section 1000.05(4)(a) (2022).

51. Florida Statute Section 1000.05 (4)(b).

52. Sweezy v. New Hampshire, 263 (Frankfurter, J., concurring).

53. Pernell v. Florida Board of Governors of the State University System 37–39 (Case No.: 4:22cv304-MW/MAF), and Novoa v. Diaz (Case No.: 4:22cv324-MW/MAF) (N.D. Fla. 2022). See also Pernell v. Florida Board of Governors, 55–69.

54. Parnell v. Florida Board of Governors, 2, 9–10.

55. Oral Argument in University of Pennsylvania v. E.E.O.C, 493 U.S.182 (1990), Nov. 7, 1989, 9, https://www.oyez.org/cases/1989/88-493, 9–11.

56. Kathleen J. Frydl, "Trust to the Public: Academic Freedom in the Multiversity," in *Academic Freedom after September 11,* ed. Beshara Doumani (New York: Zone Books, 2006), 175, 185–186.

57. See Michelle Goldberg, "This Is What the Right-Wing Takeover of a Progressive College Looks Like," *New York Times,* April 29, 2023.

58. Lovelace v. Southern Massachusetts University, 425–426.

59. Central State University v. American Association of University Professors, Central State University Chapter, 526 U.S. 124, 125 (1999).

60. J. Peter Byrne, "The Threat to Constitutional Academic Freedom," *Journal of College and University Law* 31 (2004): 79, 116.

61. Texas Education Code Ann. Sections 51.301, 51.302 (Vernon 2020).

62. Ronald Dworkin, "We Need a New Interpretation of Academic Freedom," in *The Future of Academic Freedom,* ed. Lewis Menand (Chicago: University of Chicago Press, 1996), 187, 197n1.

63. Post, *Democracy, Expertise, Academic Freedom,* 97–98, 160n8.

64. Matthew W. Finkin and Robert C. Post, *For the Common Good: Principles of American Academic Freedom* (New Haven, CT: Yale University Press, 2009), 103.

65. Post, *Democracy, Expertise, Academic Freedom,* 97–99.

66. Robert Post, "The Structure of Academic Freedom," in Doumani, *Academic Freedom after September 11,* 61, 89, 105n3.

67. Letter from American Israel Public Affairs Committee et al., March 15, 2004, in Doumani, *Academic Freedom after September 11,* 288–290.

68. Post, "The Structure of Academic Freedom," 89–90.

69. Letter from David Ward, President, American Council on Education, Oct. 21, 2003, in Doumani, *Academic Freedom after September 11,* 292.

70. Letter from Joan E. Bertin, Executive Director, National Coalition Against Censorship, and Mark F. Smith, Director of Government Relations, American Association of University Professors, in Doumani, *Academic Freedom after September 11,* 295–296.

71. See Judith Butler, "Academic Norms, Contemporary Challenges: A Reply to Robert Post on Academic Freedom," in Doumani, *Academic Freedom after September 11,* 107, 117–123; Joan W. Scott, "Academic Freedom as an Ethical Practice," in Menand, *The Future of Academic Freedom,* 163, 170–175; Judith Jarvis Thomson, "Ideology and Faculty Selection," *Law and Contemporary Problems* 53, no. 3 (1990): 155, 158.

9. Can Institutional Academic Freedom Limit Free Speech?

1. See generally J. Peter Byrne, "Racial Insults and Free Speech within the University," *Georgetown Law Journal* 79 (1991): 399–443.

2. Doe v. University of Michigan, 721 F. Supp. 852, 862–863 (E.D. Mich. 1989).

3. UWM Post, Inc. v. Board of Regents of University of Wisconsin System, 774 F. Supp.1163, 1172, 1178 (E.D. Wis. 1991).

4. Cohen v. California, 403 U.S. 15, 26 (1971).

5. Cohen v. California, 26 (quoting Baumgartner v. United States, 322 U.S. 665, 673–674 (1944)).

6. Hustler Magazine, Inc. v. Falwell, 485 U.S. 46, 48, 54–55 (1988).

7. Doe v. University of Michigan, 865.

8. See Tinker v. Des Moines Independent Community School District, 393 U.S. 503 (1969).

9. Martin v. Parrish, 805 F.2d 583, 584 (5th Cir. 1986); Bonnell v. Lorenzo, 241 F.3d 800, 803 (6th Cir. 2001); Buchanan v. Alexander, 919 F.3d 847, 853 (5th Cir. 2019); Smock v. Board of Regents of University of Michigan, 353 F. Supp. 3d 651, 655 (E.D. Mich. 2018); Nichols v. University of Southern Mississippi, 669 F. Supp. 2d 684, 689 (S.D. Miss. 2009); Frieder v. Morehead State University, 2013 WL 6187786 at 5 (E.D. Ky. 2013), aff'd, 770 F.3d 428 (6th Cir. 2014).

10. See Doe v. University of Michigan, 858.

11. See Grutter v. Bollinger, 539 U.S. 306, 362, 372–373 (Thomas, J., concurring in part and dissenting in part) (discussed in Chapter 7).

12. Brandenburg v. Ohio, 395 U.S. 444, 447 (1969).

13. Hardy v. Jefferson Community College, 260 F.3d 671, 674–675 (6th Cir. 2001).

14. Dibona v. Matthews, 269 Cal. Rptr. 882, 884 (Cal. App. 1990).

15. Cohen v. California, 403 U.S. 15 (1971).

16. See Jeannie Suk Gerson, "The Trouble with Teaching Rape Law," *New Yorker,* Dec. 15, 2014, at 86.

17. Doe v. University of Michigan, 854.

18. UWM Post, Inc. v. Board of Regents of University of Wisconsin System, 1165, 1167–1168.

19. Greg Lukianoff, *Unlearning Liberty: Campus Censorship and the End of American Debate* (New York: Encounter Books, 2012), 83.

20. Catherine Marfin, "UT Removes Anti-Muslim Posters from Campus," *Daily Texan,* Feb. 13, 2017, https://thedailytexan.com/2017/02/13/ut-removes-anti-muslim -posters-from-campus/.

21. Catherine Marfin and Kayla Meyertons, "Racist Posters Target Chinese Community in Campus Buildings, *Daily Texan,* April 4, 2017, https://thedailytexan.com /2017/04/04/racist-posters-target-chinese-community-in-campus-buildings/.

22. London Gibson, "Racist Flyers Appear around Campus," *Daily Texan,* May 3, 2017, https://thedailytexan.com/2017/05/03/racist-flyers-appear-around-campus-tuesday/.

23. Rodriguez v. Maricopa County Community College, 605 F.3d 703, 705 (9th Cir. 2010); Crawford v. Columbus State Community College, 2017 WL 5594128, 1–2 (S.D. Ohio 2017).

24. Bethel School District No. 403 v. Fraser, 478 U.S. 675, 677–678, 682–686 (majority), 691, 691n1, 696 (Stevens, J., dissenting) (1986).

25. Board of Regents of University of Wisconsin System v. Southworth, 529 U.S. 217, 236, 239n5 (2000) (Souter, J. concurring).

26. Trejo v. Shoben, 319 F.3d 878, 881–884 (7th Cir. 2003).

27. Letter from Theodore W. Ruger to Vivian L. Gadsden (June 23, 2022), 10 (quoting Wax).

28. Letter from Theodore W. Ruger, 8–9.

29. Michael Berubé and Jennifer Ruth, *It's Not Free Speech: Race, Democracy, and the Future of Academic Freedom* (Baltimore: Johns Hopkins University Press, 2022), 14–15 and cover jacket.

30. Joan Scott also observes the book's exclusive association of illegitimate views with the scholars on the right. Joan W. Scott, "Academic Freedom Has Always Been Dirty, That's a Good Thing," *Chronicle of Higher Education*, Oct. 4, 2022, https://www.chronicle.com/article/academic-freedom-has-always-been-dirty-thats-a-good-thing.

31. Levin v. Harleston, 770 F. Supp. 895, 908–909, 912–913, 921 (S.D.N.Y. 1991).

32. Letter from Theodore W. Ruger, 7–8.

33. For a similar analysis, see Jonathan Zimmerman, "My Amy Wax Problem," *Inside Higher Education*, July 26, 2022, https:www.insidehighered.com/views/2022/07/26/amy-wax-can-speak-her-mind-not-demean-students-opinion.

34. Mahoney Area School District v. B.L. by and through Levy, 141 S Ct. 2038, 2043–2044, 2055 (2021).

35. Mahoney Area School District v. B.L. by and through Levy, 2046–2048, 2047 (quoting Snyder v. Phelps, 562 U.S. 443, 461 (2011)).

36. Hustler Magazine v. Falwell, 55.

37. Doe v. University of Michigan, 856, 867.

38. UWM Post, Inc. v. Board of Regents of University of Wisconsin System, 1165.

39. Korf v. Ball State University, 726 F.2d 1222, 1227–1228 (7th Cir. 1984).

40. Riggin v. Board of Trustees of Ball State University, 489 N.E.2d 616, 628 (Ind. Ct. App. 1986). See generally David M. Rabban, "The Regrettable Underenforcement of Incompetence as Cause to Dismiss Tenured Faculty," *Indiana Law Journal* 91 (2015): 39, 50–51 (discussing these cases).

41. See, for instance, Bloedorn v. Grube, 631 F.3d 1218, 1233–1234 (11th Cir. 2011); Bowman v. White, 444 F.3d 967, 978 (8th Cir. 2006); American Civil Liberties Union v. Mote, 423 F.3d 438, 444 (4th Cir. 2005); Hershey v. Goldstein, 938 F. Supp. 2d 491, 510 (S.D.N.Y. 2013).

42. See Chapter 8.

43. State v. Schmid, 423 A.2d 615, 630–633 (N.J. 1980).

44. Perry Education Association v. Perry Local Educators' Association, 460 U.S. 37, 45–46 (1983).

45. Widmar v. Vincent, 454 U.S. 263, 267–268n5 (1981).

46. See especially Gilles v. Blanchard, 477 F.3d 466, 470 (7th Cir. 2007); Hershey v. Goldstein, 510.

47. Greer v. Spock, 424 U.S. 828, 838 (1976).

48. Bloedorn v. Grube, 1233; Bowman v. White, 978. Both decisions quoted this language from Tinker v. Des Moines Independent Community Schools District, 506.

49. Brister v. Faulkner, 214 F.3d 675, 677–678, 683 (5th Cir. 2000).

50. Bourgault v. Yudof, 316 F. Supp. 2d 411, 419 (N.D. Tex. 2004); see also Hershey v. Goldstein, 508.

51. Bowman v. White, 979 (majority), 988–990, 989n11 (Bye, J. concurring).

52. Bloedorn v. Grube, 1238; Bowman v. White, 980.

53. Hershey v. Goldstein, 510; see also Bloedorn v. Grube, 1238; Bowman v. White, 980.

54. Giles v. Garland, 281 Fed. Appx. 501, 511 (6th Cir. 2008).

55. Bowman v. White, 988 (Bye, J., concurring).

56. Bluedorn v. Grube, 1240 (citing Sonnier v. Crain, 613 F.3d 436, 445 (5th Cir. 2010)); Bowman v. White, 981–982.

57. Bowman v. White, 983; see also 990 (Bye, J., concurring).

58. Bowman v. White, 982.

59. Bloedorn v. Grube, 1240–1241.

60. Brister v. Faulkner, 675; State v. Schmid, 615; Bloedorn v. Grube, 1218; Gilles v. Blanchard, 466; Bowman v. White, 967; Bourgault v. Yudof, 411; Hershey v. Goldstein, 491.

10. Judicial Review of Conflicting Academic Freedom Claims between Professors and Universities

1. See, for instance, Regents of the University of Michigan v. Ewing, 474 U.S. 214, 226n12 (1985); Piarowski v. Illinois Community College District 515, 759 F.2d 625, 627–628 (7th Cir. 1985).

2. Turkish Coalition of America, Inc. v. Bruininks, 804 F. Supp. 2d 959, 965–966 (C.D. Minn. 2011).

3. Progressive Animal Welfare Society v. University of Washington, 884 P.2d 592, 604 (Wash. 1994); Russo v. Nassau County Community College, 554 N.Y.S.2d 774, 777–778 (Sup. Ct., Nassau County 1990).

4. See Chapter 8, the section "Who Exercises Institutional Academic Freedom?"

5. Mayberry v. Dees, 663 F.2d 502, 505 (4th Cir. 1981).

6. Hetrick v, Martin, 480 F.2d 705, 707, 709 (6th Cir. 1973).

7. Cohen v. San Bernadino Valley College, 883 F. Supp. 1407, 1419–1420 (C.D. Cal. 1999).

8. Johnson-Kurick v. Abu-Absi, 423 F.3d 590, 595 (6th Cir. 2005); Wirsig v. Board of Regents of Colorado, 739 F. Supp. 551, 554 (D. Colo. 1990).

9. Johnson v. Lincoln University, 776 F. 2d 443, 452 (3d Cir. 1985).

10. McReady v. O'Malley, 804 F. Supp. 2d 427, 440 (D. Md. 2011).

11. Johnson v. Lincoln University, 449.

12. Landrum v. Eastern Kentucky University, 578 F. Supp. 241, 244–246 (E.D. Ky. 1984).

13. McReady v. O'Malley, 440.

14. Klaassen v. Atkinson, 348 F. Supp. 3d 1106, 1176 (D. Kan. 2018).

15. Johnson v. Lincoln University, 454.

16. Franklin v. Atkins, 409 F. Supp. 439, 446 (D. Colo. 1976), aff'd, 562 F.2d 1188 (10th Cir. 1977); Starsky v. Williams, 353 F. Supp. 900, 924 (D. Ariz. 1972), aff'd in part, rev'd in part, 512 F.2d 109 (9th Cir. 1972).

17. Piarowski v. Illinois Community College District 515, 631–632.

18. Hardy v. Jefferson Community College, 260 F.3d 671, 682 (6th Cir. 2001).

19. J. Peter Byrne, "Academic Freedom: A 'Special Concern of the First Amendment,'" *Yale Law Journal* 99 (1989): 251, 305, 306; Paul Horwitz, *First Amendment Institutions* (Cambridge, MA: Harvard University Press, 2013), 114.

20. Frederick Schauer, "Is There a Right to Academic Freedom?," *University of Colorado Law Review* 77 (2006): 919.

21. Byrne, "Academic Freedom," 306.

22. Schauer, "Is There a Right to Academic Freedom?," 925.

23. Powell v. Syracuse University, 580 F.2d 1150, 1154, 1156 (2d Cir. 1978).

24. Langland v. Vanderbilt University, 589 F. Supp. 995, 1007, 1010 (M.D. Tenn. 1984), aff'd, 772 F.2d 907 (6th Cir. 1985).

25. Keddie v. Pennsylvania State University, 412 F. Supp. 1264, 1268–1270 (M.D. Penn. 1976).

26. Cooper v. Ross, 472 F. Supp. 802, 805, 811–812, 814–815 (E.D. Ark. 1979).

27. Powell v. Syracuse University, 1156.

28. Brown v. Trustees of Boston University, 891 F.2d 337, 347 (1st Cir. 1989); see also 341–342.

29. Brown v. Trustees of Boston University, 349.

30. Wagner v. Jones, 664 F.3d 259, 264, 270–272 (8th Cir. 2014).

31. Manning v. Jones, 875 F.3d 408 (8th Cir. 2017).

32. Lynn v. Regents of the University of California, 656 F.2d 1337, 1342 (9th Cir. 1981).

33. Brown v. Trustees of Boston University, 344, 344n6.

34. Wagner v. Jones, 271.

35. Whiting v. Jackson State University, 616 F.2d 116, 123–124 (5th Cir. 1980).

36. Langland v. Vanderbilt University, 1007, 1011–1013, 1015.

37. Smith v. University of North Carolina, 632 F.2d 316, 342, 345 (4th Cir. 1980).

38. Smith v. University of North Carolina, 330–331, 342, 344.

39. Lynn v. Regents of the University of California, 1979 WL 71, 2 (C.D. Calif. 1979).

40. Lynn v. Regents of the University of California, 656 F.2d 1337, 1343 (9th Cir. 1981).

41. Lynn v. Regents of the University of California, 656 F.2d, 1343n5.

42. Johnson v. Lincoln University, 448, 450.

43. McAdams v. Marquette University, 914 N.W.2d 708, 739–740 (Wis. 2018).

44. Doe v. University of Michigan, 721 F. Supp. 852, 860, 865 (E.D. Mich. 1989).

45. Kerr v. Hurd, 694 F. Supp. 2d 817, 834, 844 (S.D. Ohio 2010).

46. See Vega v. Miller, 273 F.3d 460 (2d Cir. 2001).

47. See Mahoney v. Hankin, 593 F. Supp. 1171 (S.D.N.Y. 1984).

48. See Pigee v. Carl Sandberg College, 464 F.3d 667 (7th Cir. 2006).

49. See Lopez v. Fresno City College, 2012 WL 844911 (E.D. Calif. (2012).

50. Arthur O. Lovejoy, "Harvard University and Drs. Walsh and Sweezy," *Bulletin of the American Association of University Professors* 24, no. 7 (1938): 598, 604.

51. Dube v. State University of New York, 900 F.2d 587, 590–592 (2d Cir. 1990).

52. Judith Jarvis Thomson, "Ideology and Faculty Selection," *Law and Contemporary Problems* 53, no. 3 (1990): 155, 175–176.

53. See Judith Areen, "Government as Educator: A New Understanding of First Amendment Protection of Academic Freedom and Governance," *Georgetown Law Journal* 97 (2009): 945, 1000 (advocating judicial deference under this standard).

54. Temple University Chapter, American Association of University Professors v. Temple University. AAA Case No. 14 30 1314 83H, 13, April 10, 1984 (Summers, Arbitrator) (hereafter cited as Temple Arbitration). I am grateful to Raymond Cormier for sending me a copy of this arbitration.

55. Temple Arbitration, 14, 16, 26.

56. Temple Arbitration, 7–8.

57. Temple Arbitration, 9–10.

58. Temple Arbitration, 15–16, 29.

59. Temple Arbitration, 14, 18, 29; see also 28.

60. See American Association of University Professors, *Recommended Principles to Guide Academy-Industry Relationships* (Washington, DC, 2014), 5, 124–126.

61. See AAUP, *Recommended Principles*, 71, 114–115.

62. Proposed Academic Senate Resolution, UC Policy Requiring Special Disclosure of Fossil Fuel Industry Funding. I am grateful to Professor Craig Callender for sending me a copy of this proposed resolution.

63. See Robert Gorman, "Report of Committee A, 1991–92," *Academe* 78, no. 5 (1992), 43, 49; Joan Wallach Scott, "Report of Committee A, 2002–03," *Academe* 89, no. 5 (2003) 77, 83.

64. See AAUP, *Recommended Principles,* 6, 129–132, 251.

65. AAUP, *Recommended Principles,* 123, 129.

66. Gorman, "Report of Committee A, 1991–92," 49.

67. Scott, "Report of Committee A, 2002–03," 83.

68. "Resolution of the Academic Council: Restrictions on Research Funding Sources," July 21, 2004, University of California, Office of the President, https://senate .universityofcalifornia.edu/_files/reports/acresolutionrsrchstrings0704.pdf.

69. United States v. Philip Morris USA, Inc., 449 F. Supp. 2d 1 (D.D.C. 2006).

70. AAUP, *Recommended Principles,* 39, 274n38.

71. Arthur O. Lovejoy, "To the Editor of *The Weekly Review,*" *Bulletin of the American Association of University Professors* 6, no. 6 (1920): 10–13. A slightly different version of this letter is contained in the Arthur O. Lovejoy Papers, Special Collections, Milton S. Eisenhower Library, Johns Hopkins University, box 68, file 7.

72. Rood v. Kelly, 200 N.W.2d 728, 741 (Ct. App. Mich. 1972).

73. Erica Goldberg, "Free Speech Consequentialism," *Columbia Law Review* 116 (2016): 687, 749–753; Edward T. Linenthal, in "Trauma and Trigger Warnings in the History Classroom: A Roundtable Discussion," *American Historian* (May 2015): 33, 35.

74. Katherine Rosman, "Should College Come with Trigger Warnings? At Cornell, It's a 'Hard No,'" *New York Times,* April 12, 2023, A18.

75. Jeannie Suk Gerson, "What if Trigger Warnings Don't Work?," *New Yorker,* Sept. 28, 2021, https://www.newyorker.com/news/our-columnist/what-if-trigger -warnings-dont-work, 3–4; Goldberg, "Free Speech Consequentialism," 750.

76. Jenny Jarvie, "Trigger Happy," *New Republic,* March 3, 2014, https://newre public.com/article/116842/trigger-warnings-have-spread-blogs-college-classes-thats-bad, 2 (Oberlin College, subsequently withdrawn), 5; Gerson, "What If Trigger Warnings Don't Work?," 5 (University of Michigan).

77. Nancy Bristow, Angus Johnston, and Kidada E. Williams, in "Trauma and Trigger Warnings in the History Classroom"; Gerson, "What If Trigger Warnings Don't Work?," 5; Angus Johnston, "Trigger-Happy," *Inside Higher Education,* May 29, 2014, https://www.insidehighered.com/views/2014/05/29/essay-why-professor-adding-trigger -warning-his-syllabus#, 3; Martha E. Pollack, "Resolution: SA R31: Mandating Content Warnings for Traumatic Content in the Classroom," https://assembly.cornell.edu /resolution-actions/sa-r31-mandating-content-warnings-traumatic-content-classroom (Cornell president rejects mandatory trigger warnings and student absence from class).

78. See "Trauma and Trigger Warnings in the History Classroom."

79. Erwin Chemerinsky and Howard Gillman, *Free Speech on Campus* (New Haven, CT: Yale University Press, 2017), 137.

80. Linenthal, in "Trauma and Trigger Warnings in the History Classroom," 41.

81. Michael S. Roth, *Safe Enough Spaces* (New Haven, CT: Yale University Press, 2019), 26; Chemerinsky and Gillman, *Free Speech on Campus,* 137, and see Gerson, "What If Trigger Warnings Don't Work?," 8; Roth, *Safe Enough Spaces,* 105.

82. Johnston, "Trigger-Happy," 3.

83. Goldberg, "Free Speech Consequentialism," 751.

84. AAUP, "On Trigger Warnings," (2014) (drafted by a subcommittee of Committee A on Academic Freedom and Tenure in August 2014 and approved by Committee A of the American Association of University Professors), https://www.aaup.org/report/trigger-warnings; Goldberg, "Free Speech Consequentialism," 751.

85. Goldberg, "Free Speech Consequentialism," 751. See Aaron R. Hanlon, "The Trigger Warning Myth," *New Republic,* Fall 2015, 53, 54 (though supporting trigger warnings).

86. Goldberg, "Free Speech Consequentialism," 751–753; Rosman, "Should College Come with Trigger Warnings?"

87. Keith E. Whittington, *Speak Freely: Why Universities Must Defend Free Speech* (Princeton, NJ: Princeton University Press, 2018), 61–63; Gerson, "What If Trigger Warnings Don't Work?," 6, 9; AAUP, "On Trigger Warnings."

88. Gerson, "What If Trigger Warnings Don't Work?," 7; Scott Barry Kaufman, "Are Trigger Warnings Actually Helpful?," *Scientific American,* April 5, 2019, 3.

89. Kaufman, "Are Trigger Warnings Actually Helpful?," 3–4.

90. AAUP, "On Trigger Warnings."

91. Whittington, *Speak Freely,* 62.

92. See Chapter 8, the section "Who Exercises Institutional Academic Freedom?"

93. Pollack, "Resolution: SA R31."

94. See Chemerinsky and Gillman, *Free Speech on Campus,* 137 (objecting to requiring trigger warnings but not to giving them).

95. Brian Soucek, "Diversity Statements," *UC Davis Law Review* 55 (2022): 1989, 1191n1.

96. See Daniel Ortner, "In the Name of Diversity: Why Mandatory Diversity Statements Violate the First Amendment and Reduce Intellectual Diversity in Academia," *Catholic University Law Review* 70 (2021): 515; Soucek, "Diversity Statements," 1999.

97. Ortner, "In the Name of Diversity," 544; Soucek, "Diversity Statements," 1999.

98. Soucek, "Diversity Statements," 2000.

99. Ortner, "In the Name of Diversity," 546; Soucek, "Diversity Statements," 2001.

100. Ortner, "In the Name of Diversity," 448–449; Soucek, "Diversity Statements," 2003–2004.

101. Soucek, "Diversity Statements," 2007–2010.

102. At Riverside, minority and women candidates rose from 8.3% to 23.9% of applicants, 14,3% to 46.4% of finalists, and 16.7% to 50% of hires; at Berkeley, the

percentage for minorities was 14.3% of applicants, 36.2% of finalists, and 40% of hires, and the percentage for women was 39.5% of applicants, 50% of finalists, and 46.7% of hires; at Davis, where eight positions were available, the percentage for minorities was 32.7% of applicants, 82.1% of finalists, and 100% of hires, and the percentage for women was 44.5% of applicants, 57.1% of finalists, and 87.5% of hires. Soucek, "Diversity Statements," 2004.

103. "The Math Community Values a Commitment to Diversity," letter to the editor, *Notices of the American Mathematical Society*, https://www.ams.org/journals/notices/202001/rnoti-ol.pdf, 2–9 (listing signatures; in response to "A Word from . . . Abigail Thompson," *Notices of the American Mathematical Society* 66 [Dec. 2019]: 1778–1789); Soucek, "Diversity Statements," 2004; "UC Davis Defends Its 'Diversity Statements,'" https://wsj.com/articles/uc-davis-defends its diversity statements-11577392382 (statement by Renatta Garrison Tull, Vice Chancellor for Diversity, Equity & Inclusion, and Gary S. May, Chancellor, University of California, Davis).

104. "UC Davis Defends Its 'Diversity Statements.'"

105. Conor Friedersdorf, "The Hypocrisy of Mandatory Diversity Statements," *The Atlantic*, July 3, 2023, https://www.theatlantic.com/ideas/archive/2023/07/hypocrisy-mandatory-diversity-statements/674611, 6.

106. Charlotte M. Canning and Richard J. Reddick, "In Defense of Diversity Statements," *Chronicle of Higher Education*, Jan. 11, 2019, https://www.chronicle.com/article/in-defense-of-diversity-statements/, 2–3.

107. Xander Faber, letter to the editor, *Notices of the American Mathematical Society*, https://www.ams.org/journals/notices/202001/rnoti-ol.pdf, 17.

108. Soucek, "Diversity Statements," 2021–2022.

109. See Matthew W. Finkin, "Diversity! Mandating Adherence to a Secular Creed," *Journal of Free Speech Law* 2 (2023): 463–464. Finkin himself rejects this position, differentiating disciplinary judgments from conceptions of the public good.

110. See Soucek, "Diversity Statements," 2059–2060.

111. Canning and Reddick, "In Defense of Diversity Statements," 4–5; Soucek, "Diversity Statements," 2033, 2040, 2053–2054.

112. Finkin, "Diversity!," 457, 476.

113. Soucek, "Diversity Statements," 2045, 2059.

114. Finkin, "Diversity!," 454, 466–467; Brian Leiter, "The Legal Problem with Diversity Statements," *Chronicle of Higher Education*, March 13, 2020, 5–6; Ortner, "In the Name of Diversity," 516, 578–579; Soucek, "Diversity Statements," 2011 (citing blog by John O. McGinnis), 2014–2015; Abigail Thompson, "A Word from . . . Abigail Thompson, *Notices of the American Mathematical Society* 66 (Dec. 2019): 1778–1789.

115. Statement by Academic Freedom Alliance, August 22, 2022. I am a member of the Academic Council of the Academic Freedom Alliance. See www.academicfreedom.org.

116. Leiter, "The Legal Problem," 4; Finkin, "Diversity!," 453.

117. See Leiter, "The Legal Problem," 6; Ortner, "In the Name of Diversity," 574–576 (differentiating permissible content discrimination from unconstitutional viewpoint discrimination).

118. Friedersdorf, "The Hypocrisy," 3–4, 10–11.

119. Soucek, "Diversity Statements," 2008.

120. Thompson, "A Word from . . . Abigail Thompson," 1778.

121. Leiter, "The Legal Problem," 6.

122. Lisa R. Pruitt, "Who's Afraid of White Class Migrants? On Denial, Discrediting, and Disdain (and toward a Richer Conception of Diversity)," *Columbia Journal of Gender and Law* 31 (2015): 196, 223; cited in Soucek, "Diversity Statements," 2055 and n316.

123. Ortner, "In the Name of Diversity," 561.

124. Ortner, "In the Name of Diversity," 577.

125. Finkin, "Diversity!," 463–464, 475.

126. Friedersdorf, "The Hypocrisy," 8–9.

127. Ortner, "In the Name of Diversity," 549.

128. Friedersdorf, "The Hypocrisy," 19.

129. Valentin Ovsienko, letter to the editor, *Notices of the American Mathematical Society,* https://www.ams.org/journals/notices/202001/rnoti-ol.pdf, 19.

130. Friedersdorf, "The Hypocrisy," 19; Eleftherios Gkioulekas, letter to the editor, *Notices of the American Mathematical Society,* https://www.ams.org/journals/notices/202001/rnoti-ol.pdf, 24.

131. See Soucek, "Diversity Statements," 2034, 2036, 2040–2041, 2049–2053.

11. Student Academic Freedom

1. Tinker v. Des Moines Independent Community School District, 393 U.S. 503, 506 (1969).

2. Sweezy v. New Hampshire, 354 U.S. 234, 250 (1957).

3. Barenblatt v. United States, 360 U.S. 109, 112 (1959).

4. Board of Regents of University of Wisconsin v. Southworth, 529 U.S. 217, 236, 237 (2006) (Souter, J., concurring), quoting Justice Stevens in Regents of University of Michigan v. Ewing, 474 U.S. 214, 226n12 (1985).

5. Edwards v. Aguillard, 482 U.S. 578, 610, 627 (1987) (Scalia, J., dissenting), 597, 599 (Powell, J., concurring).

6. Healy v. James, 408 U.S. 169, 174n4, 180–181, 186 (1972).

7. Baggett v. Bullitt, 377 U.S. 360, 366n5 (1964).

8. DeJohn v. Temple University, 537 F.3d 301, 314 (3d Cir. 2008).

9. McClain v. Arkansas Board of Education, 529 F. Supp. 1255, 1273 (E.D. Ark. 1982).

10. Zykan v. Warsaw Community Schools Corporation, 631 F.2d 1300, 1304 (7th Cir. 1980).

11. AAUP, "Declaration of Principles" (1915), reprinted in *Academic Freedom and Tenure*, ed. Louis Joughin, (Madison: University of Wisconsin Press, 1969): appendix A, 157, 168–169.

12. AAUP and the Association of American Colleges, "1940 Statement of Principles on Academic Freedom and Tenure," reprinted in Joughin, *Academic Freedom and Tenure*, 33, 34.

13. David Fellman, "Report of Committee A, 1960–61," *AAUP Bulletin* 47 (June 1961): 135, 139.

14. Statement on Faculty Responsibility for the Academic Freedom of Students, *AAUP Bulletin* 50 (Sept. 1964): 254–257; Statement on the Academic Freedom of Students, *AAUP Bulletin* 51 (Dec. 1965): 447–449.

15. AAUP, "Joint Statement on Rights and Responsibility of Students" (hereafter cited as Joint Statement) in AAUP, *Policy Documents and Reports*, 11th ed. (Baltimore: Johns Hopkins University Press, 2015), 381–386; reprinted in Richard A. Mullendore, "The 'Joint Statement on Rights and Freedoms of Students': Twenty-Five Years Later," *New Directions for Student Services* 59 (Fall 1992): 5, 12–23. Mullendore provides an excellent overview of the development of the Joint Statement, 6–8.

16. Mullendore, "'Joint Statement,'" 10.

17. AAUP, "Joint Statement," 381.

18. AAUP, "Joint Statement," 382.

19. AAUP, "Joint Statement," 382–383.

20. AAUP, "Joint Statement," 383–384.

21. AAUP, "Joint Statement," 382–385.

22. AAUP, "Joint Statement," 381–382.

23. Sidney Hook, "Freedom to Learn but Not to Riot," *New York Times Magazine*, Jan. 3, 1965, 8.

24. Hook, "Freedom to Learn," 8.

25. Hook, "Freedom to Learn," 8, 16–17.

26. William W. Van Alstyne, "Student Academic Freedom and the Rule-Making Powers of Public Universities: Some Constitutional Considerations," *Law in Transition Quarterly* 2 (1965): 1, 1n2, 9, 12, 22–23.

27. William W. Van Alstyne, "The Judicial Trend toward Student Academic Freedom," *University of Florida Law Review* 20 (1968): 290–304.

28. AAUP, "On Trigger Warnings," (2014) (drafted by a subcommittee of Committee A on Academic Freedom and Tenure in August 2014 and approved by Committee A of the AAUP), https://www.aaup.org/report/trigger-warnings.

29. Hook, "Freedom to Learn," 16.

30. Doe v. University of Michigan, 721 F. Supp. 852 (E.D. Mich. 1989); Grutter v. Bollinger, 539 U.S. 306, 349 (Thomas, J., concurring in part and dissenting in part).

31. Reproductive Health Services v. Webster, 851 F.2d 1071, 1084n18 (8th Cir.1988), rev'd, Webster v. Reproductive Health Services, 402 U.S. 490 (1989).

32. O'Neal v. Falcon, 668 F. Supp. 2d 979, 986–987 (W.D. TX 2009).

33. Linnemeir v. Board of Trustees of Purdue University, 260 F.3d 757, 760 (7th Cir. 2001).

34. Bhattacharya v. Murray, 515 F. Supp. 3d 436, 446, 455 (W.D. Va. 2021).

35. Doe v. University of Michigan, 854; UWM Post, Inc. v. Board of Regents of University of Wisconsin System, 774 F. Supp.1163, 1165, 1167 (E.D. Wis. 1991).

36. Brown v. Li, 308 F.3d 939, 943 (9th Cir. 2002).

Bibliographical Essay

1. William Van Alstyne, "The Specific Theory of Academic Freedom and the General Issue of Civil Liberty," in *The Concept of Academic Freedom,* ed. Edmund L. Pincoffs (Austin: University of Texas Press, 1975), 59–85, esp. 60, 62, 64.

2. Van Alstyne, "The Specific Theory," 64–65, 67–68.

3. Van Alstyne, "The Specific Theory," 61–62, 64, 68–69.

4. Van Alstyne, "The Specific Theory," 76.

5. Matthew W. Finkin, "On 'Institutional' Academic Freedom," *Texas Law Review* 61 (1983): 817–857, esp. 818, 829, 840, 850.

6. Finkin, "On 'Institutional' Academic Freedom," 849–850.

7. Finkin, "On 'Institutional' Academic Freedom," 851, 854.

8. J. Peter Byrne, "Academic Freedom: A 'Special Concern of the First Amendment,'" *Yale Law Journal* 99 (1989): 251–340, esp. 255, 262, 311, 312, and generally 262–265.

9. Byrne, "Academic Freedom," 312, 319.

10. Byrne, "Academic Freedom," 233, 255, 304–306, 308, 311.

11. Byrne, "Academic Freedom," 324, 338.

12. David M. Rabban, "A Functional Analysis of 'Individual' and 'Institutional' Academic Freedom under the First Amendment," *Law and Contemporary Problems* 53, no. 3 (1990): 227–301.

13. Rabban, "A Functional Analysis," 283–287.

14. Frederick Schauer, "Principles, Institutions, and the First Amendment," *Harvard Law Review* 112 (1998): 84–120, esp. 84, 86, 93.

15. Frederick Schauer, "Towards an Institutional First Amendment," *Minnesota Law Review* 89 (2005): 1256–1279, esp. 1274–1275.

16. Frederick Schauer, "Is There a Right to Academic Freedom?," *University of Colorado Law Review* 77 (2006): 907–927, esp. 908–910, 914, 917.

17. Schauer, "Is There a Right?," 919–920.

18. Schauer, "Is There a Right?," 925.

19. Paul Horwitz, *First Amendment Institutions* (Cambridge, MA: Harvard University Press, 2013).

20. Horwitz, *First Amendment Institutions*, 114.

21. Horwitz, *First Amendment Institutions*, 115, 117–118, 121–123, 126–127, 130–133, 139–140.

22. Judith Areen, "Government as Educator: A New Understanding of First Amendment Protection of Academic Freedom and Governance," *Georgetown Law Journal* 97 (2009): 945–1000.

23. Areen, "Government as Educator," 947, 949.

24. Areen, "Government as Educator," 989–990.

25. Areen, "Government as Educator," 957n57, 989, 995–998, 998n299, 1000.

26. Robert C. Post, *Democracy, Expertise, Academic Freedom: A First Amendment Jurisprudence for the Modern State* (New Haven, CT: Yale University Press, 2012).

27. Post, *Democracy, Expertise, Academic Freedom*, xiii, 22, 25, 33–34, 54.

28. Post, *Democracy, Expertise, Academic Freedom*, 33, 55, 60.

29. Post, *Democracy, Expertise, Academic Freedom*, 35, 43, 61–62, 73.

30. Post, *Democracy, Expertise, Academic Freedom*, 77, 80, 92.

31. Post, *Democracy, Expertise, Academic Freedom*, 79–80, 89–90.

32. Post, *Democracy, Expertise, Academic Freedom*, 81, 85, 101, 158n101.

33. Walter P. Metzger, *Academic Freedom in the Age of the University* (New York: Columbia University Press, 1955).

34. Hans-Joerg Tiede, *University Reform: The Founding of the American Association of University Professors* (Baltimore: Johns Hopkins University Press, 2015).

35. Tiede, *University Reform*, 2–3.

36. Judith Jarvis Thomson, "Ideology and Faculty Selection," *Law and Contemporary Problems* 53, no. 3 (1990): 155–176.

37. Joan W. Scott, "Academic Freedom as an Ethical Practice," in *The Future of Academic Freedom*, ed. Louis Menand (Chicago: University of Chicago Press, 1996): 163–180.

38. Judith Butler, "Academic Norms, Contemporary Challenges: A Reply to Robert Post on Academic Freedom," in *Academic Freedom after September 11*, ed. Beshara Doumani (Brooklyn: New York: Zone Books, 2006): 107–142.

ACKNOWLEDGMENTS

I have many people to thank for their help during the years I worked on this book. Alisa Holahan, Sarah George, and Zoey Miller were excellent research assistants who helped me locate and synthesize the extensive case law on academic freedom and free speech at American universities. Joe Noel, my library liaison at the University of Texas School of Law, responded quickly and effectively to my many requests for material, often ingeniously finding esoteric sources. The students in the seminars I taught based on drafts of this book had many useful reactions and suggestions on which I relied extensively while making revisions. I particularly thank Lillian Seidel, a student who suggested the charts comparing cases, which can be found at https://law.utexas.edu/faculty/david-rabban/academic-freedom. Fellowships from the John Simon Guggenheim Foundation and from the Program in Law and Public Affairs at Princeton University provided valuable time for sustained research.

Many friends and colleagues have generously read drafts of this book. Peter Byrne, Ward Farnsworth, Steve Goode, Andy Lipps, Robert Post, Fred Schauer, and Laura Weinrib made especially extensive and useful comments. I also appreciate responses from Judy Areen, Mark Ascher, Kevin Baine, Steve Collis, Matt Finkin, Jim Fleming, Willy Forbath, Abbey Gray, Andrew Kull, Jennifer Laurin, Doug Laycock, Sandy Levinson, Susie Morse, Scot Powe, Greg Scholtz, Nadine Strossen, Joerg Tiede, and Eugene Volokh. I have benefited as well from conversations following presentations based on material in the book at, in roughly chronological order, the University of Texas School of Law, Duke Law School, the University of Pennsylvania School of Law, Fordham Law School, Princeton University, the scholars conference of the Foundation for Individual Rights and Expression, the University of Chicago Law School, Northwestern School of Law, Dartmouth College, the annual meeting of the Association for University and College Counseling Center Directors, Utah Valley University, the Texas Conference of the American Association of University Professors, the Hugo L. Black Lecture at Wesleyan University, and the conference of the European Society for Comparative Legal History. Sam Stark, my editor at Harvard University Press, made extremely helpful organizational and stylistic suggestions throughout the editorial process.

I owe my greatest debt to William Van Alstyne. His brilliant distinction between the specific First Amendment right of academic freedom and the general First Amendment right of political expression in his classic essay published in 1972, "The Specific Theory of Academic Freedom and the General Issue of Civil Liberty," provides the theoretical underpinning of this book. Bill was president of the American Association of University Professors (AAUP) when I joined its legal staff in 1976, and I worked closely with him on AAUP briefs addressing issues of academic freedom and free speech. We continued to discuss our mutual interests in academic freedom until his death in 2019. I thought about him often while completing this book, wishing I could have talked with him about it and benefited from his suggestions.

INDEX

AAUP. *See* American Association of University Professors (AAUP)

academic freedom, conflicting claims between professors and universities, 11–12; in grading, 197–198; judicial competence to review academic merits, 254–266, 300; peer review in resolving, 258–266; recognized by judges, 179–180 (Stevens), 197 (Posner); regarding diversity statements, 274–280; regarding trigger warnings, 271–274; in university regulation of external funding, 266–270

academic freedom, relation to First Amendment: connected to First Amendment, 140–144; differentiated from general First Amendment doctrines, 9, 136, 139–140, 180–183; impeded by general First Amendment doctrines, 13, 113–114, 182–183; judicial inconsistency about, 131–132. *See also* academic freedom of professors; academic freedom of students; academic freedom of universities; First Amendment

academic freedom of professors: application to extramural speech, 20–24, 28–30, 109–110, 155–161; application to intramural speech, 107–109, 153–155; application to scholarship and teaching, 99–107, 144–145; challenge of antirealism, 146–148; and Communist Party membership, 54–57, 218; differentiated from political expression, 7–9, 22–23, 29–30, 65–66, 139–140, 155–156, 159, 303–304; as a distinctive First Amendment right, 93, 94–99, 114–116, 131–132, 134–135, 139–140, 168–169; implications for other professional employees, 143, 145, 301, 333n85, 333–334n8, 334n18; judicial recognition of confusion about, 94–95, 133–134, 300–301; limits of, 9, 25–26,

107, 108–109, 137–138, 140; limits on state intrusion, 105–106; overview of legal claims, 2–3; procedural protection of, 10, 161–166; as promoting democratic citizenship, 148–150; as promoting production and dissemination of knowledge, 144–145; scope of, 137–139, 168–170, 298–299; structural protection of, 10, 166–168. *See also* 1915 Declaration (AAUP)

academic freedom of students, 12–13; in the classroom, 292, 294–295; consideration within academic community, 286–291; differentiated from academic freedom of professors, 283–284; as a distinctive First Amendment right, 292–297; excluded from 1915 Declaration, 30–31; in extracurricular activities, 292–293; extramural, 293; procedural and structural protection of, 293; supportive judicial decisions, 284–286

academic freedom of universities, 10–11; in affirmative action, 173–179; in appointment and tenure, 195–197; comparisons between public and private universities, 11, 219–229; competing state interests, 222–223; differentiated from general First Amendment doctrines, 180–183, 203–204; ignoring claims about, 186–191; limiting access to university property, 244–249; limiting state intrusion, 220–221; limits of, 10–11, 208–211, 234–236, 237, 239–242, 274, 279; overview of legal claims, 3–4; in peer review, 183–186; in regulating offensive speech, 231–244; rejecting claims about, 183–186, 188, 198–202; religious universities, 26–27, 90–91, 204–205; in scholarship and teaching, 197–198; scope of, 205–211, 299; in student admission and discipline, 179–180, 192–195; who exercises, 211–218

Index

Index

Index

Metzger, Walter P.: on AAUP investigations of academic freedom cases, 338n76; on 1915 Declaration, 29, 30, 205, 314
Minnesota State Board of Education v. Knight, 84–85

National Labor Relations Board v. Yeshiva University, 91
neutrality, content and viewpoint, 182–183, 198, 200, 221–222
1915 Declaration (AAUP), 6, 8, 24–32, 151–152, 165, 204–205; criticism by university presidents, 31–32; discussed in *Urofsky*, 95, 97–98; epistemological assumptions of, 146–147; on extramural speech, 20–24, 27–29; historical background of, 17–19; on peer review, 25–26, 152–153, 154, 162; on proprietary institutions, 26–27, 204–205; on relation to First Amendment, 52, 137; on students, 286–287
1940 Statement of Principles on Academic Freedom and Tenure (AAUP-AAC), 32, 165; judicial reliance on in religion cases, 90–91; on students, 287
1964 Statement on Extramural Utterances (AAUP), 32–33
1966 Statement on Government of Colleges and Universities (AAUP, ACE, AGBCU), 153, 154–155, 211–213, 263

offensive speech, 231–244; on campus, 236–238; in classroom, 102–104, 234–236; extramural, 238–242; subjective standards for, 242–244
official duties test, 13, 83–84, 121, 128–131; Kennedy on, 83–84; Souter on, 83–84
O'Neil, Robert M., 47–48
"On the Relationship of Faculty Governance to Academic Freedom" (AAUP), 154–155
"On Trigger Warnings" (AAUP), 273, 291
Open Universities in South Africa, The, 69–71
overbreadth. *See* vagueness and overbreadth

peer review: in appointment and tenure decisions, 164, 213–215, 256–257; arbitral deference to, 264–266; as central to academic freedom, 8, 10; in conflicting academic freedom claims, 258–266; disclosure of confidential material from, 183–186; in evaluating students, 213–214; in 1915 Declaration, 25–26; paradox of, 150–153
Pickering v. Board of Education, 120, 282
political expression, differentiated from academic freedom. *See* academic freedom of professors: differentiated from political expression

Posner, Richard: on conflicting academic freedom claims, 197; on due process for students, 195; relating institutional academic freedom to due process, 253; on relative strength of claims to institutional academic freedom, 196; ridiculing law professors in *Rumsfeld*, 344n49; on student performance of controversial play, 295–296
Post, Robert C.: on democratic competence, academic freedom advancing, 312–313; on democratic competence, commercial speech advancing, 312, 334n12; on democratic competence, reconciled with democratic legitimacy, 311–312; on intramural expression, 167–168, 338n78; opposing judicial deference to university administrators, 313; on required balance or neutrality, 227; on state regulation of expert professional speech, 227
Powell, Lewis F., Jr.: opinion in *Bakke*, 173–176; opinion in *Healy*, 284–285
Pound, Roscoe, 24, 159
"Preliminary Statement on Judicially Compelled Disclosure in the Nonrenewal of Faculty Appointments, A" (AAUP), 184, 207
Princeton University v. Schmid, 188–191, 344n60
private and public universities compared, 4, 11, 36; in applying state action doctrine, 46–51; under impairment of contracts clause, 35, 38–45; implications for institutional academic freedom, 219–229; in 1915 Declaration, 26–27
public concern test, 120–127

Rabban, David M.: involvement with AAUP, 6, 318n64, 343n48; on relationship between individual and institutional academic freedom, 307–308
"Recommended Principles to Guide Academy-Industry Relationships" (AAUP), 266–267
Regents of the University of Michigan v. Ewing, 179–180
Rehnquist, William, 88–90, 134
religious universities, 26–27, 90–91, 204
Ross, Edward A., 18–19
Royce, Josiah, 145
Rumsfeld v. Forum for Academic & Institutional Rights, 186–188, 343n48
Russell, Bertrand, 58
Rust v. Sullivan, 88–90, 116, 134

Schauer, Frederick, 254, 308–309
Scott, Joan Wallach: on academic freedom as ethical practice, 152; on paradox of peer review, 150